Language and Identities

LANGUAGE AND IDENTITIES

Edited by Carmen Llamas and Dominic Watt

EDINBURGH UNIVERSITY PRESS

Edinburgh University Press Ltd
22 George Square, Edinburgh

www.euppublishing.com

Typeset in 10/12 Ehrhardt MT and Gill Sans
by Servis Filmsetting Ltd, Stockport, Cheshire, and
printed and bound in Great Britain by
CPI Antony Rowe, Chippenham and Eastbourne

A CIP record for this book is available from the British Library

ISBN 978 0 7486 3576 4 (hardback)
ISBN 978 0 7486 3577 1 (paperback)

Contents

Acknowledgements

We have Judy Dyer to thank for the idea for this book, the seed for which was sown at a workshop on language and national identity that the three of us participated in as part of the 11th Methods in Dialectology Conference in Joensuu, Finland, in August 2002. For their willingness to read and comment on draft chapters (often at very short notice) and to volunteer an abundance of useful suggestions in terms of the volume's contents and format, we also wish to express our gratitude to Joan Beal, Alicia Beckford Wassink, Dave Britain, Lynn Clark, Bethan Davies, Gerry Docherty, Anne Fabricius, Paul Foulkes, Peter French, Bill Haddican, Damien Hall, Barry Heselwood, Tyler Kendall, Paul Kerswill, Ghada Khattab, John Laver, Warren Maguire, Máiréad McElligott, Sara Mills, Lesley Milroy, Jennifer Nycz, Peter Patrick, Phil Rose, Catherine Sangster, Jeremy Smith, Jos Vermeulen, Esmé Watson, Enam al-Wer, Stuart Whitfield and Malcah Yaeger-Dror. Special thanks are due to Victoria Watt for her generously given bibliographical expertise, and her seemingly inexhaustible patience while the book was in preparation.

For their permission to use previously published material that appears in this book we would like to thank Sage Publishers, Cambridge University Press, The Ordnance Survey, James Milroy, Lesley Milroy, Paul Foulkes and Gerry Docherty.

List of Tables and Figures

Tables

Figures

Notes on Contributors

Joan Beal is Professor of English Language at the University of Sheffield. She has research interests in the history of Late Modern English (1700–1945) and dialect and identity in northern England. Recent publications include *English in Modern Times 1700–1945* (Arnold, 2004) and *Language and Region* (Routledge, 2006). She is currently writing *An Introduction to Regional Englishes: Dialect Variation in England* and (with Lourdes Burbano-Elizondo and Carmen Llamas) *Urban North-Eastern English: Tyneside to Teesside*, both to be published by Edinburgh University Press.

Alicia Beckford Wassink is Howard and Frances Nostrand Endowed Professor of Language and Cultural Competence and director of the Sociolinguistics Laboratory in the Department of Linguistics, University of Washington, Seattle. Wassink's research interests lie in language ideology, social network modelling, dialect contact, acoustic phonetics, development of sociolinguistic competence in children, and creole linguistics. Her writings in sociolinguistics have appeared in *Language in Society*, *Language Variation and Change* and the *Journal of English Linguistics*.

David Bowie is an assistant professor of English and linguistics at the University of Alaska Anchorage, where he works on issues of language and ageing, as well as the historical development of language varieties. He has recently begun a project to trace the historical development of Alaskan Englishes from the region's initial English-speaking settlement to the present.

David Britain is Professor of Modern English Linguistics at the University of Bern in Switzerland. He is an associate editor of the *Journal of Sociolinguistics*, editor of *Language in the British Isles* (Cambridge University Press, 2007), co-author (with Andrew Radford, Martin Atkinson, Harald Clahsen and Andrew Spencer) of *Linguistics: An Introduction* (Cambridge University Press, 2009) and co-editor (with Jenny Cheshire) of *Social Dialectology* (Benjamins, 2003). His research interests include language variation and change, the linguistic consequences of dialect contact and isolation, and the interface between dialectology and human geography.

Mary Bucholtz is Professor in the Department of Linguistics at the University of California, Santa Barbara. Her research focuses on language and identity, with special attention to gender and sexuality, race and ethnicity, and youth. She is the editor or co-editor of several volumes focused on language and gender, including *Gender Articulated* (with Kira Hall) and *Reinventing Identities* and is author of the forthcoming book *Styling: Language and White Youth Identities* (Cambridge University Press).

Nikolas Coupland is an elected member of the UK Academy of Social Sciences and Research Director of the Centre for Language and Communication Research at Cardiff University. He was founding editor, with Allan Bell, of the *Journal of Sociolinguistics*, published by Blackwell. With Adam Jaworski he edits the Oxford University Press book series, *Oxford Studies in Sociolinguistics*. His research interests include sociolinguistic theory, the sociolinguistics of Wales, of globalisation, of speech style, and of later life.

Judy Dyer is a lecturer in the English Language Institute at the University of Michigan, Ann Arbor. In addition to her research interest in dialect contact and identity, she is currently working on a corpus project investigating the rhetorical features of the academic writing of Korean and Chinese undergraduates, with particular emphasis on the characteristics of Generation 1.5 writers.

Anders Eriksson is Professor of Phonetics in the Department of Linguistics, Gothenburg University. He received his MSc in solid state physics from Gothenburg University in 1965 and taught physics and mathematics before turning to linguistics. In the late 1980s he worked on speech synthesis at Swedish Telecom. He received his PhD in linguistics from Gothenburg University in 1991. After working first at Umeå University and later Stockholm University, he joined the Linguistics Department in Gothenburg as a Professor in 2001. His scientific work has focused on speech rhythm, perception, paralinguistic phonetics and forensic phonetics.

Sue Fox is a Research Fellow at Queen Mary University of London. Her research interests include language variation and change, language contact, language and identity and the speech of adolescents. She is currently working on a three-year ESRC-funded project *Multicultural London English.*

Kira Hall is Associate Professor of Linguistics and Anthropology at the University of Colorado at Boulder. Her research focuses on the relationship between language and social identity, particularly as it materialises within hierarchies of gender, sexuality and socio-economic class in northern India. Among her publications are the edited volumes *Gender Articulated* (Routledge 1995), *Queerly Phrased* (Oxford University Press, 1997) and *Studies in Inequality and Social Justice* (Archana, 2009), as well as numerous journal articles and book chapters on the subject of language and identity.

Barbara Johnstone is Professor of Rhetoric and Linguistics at Carnegie Mellon University, Pittsburgh, and is Editor of *Language in Society*. In many books and articles, she has explored the links between discourse, place and the individual. Her current work, with Scott F. Kiesling, is about local speech and local identity in Pittsburgh, Pennsylvania.

John E. Joseph is Professor of Applied Linguistics at the University of Edinburgh. From 2005 to 2008 he held a Major Research Fellowship from the Leverhulme Trust. His books include *Eloquence and Power* (Blackwell, 1987), *Limiting the Arbitrary* (Benjamins, 2000), *From Whitney to Chomsky* (Benjamins, 2002), *Language and Identity* (Palgrave Macmillan, 2004) and *Language and Politics* (Edinburgh University Press, 2006). He has edited a four-volume collection on language and politics, to be published by Routledge in 2009.

Carmen Llamas is Lecturer in Sociolinguistics at the University of York. Her research to date has been principally on phonological variation and change, especially in connection with diffusion and levelling in the North-East of England, and she has a particular interest in the identity-making and -marking functions of language and the development of innovative sociolinguistic fieldwork methods. She is co-editor (with Louise Mullany and Peter Stockwell) of *The Routledge Companion to Sociolinguistics* (Routledge, 2007).

Robert McColl Millar is Senior Lecturer in Linguistics at the University of Aberdeen. His most recent books include *Language, Nation and Power* (Palgrave Macmillan, 2005) and *Northern and Insular Scots* (Edinburgh University Press, 2007). He has published widely on the interface between Gaelic and Scots in Northern Scots, lexical attrition in Modern Scots, rapid language change and its connection with attitudes in modern Scotland, language policy towards Scots, and the connection between language standardisation and the development of the nation state.

Norma Mendoza-Denton is Associate Professor in the Department of Anthropology, University of Arizona. She specialises in linguistic anthropology, sociolinguistics and multimedia anthropology, with an emphasis on youth, language diversity and migration. Her recent research interests include gangs' use of the internet, discourse markers and creaky voice, political speech, and minority identities among Western European migrant youth. She is author of *Homegirls: Language and Cultural Practice among Latina Youth Gangs* (Wiley/Blackwell, 2008).

Nick Miller is attached to the Institute of Health and Society at Newcastle University. His main teaching and research interests lie in the area of speech motor control and motor speech disorders, from studies of impairment through to issues of psychosocial impact. He has previously authored books on bilingualism and language disability and clinical aspects of apraxia.

Emma Moore is Lecturer in Sociolinguistics at the University of Sheffield. Her published work is concerned with the social meaning of linguistic variation and addresses issues of style, identity and social practice. She predominantly employs ethnographic methodologies and is currently pursuing a community collaboration project on the Isles of Scilly.

Louise Mullany is Associate Professor of Sociolinguistics in the School of English Studies at the University of Nottingham, UK. Her main research interests lie in the sociolinguistics of institutional and professional discourse and she has conducted studies in business, medical and media contexts. Recent publications include the monograph *Gendered Discourse in the Professional Workplace* (Palgrave, 2007) and the co-edited *Routledge Companion to Sociolinguistics* (2007).

Tope Omoniyi is Professor of Sociolinguistics at Roehampton University, London. His research interests are in language and religion, multilingualism, language policy and development in postcolonial Africa. These are reflected in his publications, which include *The Sociolinguistics of Borderlands: Two Nations, One Community* (Africa World Press, 2004), and the co-edited (with Goodith White) *The Sociolinguistics of Identity* (Continuum, 2006).

Dana Osborne is a doctoral student at the University of Arizona. Research interests include linguistic anthropology, memory and the intersection between thought and language particularly regarding cognitive representations of time and space. Recent research has examined the influence of experience in the world on systems of deixis, providing a way to link language to mental representations of the outside world. She plans in future research to expand on these themes with attention to time and other fundamental categories of representation.

Ben Rampton is Professor of Applied Sociolinguistics and Director of the Centre for Language Discourse and Communication at King's College London. He does interactional sociolinguistics, and his interests cover urban multilingualism, ethnicity, class, youth and education. He is the author of *Crossing: Language and Ethnicity among Adolescents* (Longman, 1995/St Jerome, 2005) and *Language in Late Modernity: Interaction in an Urban School* (Cambridge University Press, 2006), and co-author of *Researching Language: Issues of Power and Method* (Routledge, 1992).

Jane Stuart-Smith is a Reader in English Language who works on sociophonetics, understanding linguistic phenomena at the intersection between sociolinguistics and phonetics. Her recent published papers are on regional and social accent features, especially of Scottish English, and on British Asian varieties. She is currently working on the impact of the media on phonological variation and change, articulatory phonetic methods in sociolinguistics, and emerging regional ethnic accents.

Erik R. Thomas is a Professor in the English Department at North Carolina State University. His research specialises in sociophonetics, or the interface between phonetics and sociolinguistics, and he has written several papers on the sociophonetics of minority groups in the United States. He has authored or co-authored two books and is currently working on a third, *Sociophonetics: An Introduction*.

Claire Timmins is a researcher in speech science at Queen Margaret University, Edinburgh, and an Associate Lecturer in Phonetics at Strathclyde University. She also holds an honorary research fellow position at Glasgow University. She works on clinical speech (Down's syndrome, ataxia) and sociophonetics (particularly the Glaswegian accent). Her recent published papers are on aspects of the assessment and treatment of speech difficulties in Down's syndrome.

Dominic Watt is Senior Lecturer in Forensic Speech Science at the University of York. His research interests are in sociophonetics, forensic phonetics, vowel production and perception, phonological acquisition, and language and identity studies, the last of which focuses on the relationship between phonological variation and social, regional and national identity and attitudes along the Scottish/English border. He is co-author, with Arthur Hughes and Peter Trudgill, of the fourth edition of *English Accents and Dialects* (Hodder Arnold, 2005).

Lal Zimman is a PhD student in Linguistics at the University of Colorado at Boulder, where he is also affiliated with the programs in Culture, Language and Social Practice and in Women's and Gender Studies. His research focuses on issues of language and identity within transgender communities, and he has previously published on coming-out narratives among transgender speakers. His dissertation research is on identity, socialisation and the voice among female-to-male transsexuals.

Introduction

Carmen Llamas and Dominic Watt

The connection between language and identity is a fundamental element of our experience of being human. Language not only reflects who we are but in some sense it *is* who we are, and its use defines us both directly and indirectly. We use language in a direct way to denote and describe who a person is through use of naming and kinship terms, descriptions based on appearance, behaviour, background, and so on, and we use language to assign identities indirectly when we base our judgements of who people are on the way they speak. Language-mediated attribution of identity to individuals is so ingrained in human social affairs that we consider a person lacking a name to also lack an identity.

Neither our identities nor our language are static, however. Both are constantly shifting and being re-negotiated in response to the ever-changing contexts of our interactions. Yet for both our identity and our language there are elements which remain essences. Our DNA, our fingerprints, our unique facial characteristics and body markings remain constant, rare exceptions apart, and form the basis of our individual identities. Like fingerprints, human vocal tracts are to the best of our knowledge anatomically unique to each individual. The combination of features they produce in spoken language allows listeners to recognise a sample of speech as belonging to a particular talker, and prevents others from reproducing his or her speech patterns precisely. These fundamentals can be seen as marking us out as unique individuals. But in addition to personal identity, we are also social beings with social identities. The variations in our dress, appearance and behaviour, and the constant variability in our language use, mark us out as belonging to social groups. We can be members of a potentially infinite number of intersecting social groups, be they local (friends, family, colleagues, and so forth) or global (gender, class, ethnicity, nationality), whose membership is reflected in our shared linguistic behaviour. Any interaction we experience can be characterised and perceived along both intergroup and interindividual dimensions, a duality which accounts for some of the extraordinary complexity of language use. All sociolinguistically competent language users can draw upon an array of linguistic resources for foregrounding different aspects of their identities in particular contexts at particular times. Through the following chapters by leading researchers in the field, this volume investigates the connections and correlations between different levels of our linguistic behaviour and diverse facets of our identities.

The relation between how we use language and who we are is not a recent revelation, nor is it one restricted to academic discourse. We can trace examples of the explicit description of the association of linguistic habits with group and individual identities back to antiquity. The story of the Gileadites and the Ephraimites recounted in the biblical Book of Judges, in which tens of thousands of refugees were allegedly executed as a result of their non-nativelike pronunciation of the initial sound of the word 'shibboleth', is proverbial to the point that the word now denotes the direct link between the groups we belong to and how we speak. Foreshadowing modern forensic speech analysis, the Roman philosopher and lawyer Quintilian (*c*.40–120AD) contended that 'The voice of the speaker is as easily distinguished by the ear as the face is by the eye.' But it is only relatively recently that the connections between language use and identity – at the level of both the individual and the group – have become the object of scholarly empirical investigation.

Within the field of linguistics, we see an appeal to identity factors in the interpretation of patterns of variable linguistic behaviour in what can be considered the first systematic study undertaken in variationist sociolinguistics – Labov's seminal study of phonological patterns on Martha's Vineyard (Labov 1963). The work that followed in this paradigm shifted the focus of inquiry away from structural properties of language abstracted from use, as per the mentalist/cognitive approaches that dominated linguistic research at the time, placing greater emphasis on the socio-indexical information carried within language variation. It also stressed how language users are not passive, but are in fact agents capable of deploying language variation for identity-making and -marking purposes. Theorisation of how speakers exploit available language choices as a function of identity-marking – including for example Le Page and Tabouret-Keller's (1985) model of 'acts of identity' – refined and extended our knowledge of the speaker's ability to consciously manipulate the connections between language use and identity attribution. Interest in the nature of this interdependence has not waned since, and indeed recent years have seen a dramatic upsurge in the number of publications, conferences and university courses exploring the language–identity nexus. In the chapters that follow we will see how far this interest has come, and will gain an appreciation of the all-encompassing nature of the relationship between language and identity.

Language use as it relates to the individual identity of the speaker and the shared linguistic behaviour that comes to be associated with (and indeed to define) group identities are both considered in this volume. As such, its chapters deal with disparate aspects of identity, but are arranged systematically to follow a progression through the different levels of identity, beginning with the individual, moving next to consider groups and communities, and finishing with regions and nations. The focus of several chapters is on contexts in which a heightened sense of identity may be expected. As a consequence of a host of factors (social, historical, psychological, medical) people's identities may be disputed, altered, blurred, peripheralised or imposed. This concentration on the analysis of sites of linguistic interaction in which the notion of identity is unusually complex and problematic brings the identity-making and -marking functions of language more visibly to the fore. Given the variety of perspectives taken, the range of theoretical frameworks and models employed in the chapters is thus necessarily broad and varied. Some derive from research in social theory and linguistic anthropology, while others are centrally placed in (socio)linguistic theory. Varying methodological approaches are also illustrated in the chapters, with a combination of qualitative and quantitative analytic techniques

being exemplified. Data are analysed at various linguistic levels, from fine-grained phonetic and phonological descriptions of speech productions, through narrative and discourse analysis, to examination of patterns in morphosyntactic and lexical variation.

The volume begins with an in-depth exposition of theoretical issues implicated in the
links between language and identity. The indexical functions of language, in terms of
both differing orders of indexicality and direct versus indirect indexicality, are explored
by the authors of the chapters in Part I. They give detailed consideration to how social
meaning attaches to linguistic forms, and how linguistic forms can become associated
with social identities of various kinds, thereby giving an explicit account of the theoretical grounding for the work presented in subsequent sections. In Chapter 1, John Joseph
offers an overview of the heavily theorised notion of identity from a maximally general
perspective, describing and evaluating some of the major theoretical contributions to
our understanding of identity that have emerged from social scientific research. The
central argument presented by Mary Bucholtz and Kira Hall in Chapter 2 – namely, that
identity is the constructed product of intersubjective interaction – provides a framework
structured around the principles *emergence, positionality, indexicality, relationality* and
partialness. Barbara Johnstone develops the linkage between language and identity from a
complementary angle in Chapter 3. She discusses the process of *enregisterment*, whereby
a linguistic form becomes associated with a social meaning, through description and
exemplification of the stages involved in the layering of indexicality. The chapters in this
section demonstrate that in spite of the ubiquity of the notion of identity in linguistic
discourse, its exact nature remains elusive and its manifestations through language use are
as varied as they are complex. The recent theoretical advances described in this section
allow us to operationalise the notion of identity as it relates to linguistic behaviour. This
set of chapters thereby provides us with an essential toolkit with which to examine the
explanatory potential afforded by this relationship to the furthering of our understanding
of the social meaning attached to linguistic variation. Detail of the connections between
language use and our multifaceted identities seen from a broad spectrum of perspectives
in the later sections can thus be situated within the theoretical background provided in
this first Part. We begin with an examination of the individual identity of the speaker,
discussing the extent to which such identities are unique and immutable.

Part II investigates identity at the personal level and individual linguistic behaviour
from forensic and clinical perspectives, as well as from a sociolinguistic vantage point.
Jane Stuart-Smith and Claire Timmins begin, in Chapter 4, by looking at the individual's propensity to adopt linguistic innovations and how different adopter categories
of individuals respond to the broadcast media in participation in the diffusion of innovations. In Chapter 5, David Bowie charts the individual's movement through time in an
investigation of whether individuals alter their linguistic behaviour to reflect changes in
their social identities as they progress, post-adolescence, through the ageing process. The
unusual clinical condition of Foreign Accent Syndrome is explored in Chapter 6 by Nick
Miller. Drawing on a variety of case studies he outlines the disturbing implications of
this condition for those experiencing the syndrome in terms of changes to their identities,
and in many instances the sense of a complete loss of personal identity. Dominic Watt, in
Chapter 7, discusses how language use is approached in the forensic domain by examining techniques used by forensic phoneticians in criminal investigations, and by lay speakers in everyday contexts, when attempting to resolve an individual's identity using his

or her speech patterns. Chapter 8, by Anders Eriksson, continues the forensic theme by considering how natural variation in language, accent and dialect can affect speaker recognition, and how, and with what degree of success, deliberate imitation and impersonation can be used to conceal the speaker's identity.

In Part III we turn to view the speaker with an emphasis on his or her social identities manifested through membership of various social groupings. The ubiquitous notion of the 'speech community' is examined by Nikolas Coupland in Chapter 9. New light is shed on this highly debated concept through interrogation of the notion of authenticity and the process of deauthentication. Norma Mendoza-Denton and Dana Osborne, in Chapter 10, consider how bilingualism relates to identity-marking, and they exemplify the strategic uses of two languages by bilingual speakers to construct personas through the switching of codes and the exploitation of the expectation of such switches. A similar ethnographic approach to the deconstruction of social dynamics and relations within an adolescent 'community of practice' is taken by Emma Moore in Chapter 11. Here, Moore explores peripherality by contrasting the statuses and roles of marginal and peripheral community members with those more centrally placed, through analysis of group members' varying use of discourse markers. An account of the practice of 'crossing' among ethnically diverse adolescents in England is presented in Chapter 12, in which Ben Rampton documents rapid and frequent switches between linguistic codes that demonstrate these young speakers' nuanced awareness of the interplay of class and ethnic identities. Sue Fox pursues the ethnicity theme in Chapter 13, but focuses here on how it interacts with religious identities among a group of Bangladeshi adolescents in London. Correlations between the distribution of phonological features with levels of engagement with religion and social practices more generally are assessed. How ethnicity relates to language in terms of identifiable ethnic varieties is the topic of Chapter 14, by Erik Thomas and Alicia Beckford Wassink. These authors elucidate how the use of African-American English can be seen as a performance of a particular ethnic identity, and examine whether the variety in question retains homogeneity across wide geographical space.

We turn to the theme of gender in the final two chapters of Part III. In the first of these, Chapter 15, Lal Zimman and Kira Hall challenge the existence of a fixed dichotomy between male and female and, through recourse to the category 'third sex', demonstrate how language can be used creatively to reclaim and reallocate terms conventionally agreed to denote fixed biological categories. They also illustrate how gesture in the form of stylised handclaps can be used to index alternative gendered identities. In Chapter 16, the gendered identities available to women in professional settings are discussed by Louise Mullany with reference to identity performances through narratives from women whose career prospects may be constrained by the existence of the so-called 'glass ceiling'.

In the final Part of the volume we again adjust the focus to look at more locally defined identities that cut across many of the global categorisations discussed in the previous section – those associated with the region and the nation. In Chapter 17, David Britain investigates the maintenance of local and regional dialect forms in the face of supralocalisation and regional dialect levelling, in the context of actual and perceived geographical distance and the routinisation of mobility. Longer-term mobility in the case of migration and its effects on linguistic behaviour are appraised by Judy Dyer in Chapter 18. Her study of Scottish migrants to an English steel town exemplifies the process of reallocation of the indexicality of phonological forms. The notion of belonging to one regional or national group versus another (or indeed to more than one) is continued in the following two chapters. Joan Beal, in Chapter 19, relates changes in local administrative boundaries in the UK to changes in linguistic behaviour and social attitudes, revealing that alterations in governmental structure which ostensibly appear unlikely to affect patterns of language use can in fact materially affect people's sense of regional identity. This is shown to have implications in terms of the impact of processes of language convergence and divergence. Carmen Llamas investigates such phenomena across the Scottish/English border in Chapter 20, wherein the coincidence of a national boundary and a sharp and long-standing linguistic divide is interpreted in the light of the fluidity of national and regional identity and language use in this liminal area. Looking further afield, Tope Omoniyi scrutinises the post-colonial linguistic landscape of Nigeria in Chapter 21. The degree to which the crystallisation of a Nigerian national identity has been catalysed by the institutionalisation of common shared (and in the case of English, historically non-indigenous) languages is set against the enormity of the task of uniting the citizens of this unusually linguistically and ethnically diverse state. The issue of national identity as it relates to a shared language is also considered by Robert McColl Millar in the final chapter (Chapter 22). The case for Scots as a national language is assessed from both historical and contemporary angles, and the fate of the variety in competition with English – which has *de facto* official status in Scotland – is speculated upon in light of the degree to which use of Scots functions, and has functioned, as a marker of Scottish national identity.

The broad range of perspectives on issues in the study of language and identities that is offered by the varied contributions in this collection demonstrates the complexity and diversity of the interdependence of language use and its roles in identity-making and -marking. The research presented here by world-leading scholars demonstrates our increasingly sophisticated state of knowledge of the language/identity interface in this ever-expanding field. The rich explanatory potential possessed by contemporary models of the socioindexicality inherent in language brings us closer to a full appreciation of the functions of linguistic variation in human social relations. Additionally, and as is evident from the topics covered in several of the following chapters, an understanding of the connections between language and identity has very obvious value in applied contexts, such as in the clinical, forensic, language planning/policy, media and technological domains.

We believe that one of the key strengths of this volume lies in its demonstration of the advantages accruing from systematic, empirical approaches to the notion of identity undertaken through triangulation of appropriate models and methods. This reduces the risk of uncritically invoking identity as an umbrella explanatory factor accounting for speakers' motivations for linguistic behaviour without supporting evidence. Our goal in putting together this collection is to offer firmer foundations for how and where to position identity among the external motivations appealed to in explanations of linguistic variation and change.

Part I
Theoretical Issues

I

Identity

John E. Joseph

In recent years an emerging strand of research has been concerned with how languages function as more than cognitive systems, and texts as more than squiggles on a page. Languages and texts are so fundamental to our day-to-day interactions with others that it is easy to take them for granted, and to imagine that they are simply tools for conveying ideas. In reality, our very sense of who we are, where we belong and why, and how we relate to those around us, all have language at their centre.

The recognition of this deep linkage of languages and texts with identity – national, ethnic and religious on the grand scale, but operating no less crucially on more local levels – unites a wide range of research projects. Some of these are aimed at understanding the nature of a particular identity from the inside, others at overcoming problems that arise when two or more identities come into conflict.

Researchers have been analysing how people's choice of languages, and ways of speaking, do not simply *reflect* who they are, but *make* them who they are – or more precisely, allow them to make themselves. In turn, the languages they use are made and re-made in the process. If communication were the only function of language, we could expect all mother-tongue speakers of English or any other language to sound more or less the same. The differences in regional and social-class dialects can only be obstacles to efficient conveyance of a message. But dialect differences exist everywhere – so it is rational to suppose that this is not a 'design error' in human language. The differences too fulfil a function. They signal social belonging.

Suppose you stop me to point out that my shoelaces are untied. You are communicating more than just the fact embodied in your message. By expressing concern for my well-being, you are creating a social bond. Simultaneously, in the way you speak – your accent, how you address me (*Oi pal/mate/love/guv* versus *I beg your pardon*), your word choice and even your intonation patterns – you communicate information about yourself. A slight change of intonation can change your concern into ridicule, and turn my interpretation of you on its head. As speakers of English we have been through a lifelong socialisation that leaves us instinctively able to interpret one another's background, where we come from, our level of education, our trustworthiness, our aspirations.

Conversations in which visual clues are lacking, such as those held over the telephone, make it evident that we also communicate information about our gender, age and race. Studies suggest that we make up our minds about these things within hearing a syllable or two (see further, Watt, this volume). Even in e-mails and text messaging, readers are able to pick up on very subtle signals in messages from strangers, and to construct an identity, an image, of the sender based upon them. The members of a community, however defined, instinctively develop ways of sending and interpreting signals that do not merely show, but actually create, maintain and perform the bonds they have with one another. Some prominent researchers on the origins of language have proposed in the last few years that this was the main impetus for the evolution of language: the need not merely to transmit messages, but to identify potential allies and enemies.

In his book *Grooming, Gossip and the Evolution of Language* Robin Dunbar argues that language 'allows you to say a great deal about yourself, your likes and dislikes, the kind of person you are; it also allows you to convey in numerous subtle ways something about your reliability as an ally or friend'; it 'thus seems ideally suited in various ways to being a cheap and ultra-efficient form of grooming . . . language evolved to allow us to gossip' (Dunbar 1996: 78–9). Jean-Louis Dessalles, in *Why We Talk*, similarly locates the origins of language in the need to form communities: 'We humans speak because a fortuitous change profoundly altered the social organisation of our ancestors, who found themselves faced with the necessity, if they were to survive and procreate, of forming sizeable coalitions. Language then arose as a way in which individuals might show off their value as members of these' (Dessalles 2007: 363).

The signs by which we interpret each other's identity in modern society are not different in kind from those by which our remote ancestors distinguished friend from foe. They are still what bind together communities, from the family to the nation, or fail to bind them. The essential questions can be stated quite simply: What is it that holds together a people, a nation, a community? What is the glue, the bond, that makes many stand together and label themselves as one? And what is the solvent that dissolves that glue?

The last question seems the easier one to answer. Oppression, resistance, war. Famine, drought, dispersion, diaspora. These are what break up a once united people, sending them in their separate directions, carrying with them their hatreds and resentments. Eventually they forget them, or at least let them cool to a point where they can be set aside. Still, they never go entirely cold. At a remove of decades, even centuries, they can rear their heads, and neighbours who have been close friends from childhood, intrigued and attracted by their differences, are ready to attack one another to avenge hurts they remember only as transmitted texts.

The paradox is that those texts – the stories, histories, inscriptions, rites, ceremonies, dances, parades, carvings, weavings, tattoos and coins – are also what make them a people. In transmitting the memory of who is not part of us, they transmit as well the meaning of who we are. The fascination with war, although predominantly male, derives less from machismo and bloodlust than from the fact that accounts of war offer the distilled essence of national identity. If the most popular books and films are about wars in which one's own side was victorious, those in which we lost run a close second. They too are about binding us together as a people, and are not all negative, any more than accounts of victory – which always include gut-wrenching losses – are pure drum-beating. The archetypal war-identity text is *England expects*, uttered by a commander who would himself not live out the day.

One of the current threads of discourse research has to do with how the metaphorical arsenal of war accounts is deployed in other areas, most obviously politics – war by other means. In medicine and education too, 'wars' are being waged against obesity and illiteracy and on countless other fronts. A key part of this discourse is comparisons with other countries, particularly in Europe. Nothing gets a headline faster than an announcement that schoolchildren in the UK have been 'beaten' by their healthier or more literate counterparts in some part of the world formerly considered less developed. Health issues, let alone intellectual ones, do not get the same level of emotional response as threats to national pride.

The idea that the existence of communities is largely textual has not simply been invented by academics. The linguistic and discursive nature of *race* was established in law by the House of Lords in 1983, in the case of *Mandla v. Dowell Lee*, in which a Sikh boy won the right to wear his top knot and turban despite its violating his school's uniform code. The opinion stated that a number of criteria make a race, of which two are essential:

- a long shared history, of which the group is conscious as distinguishing it from other groups, and the memory of which it keeps alive;
- a cultural tradition of its own, including family and social customs and manners, often but not necessarily associated with religious observance.

Among the five other criteria cited as relevant were

- a common language, not necessarily peculiar to the group;
- a common literature peculiar to the group.

Sikhs were given recognition as a race under the law by virtue of being 'a distinctive and self-conscious community . . . although they are not biologically distinguishable from the other peoples living in the Punjab.' A crucial piece of evidence for their distinctiveness lay in a surprisingly fine-grained fact about their literary language, Punjabi: 'They have a written language which a small proportion of Sikhs can read but which can be read by a much higher proportion of Sikhs than of Hindus' (http://mandladowell.notlong.com).

The law recognises that race is not a genetic given but a historical, cultural, textual and linguistic construct. What differentiates it from, say, religion, is the physical nature of the signs by which it is interpreted – skin colour, hair texture, the shape of facial and other bodily features. But these things are never fixed. They overlap, as we should expect them to do given that people have always tended to marry outside their genetic group. Indeed, many cultures require exogamy. And the interpretation of racial features itself takes place within a culture-specific context.

Self-identity has long been given a privileged role in identity research. But the identities we construct for ourselves and others are not different in kind, only in the status we accord to them. The gap between the identity of an individual and of a group – a nation or town, race or ethnicity, gender or sexual orientation, religion or sect, school or club, company or profession, or the most nebulous of all, a social class – is most like a true difference of kind. Group identities seem more abstract than individual ones, in the sense that 'Brazilianness' doesn't exist separately from the Brazilians who possess it, except as an abstract concept. Yet combinations of such abstractions are what our individual identities are made up of, and group identity frequently finds its most concrete manifestation in a single, symbolic individual. The group identities we partake in nurture our individual sense of who we are, but can also smother it.

Pierre Bourdieu, discussing regional and ethnic identities, makes an important point that applies to many other types of identity as well: although they essentialise what are actually arbitrary divisions among peoples, and in this sense are not 'real', the fact that, once established, they exist as mental representations makes them every bit as real as if they were grounded in anything 'natural':

> One can understand the particular form of struggle over classifications that is constituted by the struggle over the definition of 'regional' or 'ethnic' identity only if one transcends the opposition . . . between representation and reality, and only if one includes in reality the representation of reality, or, more precisely, the struggle over representations . . .
>
> Struggles over ethnic or regional identity – in other words, over the properties (stigmata or emblems) linked with the *origin* through the *place* of origin and its associated durable marks, such as accent – are a particular case of the different struggles over classifications, struggles over the monopoly of the power to make people see and believe, to get them to know and recognize, to impose the legitimate definition of the divisions of the social world and, thereby, to *make and unmake groups*. (Bourdieu 1991: 221)

Modern linguistics has moved slowly but steadily toward embracing the identity function as central to language. The impediment has been the dominance of the traditional outlook which takes representation alone to be essential, with even communication relegated to a secondary place. This outlook was never the only one available, however, and when early twentieth-century linguists such as Jespersen and Sapir came to investigate how language functions to define and regulate the role of the individual within the social unit at the same time as it helps to constitute that unit, they were not without predecessors. It was just that mainstream linguistics as it had developed within the nineteenth century was not inclined to see such questions as falling within its purview.

An overview of the development of such inquiry within linguistics and adjacent fields can be found in Joseph (2004), from which some key moments will be excerpted here. The first is Labov's 1963 study of the English dialect of Martha's Vineyard, an island off the coast of Massachusetts, where the diphthongs in words like *right* and *house* are pronounced as [əy] and [əw] rather than [ay] and [aw]. This feature is not found in the dialects of the mainlanders who 'summer' on Martha's Vineyard, and with whom the Vineyarders (year-round residents) have a complex relationship of dependency and resentment. 'It is apparent that the immediate meaning of this phonetic feature is "Vineyarder". When a man says [rəyt] or [həws], he is unconsciously establishing the fact that he belongs to the island: that he is one of the natives to whom the island really belongs' (Labov 1963: 307). This is very much the sort of analysis of the effect of linguistic identity on language form that would characterise work in the 1990s and since, though it would be sidelined in the mid-1960s by the statistical charting of variation and change.

In the meantime, one particular identity focus – gender – led the way in directing atten-tion to the reading of identity in language. Lakoff (1973) argued that, in both structure and use, languages mark out an inferior social role for women and bind them to it. Gender politics is incorporated directly into the pronoun systems of English and many other lan-guages, through the use of the masculine as the 'unmarked' gender (as in 'Everyone take his seat'). Lakoff points to features that occur more frequently in women's than in men's English, such as tag questions, hedges, intensifiers and pause markers, which as marks of insecurity and of the role women are expected to occupy are fundamental to maintaining the status quo in gender politics.

As the notion of separate men's and women's language was accepted, the more general notion of the language–identity link was let in through the back door, leaving the way open for the study of group identities of all sorts beyond those national and ethnic ones traditionally associated with language difference. This was a challenge to a sociolinguis-tics that had been fixated on class differences. By the mid-1980s this shift was under-way in the work of, for example, Gumperz (1982), Edwards (1985) and Le Page and Tabouret-Keller (1985), though it was really in the 1990s that it would come to occupy the mainstream of work in sociolinguistics and linguistic anthropology. (For a small but representational sample of studies see, on the sociological end, Fishman 1999; on the anthropological, Schieffelin et al. 1998; and in discourse analysis, Wodak et al. 1999; Benwell and Stokoe 2006).

This work also received significant input from social psychology, where one approach in particular needs to be singled out: Social Identity Theory, developed in the early 1970s by Tajfel. In the years following his death in 1982 it came to be the single most influen-tial model for analysing linguistic identity. Tajfel defined social identity as 'that part of an individual's self-concept which derives from his knowledge of his membership of a social group (or groups) together with the value and emotional significance attached to that membership' (Tajfel 1978: 63). Within this simple definition are embedded at least five positions which in their time were quite revolutionary: that social identity pertains to an individual rather than to a social group; that it is a matter of *self-concept*, rather than of social categories into which one simply falls; that the fact of *membership* is the essen-tial thing, rather than anything having to do with the nature of the group itself; that an individual's own knowledge of the membership, and the particular value they attach to it – completely 'subjective' factors – are what count; that emotional significance is not some trivial side effect of the identity belonging but an integral part of it.

Beyond this, Social Identity Theory marked a break with other approaches in the fact that it was not concerned with analyses grounded in a notion of 'power', but simply in the relative hierarchisations that we seem instinctively to impose on ourselves, most particularly in our status as members of 'in-groups' and 'out-groups', which would come into even greater prominence in the 'Self-Categorization Theory' that developed as an extension of the original model, notably in the work of Tajfel's collaborator Turner (see Tajfel and Turner 1979; Turner et al. 1987; Turner 1991).

Partly under the influence of such work, sociolinguists were beginning to re-orient their own object of investigation. Milroy (1980) reported data from studies she conducted in Belfast showing that the 'social class' of an individual did not appear to be the key variable allowing one to make predictions about which forms of particular linguistic variables the person would use. Rather, the key variable was the nature of the person's 'social network', a concept borrowed from sociology, which Milroy defined as 'the informal social relation-ships contracted by an individual' (Milroy 1980: 174). Where close-knit localised network structures existed, there was a strong tendency to maintain nonstandard vernacular forms of speech – a tendency difficult to explain in a model such as Labov's, based on a scale of 'class' belonging where following norms of standard usage marked one as higher on the hierarchy and entitled to benefits that most people desire. Labov's early work on Martha's Vineyard had suggested that the answer lay in identity, specifically in the value of belonging to a group who, although not highly placed in socio-economic terms, could nevertheless claim something valuable for themselves (in the Martha's Vineyard case, authenticity). Milroy's book provided statistical backing for such an explanation.

Although the inner workings of the social network depend somewhat on amount of personal contact, the essential thing is that its members share *norms*. As attention turned to understanding the nature of these norms, two much publicised views had an impact. Fish (1980) had devised the concept of the 'interpretative community' to account for the norms of reading whereby people evaluate different readings of the same text as valid or as absurd. An interpretative community is a group sharing such a set of norms; its members may never come into direct physical contact with one another, yet they share norms spread by the educational system, books or the media. Soon after, Anderson (1991, first published in 1983) proposed a new understanding of the 'nation' as an 'imagined commu-nity', whose members, like that of the interpretative community, will never all meet one another let alone have the sort of regular intercourse that creates a 'network'. What binds them together is the shared belief in the membership in the community.

Notably with the work of Eckert, sociolinguistic investigation of groups ideologically bound to one another shifted from statistically–based examination of social networks to more interpretative examination of 'communities of practice', defined as 'an aggregate of people who come together around mutual engagement in an endeavor' (Eckert and McConnell-Ginet 1992: 464) (see further, Moore, this volume). In the course of this endeavour there emerge shared beliefs, norms and ideologies, including though not limited to linguistic and communicative behaviour. The advantage of the 'community of practice' concept is its openness – any aggregate of people can be held to constitute one, so long as the analyst can point convincingly to behaviour that implies shared norms, or, better still, elicit expression of the underlying ideologies from members of the com-munity. This line of research is thus continuous with another one that has focused more directly on the normative beliefs or ideologies by which national and other group identi-ties are maintained. Some early work along these lines was published in Wodak (1989) and Joseph and Taylor (1990), and subsequently a great deal more has appeared, for example in Verschueren (1999), Blommaert (1999), Kroskrity (2000).

Other features of recent work on language and identity include the view that identity is something constructed rather than essential, and performed rather than possessed – features which the term 'identity' itself tends to mask, suggesting as it does something singular, objective and reified. Each of us performs a repertoire of identities that are con-stantly shifting, and that we negotiate and re-negotiate according to the circumstances.

Billig, a colleague and collaborator of Tajfel, has explored how the 'continual acts of imagination' on which the nation depends for its existence are reproduced (Billig 1995: 70), sometimes through purposeful deployment of national symbols, but mostly through daily habits of which we are dimly aware at best. Examples include the national flag hanging in front of the post office, the national symbols on the coins and banknotes we use each day. Billig introduced the term *banal nationalism* to cover the ideological habits which enable the established nations of the West to be reproduced (see also Llamas, this volume). In Billig's view 'an identity is to be found in the embodied habits of social life' (1995: 8), including language. Smith (1998) has emphasised how much of the effort of nationalism construction is aimed at reaching back to the past in the interest of 'ethno-symbolism', and this can be seen particularly in the strong investment made by modern cultures in maintaining the 'standard language', by which is meant a form resistant to change, hence harking backward.

Hobsbawm places great stress on the fact that enthusiasm for linguistic nationalism has historically been a phenomenon of the *lower middle class*: 'The classes which stood or fell by the official use of the written vernacular were the socially modest but educated middle strata, which included those who acquired lower middle-class status precisely by virtue of occupying non-manual jobs that required schooling' (Hobsbawm 1990: 117). These are also the people who become the mainstay of nationalism – not just by active flag-waving on symbolic occasions, but daily in the banal ways pointed to by Billig, including their use of 'proper language' and their insistence on its norms, for instance in conversation with their own children. Hobsbawm has suggested that, in Victorian times, the pattern was established whereby the lower middle classes (artisans, shopkeepers and clerks) enacted their national belonging by showing themselves to be 'the most "respectable" sons and daughters of the fatherland' (1990: 122). In other words, although their real identity was that of a social class, they masked it for themselves and others in a nationalistic guise. The mask was double-sided: in their obsession with 'speaking properly' as a mark of respectability, they were contributing to the linguistic construction of their nation.

Language has traditionally been a key ingredient in this process of national identity formation and reproduction for at least five reasons:

1. Groups of people who occupy contiguous territory and see themselves as having common interests tend to develop, over long stretches of time, ways of speaking that are distinctive to them, marking them out from groups who either are not geographically adjacent to them or else are perceived as having different, probably rival interests. In other words, language does tend to mark out the social features on which national belonging will come to be based – but it is only a tendency, because it also happens very frequently that the same way of speaking is shared by people with very different interests (religious ones, for instance), and that markedly different ways of speaking exist among a group of people who nonetheless see themselves as part of the same nation.

2. The ideology of national unity has favoured a view that nations are real because those within them share a deep cultural unity, and this has co-existed with a widespread – indeed, nearly universal – belief that deep cultural unity is the product of a shared language. This is what Fichte (1808) meant by the 'invisible bonds' by which nature has joined those who speak the same language. Again, as with (1), it cannot be more than a tendency, since it is not the case that people who identify themselves as belonging to the same culture or nation think identically. Yet language is central to the *habitus* (a traditional term revived by Bourdieu): the fact that we spend our formative years attending long and hard

to the task of learning words and their meanings from those around us results in our acquiring tastes, habits, ways of thinking from them that will endure into adult life. The language does not somehow transmit culture and identity to its speakers – rather, it is that *text* in constant interaction with which older speakers transmit culture and identities (local and personal as well as national, ethnic and religious) to the young. (In many cases the young will want an identity of their own, and will attain it first of all by resisting the imposition of culture upon them by their elders.)

3. In addition to being the text of cultural transmission, the language is the principal medium in which texts of national identity in the more usual sense will be constructed. It is not the only such medium, nor the only powerful one, as Billig's exposition of 'banal nationalism' has shown. But the particular concepts which constitute a national identity correspond to words in the national language, embodied in 'sacred texts' of the nation such as a constitution or key works of the national literature, including the national anthem.

4. As universal education is adopted throughout the nation, inculcating standards of 'correct' language assumes a central role. Overtly, this is out of a perceived duty to maintain the culture. However, as Hobsbawm has shown, such is the force of the language-culture-nation-class nexus that, especially for the upwardly mobile members of the lower middle class, being a 'proper' citizen and member of the community is inseparable from using 'proper' language.

5. In so far as nations are not the historical essences they purport to be, but are constructs which inevitably involve a certain amount of arbitrary and even capricious divisions and classifications, when a nation wants to control who can live in it, vote in it and enjoy state benefits, language can appear to be the most obvious test for deciding whether particular individuals belong to the nation or not. Most nations no longer have laws based upon 'racial' classification – which are rarely easy to apply in any case – yet many do require cultural qualifications to be met, which are likely to include language either overtly or indirectly.

Each of these factors has reinforced the others in giving the national language the force of a cultural-historical 'ethno-symbolic' myth as suggested by Smith (see above). Within each, too, there is a contradiction or a caveat that has periodically pendulum-swung to prominence, such that the loss of belief in the national language and all it stands for is always potentially there, and is bound to come to the fore at least on occasion. The question that is unanswerable for now is whether national languages, together with the nations to which they are attached, represent a historical phase that is now on a course of decline heading for eventual disappearance, to be replaced with 'glocalisation' – a term that has been coined to denote the combination of globalisation with the resurgence of local, sub-national sites of belonging – or whether they are an invention that has proven too useful for human social organisation to be given up.

A model that has recently become prominent in sociolinguistic discussions of identity is that of *indexical order*, first proposed in its current form by Michael Silverstein (2003) though in fact going back to work of his from the 1970s. It is inspired by the semiotic theory of Charles Sanders Peirce, for whom a key property of linguistic and other signs is indexicality, the fact that they point towards associations that do not have to be in the same existential realm. Thus smoke is an index of fire, and in much the same way, pronouncing *path* as /pɑːθ/ ('pahth') rather than /paθ/ is an index of southern Englishness, or of education in a posh school where Received Pronunciation was *de rigueur* (see further Johnstone, this volume). Silverstein has argued that such indices pursue an ordered path of development. They begin as 'first order' markers of relatively value-free associations such as geographical identity (for example, southern England), then proceed to become 'second order' indices of ideologically loaded information, such as the eliteness of a speaker's education. This ordering can proceed up to an unlimited number of layers, but the crucial point for Silverstein is always the relationship between a particular level in the order (*n*) and the one just above it (*n* + 1), for it is in the interplay between these two that identity is dialectically constructed. Silverstein calls this approach 'ethno-pragmatics', and identifies its goal as analysing 'the n-th order indexical token as a direct (causal) consequence of the degree of (institutionalized) ideological engagement users manifest in respect of the n-th order indexical meaningfulness' (Silverstein 2003: 194).

In still more recent work, Blommaert (2007) has reformulated this model into what he calls 'orders of indexicality'. It is self-consciously inspired by Silverstein's indexical order, but tries to supply what Blommaert and others (including the present author) see as crucially missing from Silverstein's model: an explanation of where it exists, how it is manifested, and above all how speakers become aware of it and 'play' with it. Where Silverstein's analysis is focused on the play of signs, Blommaert grounds his approach in the social theory of Foucault and looks specifically for the institutional context in which orders of indexicality operate, and how speakers make use of the affordances they provide to achieve the speakers' own agentive ends.

Silverstein and Blommaert agree, however, on the point that identities of all sorts, including linguistic ones, are constructed at the interstices and margins of the categories and places to which they are tied. It is for those at the margins that identities matter most. But no one occupies the 'centre' all the time. *Who's he when he's at home?* is the hardest question to answer, and the least interesting, because when he's at home, he doesn't need to be anybody. It's when he's *not* at home that his identity matters. Indeed, in a significant sense, it is only then that his identity exists.

2

Locating Identity in Language[1]

Mary Bucholtz and Kira Hall

1. Introduction

In this chapter, we propose a framework for the analysis of identity as constituted in linguistic interaction. The need for such a framework has become apparent in recent years, as linguistic research on identity has become increasingly central within sociolinguistics, linguistic anthropology, discourse analysis and social psychology. But the concomitant development of theoretical approaches to identity remains at best a secondary concern, not a focused goal of the field. We argue for the analytic value of approaching identity as a relational and socio-cultural phenomenon that emerges and circulates in local discourse contexts of interaction rather than as a stable structure located primarily in the individual psyche or in fixed social categories. We believe that the approach we propose here, which draws together insights from a variety of fields and theorists, allows for a discussion of identity that permits researchers to articulate theoretical assumptions about identity often left implicit in scholarship, while avoiding the critiques of this concept that have arisen in the social sciences and humanities in the past two decades. Given the scope of such scholarly research, our definition of identity is deliberately broad and open-ended: *identity is the social positioning of self and other.*

The framework we outline here synthesises key work on identity from a number of scholarly traditions to offer a general socio-cultural linguistic perspective on identity – that is, one that focuses on both the details of language and the workings of culture and society. By *socio-cultural linguistics*, we mean the broad interdisciplinary field concerned with the intersection of language, culture and society. This term encompasses the disciplinary subfields of sociolinguistics, linguistic anthropology, socially oriented forms of discourse analysis (such as conversation analysis and critical discourse analysis) and linguistically oriented social psychology, among others.[2] In incorporating these diverse approaches under a single label, our purpose is neither to deny the differences among them nor to impose new disciplinary boundaries; rather, it is to acknowledge the full range of work that falls under the rubric of language and identity and to offer a shorthand device for referring to these approaches collectively. The interdisciplinary perspective taken here is intended to help scholars recognise the comprehensive toolkit already available to them for analysing identity as a centrally linguistic phenomenon. Identity does not emerge at a single analytic level – whether vowel quality, turn shape, code choice or ideological structure – but operates at multiple levels simultaneously. Our own approach privileges the interactional level, because it is in interaction that all these resources gain social meaning. Our goal is to assemble elements of socio–cultural linguistic work on identity into a coherent model that both describes the current state of research and offers new directions for future scholarship.

We propose five principles that we see as fundamental to the study of identity. The first and second principles challenge narrowly psychological and static views of identity that have circulated widely in the social sciences. We argue instead, in line with abundant socio–cultural linguistic research, that identity is a discursive construct that emerges in interaction. Further, we expand traditional macrosociological views of identity to include both local ethnographic categories and transitory interactional positions. The third principle inventories the types of linguistic resources whereby interactants indexically position self and other in discourse. The heart of the model is described in the fourth principle, which highlights the relational foundation of identity. To illustrate this principle, we briefly outline our own recently developed framework for analysing identity as an intersubjective accomplishment. Finally, the fifth principle considers the limits and constraints on individual intentionality in the process of identity construction, while acknowledging the important role that deliberate social action may play in producing identity. Throughout the chapter, we argue for a view of identity that is intersubjectively rather than individually produced and interactionally emergent rather than assigned in an *a priori* fashion.

2. The emergence principle

The first principle that informs our perspective addresses a traditional scholarly view of identity as housed primarily within an individual mind, so that the only possible relationship between identity and language use is for language to reflect an individual's internal mental state. While individuals' sense of self is certainly an important element of identity, researchers of individuals' language use (for example, Johnstone 1996) have shown that the only way that such self-conceptions enter the social world is via some form of discourse. Hence, accounts that locate identity inside the mind may discount the social ground on which identity is built, maintained and altered.

Our own view draws from the sustained engagement with the concept of emergence both in linguistic anthropology, where it is linked to performance and culture, and in interactional linguistics, where it informs a usage-based theory of grammar. We extend the insights of this previous linguistic work on emergence to the analysis of identity. As with performance, culture and grammar itself, we maintain that identity emerges from the specific conditions of linguistic interaction:

> 1. Identity is best viewed as the emergent product rather than the pre-existing source of linguistic and other semiotic practices and therefore as fundamentally a social and cultural phenomenon.

This is a familiar idea within several very different branches of socio–cultural linguistics: the ethnomethodological concept of 'doing' various kinds of identity (for example,

Fenstermaker and West 2002; West and Zimmerman 1991) and the related conversation-analytic notion of identity as an interactionally relevant accomplishment (for example, Antaki and Widdicombe 1998); the poststructuralist theory of performativity (Butler 1990), developed from the work of J. L. Austin (1962), as taken up by researchers of language, gender and sexuality (for example, Livia and Hall 1997); and more generally the semiotic concepts of creative indexicality (Silverstein 1979) and referee design (Bell 1984). Despite fundamental differences among these approaches, all of them enable us to view identity not simply as a psychological mechanism of self-classification reflected in people's social behaviour but rather as something constituted through social action, and especially through language. Of course, the property of emergence does not exclude the possibility that resources for identity work in any given interaction may derive from resources developed in earlier interactions (that is, they may draw on 'structure' – such as ideology, the linguistic system, or the relation between the two).

Although nearly all contemporary linguistic research on identity takes this general per-spective as its starting point, it is perhaps easiest to recognise identity as emergent in cases where speakers' language use does not conform with the social category to which they are normatively assigned. Cases of transgender identity and cross-gender performance (for example, Barrett 1999; Hall and O'Donovan 1996) and ethnic, racial and national bound-ary crossing (for example, Bucholtz 1995, 1999a; Rampton 1995) illustrate in diverse ways that identities as social processes do not precede the semiotic practices that call them into being in specific interactions. Such situations are striking only because they sever the ideologically expected mapping between language and biology or culture; that is, they subvert essentialist preconceptions of linguistic ownership. While the emergent nature of identity is especially stark in these cases, identity is discursively produced even in the most mundane and unremarkable situations.

3. The positionality principle

The second principle challenges another widely circulating view of identity, namely that it is simply a collection of broad social categories. This perspective is found most often in the quantitative social sciences, which correlate social behaviour with macro identity cat-egories such as age, gender and social class. Within socio-cultural linguistics, the concern with identities as broader social structures is particularly characteristic of early variation-ist sociolinguistics (for example, Labov 1966) and the sociology of language (see Fishman 1971, among others). The traditional forms of these approaches have been valuable for documenting large-scale sociolinguistic trends; they are often less effective in capturing the more nuanced and flexible kinds of identity relations that arise in local contexts (but see, for example, Labov 1963). This analytic gap points to the importance of ethnogra-phy. Linguistic ethnographers have repeatedly demonstrated that language users often orient to local identity categories rather than to the analyst's sociological categories, and that the former frequently provide a better empirical account of linguistic practice.

In addition, more recent socio-cultural linguistic work has begun to investigate the micro details of identity as it is shaped from moment to moment in interaction. At the most basic level, identity emerges in discourse through the temporary roles and orientations assumed by participants, such as evaluator, joke-teller or engaged listener. Such interactional posi-tions may seem quite different from identity as conventionally understood; however, these temporary roles, no less than larger sociological and ethnographic identity categories, contribute to the formation of subjectivity and intersubjectivity in discourse. On the one hand, the interactional positions that social actors briefly occupy and then abandon as they respond to the contingencies of unfolding discourse may accumulate ideological associations with both large-scale and local categories of identity. On the other, these ideological associations, once forged, may shape who does what and how in interaction, though never in a deterministic fashion. Our own perspective therefore broadens the traditional referential range of *identity* to encompass not only more widely recognised constructs of social subjectivity but also local identity categories and transitory interactional positions:

> 2. Identities encompass (a) macrolevel demographic categories; (b) local, ethnographically specific cultural positions; and (c) temporary and interactionally specific stances and participant roles.

These different kinds of positions typically occur simultaneously in a single interaction. From the perspective of the analyst, it is not a matter of choosing one dimension of identity over others, but of considering multiple facets in order to achieve a more complete understanding of how identity works.

4. The indexicality principle

While the first two principles we have discussed characterise the ontological status of identity, the third principle is concerned with the mechanism whereby identity is constituted. This mechanism, known as *indexicality*, is fundamental to the way in which linguistic forms are used to construct identity positions. In its most basic sense, an *index* is a linguistic form that depends on the interactional context for its meaning, such as the 1st person pronoun *I* (Silverstein 1976). More generally, however, the concept of indexicality involves the creation of semiotic links between linguistic forms and social meanings (Ochs 1992; Silverstein 1985). In identity formation, indexicality relies heavily on ideological structures, for associations between language and identity are rooted in cultural beliefs and values – that is, ideologies – about the sorts of speakers who (can or should) produce particular sorts of language.

Indexical processes occur at all levels of linguistic structure and use. The third principle outlines some of these different linguistic means whereby identity is discursively produced:

> 3. Identity relations emerge in interaction through several related indexical processes, including: (a) overt mention of identity categories and labels; (b) implicatures and presuppositions regarding one's own or others' identity position; (c) displayed evaluative and epistemic orientations to ongoing talk, as well as interactional footings and participant roles; and (d) the use of linguistic structures and systems that are ideologically associated with specific personas and groups.

The most obvious and direct way that identities can be constituted through talk is the overt introduction of referential identity categories into discourse. Indeed, a focus on social category labels has been a primary method that nonlinguistic researchers have used to approach the question of identity. Researchers in socio-cultural linguistics contribute to this line of work a more precise and systematic methodology for understanding labelling and categorisation as social action. The circulation of such categories within ongoing discourse, their explicit or implicit juxtaposition with other categories, and the linguistic elaborations and qualifications they attract (predicates, modifiers, and so on) all provide important information about identity construction. Less direct means of instantiating identities include such pragmatic processes as implicature and presupposition, both of which require additional inferential work for interpretation.

Recent work on stance – that is, the display of evaluative, affective and epistemic orientations in discourse – has made explicit the ways in which other dimensions of interaction can be resources for the construction of identity. In his framework for the analysis of stance as both a subjective and an intersubjective phenomenon, John Du Bois characterises stance as social action in the following terms: 'I evaluate something, and thereby position myself, and align [or disalign] with you' (Du Bois 2007: 163). Stance and related concepts that have developed in various fields of socio-cultural linguistics are productive for the study of identity because they show how, even in the most fleeting of interactional moves, speakers position themselves and others as particular kinds of people. Moreover, stances can build up into larger identity categories. In an influential paper, Ochs (1992) extends the concept of indexicality by arguing that the indexical connection between a given linguistic form and a particular social identity is not direct. Rather, linguistic forms that index identity are more basically associated with interactional stances such as forcefulness, uncertainty, and so on, which in turn may come to be associated with particular social categories, such as gender. Within interactional linguistics, Rauniomaa (2003) has developed Du Bois's (2002) concept of stance accretion to capture the way in which stances accumulate into more durable structures of identity.

It is important to emphasise that the process of creating indexical ties of this kind is inherently ideological, creating in bottom-up fashion a set of interactional norms for particular social groups. Conversely, in the process of indexical inversion described by Inoue (2004), indexical associations can also be imposed from the top down by cultural authorities such as intellectuals or the media. Such an imposed indexical tie may create ideological expectations among speakers and hence affect linguistic practice.

A somewhat related set of insights comes from the concept of style in variationist sociolinguistics. This term traditionally refers to intraspeaker variation in language use (Labov 1972a), but more contemporary approaches (for example, California Style Collective 1993; Eckert 2000), along with earlier work by Bell (1984) and Coupland (1980), understand style as a repertoire of linguistic forms associated with personas or identities. Whereas scholars concerned with stance concentrate on conversational acts such as evaluative expressions, sociolinguists of style typically look instead to linguistic structures below the discursive level, such as grammar, phonology and lexis. In an indexical process similar to what both Ochs and Rauniomaa describe for stance, these features become tied to styles and hence to identity through habitual practice (Bourdieu [1972] 1977). One of the important insights of the style literature is that the social meanings of style often require ethnographic investigation to uncover groups that may seem homogeneous when seen through a wider analytic lens, but become sharply differentiated when ethnographic details are brought into close focus.

In addition to microlevel linguistic structures like stance markers and style features, entire linguistic systems such as languages and dialects may also be indexically tied to identity categories. This phenomenon – long the mainstay of a wide range of socio-cultural linguistic scholarship – has been especially well theorised in the literature on language, nationalism and ideology (for example, Gal and Irvine 1995). Work on language choice has also begun to appear in the emerging field of language and glo-balisation. Given the vast scale of such phenomena as nationalism and globalisation, much of the research on these issues is not interactional in its approach. However, some current studies, especially on the latter topic (for example, Besnier 2004; Hall 2003a), consider how large-scale social processes such as globalisation shape identity in interaction.

The range of phenomena discussed in this section attests to the wealth of linguistic resources that contribute to the production of identity positions. Disparate indexical processes of labelling, implicature, stance-taking, style-marking, and code-choice work to construct identities, both micro and macro, as well as those somewhere in between. By considering identity formation at multiple indexical levels rather than focusing on only one, we can assemble a much richer portrait of subjectivity and intersubjectivity as they are constituted in interaction.

5. The relationality principle

The first three principles we have discussed focus on the emergent, positional and indexi-cal aspects of identity and its production. Building on these points, the fourth principle emphasises identity as a relational phenomenon. In calling attention to relationality, we have two aims: first, to underscore the point that identities are never autonomous or inde-pendent but always acquire social meaning in relation to other available identity positions and other social actors; and second, to call into question the widespread but oversimpli-fied view of identity relations as revolving around a single axis: sameness and difference. The principle we propose here suggests a much broader range of relations that are forged through identity processes:

> 4. Identities are intersubjectively constructed through several, often overlap-ping, complementary relations, including similarity/difference, genuineness/artifice and authority/delegitimacy.

We have described these relations at length elsewhere as what we have termed *tactics of intersubjectivity* (Bucholtz and Hall 2004a, 2004b), and we briefly summarise those dis-cussions here. The list of identity relations we outline in this and our earlier work is not intended to be exhaustive but rather suggestive of the different dimensions of relationality created through identity construction. In addition, it is important to note that although we separate the concepts for purposes of exposition we do not view them as mutually exclusive; indeed, since these are relational processes, two or more typically work in conjunction with one another.

5.1 Adequation and distinction

The first two complementary identity relations we describe – similarity and difference –
are also the most widely discussed in social-scientific research on identity. To highlight
the ways in which we depart from traditional views of these relations, we use the terms
adequation and *distinction*.

The term *adequation* emphasises the fact that in order for groups or individuals to be
positioned as alike, they need not – and in any case cannot – be identical, but must merely
be understood as sufficiently similar for current interactional purposes. Thus, differences
irrelevant or damaging to ongoing efforts to adequate two people or groups will be down-
played, and similarities viewed as salient to and supportive of the immediate project of
identity work will be foregrounded.

The counterpart of adequation, *distinction*, focuses on the identity relation of differentiation.[3] The overwhelming majority of socio-cultural linguistic research on identity has
emphasised this relation, both because social differentiation is a highly visible process and
because language is an especially potent resource for producing it in a variety of ways. Just
as adequation relies on the suppression of social differences that might disrupt a seamless
representation of similarity, distinction depends on the suppression of similarities that
might undermine the construction of difference.

5.2 Authentication and denaturalisation

The second pair of relations, *authentication* and *denaturalisation*, are the processes by
which speakers make claims to realness and artifice, respectively. While both relations
have to do with authenticity, the first focuses on the ways in which identities are discursively verified and the second on how assumptions regarding the seamlessness of identity
can be disrupted. Like the focus on distinction, a concern with authenticity – that is, what
sorts of language and language users count as 'genuine' for a given purpose – has per-
vaded the socio-cultural linguistic literature, although analysts have not always separated
their own assumptions about authenticity from those of the speakers they study (Bucholtz
2003; see also Coupland, this volume). We call attention not to authenticity as an inherent
essence, but to authentication as a social process played out in discourse.

In denaturalisation, by contrast, such claims to the inevitability or inherent rightness
of identities are subverted. What is called attention to instead are the ways in which identity is crafted, fragmented, problematic or false. Such aspects often emerge most clearly
in parodic performance and in some displays of hybrid identity, but they may also appear
whenever an identity violates ideological expectations.

5.3 Authorisation and illegitimation

The final pair of intersubjective relations considers the structural and institutional
aspects of identity formation. The first of these, *authorisation*, involves the affirmation
or imposition of an identity through structures of institutionalised power and ideology,
whether local or translocal. The counterpart of authorisation, *illegitimation*, addresses
the ways in which identities are dismissed, censored or simply ignored by these same
structures.

The tactics of intersubjectivity outlined here not only call attention to the intersubjective basis of identity, but also provide a sense of the diverse ways that relationality works through discourse. Relationality operates at many levels. As many socio-cultural linguists have argued, even genres traditionally thought of as monologic are fundamentally interactional. Identities emerge only in relation to other identities within the contingent framework of interaction.

6. The partialness principle

The final principle draws from a voluminous literature in cultural anthropology and feminist theory over the past two decades that has challenged the analytic drive to represent forms of social life as internally coherent. This challenge, inspired by the postmodern critique of the totalising master narratives characteristic of previous generations, surfaces in ethnography in the realisation that all representations of culture are necessarily 'partial accounts' (Clifford and Marcus 1986). This idea has long been central to feminist analysis, in which there is an ethical commitment to recognising the situatedness and partialness of any claim to knowledge (see Behar and Gordon 1995; Visweswaran 1994). The feminist commitment to explicitly positioning oneself as a researcher rather than effacing one's presence in the research process, a practice which echoes the politics of location in reflexive ethnography, has exposed the fact that reality itself is intersubjective in nature, constructed through the particulars of self and other in any localised encounter. This idea fits well with postmodern theorisings of identity as fractured and discontinuous, for as anthropologist Kamala Visweswaran has noted, 'identities are constituted by context and are themselves asserted as partial accounts' (1994: 41).

Whereas the critique of ethnography has been most interested in the partialness construed by one kind of identity relation – that of researcher and subject – our fifth principle attempts to capture not only this dynamic, but the entire multitude of ways in which identity exceeds the individual self. Because identity is inherently relational, it will always be partial, produced through contextually situated and ideologically informed configurations of self and other. Even seemingly coherent displays of identity, such as those that pose as deliberate and intentional, are reliant on both interactional and ideological constraints for their articulation:

> 5. Any given construction of identity may be in part deliberate and intentional, in part habitual and hence often less than fully conscious, in part an outcome of interactional negotiation and contestation, in part an outcome of others' perceptions and representations, and in part an effect of larger ideological processes and material structures that may become relevant to interaction. It is therefore constantly shifting both as interaction unfolds and across discourse contexts.

Particular kinds of analysis will often bring to the forefront one of these aspects over others. However, the rich possibilities of the broad interdisciplinary research we include under the rubric of socio-cultural linguistics are most fully realised when multiple dimensions of identity are considered in a single analysis or when complementary analyses are brought together.

The principle stated above helps to resolve a central and long-standing issue regarding research on identity: the extent to which it is understood as relying on agency. From the perspective of an interactional approach to identity, the role of agency becomes problematic only when it is conceptualised as located within an individual rational subject who consciously authors his identity without structural constraints. (Our gendered pronoun choice here is quite deliberate and corresponds to the fact that male subjectivity was taken as unmarked by many scholars in earlier generations.) Numerous strands of social theory from Marxism to poststructuralism have rightly critiqued this notion of agency, but the litany of dubious qualities associated with the autonomous subject now functions more as caricature than critique of how agency is currently understood. Indeed, current researchers, particularly within socio-cultural linguistics, have found ways of theorising agency that circumvent the dangers identified by critics while exploiting its utility for work on identity. Socio-cultural linguists are generally not concerned with calibrating the degree of autonomy or intentionality in any given act; rather, agency is more productively viewed as the accomplishment of social action (cf. Ahearn 2001). This way of thinking about agency is vital to any discipline that wants to consider the full complexity of social subjects alongside the larger power structures that constrain them. But it is especially important to socio-cultural linguistics, for the very use of language is itself an act of agency (Duranti 2004). Under this definition, identity is one kind of social action that agency can accomplish.

Such a definition of agency does not require that social action be intentional, but it allows for that possibility; habitual actions accomplished below the level of conscious awareness act upon the world no less than those carried out deliberately. Likewise, agency may be the result of individual action, but it may also be distributed among several social actors and hence intersubjective. The phenomenon of what could be called distributed agency, though not as well documented as that of distributed cognition (Hutchins 1995), has begun to receive attention in some areas of socio-cultural linguistics, often under the label of *joint activity* or *co-construction*. Finally, agency may be ascribed through the perceptions and representations of others or assigned through ideologies and social structures. As we have emphasised throughout this chapter, it is not a matter of choosing one of these aspects of identity over others, but of considering how some or all of them may potentially work with and against one another in discourse.

The interactional view that we take here has the added benefit of undoing the false dichotomy between structure and agency that has long plagued social theory (see the discussion in Ahearn 2001). On the one hand, it is only through discursive interaction that large-scale social structures come into being; on the other hand, even the most mundane of everyday conversations are impinged upon by ideological and material constructs that produce relations of power. Thus both structure and agency are intertwined as components of micro as well as macro articulations of identity.

7. Conclusion

Different research traditions within socio-cultural linguistics have particular strengths in analysing the varied dimensions of identity outlined in this chapter. The method of analysis selected by the researcher makes salient which aspect of identity comes into view, and such 'partial accounts' contribute to the broader understanding of identity that we advocate here. Although these lines of research have often remained separate from one another, the combination of their diverse theoretical and methodological strengths – including the microanalysis of conversation, the macroanalysis of ideological processes, the quantitative and qualitative analysis of linguistic structures, and the ethnographic focus on local cultural practices and social groupings – calls attention to the fact that identity in all its complexity can never be contained within a single analysis. For this reason, it is necessary to conceive of socio-cultural linguistics broadly and inclusively.

The five principles proposed here – Emergence, Positionality, Indexicality, Relationality and Partialness – represent the varied ways in which different kinds of scholars currently approach the question of identity. Even researchers whose primary goals lie elsewhere can contribute to this project by providing sophisticated conceptualisations of how human dynamics unfold in discourse, along with rigorous analytic tools for discovering how such processes work. While identity has been a widely circulating notion in socio-cultural linguistic research for some time, few scholars have explicitly theorised the concept. The present article offers one way of understanding this body of work by anchoring identity in interaction. By positing, in keeping with recent scholarship, that identity is emergent in discourse and does not precede it, we are able to locate identity as an intersubjectively achieved social and cultural phenomenon. This discursive approach further allows us to incorporate within identity not only the broad sociological categories most commonly associated with the concept, but also more local positionings, both ethnographic and interactional. The linguistic resources that indexically produce identity at all these levels are therefore necessarily broad and flexible, including labels, implicatures, stances, styles and entire languages and varieties. Because these tools are put to use in interaction, the process of identity construction does not reside within the individual but in intersubjective relations of sameness and difference, realness and fakeness, power and disempowerment. Finally, by theorising agency as a phenomenon broader than simply individualistic and deliberate action, we are able to call attention to the myriad ways that identity comes into being, from habitual practice to interactional negotiation to representations and ideologies.

It is no overstatement to assert that the age of identity is upon us, not only in socio-cultural linguistics but also in the human and social sciences more generally. Scholars of language use are particularly well equipped to provide an empirically viable account of the complexities of identity as a social, cultural and – most fundamentally – interactional phenomenon. The recognition of the loose coalition of approaches that we call socio-cultural linguistics is a necessary step in advancing this goal, for it is only by understanding our diverse theories and methods as complementary, not competing, that we can meaningfully interpret this crucial dimension of contemporary social life.

Acknowledgements

We are grateful to the many audiences and readers who have provided feedback at various stages in the development of this project, and particularly to Dick Bauman, Niko Besnier, Elaine Chun, Barbara Fox, Barbara Johnstone, and Sally McConnell-Ginet for suggestions and encouragement. Special thanks are also due to Sandro Duranti for incisive comments as well as for his original invitation to us to present our joint work at the UCLA symposium *Theories and Models of Language, Interaction, and Culture*, which spurred us to think more deeply about the interactional grounding of identity. We also thank the editors for encouraging us to include our work in this volume. Naturally, we alone are responsible for any remaining weaknesses.

Notes

1. This chapter is an abbreviated and slightly revised version of Bucholtz and Hall (2005). Although due to space limitations we are unable to include data examples and comprehensive references, it is important to note that the theoretical framework we present here rests on the foundation of a wide range of empirical studies, the insights of which it builds upon.
2. The term *sociolinguistics* sometimes carries this referential range, but for many scholars it has a narrower reference. *Socio-cultural linguistics* has the virtue of being less encumbered with a particular history of use.
3. We take the term *distinction* from Pierre Bourdieu (1984), whose own conceptualisation of it is concerned with the production of social-class difference by members of the bourgeoisie. We broaden its reference to include any process of social differentiation.

3

Locating Language in Identity

Barbara Johnstone

1. Introduction

How do linguistic forms and patterns come to be associated with identities? What is it about the social practice we call language that enables linguistic forms to point to 'social meanings' like identity without necessarily referring to them? This chapter explores these questions. I describe how links between forms and social meanings are made, often fleetingly, in interaction and how such links can sometimes stabilise and coalesce into styles of discourse associated with identities. In the process, I discuss four key concepts: *indexicality*, *reflexivity*, *metapragmatics* and *enregisterment*. I first show how the concept of indexicality helps account for the way in which linguistic forms and social meanings are related (section 2). In section 3, I discuss reflexivity and metapragmatics, the general and more specific mechanisms that allow indexical relationships to be created. Section 4 sketches how indexical links between form and social meaning can stabilise, becoming reusable and accreting into sets of links sometimes called styles. For this, I draw on the concept of enregisterment.

My exposition of these concepts follows current thought in sociolinguistics and linguistic anthropology, and readers of this chapter should come to be able to use the terms the way many students of language and identity use them. However, I end the chapter, in section 5, with a critique of this way of thinking about meaning, suggesting that if we take the ideas of indexicality, reflexivity, metapragmatics and enregisterment seriously we should be drawn to a way of thinking about language that does not distinguish 'social' or 'pragmatic' meaning from meaning of any other sort.

2. Meaning and indexicality

For most of its history, linguistics has focused on denotation, or the relationship between linguistic signs and things in the world. From the point of view of denotation, it has typically been thought that the meaning of a sentence can be recovered by parsing its structure and looking up its words in a mental dictionary. This level of meaning is thought not to vary across contexts; a sentence means the same thing, on this abstract level, no matter who utters it, in what situation.

Clearly, though, what a sentence is actually taken to mean does vary according to the context in which it is uttered. A sentence that would be appropriate if uttered in one context can seem rude or crazy in another. To account for this, philosophers and linguists began to develop theories of 'pragmatic' meaning (see, for example, Levinson 1983) that purport to account for how people actually interpret each others' utterances. There are many versions of pragmatic theory, but the basic notion is that speakers and hearers add a layer of calculations about the context on top of calculations about lexical and structural meaning that are needed to figure out the utterance's 'literal', denotational meaning. For example, according to Speech Act theory (Searle 1969), in order to decide whether 'It's chilly in here' is to be taken as a request to close a window or simply an assertion of fact, the addressee makes calculations about whether the speaker would benefit from the addressee's taking action, whether the addressee is able to take action, whether the speaker really desires the action (or, alternatively, is being ironic), and so on.

Whether or not one person can request another's compliance in the first place has to do with power relations associated with culture- and situation-specific identities. It is easier for a superior to make a request of a social inferior than the other way around, and social superiority and inferiority are connected with identities like boss, teacher, sergeant, and sometimes male or white, versus identities like employee, student, private, or female or black. It is easier to make a request of someone socially closer than someone socially more distant, and social closeness is connected with identities like spouse, neighbour and friend. And some individuals are more intimidating, some more approachable. So linguists need a way of thinking about how social and personal identities and linguistic forms are related.

Sociolinguists have, in fact, talked about 'social meaning' for some time. Beginning in the 1960s, William Labov's (1963) research showed how facts about speakers' identities could be correlated with how they talked in various situations. Since then, new ways of thinking about identity and new reasons for talking about it have deepened our understanding of what language can accomplish in addition to denotation and pragmatic illocution. We know, for example, that when people say 'It's chilly in here' they are not only uttering a string of words that can be heard as having a literal, denotative, meaning and that are aimed at accomplishing some pragmatic action, but they are also displaying something, potentially, about the sort of person they are (or the sort of persona they are adopting) in the situation at hand, and we know that this display is essential to the work the utterance does in the interaction. However, sociolinguists have only fairly recently started to ask exactly what 'social meaning' is and how linguistic forms acquire meanings of this sort.

One influential model of this process begins with the concept of *indexicality* (see further Bucholtz and Hall, this volume). The idea of indexicality originates with American philosopher Charles Sanders Peirce (pronounced 'purse'). Peirce distinguished among three ways in which phenomena (including linguistic ones) could be taken as meaningful signs. A phenomenon can be taken as an iconic sign if it resembles what it is taken to mean. When ✐ is used to refer to a pencil, it is functioning as an iconic sign. A sign is *symbolic* if it is related to its meaning by convention rather than by resemblance. The word *pencil* is functioning as a symbol when it is taken to refer to a pencil, and because the sign does not resemble its referent, the word *pencil* can also be used for other things that may or may not actually involve a pencil: you can 'pencil someone in' for an appointment via keyboard or pen rather than by using a pencil. A sign is *indexical* if it is related to its meaning by virtue of co-occurring with the thing it is taken to mean. When we hear thunder, we often experience lightning, rain and a darkening sky, so the sound of thunder may lead us to expect a storm. Because the sound of thunder evokes storminess in this way, thunder noise can be used to evoke a storm in a staged play. Likewise, if hearing a word pronounced a particular way is experienced in connection with a particular style of dress or grooming, a particular set of social alignments, or a particular social activity, that pronunciation may evoke and/or create a social identity. The relationship between the pronunciation and the identity is an *indexical* relationship; we can say that the pronunciation *indexes* the identity; the pronunciation can be called an *indexical* (or an *index*) when it serves this purpose. Just as pronunciations can index identities, by virtue of being experienced together with other evidence of them, so can any other kind of linguistic form: words, phrases, grammatical patterns, patterns of discourse, even linguistic consistency or inconsistency over a lifetime (see Johnstone, forthcoming).

According to the linguistic anthropologists who first brought the concept of indexicality into sociolinguistics (Ochs 1992; Silverstein 2003), indexical relationships between linguistic form and social meaning can emerge at various levels of abstraction. Few, if any, linguistic forms exclusively index one particular social identity. For example, with relation to gendered identities, 'many of the linguistic features that in the literature are associated primarily with either men or women have as their core social meaning a particular affective stance' (Ochs 1992: 341) like toughness or softness. In some societies, styles of linguistic politeness (Brown and Levinson 1987) – that is, how people attend to their addressees' face needs – can come to index gender. Language that comes to seem gendered in a particular socio-cultural milieu arises out of contexts in which people use certain linguistic forms in the process of performing particular pragmatic, interactional practices. The same observations apply to how identities other than gendered ones are indexed. Table 3.1 sketches how indexical meanings can be layered and provides several examples.

Indexical forms can both evoke and construct identities, and they always potentially do both. Thus any of the indexical relationships described in the right-most column of Table 3.1 can themselves become tools for pragmatic, interactional practices that index other social identities. For example, if a woman uses baby talk in a romantic situation it might then index femininity; if an Australian used features of what Kiesling (2005) refers to as 'wogspeak' to parody an immigrant it might index a political affiliation. Every *n*+1-th-order index, in Silverstein's terms, can itself function as an *n*-th-order index when the context that the form presupposes (for example, mother speaking to child) gets evoked in order to shape (Silverstein uses 'entail') a new identity (for example, feminine flirt).

3. Creating indexicality: reflexivity and metapragmatics

How do indexical meanings get attached to linguistic forms? In other words, how do *correlations* between form and context become *indexical relationships* between form and context? How do people come to share the idea that, in the US, people who pronounce /æ/ as [a] in some contexts sound upper-class? How do we learn that words like *heretofore* are examples of 'legalese'? How does *wicked*, used as an adverbial intensifier in phrases like *wicked good*, get associated with New Englanders, and how does *hella*, used the same way, get associated with Northern California youth? The answer is surprisingly simple:

Table 3.1 Layering of indexicality

	A linguistic form is used by a particular person in performing an . . . ⟶	. . . interactional, pragmatic activity, which can then come to index a . . . ⟶	. . . social identity
Ochs's (1992) terms		'direct indexicality'	'indirect indexicality'
Silverstein's (2003) terms	'*n*-th-order indexicality'	'*n*+1-th order indexicality'	'(*n*+1)+1-th order indexicality'
example	A mother uses 'baby talk' (raised pitch, simplified words, etc.).	This comes to be heard as accommodating a child's (perceived) needs and wants,	which comes to index the social identity of caregiver to children (example from Ochs 1992)
example	A person with a Greek name uses high rising tone on word-final *-er*.	This comes to be heard as projecting forceful solidarity, as someone with relatively little power in Australian society,	which comes to index the social identity of recent immigrant (example from Kiesling 2005)
example	A person from Pittsburgh monophthongises (aw).	This comes to be heard as speaking casually, showing solidarity with neighbours,	which comes to index the social identity of authentic Pittsburgher (example from Johnstone et al. 2006)

people learn to hear linguistic variants as having indexical meaning by being told that they do, and they continue to share ideas about indexical meaning as long as they keep telling each other about them.

On the most general level, we are able to tell each other about the indexical meanings of linguistic forms because language is *reflexive* – language is always about itself, no matter what else it is also about. Every utterance is an example of how an utterance can be structured, how it can sound, and what it can accomplish. Every time we say something we are potentially modelling to our hearers how someone with the identities that are being oriented to at the moment would say it. As Talbot Taylor puts it, '[w]e ourselves are the sources of our own verbal regularity' by virtue of 'the normative character of the situated events of linguistic production' (1997: 165).

More specifically, connections between linguistic form and indexical meaning can be highlighted as people interact. These strategies are sometimes referred to under the rubric of *metapragmatics* (Silverstein 1993; Agha 2007). Metapragmatics encompasses all the ways in which an utterance can be *framed* (Goffman [1974] 1986; Tannen 1993) or *contextualised* (Gumperz 1982): that is, linked with a particular context. Forms can be metapragmatically linked with social identities explicitly, in utterances like 'You know you're from Maine if you say *wicked* instead of *very*' or 'She sounds like such a nerd.'

Slightly less direct metapragmatic links can also involve words or phrases that refer to social identities. For example, in answer to a question about a clematis vine, the pronunciations [klə'mærəs] and ['klɛmərəs] were suggested. A third pronunciation was introduced by another speaker, who said 'It's [klə'marəs] if you're in the garden club.' With this move, she linked the pronunciation [klə'marəs] with a social identity (being 'in the garden club') associated with expertise in the area of plant-name pronunciation but also with the upper-class snobbery that can be evoked in the US by pronouncing words in the BATH class (*bath, path, grass, dance, plant*, and so on; Wells 1982) with [a] rather than [æ].

But not all metapragmatic framing occurs explicitly as talk about talk. 'Text-metricality' is perhaps the most basic metapragmatic practice. The idea of text-metricality originated with linguist and philologist Roman Jakobson (1960), who pointed out that, in traditional poetic language in Europe and elsewhere, terms with similar meanings appear in parallel places. Parallelism is the re-use of the same or similar structure. Rhyme and metre are common types of parallelism in traditional poetry; grammatical parallelism is common in oratory. Parallelism provides a frame in which the item or items that differ from line to line are highlighted and semantically juxtaposed. Because the items occur in the same context, we are led to compare or contrast them. As Tannen (1987) points out, people also do this collaboratively in spontaneous everyday talk, re-using bits of others' sounds and grammar and so making the places where their contributions differ stand out. Variation in the context of repetition is arguably the most fundamental human meaning-making practice (Koch 1984; Johnstone 1994). And just as text-metricality can draw on and create links between denotational meanings (connecting love with doves on countless greeting cards, for example, by using the words *love* and *dove* as a rhyming pair), it can create indexical links between form and social meaning. Think again about the 'clematis' example above. Here is the interchange:

Ruth:	What's that one called?		
Anne:	That's called	[klə'mærəs] or ['klɛmərəs],	depending how you pronounce it.
Bess:	It's	[klə'marəs]	if you're in the garden club.
		pronunciation	*identity attribution*

Anne and Bess's contributions, framed in parallel structures, collaboratively set up two slots: a slot for possible pronunciations of the name of the vine, and a slot for attributing pronunciations to personas. Anne's generic *you* suggests that the alternative pronunciations she proposes are in free variation ('depending how you pronounce it'). Bess is able to take advantage of the metrical structure that has been set up to link a third alternative to a stereotypical persona, the knowledgeable but snobbish garden club member. (Note how this move also positions Bess as an expert, but without linking her own identity to the garden club stereotype.)

If we think of 'text' more inclusively (as any strip of interaction rather than only a verbal exchange) and extend the notion of parallelism to include more loosely structured juxtapositions, we can use the idea of text-metricality as a cover concept for other ways of linking linguistic forms and social identities. 'Interactional texts' are more often than not multimodal, involving verbal discourse but also modes of dress, carriage, or gesture.

A person who uses a particular form while looking a particular way can link the linguistic form to the look, if co-participants are able to attend to the form and make the link. Written texts and pictures can also help link linguistic form and social identity, as when a folk dictionary of 'Pittsburghese' is illustrated with sketches of working-class men doing things like napping on the 'cahch ('couch')' or cheering for the 'Stillers ('Steelers')'.

4. Stabilising indexicality through enregisterment

Consider the *clematis* example once again. I claimed that Bess's proffered pronunciation, explicitly linked by her to garden club members, also sounded upper-class by virtue of an already circulating way of indexing upper-class identity by means of pronunciation in the US. In other words, I described not just a momentary linking of linguistic form and social identity in a particular interaction ([klə'marəs] ↔ garden club member), but also a fairly stable, familiar, re-usable way of indexing class, namely by pronouncing words like *clematis* (or *class*) with [a] rather than the usual (in North America) [æ]. How do linguistic forms get linked with social identities in more permanent ways like this?

To talk about this, it is useful to use Asif Agha's (2003; 2007) concept of 'enregisterment'. 'Registers', for Agha, 'are cultural models of action that link diverse behavioral signs to enactable effects, including images of persona, interpersonal relationship, and type of conduct' (Agha 2007: 145). (Note that Agha uses the term *register* much more broadly than do many linguists.) Registers are like what Eckert (2000) calls 'styles', although a register may be associated with a situation or a set of social relations rather than or in addition to being associated with a social identity like 'jock' or 'burnout'. A register emerges when a number of indexical relationships begin to be seen as related; a particular linguistic form (or nonlinguistic sign) is 'enregistered' when it becomes included in a register. To see how this can work, we need to take an historical perspective on indexicality.

In Pittsburgh, a post-industrial US city, various nonstandard English forms can be heard, for various historical reasons (see Johnstone et al. 2006). Until the 1960s, the use of these forms could have been correlated with a person's being from the Pittsburgh area, and they were more likely in males' speech than in that of females (Johnstone et al. 2002; Kiesling and Wisnosky 2003). However, most Pittsburghers did not notice these correlations and were thus unable to associate them with identities. Only when the right historical, geographical and ideological conditions were in place, beginning in the 1960s, did most members of this speech community become able to notice these correlations between form and identity. They gained the ability to notice the correlations and interpret them as indexical relations because of metapragmatic activities that called attention to the correlations and imbued them with meaning, in contexts such as moving into jobs where speaking 'correctly' was required, travelling on holiday and returning with stories about other people's reactions to their speech, or seeing newspaper articles that described the oddities of the local 'dialect'.

Pittsburghers could then begin to vary the usage of regional forms in their own speech, depending on what they needed to accomplish or were heard as accomplishing in interaction: whether they were trying to sound more local or more supra-local, more careful or more relaxed, more working class or less so. In other words, at this stage local features began to function as $n+1$-th-order indexicals assigned 'an ethno-metapragmatically driven native interpretation' (Silverstein 2003: 212) – that is, a meaning in terms of one or more native ideologies (including the idea that certain people speak more correctly than others, and the idea that class and speech are related). As Pittsburgh-area linguistic forms became enregistered, they became linked with styles of speech associated with identities, and they could be used to create contexts for those styles. For example, a person could make use of a feature correlated with being working class in order to create rapport with a working-class speaker or annoy an English teacher.

As this example suggests, an n-th-order indexical can have meaning along a variety of ideological dimensions: the same form can be enregistered in multiple ways. Different members of a community, differently placed by class, education, gender, mobility and the like, can use locally-available features to do different kinds of social work and can hear them as doing different kinds of work. (For example, women may be more likely to hear local features as sloppy, ugly and uneducated, lining them up with one end of an ideological cline of correctness; men may be more likely to hear local features as suggesting local-ness, solidarity, friendliness or masculinity, lining them up with one end of an ideological cline from self to other.)

The same process can recur. A feature with $n+1$-th-order meaning for some people may, for them or for others, come to be enregistered in terms of a new ideological schema. For example, because particular variants are correlated, in some Pittsburghers' experience, with being working class and male, a subset of these features has come to be enregistered as indexing the persona of the authentic Pittsburgher. The ideological schemata in play here include the idea that places have dialects and that the most authentic Pittsburghers are working-class men. People who want to create the sense that they are authentic Pittsburghers can use this register of features to set the scene, and people whose perceptions are shaped according to an ideological cline of authenticity may hear people using these features as authentic Pittsburghers (whether or not the people they hear are using the features for this purpose; cf. Johnstone and Kiesling 2008). The forms that have been resemioticised (given new meaning) in this way are, from an analyst's-eye perspective, now $(n+1)+1$-th-order indexicals.

The process of re-enregisterment can continue indefinitely. For example, if it is noticed that Pittsburghers are people who talk about 'Pittsburghese' (as intense media coverage of the topic has made increasingly likely), and if people associate cities that have dialects with the post-industrial 'rust belt' and cities that do not (or are thought not to) have dialects with the new economy, then forms hearable in Pittsburgh have come to have indexical meaning on yet another level.

5. 'Social meaning' or 'meaning'?

Stepping back to look at the process as a whole, it becomes evident that what we are describing is not simply 'social meaning', but meaning in general. A few suggestions will have to sketch this possibility here. Words acquire meanings by virtue of being used together with their referents (a child sees Daddy and hears 'Daddy's here') or (in some socio-cultural settings) by being explicitly juxtaposed with them in repeated metaprag-matic activities like labelling or definition. ('What's that? / A fire engine. / Very good!'.) Like meanings associated with identities, words can be said to be 'enregistered' in terms of ideological structures. (These have been called 'cognitive metaphors' in some accounts; cf. Lakoff and Johnson 1980.) Once a word is learned, it can sometimes be detached from its indexical anchoring in a context and treated as if it had meaning outside of any context. If this happens, we may think of the word, originally a context-tied indexical, as a conventional, 'arbitrary' symbol. (Our tendency to do this is arguably tied to our literacy.) All linguistic signs are 'mixed' in Peirce's sense, consisting, to varying degrees, of indexical, symbolic and iconic elements (Clark 1997: 590–2).

Grammar, likewise, according to contemporary functional and interactional theories, consists of enregistered sets of structural patterns encountered in juxtaposition with their functions. As Joan Bybee puts it (2006: 714; see also Becker 1979; Hopper 1988; Johnstone 1996), grammar is 'the cognitive organization of one's experiences with language', and 'the apparent structure emerges from the repetition of many local events'. 'Local events' – the interactions in which actual bits of language and other behaviours are taken as meaningful, and meanings come to stabilise – are always social (Ochs et al. 1996). Discourse is a continual process of mutual coordination in making sense of the world; 'languages', 'grammars' and 'identities' emerge in the course of this process, as humans' reflexivity – our ability to see what people do as an illustration of how to do it, and to arrange things in ways that encourage others to attend to these illustrations – links together sets of actions, linguistic and otherwise, into registers of conduct. From this perspective, the difference collapses between the effects of identity and other aspects of meaning we might think of as 'social' as opposed to 'pragmatic' or 'denotational' meaning.

Part II
Individuals

4

The Role of the Individual in Language Variation and Change

Jane Stuart-Smith and Claire Timmins

1. Introduction

Leeann and Debbie, two thirteen-year-old teenagers from one of Glasgow's inner city districts, are being recorded in conversation in a schoolroom as part of our sociolinguistic study. Leafing through a magazine, Leeann notices a story about *EastEnders*, a soap drama set in London:

1.	Leeann:	Oh my God!
2.	Debbie:	What?
3.	Leeann:	Mark tries to kill hissel'!
4.	Debbie:	What?
5.	Leeann:	Don't do it Mark. He's a bit shy. [*inaudible*]
6.	Debbie:	[*high voice*] Don't do it Mark! Don't kill yourself!
7.	Leeann:	Oh, but Kat's pregnant, that's just pure, d' you no' think he's nice lookin'?
8.	Debbie:	Is that who she's pregnant tae?
9.	Leeann:	No, I think it's Anthony's.
10.	Debbie:	I think . . .
11.	Leeann:	But d' you no' think he's kinda nice lookin'?
12.	Debbie:	No, I do–
13.	Leeann:	I just [*inaudible*] the way I see him
14.	Debbie:	I think wee Spencer's nice.
15.	Leeann:	Hm, he's a wee bit annoyin'.

Here Leeann confirms what she reported in a formal questionnaire, that she is deeply engaged with the characters and plot of this particular TV show. Initially, this might seem an obvious illustration of a finding which applies to the larger cohort of adolescents these girls belong to: that they lead the use of innovative phonetic variation within Glaswegian, and that this linguistic behaviour is linked to a range of social factors, including engagement with the TV show that they are discussing. But this assumption is problematic:

Leeann's use of TH-fronting and DH-fronting, two features claimed to be associated with London and south-east England, reveals minimal usage of [f] and [v] for (θ) and (ð). Every instance of (θ) in the extract (*think* in lines 7, 9, 11) is realised with the local, nonstandard [h]. What accounts for this apparent anomaly? Are linguistic variation and personal engagement with television straightforwardly linked? And, more generally, how does modelling individuals' behaviour contribute to our accounts of linguistic variation and the transmission of language change?

In this chapter, we discuss identity and language at the level of the individual by evaluating an alternative way of characterising personal responses to participation in language change. We explore the usefulness of a model of individuals' propensities to adopt innovations over time – Rogers' (2003) 'adopter categories' – by examining its applicability to two ongoing sound changes in Glaswegian. Rogers' model is not new to sociolinguistic theory (Milroy 1987: 202f); we revisit it here because the changes are linked with media influence, and we make specific observations about how different adopter categories may respond to the media in the diffusion of innovations.

2. Individuals and language variation and change

Individuals are inevitably at the heart of language variation and change, because it is the conscious or (more usually) subconscious adjustments in individuals' linguistic behaviour which constitute variation, and potentially change. Unsurprisingly, then, we discover modelling of individuals' social and linguistic traits, albeit from differing perspectives, permeating quantitative sociolinguistic research from the outset, starting with Labov (1963). While Labov's early studies are known for concentrating on language variation and social groups, his major work on social factors in language change culminates in detailed discussion of the personal histories, characteristics and revealed identities of identified leaders of linguistic change. He notes: '[t]o understand the forces operating in linguistic change, we will necessarily be focusing upon a handful of individuals' (Labov 2001: 33).

This shift toward abstract social ties binding individuals together (for example Milroy 1987) moved the focus of quantitative sociolinguistics closer to individual speakers, through the use of ethnography and by developing a deeper understanding of social relationships (see Eckert 2005 on 'second wave' research). How social network ties may relate to language change is explored by Milroy and Milroy (1985a), and J. Milroy (1992). Recent 'third wave' work (Eckert 2005) explicitly foregrounds the individual and identity, permitting insight into how individuals negotiate meaning by developing social and linguistic practices, and thereby shared and personal sociolinguistic identities (Eckert 2000). Stylistic variation, particularly seen from the perspective of speaker design/ persona construction, hinges on individual speakers exploiting arrays of linguistic variation (Eckert and Rickford 2001; Eckert 2005; Coupland 2007), which may entail shifting in language norms.

To understand the complex motivations underpinning the linguistic behaviour of individuals as they negotiate their identities, locating themselves 'in a highly complex multi-dimensional social space' (Hudson 1996: 147), we need several complementary, but probably different, theoretical approaches. Cheshire et al. (in press) discuss the intersection of multi-ethnic networks, brokering and personality traits among linguistic innovators in London; this chapter considers another possible addition to the theoretical arsenal.

3. The context: variation and change in Glaswegian

The results discussed belong to a larger study on language variation and change in Glaswegian which contributes to broader debates concerning the potential influence of the broadcast media, especially television, on changes to core features of language (Stuart-Smith 2006). TH-fronting ([f] for (θ), as in *think*) and DH-fronting ([v] for (ð), as in *brother*) are spreading through UK urban accents from London (Foulkes and Docherty 1999a), and as such look to be prime illustrations of linguistic diffusion through dialect contact (Kerswill 2003). However, the predominance of [f] and [v] among working-class adolescents with few apparent opportunities for mobility (passive or active) suggests we should consider factors such as limited contact between weakly tied individuals, in conjunction with positive attitudes towards London accents (Trudgill 1988; Milroy 1987: 203), and/or orientation towards 'youth norms' experienced partially via exposure to the broadcast media (Williams and Kerswill 1999).

Neither change is historically expected in Scottish English, where varieties towards the Scots end of the continuum (see Millar, this volume) also have local nonstandard variants for these phonemes – [h] for (θ) in a restricted set of lexemes such as *think*, and [ɾ] for (ð) intervocalically, in for example *bother*. However, there are informal reports of [f] from the 1950s, and [f] and [v] were sporadic in the early 1980s (Macafee 1983: 34). Analysis of the variables in a Glaswegian corpus collected in 1997 revealed a similar distribution to elsewhere in the UK, showing both changes were only apparent among younger working-class speakers, and more TH-fronting than DH-fronting. Lacking direct evidence for factors external to Glasgow, we examined the role of the local context, and concluded that local network history and accompanying class-based language ideologies relating to recent changes to the city itself were important in understanding how speakers exploited these resources (Stuart-Smith et al. 2007).

A subsequent multidisciplinary project on Glasgow accent confirmed these patterns as language change. We related them to a wider range of social factors, internal and external to the city, including for the first time a systematic consideration of the potential role of the media. We worked with 36 adolescents and 12 adults from the same inner-city area (Maryhill) as in our previous study, recruiting our younger informants from the same secondary school and a feeder primary, and men and women from local pubs and the same women's centre respectively (see Table 4.1).

Later, the same fieldworker recorded wordlists for each speaker and further conversations from same-sex self-selected pairs. We also collected additional information (demographic, social, attitudinal, dialect contact-related, media-related) from the adolescents using a questionnaire, a one-to-one informal interview, and participant observation over the four-month data collection periods. We used several complementary methods from sociolinguistics and media studies research to investigate the role of the media in these changes, including a large-scale multi-factorial correlational study (Stuart-Smith 2005; Stuart-Smith et al. in progress, a). We narrowly transcribed every instance of (θ) and (ð) in the wordlists, and (θ) in the conversations; [v] for (ð) in the conversations was very rare, so the results for the variable in that style are not presented here.

Table 4.1 Profile of the forty-eight working-class Glaswegian informants from year one

Age group	Chronological age	Number of informants	Gender	School
1	10–11 years	12	6 M 6 F	Primary school
2	12–13 years	12	6 M 6 F	Secondary school
3	14–15 years	12	6 M 6 F	Secondary school
4	40+ years	12	6 M 6 F	Adults from same area

The overall (θ) and (ð) results for the 1997 and 2003 groups of working-class adolescents appear in Table 4.2. Real-time change is apparent in the increased use of [f] in both speech styles (read, χ^2 (1, N = 733) = 14.05, p = 0.0002; spontaneous, χ^2 (2, N = 1654) = 24.44, p < .005). Scarcity of [v] in 1997 hinders statistical analysis across the samples, but proportionally, its use seems similar (even slightly higher in 1997), but the 1997 figures represent only 7 instances of a potential 46, with 6 out of 8 speakers using [v] for *smooth*, and only one using it intervocalically. In 2003, we gave our informants more opportunities in the wordlist (21 /ð/ words), and more were taken; 29 of the 36 children showed [v], with 11 also using it intervocalically. In 1997, there were no instances of [v] in the conversations; in the 2003 recordings, [v] was used 6 times by 3 speakers, for word-final /ð/ (*breathe*), and in *breathing, either, other, neither*. We interpret these, particularly the extension of [v] into intervocalic position even in spontaneous speech despite the strong presence of local [r], to indicate that DH-fronting is, like the more advanced TH-fronting, a change in progress in Glaswegian vernacular.

Our first attempt to account for these patterns was a large-scale regression analysis of [f] and [v] for all speakers as a group, with respect to the key linguistic factor of position in word, and numerous extra-linguistic factors derived from information gained during the study (potential for dialect contact within and beyond Glasgow, attitudes to urban accents, social practices and identity, entertainment preferences, engagement with computers and the internet, involvement in sport, and exposure to and engagement with television, both generally and with specific programmes; see Stuart-Smith et al., in progress, a). Briefly, the correlational study shows robust links with linguistic factors for TH-fronting and DH-fronting, and also with a range of extra-linguistic factors, including strong relationships with variables relating to anti-establishment social practices, contact with relatives in southern England, and engagement with the TV soap, *EastEnders*. Links with positive attitudes towards the London accent are less robust, and only for TH-fronting. Furthermore, the final models with the full range of social factors show an explanation of variance at least three times better than any single category model alone (for example just dialect contact, or attitudes, or social practices).

Interpreting significant correlations for extra-linguistic factors in the model in terms of causality, especially those of theoretical importance such as social practices or dialect contact, requires assuming an underlying mechanism which allows the translation of the statistical links between linguistic and extra-linguistic variables. For example, consider our regression results for social practices and identity, where greater [f] usage is linked with disliking school. We could take the link partly as the product of class-based language ideologies indexing [f] as 'us' [= local kids], 'normal', and [θ] as 'them' [= school], 'posh'

Table 4.2 Main phonetic variants for (θ) and (ð) across all word positions in the read and spontaneous speech of eight working-class Glaswegian adolescents recorded in 1997 and thirty-six working-class Glaswegian adolescents recorded in 2003

	1997		2003	
(θ) wordlists	%	n	%	n
[θ]	53.5	46	37.0	270
[f]	30.2	26	55.4	391
(θ) conversations				
[θ]	28.3	88	15.5	194
[h]	43.4	151	49.1	710
[f]	26.2	102	34.5	409
(ð) wordlists				
[ð]	65.2	30	66.0	484
[ɾ]	15.2	7	16.4	120
[v]	15.2	7	9.5	70

(Stuart-Smith et al. 2007), though other explanations might be relevant. That we cannot easily supply processes behind the links between linguistic variation and engagement with television does not in itself negate a causal relationship, but rather makes an explanation more difficult.

However we try to interpret the model, two additional points must be made. First, the results of the correlational study represent a summary of relationships for all our informants as a group, explaining why the changes might be operating at the group level. Second, for all linguistic variables the models require several different kinds of factors together, suggesting that particular individuals' linguistic performance may relate to one or more factors, or 'causal pathways' (Figure 4.1). To identify which pathways might be relevant for specific individuals, and to consider reasons for these changes to occur at the individual level, necessitates scrutinising our informants more closely. We structure our discussion from a perspective drawn from diffusion research on individuals' potential responses to innovations.

4. Individuals and the diffusion of innovations

Rogers (2003: 35–37) summarises the diffusion of innovations as the communication of new ideas/practices/objects over time among members of a social system through two channels: interpersonal or mass media. Individuals encountering an innovation follow a multi-step process: knowledge, persuasion, decision, implementation and confirmation. The decision step is crucial, since at this stage the innovation may be adopted or rejected.

Members of a social system can be categorised in terms of their 'innovativeness': 'the degree to which an individual . . . is relatively earlier in adopting new ideas than other members of a social system' (Rogers 2003: 37). Diffusion research has led to the specification of 'adopter categories' based on the S-curve of cumulative innovation adoption over time (272f.). Initially, few individuals adopt, and the number of adoptions rises slowly, but it then increases rapidly and with a cumulative effect on the system until around half

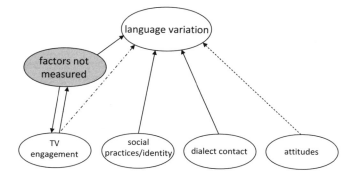

Figure 4.1 Schematic diagram of causal pathways relating social factors to linguistic variation. Bundles of the key theoretical social factors are indicated within the ovals at the bottom of the figure. The shaded oval indicates potential alternative factors not included in the model which may be interposed between language and TV engagement factors. Arrow connectors indicate the presence of a significant correlation within the regression models, and the inference of a causal link. Solid lines indicate factors for which accepted mechanisms/processes exist; the light dashed line connecting attitudinal factors indicates the weaker statistical evidence for a relationship. The dotted/dashed line connecting TV engagement factors indicates the likelihood of a causal relationship whose mechanisms are still far from clear.

the individuals in the system have adopted, after which the rate slows as the remaining members adopt. Adoptions over time tend towards a bell-shaped distribution approaching normality, justifying an abstract distribution of the innovativeness dimension which is then divided into five adopter categories as standard deviations from the mean adoption time (Figure 4.2). The five adopter categories are (282–5)

Innovators: 'venturesome': the few innovators are daring and risky, existing at the edge of the local system, and communicating with other innovators across systems. They can cope with significant uncertainty about an innovation, especially since some can prove unsuccessful. They '[launch] the new idea in the system by importing the innovation from outside' (283).

Early adopters: 'respect': early adopters are a small number of respected members of the local social system that other potential adopters solicit for advice and information before adopting new ideas themselves. They 'put their stamp of approval on a new idea by adopting it' (283).

Early majority: 'deliberate': this is a large adopter category, engaged in frequent interaction with peers in the local system. Longer deliberation before adopting the innovation is characteristic. Their 'unique location between the very early and the relatively late to adopt makes them an important link in the diffusion process' (283–4).

Late majority: 'sceptical': like the early majority, the late majority constitutes a third of the social system, but they wait cautiously until at least half of the overall system has adopted before they venture. 'The weight of system norms must definitely favor an innovation before the late majority are convinced . . . most of the uncertainty about a new idea must be removed before the late majority feel that it is safe to adopt' (284).

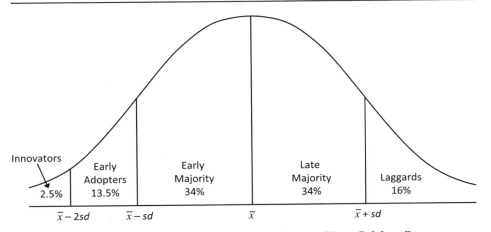

Figure 4.2 Adopter categorisation on the basis of innovativeness, Figure 7–3 from Rogers (2003: 281).

Laggards: 'traditional': in the tail of the adopters are the laggards, who are most local in their outlook, mixing largely with those who also have traditional values, and whose reference point for decisions is past experience. 'Resistance to innovations . . . may be entirely rational from the laggards' viewpoint, as their resources are limited and they must be certain that a new idea will not fail before they can adopt' (284–5).

Diffusion of innovations research has already attracted attention from sociolinguists, notably James and Lesley Milroy. An objection they raise concerning the influence of the broadcast media on language (Milroy and Milroy 1985a: 30) is that speakers are far more likely to be influenced by their everyday personal contacts, an argument based on Rogers and Shoemaker's (1971) generalisation that interpersonal channels of communication are relatively more important at the persuasion stage, whereas mass media channels count for more at the knowledge stage (Rogers 2003: 205). A key aspect of the theoretical model of social networks and language change outlined by Milroy and Milroy (1985a) is their depiction of weak ties as 'bridges' across which innovations may pass between close-knit networks, which draws on the roles of 'innovators' and 'adopters' in the process. Milroy (1987: 202) revisits these roles in the context of social network theory, assessing their value for understanding the transmission of linguistic innovations, given that these also tend to show an S-curve distribution over time. J. Milroy (1992: 183f) offers some useful critique: that the diffusion of linguistic forms may be more complex than that of other innovations; that the schema relates not to personality types but to relations between groups and individuals; and that people may be innovative in certain respects and not in others (see Rogers' discussion of the Amish as an example).[1]

Adopter categorisation is particularly interesting for the Glaswegian changes in that we observe differences in how communication channels function in the diffusion process for the different categories. Rogers' Generalization 5–13 states that: 'Mass media channels are relatively more important than interpersonal channels for earlier adopters than for later adopters' (Rogers 2003: 211). Figure 4.3 shows both channels functioning at all stages, but at the knowledge stage all categories bar laggards use interpersonal channels

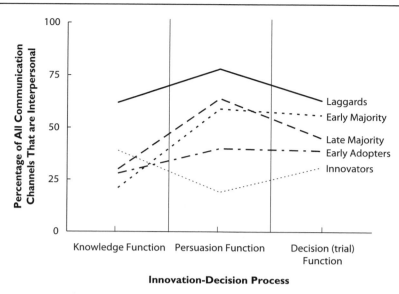

Figure 4.3 Use of interpersonal channels in the diffusion of 2,4-D weed spray in Iowa, according to stages of the innovation-decision process and adopter category; Figure 5–3, Rogers (2003: 212).

less and media channels more. There is then a separation at the persuasion stage between laggards, late majority, and early majority favouring interpersonal channels, and early adopters and especially innovators favouring media channels. Assuming that linguistic diffusion operates similarly, we might expect the media to be involved in the diffusion of linguistic innovations in general, and to influence some individuals more than others.

With respect to the Glasgow data, then:

1. How does our informant sample pattern in terms of adopter category?
2. Does adopter category relate to linguistic change in progress?
3. How does adopter category intersect with the causal pathways arising from the regression results, and in particular:
   a. with those relating to communication channel, dialect contact (interpersonal) and engagement with specific television programmes (mass media)?
   b. with that relating to social identity?

5. Individuals and linguistic diffusion in Glasgow

5.1. Adopter categories

Using Rogers' listing of structural, social and personality traits as a guide, and independently of any linguistic analysis, the second author assigned each informant to an adopter category based on: their observed participation in social relationships; their social behaviour towards each other during the course of the project (who respected and followed whom); their innovativeness regarding social pursuits and technology; their observed personality traits.

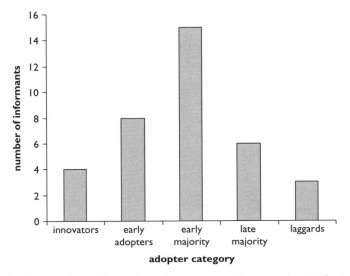

Figure 4.4 Distribution of the Glaswegian informants according to assigned adopter category.

Figure 4.4 shows the structure of our (small) sample by adopter category. Size notwithstanding, there are similarities with the expected 'ideal' distribution in Figure 4.2. We have more innovators/early adopters/early majority, and fewer late majority and laggards, than expected. This probably reflects our recruitment method, which depended on volunteers and may thus have favoured more innovative individuals.

Adopter categories and the basic social relationships in the sample for the three age groups are shown in Figure 4.5. Our sampling caught some existing networks, fragments of others, and some more peripheral individuals. Innovators are unconnected to the main networks, and in three cases chose to talk to laggards. Early adopters are largely members of dense networks.

Table 4.3 shows adopter categorisation and social identification. We explored 'identifying self' and 'identifying others' with informants in the study's second year. The adolescents used three social categories when discussing each other:

- 'ned': applied pejoratively to someone involved in antisocial, often violent, behaviour, and wearing particular clothing:

  'They wear . . . like the neds wear the trackies [tracksuits] an' Lacoste [a clothing brand] stuff'. Kate (1F6)

  15 of our 23 year two informants were labelled neds (or 'tarts') by others, but none self-identified as a ned, preferring 'normal' or avoiding self-labelling altogether:

  'I'm a wee Glasgow person. I wouldnae say I'm a ned 'cause I don't like go oot and start fights'. Declan (2M3)

Being a ned was also associated with particular speech patterns:

'. . . when I talk, my pals go – you pure talk like a wee ned'. Catherine (2F1) (self-identifies as 'normal')

We found significant links between being identified as a ned/tart and TH-fronting in regressions which modelled social practices and identification for this group of speakers.

- 'geek/wimp': another negative term, also linked with speech, but the polar opposite of ned:

  'see when you hear them, man, they just talk dead . . . posh, man'. Declan (2M3)

  We shall see that this is also reflected in our sample.

- 'goth': a separate category for a rival group to the neds (with whom they fought), and associated with particular dress:

  'An' the goths wear like rock tops wi' skeletons on it an' big baggy troosers . . . and the purple hair.' Kate (1F6)

Four of our informants were identified as goths by others, but only two self-identified as such (Martin, 1M4 and Rory, 2M1).

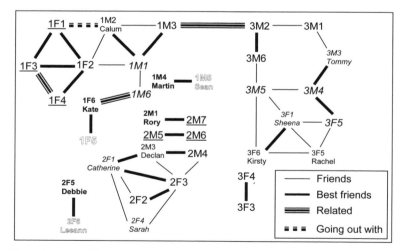

Figure 4.5 Sociogram of the three age groups of thirty-six Glasgow adolescent informants shaded according to adopter category: **innovator**, *early adopter*, early majority, <u>late majority</u>, laggards. The code for each individual is constructed of (a) 1, 2, 3 = age group, (b) F/M = female/male, and (c) an informant number.

Table 4.3 Adopter categories and social identification – of self and by others – for the twenty-three informants who continued into year two of the study. Dashes indicate that an informant did not offer a label/grouping for him-/herself or others

Self identification	Identification by others	Adopter category	Informant code
–	goth	laggards	1F5
don't know	geek/wimp	laggards	1M5
normal	goth	laggards	2F6
–	geek/wimp	late majority	2M7
–	ned	late majority	1F1
–	ned	late majority	2M5
don't know	ned	late majority	1F3
–	ned	late majority	2M6
–	ned	late majority	1F4
normal	ned	early majority	2F3
normal	ned	early majority	1F2
–	ned	early majority	2M3
don't know	ned	early majority	1M3
–	ned	early majority	2M4
normal	ned	early majority	2F1
normal	ned	early majority	2F2
don't know	ned	early majority	1M2
–	–	early adopter	1M6
normal	ned	early adopter	1M1
–	ned	early adopter	2F4
[not in year 2]	[not in year 2]	innovators	2F5
goth	goth	innovators	2M1
don't know	–	innovators	1F6
punk/normal	goth	innovators	1M4

Social identification and adopter categories align at the edges of the distribution, so that innovators and laggards are goths or geek/wimps (one geek/wimp is a late majority), while late and early majority and early adopters are mainly neds. While laggards might well be geek/wimps, it seems odd that two laggards are classed as goths beside the two goth innovators. But the latter self-identify as something different (goth and 'punk'), while the laggards consider themselves 'normal', or don't identify. Certainly, their dress did not mark them as goths, as both adhered closely to school uniform. They may have been classed as goths partly to signal their peripherality to the main group.

5.2. DH-fronting

We begin by considering the change which is least advanced in Glaswegian: [v] constitutes under 10 per cent of the overall variation for the wordlists, and only occurs six times in spontaneous speech. Table 4.4 presents the overall results by adopter category. The

Table 4.4 Overall percentages of DH-fronting in wordlists, and TH-fronting in wordlists and conversations, for each speaker, according to adopter category. For each linguistic variable percentage scores within each adopter category are ordered in ascending order. Counts follow each percentage column. * indicates the three speakers who show instances of [v] in the conversations; dashes indicate speakers using an overall token count of ten or less, for whom percentages are not given.

	(ð) wordlist			(θ) wordlist			(θ) conv.		
		[v] %	n		[f] %	n		[f] %	n
laggards	1F5	0.0	0	1F5	0.0	0	1M5	0.0	0
laggards	1M5	0.0	0	1M5	0.0	0	2F6	3.7	1
laggards	2F6	0.0	0	2F6	33.3	7	1F5	39.1	9
late maj.	2M7	0.0	0	1F4	0.0	0	2M7	4.5	1
late maj.	1F1	4.8	1	2M7	47.4	9	1F1	19.0	12
late maj.	2M5	5.0	1	2M5	61.9	13	1F4	30.8	12
late maj.	1F3	5.3	1	2M6	71.4	15	2M6	32.1	9
late maj.	2M6	9.5	2	1F3	81.0	17	1F3	33.3	10
late maj.	1F4	14.3	3	1F1	94.4	17	2M5	40.0	14
early maj.	2F3	0.0	0	3F3	0.0	0	3F1	14.9	7
early maj.	1F2	0.0	0	1F2	0.0	0	2F2	17.4	4
early maj.	2M3	4.8	1	1M3	28.6	6	2M4	20.0	7
early maj.	3F4	4.8	1	2M4	30.0	6	3F2	22.0	13
early maj.	3M1	4.8	1	2F1	38.1	8	3M1	23.5	12
early maj.	3M6	4.8	1	3M1	47.4	9	2F1	30.0	12
early maj.	1M3	5.0	1	3F2	52.4	11	3F4	31.0	13
early maj.	2M4	5.0	1	3M6	57.9	11	3F6	33.3	5
early maj.	3F2	5.0	1	3F6	60.0	12	3M6	33.9	21
early maj.	3M2	9.5	2	2F2	71.4	15	2F3	36.7	18
early maj.	2F1*	10.0	2	3M2	75.0	15	3M2	40.0	20
early maj.	2F2	10.0	2	2F3	88.2	15	2M3	45.2	14
early maj.	3F3	14.3	3	2M3	89.5	17	3F3	49.2	31
early maj.	1M2	15.0	3	3F4	89.5	17	1M2	–	9
early maj.	3F6	19.1	4	1M2	100.0	21	1M3	–	3
early ad.	3F5	0.0	0	3M4	47.6	10	3M4	18.2	6
early ad.	3M5*	4.8	1	1M1	47.6	10	1F2	22.2	14
early ad.	1M6	7.1	1	3M3	47.6	10	3M5	23.1	6
early ad.	3M4	9.5	2	3F1	57.1	12	3M3	25.5	14
early ad.	1M1	10.5	2	3M5	66.7	8	2F4	31.0	13
early ad.	2F4	14.3	3	3F5	76.5	13	1M1	32.5	13
early ad.	3F1	19.1	4	1M6	85.0	17	3F5	49.1	27
early ad.	3M3	23.8	5	2F4	90.5	19	1M6	83.9	26
innovators	2F5	4.8	1	1F6	15.0	3	2F5	11.1	8
innovators	2M1	5.6	1	2F5	71.4	15	1M4	23.5	4
innovators	1F6	9.5	2	2M1	76.2	16	2M1	–	6
innovators	1M4*	81.0	17	1M4	94.4	17	1F6	71.4	15

coincidence of [v] frequency and adopter category is striking. The laggards avoid [v] altogether; the late majority show more, but use only 14 per cent; several of the early majority use little [v], with usage peaking at 19 per cent; the early adopters show a range, but use [v] more frequently overall; finally, the innovators have both the highest score and three low-rating speakers. Conversational [v] tokens are used infrequently by one member of each of the early majority, early adopter and innovator categories.

As with TH-fronting, we cannot unpack results for individual informants in detail, and limit discussion to specific aspects of interest: the behaviour of the innovators, second adopter category and social identification, and then the intersection of linguistic usage with adopter category and peer networks in the oldest informants.

The heaviest [v] user is also an innovator. Martin (1M4) appears opinionated and confident, shows active interest in technology, and has social pursuits including skateboarding, which facilitate contact with individuals outside Glasgow, if only via the internet. He reports no active mobility beyond occasional visits to Edinburgh, and all his family live in Glasgow. Martin is identified as a goth, but in conversation with his friend Sean (1M5) describes himself as 'a punk', a label not used by any other informants. Martin shows enthusiastic engagement with several TV programmes, his favourites being *Buffy the Vampire Slayer* and *The Simpsons*. He likes the local comedy *Chewin' the Fat*, and London-based *EastEnders* and *Grange Hill*. An indication of his strong engagement with *EastEnders* emerged during the imitation task. He was shown a photo of a key character ('Phil Mitchell') and asked to imitate and discuss the character's accent. Martin knows that *EastEnders*, or at least Phil Mitchell's character, is located in England, but the place name he gives ('Walford') is the fictional location of the drama. Martin's high degree of DH-fronting fits with his adopter categorisation as an innovator, and as such, his engagement with London-based dramas, in the absence of opportunities for direct dialect contact, seems likely to be one of the causal pathways accounting for his linguistic behaviour.

Innovators do not always have to innovate; their profile means they are more marginal and refer less to others in the social system, allowing their behaviour to be independent in either direction. The innovator showing the lowest [v] use, Debbie (2F5), whom we saw talking in the opening extract, may be such an example. Debbie comes across as an independent girl who does as she pleases. She reports high engagement with London-based programmes, especially *EastEnders* and *Only Fools and Horses*, but is also very engaged with *The Simpsons* and with local comedienne *Karen Dunbar*. Unlike Martin, Debbie has opportunities for dialect contact beyond Glasgow. She has relatives in Bolton (Lancashire) and has visited several other English cities, including London. As an innovator, Debbie could use both channels, media and interpersonal, in acquiring [v]; she seems to be using neither.

Social identification and adopter category intersect and roughly align with linguistic variation at the periphery: the most prolific use of [v] is by Martin (1M4) – an innovator, a goth and a self-identified punk – while at the other end, neither geek/wimp nor the two socially-peripheral goths (laggards and a late majority) use [v].

We can explore how far adopter category fits with dialect contact and engagement with television by considering members of the third age group. All bar two informants belong to a dense network (Figure 4.5). Tommy (3M3) is the early adopter with most [v]; he reports several visits to cousins in Warrington (Cheshire) and relatives in London. Dialect contact seems a likely causal pathway for his use of [v], probably in conjunction with engagement with TV given his reported interest in *EastEnders*. Sheena (3F1), also an early adopter, talks with her friend Kirsty (3F6; early majority). Both show high [v] use. Neither girl has many opportunities for contact with non-Glaswegians, but both are very engaged with London-based dramas (especially Kirsty). We could speculate that Sheena's early adopter status helps her cross the decision threshold to use [v], and that Kirsty's usage reflects her reference to Sheena's behaviour.

But the model's predictions are sometimes inaccurate: Rachel (3F5) is an early adopter, immensely engaged with *EastEnders*, and she has frequently visited London because her father lives there. But she categorically avoids [v]. However, by adhering to the model we could suggest that [v] is incompatible with her existing arrays of sociolinguistic variants, their ranges of social symbolic functions, and the ideologies and beliefs underlying them, which we loosely call her 'sociolinguistic system'. Rogers (2003: 240f) emphasises the importance of compatibility of innovations with existing belief systems for their successful adoption.

5.3. TH-fronting

The fit between adopter category and TH-fronting levels in either speech style is markedly weaker than is the case for DH-fronting. The former change is more advanced, and another factor is involved in the diffusion of [f] in Glaswegian. In spontaneous speech, as in the 1997 data, TH-fronting for most speakers is limited, largely because the local (stigmatised) variant [h], which occurs in *think*, *thing* and related words, is so tenacious. In the wordlists [h] is blocked by several constraints including the influence of standard orthography and the fact that the words are citation forms; TH-fronting is much commoner (Stuart-Smith and Timmins 2006).

In read speech only an approximate relationship between adopter category and TH-fronting seems to exist, possibly for laggards, early majority and innovators. In spontaneous speech only the edges of the adopter category distribution seem to fit; [f] is used least by two laggards and a late majority informant; the highest score is for an innovator. Again at the edges, social categorisation fits roughly with adopter category: the two 'geek/wimps' avoid [f] in wordlist style and show only one instance in the conversations, while Martin (1M4), the innovator 'goth'/'punk', uses most [f] in the wordlists.

Nevertheless, as for DH-fronting, closer inspection suggests that individuals could be using causal pathways for TH-fronting which may relate to adopter category. Kate (1F6) uses [f] most in spontaneous speech. Classified as an innovator, confident and knowledgeable, Kate has negligible opportunities for dialect contact, but is a highly engaged viewer of *EastEnders* and *The Bill*. Sarah (2F4) is an early adopter with the highest amount of [f] in read speech. It seems likely that dialect contact and associated positive attitudes she expresses towards southern English accents (her father lives with his English girlfriend in the south of England and comes up to Glasgow to visit her) are at least as important for her TH-fronting as are her TV preferences.

We conclude this section by returning to Leeann (2F6) and Debbie (2F5). As we saw, Debbie is an innovator, who avoids [v]; [f] is also rare in her conversation. Debbie's usage seems consistent with her categorisation as an innovator, who sets her own standards for behaviour. Leeann, however, is a laggard with few opportunities for dialect contact, but is extremely engaged with London-based dramas, especially *EastEnders*. Leeann's reluctance to use [f] and [v] ('I like to talk nice'), despite this engagement, may relate to her laggard status both generally and possibly also in response to her interlocutor, Debbie.

5.4. Summary and critique

To summarise our answers to the questions posed earlier:

1. We can assign the Glasgow informants to adopter categories, and the resulting distribution bears similarity to the ideal distribution.
2. There is evidence that adopter categorisation relates to these two ongoing sound changes, though the patterning is better for the more recent change (DH-fronting) than the more advanced one (TH-fronting).
3. (a) Adopter category relates to communication channels, and so to causal pathways for dialect contact and engagement with specific television programmes, partly as predicted, though different speakers use different pathways or combinations thereof. But adopter category and communication channel do not always align with linguistic behaviour.

   (b) Adopter category broadly relates to social identity, in terms of the social categories used by our informants, and these align with linguistic variation at the edges of the distribution.

Assuming that our implementation of adopter categorisation was appropriate – and it was sometimes difficult to assign informants to categories – it seems that this model does help account for the linguistic behaviour of our sample, thus lending substance to a possible causal pathway for engagement with TV and for the dialect contact links, as previously assumed. But there are limitations: we only viewed static snapshots of speakers' behaviour at one point in the process, and only considered overall scores for each speaker. While we gathered some information about our informants, we lacked the in-depth understanding required when examining, for example, compatibility of innovations with particular individuals' sociolinguistic systems (see our discussion of Rachel above). Again, we need detailed insights from ethnographic research with our informants to better apprehend both the kinds of social categories that were discussed, and how these more subtly relate to adopter categorisation.

The model is limited too, as summarised already by J. Milroy (1992: 185). Certainly, the diffusion of linguistic innovations is fundamentally different from the diffusion of many innovations in that communication about them is often characteristic of the later stages of a language change, whereas the important role of interpersonal channels at the persuasion stage is often emphasised in terms of potential adopters overtly discussing and evaluating a new idea/object/practice. Rogers himself identifies a crucial but inadequately understood obstacle – the pro-innovation bias – which promotes a tendency 'to underemphasize the rejection or continuance of innovations' (Rogers 2003: 107).

6. Conclusions

In this chapter we have taken a particular view towards modelling individuals and language change. The notion of adopter categories from diffusion research presents an additional, potentially useful, theoretical dimension to understanding how individuals respond to the transmission of linguistic innovations through different kinds of influence, in conjunction with their perceived social identities. But these insights should be integrated with results from further work at the level of the individual. An important factor in these two changes is stylistic differentiation (Stuart-Smith et al. in progress, b), which also deserves more attention given the large body of qualitative sociolinguistic research on the appropriation of linguistic material from media resources (Androutsopoulos 2001).

Returning finally to our underlying theme, we must accept that individuals occupy the centre of any model attempting to account for media influence on language, just as they are for language change in general. This is because we must reject any definition of 'influence' which equates to a kind of blanket transmission from media source to passive speaker/viewers, a notion long abandoned within media effects research. Rather, it is more helpful to conceptualise media influence in terms of individual speaker/viewers appropriating media material: that is, each speaker/viewer appropriates aspects of the media experience while engaging with the media, given their own particular experience of the world (Holly et al. 2001). Unpacking precisely what linguistic appropriation from the media entails is not trivial. But, whether at the level of processing speech from mediated signals, in the sociolinguistic alignment of incoming material, or in the locally-embedded exploitation of appropriated innovations at specific stylistic opportunities, understanding individual behaviour will always be vital.

Acknowledgements

We thank our informants for their participation, the Economic and Social Research Council for providing funding (R000239757, 2002–5), the Royal Society of Edinburgh for funding research time at the University of Hannover (courtesy of Jannis Androutsopoulos), the audiences at UKLVC6 (Lancaster) and NWAV36 (Philadelphia), and our two patient editors for constructive feedback on earlier presentations of this material.

Note

1. Another aspect of diffusion theory which we do not discuss here, but which Labov (2001: 356f) regards as central to the transmission of linguistic variation, is 'opinion leadership'; cf. Rogers (2003, Chapter 8).

5

The Ageing Voice: Changing Identity Over Time

David Bowie

1. Language and ageing

There is an extensive research literature on language and identity, and a similarly extensive one on ageing and identity. However, while age and lifestage as they relate to language and identity have been the subject of theoretical discussion (see, for example, Eckert 1997; Coupland 2001a; Llamas 2007a) much of the empirical research on which it is based is limited to adolescence, a developmental stage at which individuals clearly mark themselves as members of social groups by their use of different linguistic features (Eckert 1989, 2000; but see sources on communication and the elderly by, for example, Coupland and Ylänne 2006). As adolescents change their social affiliations (which they do with some frequency), they can also change their linguistic behaviour to reflect their new social reality (Mendoza-Denton 1997, 2008) – in effect, they mark their own changes in identity through language. This, of course, leads to a question: if adolescents can alter their linguistic behaviour to reflect changes in their social identities, does it also happen over the course of the lifespan beyond adolescence?

This is a complicated question on many levels, it turns out. Firstly, there is the question of whether individuals exhibit any meaningful post-adolescent changes in their linguistic behaviour at all. The idea that they do not is based on the claim of a critical period for language acquisition (Lenneberg 1967), and it has developed into a widespread assumption in sociolinguistics. For example, the apparent time construct, the usual framework used for quantitative analyses of language change over time, relies on the assumption that post-adolescent language change does not occur (Bailey et al. 1991; Bowie 2005).

The problem is that post-adolescent language change quite clearly does occur. Most obviously, individuals' linguistic behaviours can change due to an injury or disease affecting the speech centres of the brain or the vocal tract (see Miller, this volume). However, since these cases do not generally involve a socially motivated change, I will not consider them further in this chapter (even though they are often associated with ageing, and they certainly have an effect on identity). Linguistic changes can occur for other, more socially motivated, reasons – for example, if individuals relocate so that they are constantly exposed to a variety other than their native one (Bowie 2000).

These facts have led a number of researchers to accept that post-adolescent changes in linguistic behaviour do occur, but to propose that the changes that can occur are extremely limited and, probably, non-systematic (see, among others, Bhat 1970; Bowie, 2000; Blondeau 2001; Sankoff et al. 2001; Nahkola and Saanilahti 2004). However, recent work casts doubt on this claim, leading some to conclude that post-adolescent change is more pervasive than previously assumed (see, for example, Bowie 2005 and forthcoming; Buchstaller 2006; Sankoff and Blondeau 2007). This raises the issue of how stable we can expect individuals' post-adolescent linguistic behaviours to be. If they are not, the question becomes not just what limits there are on adult linguistic stability, but also how and why individuals' linguistic behaviours change as they age. We must start, though, by determining whether such changes occur and what the parameters of the changes might be, which will allow the development of a baseline permitting us to figure out how speakers are using such stability or change.

2. Data

To investigate the above questions we need a longitudinal sample, which will provide us with the opportunity to ascertain whether individuals actually change their linguistic systems as they age. However, as Tillery and Bailey (2003) point out, longitudinal samples are fraught with potential difficulties that make them problematic for testing these issues. This is particularly true given that external factors can affect the extent to which an individual remains linguistically stable over the course of adulthood (Bowie 2000; Nahkola and Saanilahti 2004). We therefore need a longitudinal sample composed of people who were recorded repeatedly while they remained relatively stable both socially and geographically during their entire adult lives. It obviously should contain only individuals free from pathologies or physical traumas affecting their language abilities, and who haven't been continuously surrounded by varieties or languages other than their native one. Additionally, it would be best if the data were collected in such a way that the influence of the interviewer, audience or survey instrument could not bias the results (Trudgill 1988; Bailey and Tillery 1999; Tillery and Bailey 2003), and our results would be strongest if we could obtain several recordings of multiple individuals over a long timespan, rather than just two or three over the course of a couple years or so.

Such data are not widely available for linguistic studies, but can be found in a number of places, particularly archives of public speeches, and to a lesser extent in oral history archives. For this study, I use an archive of public speeches originally broadcast over the radio (and, for the most recent decades of the archive, also via television). It is a collection of recorded religious addresses delivered at the semiannual conferences of The Church of Jesus Christ of Latter-day Saints (the Mormon Church) from 1940 to 2000. This archive consists primarily of semi-extemporaneous religious addresses delivered by church leaders to audiences made up mostly of adherents of the same religion. The archive also includes prayers, songs and transactions of church business, but these are not analysed here. Since the addresses were delivered in the same place (Salt Lake City, Utah, US) to similar audiences, and have consistently similar content, it seems reasonable to suppose that we can use this archive to investigate the way individuals change their linguistic behaviour over time without interference from complicating factors such as changes in setting, survey forms, interviewer or audience. Also, this archive contains speeches by

Table 5.1 Speakers analysed, with birth year and year of recording.

Speaker	Year of birth	Years recorded
JRC	1871	1940, 1950, 1960
DOM	1873	1940, 1950, 1960
LGR	1886	1940, 1950, 1960, 1970, 1980
JLW	1893	1940, 1950, 1960
MEP	1900	1950, 1960, 1970 ,1980
DBH	1906	1970, 1980, 1990, 2000
GBH	1910	1960, 1970, 1980, 1990, 2000
BRM	1915	1950, 1960, 1970, 1980
MJA	1915	1970, 1980, 1990
TSM	1927	1970, 1980, 1990, 2000

several individuals who appear repeatedly over the course of several years, some every year (or nearly so) for a period exceeding four decades. This allows us to track changes in individuals' linguistic behaviour in real time, rather than relying on apparent-time analysis (for discussion of differences between these approaches, see Buchstaller 2006; Bowie 2005; Tillery and Bailey 2003). Unfortunately, other than a few female speakers who were recorded in more recent decades but did not fit into the sample for other reasons, only educated white male speakers were recorded for this archive. Social factors like race/ethnicity, social class and sex could therefore not be analysed, but this allows us to focus more intensely on changes associated with ageing in this particular social group.

Those at the church's highest levels of leadership consistently move to the Salt Lake City area, presumably to allow them to conduct church business more efficiently, so if we wish to track their linguistic behaviour over time while avoiding artefacts resulting from dialect contact we must confine investigation to the linguistic behaviour of individuals originating from the region where the speeches were given. Also, they should be adequately represented in the archive by having been recorded multiple times over a reasonably long period. If the archive is sampled at decade intervals (a timespan chosen mainly for convenience, but also because it would seem to give more than enough time for linguistic changes to occur between each sampling point), there are ten speakers who were recorded three or more times and were also from the region where the speeches were delivered. These speakers are listed in Table 5.1, along with the year of recording; speakers were not recorded in all years, either because they died during the sampling period, they were not recorded in the earliest decades of the archive, or both.

This analysis focuses on phonological behaviour, specifically the deletion of post-vocalic /r/ and the aspiration of syllable-initial /ʍ/. Although the speeches in this archive were delivered in a fairly formal setting, there is still plentiful variation in the realisation of these variables in the material.

The deletion of post-vocalic /r/, or r-lessness, involves the optional deletion of an instance of /r/ in which the /r/ occurs in a syllable coda and does not precede a vowel. It has been studied in numerous varieties of English, but it is not generally recognised as a feature of any western variety of American English, including Utah English. Lillie (1998) does not include /r/-deletion in her list of Utah English features, and Labov et al. (2006)

Table 5.2 Tokens of historical /ʍ/ collected, by speaker and year.

Speaker	1940	1950	1960	1970	1980	1990	2000
JRC	68	73	49				
DOM	42	97	73				
LGR	36	32	22	46	24		
JLW	25	33	40				
MEP		33	31	25	46		
DBH				11	27	29	41
GBH			43	43	31	81	73
BRM		21	29	30	39		
MJA				26	32	28	
TSM				25	21	88	68

only mention *r*-lessness in connection with some parts of the eastern and southern US. Whether this means that the feature existed in early Utah English (as evidenced by its existence in the speech of the speakers studied here) but had disappeared when fieldwork was conducted in the 1990s, or that it prevails only in contexts that later studies have not examined, remains uninvestigated.

However, *r*-lessness is clearly a feature of the archive speakers' productions, with the *r*-less variant used, on average, 30.1 per cent of the time. To investigate how this might have changed over the sampled speakers' adult lives, I took the first 60 post-vocalic /r/ tokens uttered by each speaker in each year as sampled at decade intervals. A total of 2,344 tokens was collected. To gauge its usefulness a first run of this method was done on two speakers' productions (GBH and TSM), and so more than 60 tokens were collected for them for some of the sampled years, which accounts for the fact that the sample total is somewhat larger than the expected 2,280 tokens (60 tokens × 38 speeches). I then obtained formant values for each instance of post-vocalic /r/ to calculate an 'index of *r*-fulness' (IR) value for each utterance using Ocumpaugh's (2001) formula, which is based on the relationship between F1, F2 and F3 in Bark units (Traunmüller 1990).

Similarly, the preservation of the /ʍ/~/w/ distinction has generally not been recognised as a feature of English in Utah. The feature involves the maintenance of the historical contrast between the two consonants, so that *whale* (with a voiceless onset) is not homophonous with *wail* (with a voiced onset). Lillie (1998) does not include this feature in her list of markers of Utah English, and Labov et al. (2006) did not find this feature in their (small) sample of northern Utah speakers. Since few varieties of English retain this distinction, it may seem unusual to claim that it exists among these speakers. To check this, all instances of /w/ and (historical) /ʍ/, as sampled at decade intervals, were collected. The latter sound is clearly in use among the speakers in this sample, although it generally does not involve the realisation of /ʍ/ as a voiceless [ʍ], but rather as a preaspirated cluster [hw]. All tokens were coded as preaspirated or fully voiced, using spectrograms to clarify ambiguous cases. Because the lengths of each individual's speeches varied enough in each decade's sample that token counts were widely divergent for each speaker in each sampled year, a list of the number of tokens collected by speaker and year is shown in Table 5.2 (total N = 1,581).

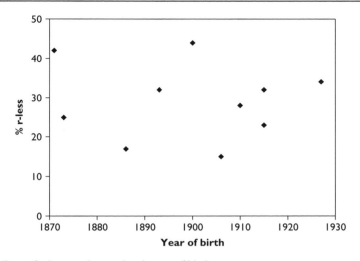

Figure 5.1 Rate of *r*-lessness by speakers' years of birth.

3. Results

3.1 r-lessness

Before looking at individuals and how their patterns of *r*-lessness may have changed linguistically over their adult lives, it's worth taking a moment to look at the group as a whole over time. Of course, there is an interaction between speakers' year of birth (the basis of any apparent-time analysis) and the year the speech was delivered (which would be the basis of any real-time analysis). For example, no speakers born in 1900 or earlier were recorded in 1990 or 2000, and no speakers recorded in 1940 were born after 1893, so earlier-born speakers are over-represented in the early years of the archive, and later-born speakers are over-represented in later years. This is probably unavoidable, because the data were collected over the course of decades, but it does mean that we need to consider both of these measures at once when looking at the behaviour of the group over time.

With this in mind, Figure 5.1 gives the overall *r*-lessness rates for individual speakers arranged by birth year, and Figure 5.2 gives the overall *r*-lessness rates for each year that speech samples were taken. The cutoff for *r*-lessness was set at Ocumpaugh's (2001) suggested level of IR > 1.28. It should be noted that where *r*-lessness rates are used in this chapter, parallel analyses were also conducted using Ocumpaugh's cutoffs for full and marginal *r*-fulness (IR < 0.56 and IR ≤ 1.28, respectively), as well as raw IR values. The overall results (that is, the lack of any identifiable intraspeaker or interspeaker trajectories of change over time) were consistently the same, no matter which of these methods was used.

Looking at the figures, the lack of any pattern is obvious. We see neither apparent-time nor real-time change in progress in these data.

This is all based on averages, however, and tells us nothing about either the behaviour of the individuals in the sample or any correlation between changes in their linguistic behaviour and ageing. Such information is shown in Figure 5.3, which shows the rate of

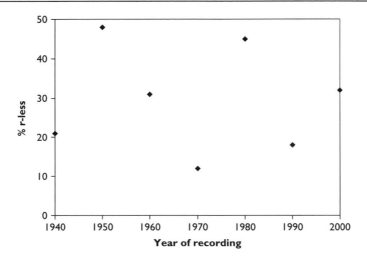

Figure 5.2 Rate of *r*-lessness by year of recording.

r-lessness for each speaker in each of the years he was recorded (note that LGR and BRM were both recorded in 1970, but they both exhibited categorical *r*-fulness in that year).

Here again, a pattern is basically absent. All ten speakers show statistically significant (p < .05) swings in *r*-lessness from decade to decade, but these are not in the same direction across speakers. DOM's *r*-lessness progressively increases across the decades, JLW and MJA also move from low rates of *r*-lessness to higher ones, and LGR, GBH, and possibly also TSM show the same general trend, if we ignore specific years with outlying rates in the midst of the trend. However, JRC and MEP seem to exhibit a *downward* trend, while DBH and BRM show no identifiable change with the passage of time.

3.2 / ʍ/-voicing

At first glance, the /ʍ/-voicing results (Figures 5.4 and 5.5) appear to hint at change over time. Figure 5.4 indicates the rate of /ʍ/-voicing by speaker (collapsing together all the different years in which each speaker was recorded), and arranged by birth year to show changes over apparent time. It shows what appears to be an upward trend over apparent time, though the correlation lacks the regularity needed to achieve statistical significance. Similarly, Figure 5.5 shows the results arranged by each year sampled from the archive (with each speaker's utterances for each year collapsed together), giving a real-time picture of any changes there might have been for this variable. Once more, there appears to be a trend towards more voicing over time, though this also falls short of statistical significance, which may well be a function of the small number of points involved here. Of course, even if there had been significant changes over real or apparent time, it would have been difficult or impossible to tease them apart, since the measures used for them interact with each other. For completeness, VARBRUL runs done separately with each measure of change over time (birth year and year of recording) found that the real-time measure provided a model that fit the data better.

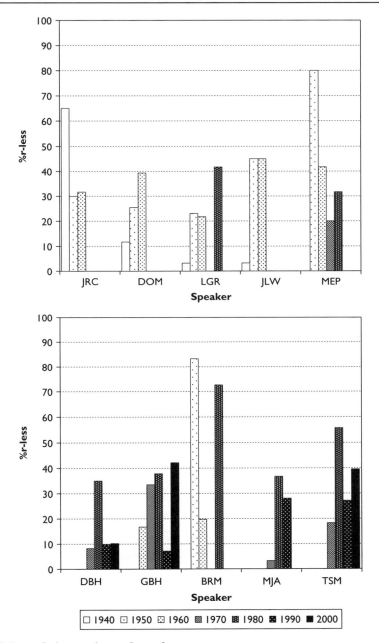

Figure 5.3 Rate of *r*-lessness by speaker and year.

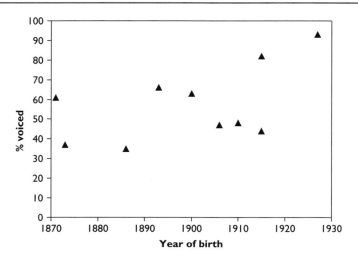

Figure 5.4 Rate of voicing of historical /ʍ/ by year of birth.

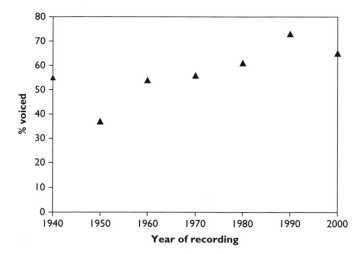

Figure 5.5 Rate of voicing of historical /ʍ/ by year of recording.

Since the real- and apparent-time measures for the entire group both yielded non-significant results, we focus next on each individual's behaviour in real time, as we did with *r*-lessness. This information is given in Figure 5.6. As per what was done for *r*-lessness in Figure 5.3, /ʍ/-voicing rates are given for all years each speaker was recorded.

Unlike *r*-lessness, not all speakers show marked changes in /ʍ/-voicing. MEP, DBH, GBH, BRM and TSM exhibit no meaningful change in voicing with the passage of time. Among the rest, a U-shaped pattern can be discerned. This is descriptive rather than explanatory, however: the U-curve may simply reflect the fact that four of the five speakers with significant changes were recorded at only three points in time, making a

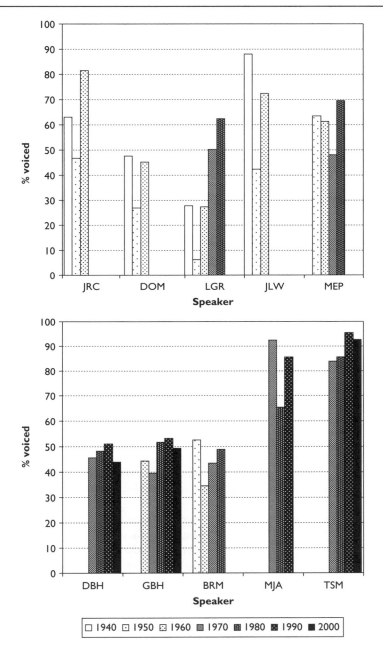

Figure 5.6 Rate of voicing of historical /ʍ/ by speaker and year.

high-low-high pattern more likely. Note that the one speaker with significant changes who was sampled at more than three points (LGR) showed a less transparently U-shaped pattern.

Overall, it is safest to say that the findings for /ʍ/-voicing are the same as those for r-lessness: there is no consistent pattern of change across the entire group, nor does each change (or the lack thereof) follow the same pattern from speaker to speaker. It is true, all the same, that all individual speakers do exhibit variation of some kind over time with respect to both variables examined.

4. Discussion and conclusions

The r-lessness and /ʍ/-voicing results reported above parallel other studies of this group of speakers in that the only common trend across speakers and over time is the lack of a pattern (Bowie 2005, forthcoming). However, the issue at stake here is what the effects of age on an individual speaker's linguistic behaviour might be, and it would seem that the lack of patterns in the present data preclude finding an answer to this question. That is, if all (or even most) of the speakers had followed similar patterns for the variables studied, the conclusion would be clear: the relationship between ageing and linguistic behaviour would be straightforward, with people tending to change their linguistic behaviour in particular ways as they age. This, though, is quite clearly not what was found in this study, so we must probe deeper. Perhaps the simplest conclusion to draw from this – though it is not a terribly satisfying possibility – would be that ageing has no predictable effect on linguistic behaviour of a sort that would lead us to infer that a real-time change is taking place. Since the claim that would follow from this is that those linguistic changes which are observed are effectively random, the implication would be that changes in individuals' post-adolescent linguistic behaviour have no relationship to the actual experience of ageing. Though this seems plausible at first glance, it is actually rather unlikely given the tight connection between adolescent linguistic behaviour and identity (Mendoza-Denton 1997, 2008). It seems more probable that this connection would not necessarily disappear with the transition out of adolescence into adulthood, even if the nature of the connection did change. Therefore, it is reasonable to look for other explanations for this apparent lack of patterning.

Of course, the seeming randomness of post-adolescence changes is only problematic if we try to interpret them as evidence of changes in progress, when perhaps these apparently large changes aren't in fact changes in the ordinary sense at all. There is a tendency in the sociolinguistics literature to try to attribute changes like those described in this chapter to changes in community norms or to age-grading (Bhat 1970; Nahkola and Saanilahti 2004). It is entirely possible, however, that what we have here is due neither to one of these causes nor to random variation, but rather that the variation we see could simply be due to ordinary everyday intraspeaker variation.

The psychological literature on ageing supports this claim. It has been shown that as people age they become increasingly diverse as a group, with individuals in the same age cohort showing a large amount of variation and generally becoming more dissimilar from each other over time (for examples see Christensen et al. 1999; Novak and Mather 2007; Gerstorf et al. 2008). Though these studies generally deal with cognitive processes and attitudes rather than linguistic production, it seems reasonable to suppose that the use of language would be similarly divergent with age, since language use is grounded in cognitive processes. It is therefore not actually surprising that the speakers in this study followed very different linguistic trajectories. It seems that just as adolescents have a wide repertoire of linguistic behaviours from which they can choose depending on their social needs, adults – including those well beyond adolescence – also have a range of behaviours to choose from. If this is the case, then we would expect patterns precisely like those reported above: ones that look random at first glance, when what we are seeing is actually the result of individuals whose speech has been sampled at several points displaying different parts of their linguistic repertoires at each point.

The question then becomes: what leads individuals to use these different parts at different times? We currently have no complete answer to that question, but the patterns (or lack of them) discussed in this chapter can give us an idea of where to look. Note particularly that this archive was used in part because the speakers whose voices appear in it were speaking in socially constant situations over the course of decades, and that the speakers chosen from the archive for study were those who would have been the most socially constant (aside from ageing) within that group. However, changes still occurred, and in patterns that could not be directly attributed to ageing, the one clear variable at play.

On any given day, though, speakers may face both internal and external pressures that lead them, in real but subtle ways, to be socially different from how they are on other days. What affects a speaker socially on any given day isn't necessarily predictable, however, and the same things might not even have any influence on some speakers. Unfortunately, widely used quantitative methodologies with their origins in variable rule analyses are not well-suited to deal with these sorts of influences, even if they could be measured (see particularly Rousseau and Sankoff [1978] and Sankoff [1988] for a discussion of the assumptions underlying such methodologies).

Speakers certainly do behave differently at different times, but, as can be seen from the results presented in this chapter, variation at different points across the adult lifespan can't always be attributed to age itself, except in so far as increasing age may give individuals more opportunities to use and to add to their linguistic repertoires, thereby increasing their potential linguistic ranges. We could say that what seems to be random variation masks what is actually remarkable stability. Individuals draw from a palette of linguistic identities at various points in time depending on their need to express whatever facets of their social identities are most important for that day and moment, and for the interlocutor(s) or audience with whom they are interacting. This could explain the behaviour of, for example, JRC and DOM, who are arguably the two most similar speakers in the sample (Bowie 2005), and who follow different trajectories for r-lessness but follow the same trajectories – though at very different rates – for /ʍ/-voicing. Despite their demographic and social similarities, JRC and DOM were influenced by different internal and external factors which affected their need to express their identities via linguistic means, leading to initially puzzling differences in their production patterns when their speeches were recorded.

The fact that individuals actually appear to take advantage of significant levels of linguistic freedom throughout the lifespan, and that this freedom isn't lost with advanced age (recall that some of the speakers studied here were quite old by the time of their later speeches), is offered here as a final hopeful note. Most discussions of ageing tend to be situated within a rather negative narrative of decay and loss, but we should remember that a state of fixity followed by one of decline is not the only possible characterisation of language in adulthood. All sociolinguistically competent adults, no matter how old, have the ability to display different facets of their linguistic identities whenever a need to do so is perceived to arise. In a very real sense, we all possess the capacity to reinvent ourselves linguistically at any time, at any age.

6

Foreign Accent Syndrome: Between Two Worlds, At Home in Neither

Nick Miller

1. What is foreign accent syndrome?

Foreign accent syndrome (FAS) is a neurological speech disorder acquired through damage to the brain principally via stroke or head injury. Its defining characteristic is that someone is perceived by listeners to be speaking with a foreign or different regional accent (Kwon and Kim 2006), in spite of the following facts: that the person (a) has never spoken in that way before, (b) has no contact with anyone or any place where the accent is spoken, and (c) has no other social, psychological or psychiatric reason to adopt an altered speech mode.

The perceived foreign accent may last only days, weeks or months (Gurd et al. 1988; Berthier et al. 1991). For a minority, the changes persist and are impervious to all attempts on the part of the speaker and through rehabilitation to revert to his or her previous accent. Such individuals are the predominant concern of this chapter. The appearance of the foreign accent may be sudden, immediately following the trauma, or it may emerge over days or weeks. Individuals may or may not themselves initially be aware of changes, but in some cases they are painfully aware of them from the start.

2. Causes of acquired foreign accent

FAS has been associated with a range of neurological conditions, most commonly stroke but also other conditions, including head injury, dystonia and multiple sclerosis.

Novel accents, or even complete language switches, may arise for other reasons, and these aetiologies constitute differential diagnostic considerations when assessing FAS. Cases have been observed after a neurological insult where a person begins to speak with what is an apparently different accent, but which transpires to be the re-emergence of an earlier different accent that he or she had modified (Roth et al. 1997). 'Regressions' to a former accent or even a totally different language under altered states of consciousness have been reported under hypnosis or in fugue states (Glisky et al. 2004). Altered accent has also been recorded in some cases of structural change to the vocal tract (Pinto et al. 2004).

A range of neurobehavioural conditions – among them depression, bipolar disorder, schizophrenia and delirium – have associations with altered accent, including on occasions foreign-sounding ones. The vast majority of reported cases of FAS have a clear neurological root, though descriptions exist of acquired foreign accent interpreted as psychogenic in origin (for example, Gurd et al. 2001).

3. Perception of speech in FAS

There are some key features in the perception of FAS which contribute simultaneously to our understanding of the condition and also to misconceptions of what lies behind it.

Listeners typically do not hear a definite foreign or regional accent, only a hint of, say, a generic Slavic, Scandinavian or Oriental pronunciation. When placed alongside someone who has a *bona fide* Russian or Chinese accent, for example, the fact that the accent is not a 'true' foreign one is revealed (Miller et al. 2006a; Wendt et al. 2007). This was starkly illustrated in the case of Tiffany (or Judi) Roberts (http://tiffanyroberts.notlong.com) who became so upset at listeners misconstruing her American accent as British that she contemplated emigrating to Britain, only to discover that British listeners simply still heard her as American.

Those who hear a foreign accent may disagree on how marked that accent is (Southwood and Flege 1999). Furthermore, listeners do not necessarily all identify the same accent (Christoph et al. 2004; Di Dio et al. 2006). Hearing the same person, one listener labels him or her as Italian, another as French, another as Welsh, while others hear no altered accent at all, or only disordered speech. Even more problematic for speakers in trying to convince others that they have no control over the accent – that the origin is neurological rather than psychiatric – is the fact that the accent may be perceived to come and go, or to alter from one language to another.

Phonetic transcriptions of speech seem to further undermine the speaker's cause. Features that might signal the claimed accent are intermittent and inconsistent. Alongside these, sound changes occur which are not compatible with assignment to a particular accent. There may even be sounds not attested in natural languages. However, all these features – generic rather than specific accent, disagreement amongst listeners, fluctuation, presence of non-natural speech sounds, and so forth – are compatible with what is known about the perception of (foreign) accent and presentation of acquired motor speech disorders, as will be explained later.

Humans are highly sensitive to variation in speech sounds. Even young children react differentially to familiar versus unfamiliar speech patterns; adults can distinguish in toddlers' babble whether the children are from the adults' speech community or not (Engstrand et al. 2003; Rivera-Gaxiola et al. 2005; Kinzler et al. 2007). Moreover, listeners can label differences in accent on the basis of splices of speech in the order of milliseconds in duration (Magen 1998). A minor shift in vowel space, vowel length, voice onset time, aspiration or palatalisation, let alone more frank alterations, are sufficient to trigger difference judgements (Cunningham-Andersson and Engstrand 1989; Sancier and Fowler 1997). Subtle as well as more gross changes to speech rhythm, intonation, rate, pause length and pause frequency, restarts and self-corrections can equally add to the perception of a different regional or foreign accent (Critchley 1970; de Mareüil and Vieru-Dimulescu 2006).

Alterations need not be all-pervasive or constant. A minor shift in the relative degree of nasality of vowels, the proportion of spirantised plosives, the extent of phrase-final fundamental frequency movement, or in stress placement, can suffice to evoke in a listener the impression of a different accent.

Speakers with FAS typically exhibit multiple segmental and suprasegmental modifications to speech output. Each change is not necessarily equally salient to all listeners. One listener may be acutely aware of the prevalence of prevoicing of initial voiced plosives, while another's attention is drawn to a tendency to insert epenthetic schwa in word-initial and intersyllabic consonant clusters. On this basis the former hears a Russian accent, the latter an Italian one. This inter-rater variability in focus on different features in voice and speech evaluation, and the fact that different listeners do not partition perceptual continua in identical ways, is a well-attested phenomenon in speech-language pathology (Kreiman and Gerratt 2000; Southwood and Flege 1999), which is doubtless one of the main factors determining disagreement among listeners regarding the identity and strength of the accent they hear.

In so far as a listener's perceptual focus may shift, and given that the prevalence of a given output form varies continuously on the part of the speaker, listeners may well perceive one accent one day, and a different or more or less marked one the next. Also, since the relationship between changes in the speaker's productions and accent assignment by listeners is not necessarily linear, picking up an intermittent hint of an altered feature that a listener links strongly to a given language can be enough for listeners to believe they are hearing a given accent, even in the face of more constant but less salient acoustic evidence to the contrary.

4. The speech characteristics of FAS

Examination of articulatory, perceptual and acoustic modifications in FAS point precisely to the kinds of changes that signal accent differences for listeners. In one of the earlier published studies on the subject (Monrad-Krohn 1947), alterations to the speaker's realisation of Norwegian pitch accents was a key factor in determining foreignness ratings. Kurowski et al. (1996) described large pitch excursions and word–level contour changes. Ashworth et al. (2006) played listeners soundtracks stripped of all acoustic cues except fundamental frequency, and found that raters were still able to separate speakers with FAS from non-disordered native speakers, and disordered from non-disordered speakers. Modified speech is not restricted to prosodic changes: segmental deviation is also well attested (Gurd et al. 1988; Carbary et al. 2000; Dankovičová et al. 2001; Miller et al. 2006a). For example, alterations in vowel space have been commonly observed (Moonis et al. 1996). In other words, the changes noted in individuals' output have been exactly of the kind that interlocutors are likely to label as indices of a different regional or foreign accent. So how do these changes come about?

5. Speech pathological perspectives of FAS

Some have argued (for example, Blumstein and Kurowski 2006) that FAS represents a neurological disorder in its own right. The weight of evidence supports the view that it is a specific manifestation of more common speech disorders that arise in neurological illness (see above). Reports typically associate FAS with apraxia of speech, forms of dysarthria, or dysprosodia.

Apraxia of speech represents a disorder of planning and coordinating speech movements (McNeil et al. 2000; Miller 2000). In milder forms one observes problems with articulation of complex syllables or sound transitions, which increase when the person is under time or tiredness pressure. Speech rate is slowed, and one commonly finds an elevated number of hesitations and self-corrections. Stress placement, intonation and rhythm may be affected, the latter in the direction of syllabification and syllable-timed speech (Van Putten and Walker 2003). Insertion of schwa in consonant clusters may further disrupt rhythm. These articulatory derailments lead one to believe that sounds have been substituted (*pen* may sound like *Ben*, *bake* like *bike*, and *played* like *plate*). There are distortions to sounds – for example, aspiration may be perceived where one does not expect it, or vice versa – and voice onset time and vowel length can be unstable. All these characteristics are perfectly explained by the underlying apraxic impairment to speech motor planning.

A key feature of speech apraxia is inconsistency in production. Although someone may utter *pen* to sound like *Ben* on one occasion, another time they may produce it correctly, and still another time with excess or reduced aspiration. Furthermore, speech accuracy varies according to elicitation method and message content (Lum and Ellis 1999; McNeil et al. 2000; Miller 2000; Kempler and Van Lancker 2002). On the basis of this variability, people with an isolated apraxia of speech have frequently been misdiagnosed as having a functional, psychogenic speech disorder. This is all the more likely when the changes are coupled with a perceived accent change.

In the dysarthrias (Duffy 2005) articulation is disturbed due to neuromuscular changes, specifically alterations in tone, power and coordination of muscles, and consequently range, rate, strength and sustainability of movements of the speech organs. Again, in their milder forms these changes are reflected in alterations to rate and pause length, distortions of individual sounds or sound sequences, and modification to overall vowel space and stress and intonation patterns, all of which may be mistaken for a foreign accent.

Prosodic alterations arise with apraxia of speech and dysarthria (Baum and Pell 1999; Van Putten and Walker 2003; Duffy 2005). Additionally, dysprosodia may occur with right-hemisphere lesions in the absence of any overt apraxia or dysarthria (Ross and Monnot 2008). As the label dysprosodia implies, stress, intonation and rhythm output are impaired. Dysprosodia of right-hemisphere origin has also been linked to problems with prosody perception. Dysprosodic people cannot interpret the prosodic content of others' speech and may not recognise that they themselves have altered output (Pell 2006).

People with FAS frequently experience aphasia. This may manifest itself as hesitations or circumlocutions in word finding, semantic paraphasias (for example, the speaker calls a *chair* a *table*), or failures in tense or number marking and other morphosyntactic errors. Such problems doubtless interact in the listener's perception with the phonological perturbations to support the judgement that the speaker must be a foreigner.

6. Why is FAS not heard as disordered speech?

If, as claimed above, FAS arises from neurogenic speech disorders and people with FAS show all the elements of disordered speech, and possibly disordered language too, why do people with FAS not sound disordered rather than foreign? A favoured explanation lies in the direction of the probabilistic rather than absolute nature of perception and of production changes. The speech derailments made by people with FAS are fully accounted for by speech pathological mechanisms. However, the crucial separation between hearing 'foreign' as opposed to 'disordered' rests in the profile of those changes which are most prominent to the listener. If changes that the interlocutor associates with characteristics of known natural languages are more salient, then foreignness is perceived. If derailments outside of listeners' experience of natural languages or ones they associate strongly with disordered speech are to the fore, they perceive disorderedness (Gurd et al. 1988; Miller et al. 2006a). It does not matter that exemplars of both possibilities are present; the key factor is what the balance of salient evidence leads listeners to judge.

One further factor that must contribute to a perception of foreignness rather than disorder concerns viewers' expectations of how someone with a neurological condition should *appear*. A stereotypical preconception of people with a neurological disorder is that they are older, and if not older then perhaps frail, and that they are likely to show other signs of impairment (hemiplegia, contractures, or cognitive slowness; they may be expected to be wheelchair-bound or to need support for walking, to have faces distorted by weakness, with their voices faint and bodies stooped). People with FAS do not typically fit this profile. There may well be other sequelae of the underlying neurological impairment, but the conspicuous speech patterns they exhibit are all that is openly obvious to the eye and ear.

The above accounts site FAS firmly within a framework of known features and phenomenology concerning accent perception, speech output models and speech pathology. Yet for the majority of people with FAS such an account provides at most only a partial explanation of their predicament. The essence of the condition for people with FAS is found not just in its disruption to speech, but in its impact on their public and private identities.

7. FAS and identity

Identity, as the chapters in this book make clear, is a multifaceted phenomenon. Component strands develop and operate simultaneously and diachronically over many domains. One domain is spoken communication. Speech, language and accompanying gestures act both as vehicles for indexing and manipulating facets of identity (geographical or social ones, say), but also act themselves as elements of identity (for example age, gender or psychological state). As is contended throughout this book, identity is constituted and emerges in linguistic interaction; interlocutors build their profiles of an individual through interpersonal communication, but one's self-identity is also shaped by others' appraisals of the externalisation of inner concepts and beliefs through that same communication. Such an emergent, interactionist, relational perspective on the constitution, maintenance and modification of identity provides a framework within which to characterise the possible challenges faced by people with FAS. The following paragraphs consider these for the person with FAS in interaction with strangers and with familiar interlocutors, and in relation to his or her own conception of self.

To the extent that people with FAS are perceived as foreign, to interlocutors who are unfamiliar with them they are no longer identified as local but as outsiders. Accordingly, people with FAS are exposed to influences recognised to operate in people's judgements of those who have a different regional or foreign accent. Depending on the accent (its perceived prestige or stigmatised status, for instance), the listener (in terms of power relationships, rigidity of ethnic identities, stereotyping, and so on) and diverse other variables, reactions to the person with FAS may be benign or malign. They may range from positive engagement to denial, distortion or denigration of identity and intentions. The person with FAS may be perceived variously as befriendable, exotic, hostile, threatening, guilty, an outsider, less employable, uneducated, and difficult to understand (Dixon et al. 2002; Lindemann 2003; Burda and Hageman 2005; Frumkin 2007; Hosoda et al. 2007; Carlson and McHenry 2006; Allard and Williams 2008).

Any person with FAS can provide illustrations of these reactions. Strangers insist on speaking to him or her in German, Spanish, or 'foreigner talk', despite protestations that the person they are addressing is a born–and–bred local, monolingual speaker. People offer help in shops with currency, or extol local tourist attractions. Most people with FAS laugh off such incidents, but may also admit to deep–down feelings of rejection by people they identify as members of the same groups they feel they belong to, yet from whom they receive no affirmation of their belonging.

More injurious are outright prejudicial responses. One speaker with FAS from the US reported being told at her local surgery that she could not receive the treatment she was requesting, and that she would have to return to her own country. A British citizen–band radio enthusiast who sounded 'East European' after her stroke met with calls for foreign 'communist scum' (this was pre-1989) to get off the airways. Astrid L. (Monrad-Krohn 1947), who was perceived to sound German after a head injury in World War II Norway, was ostracised by her community on suspicion of fraternisation with the occupying enemy. Another post-1989 instance in Norway led to a woman with FAS being vilified as a prostitute, since that was the only reason people could imagine for her suddenly deciding to speak with a Russian accent.

Such reactions may be familiar to anyone with a 'different' accent, especially a foreign one. Possible consequences of this in relation to denial and reconstitution of self are considered below. The position is more problematic when interaction is with family and friends. Over years, perhaps decades, familiar interlocutors will have built identities of one another and laid the relational foundations of interaction. They will intimately appreciate the nuances of communication in shaping and reconfirming the status of their relationships and the bounds within which they may vary. Roles and expectations will be largely predictable and well–defined.

Communication changes consequent to neurological illness shatter this *status quo*. The diagnosis of a major illness brings with it recognised issues of impact, personal and social adjustment, and identity (Charmaz 1995; Burgener and Berger 2008; Walker et al. 2004; Murray and Harrison 2004). Parallel to the literature on the sociolinguistics of accent perception there is work documenting the effects on others' consciously and non-consciously expressed attitudes towards having a perceived disability in general, and on the individual's evaluation of self in such circumstances (Charmaz 1995; Ellis-Hill 2000; Vickery et al. 2008; Rhodes et al. 2008). Within the latter body of work, some studies have focused on attitudinal issues of this kind specifically in the context of speech disorders (Cant 1997; Allard and Williams 2008; Klompas and Ross 2004; Dickson et al. 2008; Fong et al. 2006). Again, effects may range from subtle prejudice to blatant discrimination, from well-intentioned but misplaced sympathy or condescending concern to outright hostility and exclusion.

With regard to the effects of accent change on the individual with FAS, a recurrent theme in acquired motor speech disorders concerns the effects of voice and speech changes on confidence in communication and perceptions of loss of former self – that is, of altered identity (see for example the references to perceived speech disability above and Parr 2001; Baylor et al. 2005; Miller et al. 2006b, 2008). Indeed, aphasia has been characterised in terms of identity theft (Shadden 2005). It is not uncommon that this altered identity – the loss of former roles, skills and communicative abilities – is experienced as an irrecuperable loss akin to the death of a partner, the loss of a limb, or severe disfigurement. Part of the 'grief work' in coming to terms with this loss entails coming to terms with the altered existence, moving later to acceptance of it, adaptation to the change, and renewal of self (Tanner and Gerstenberger 1988; Charmaz 1995, 2002).

Family and friends must reappraise who their conversational partner now is, and how communication with him or her should henceforth be conducted. The old 'rules' no longer seem valid. This is true where neurological illness brings about aphasia, apraxia or dysarthria. Where the only obvious manifestation of these is an altered accent, the situation is further aggravated. Realignment requires not just adjustment to another as someone with a neurological disorder (who probably does not show any other outward signs of such a condition) but also to the compounding effect of understanding the changes alongside an apparently inexplicable shift in linguistic identity.

Close family and friends can struggle to understand. In the words of EJC, 'My friends? They went away, you know. They couldn't take it, how I was. Maybe they were afraid' (Miller et al. 2006a). In the absence of obvious neurological signs, others may find that the easiest way to cope with their incredulity that a person would start to speak in a foreign-sounding fashion because of a stroke or head injury is to assume this behaviour is psychiatric in origin. Indeed, the case histories of people with FAS abound with reports of referral to psychiatrists and psychologists, who advise treatment but deny the existence of an organic disorder. Even where a clear neurological aetiology is established, the accent may be dismissed as a behavioural epiphenomenon rather than a direct physical consequence of the primary condition.

Such a view is easily bolstered by the apparent variability in the strength and perceived provenance of the accent. The individual on occasions appears to have regained his or her former speech, only to revert to sounding foreign once more (see above regarding apraxia of speech and perception of different accents), although he or she claims to have no control over these fluctuations. In the end the individual with FAS may even doubt the condition is real, at which point the label of psychiatric disorder looms even larger than the accent issues. Tiffany Roberts, the American woman with FAS mentioned in section 3, became reclusive and agoraphobic in reaction to worry over the taunts and questions that greeted her because of her 'British' accent. She took the ultimate step in identity shift and changed her name, to save her family the embarrassment of being associated with what people took to be her psychiatric condition.

Speakers may feel 'it is no longer me speaking' even before the pivotal factor in FAS of the altered accent enters into the equation. 'It was almost as if I was one of the visitors visiting myself and looking at my unfamiliar damaged body. It was as though the person confined to bed was someone else' (Cant 1997: 298).

Within the interactionist framework one can view self as something which is built up by external affirmation and reaction. Accent forms part of the construction of one's internalisation and externalisation of self – who we are, where we come from, where we belong, our geographical, social, political and psychological selves. In being robbed of our accent, against our will and against all attempts to regain that accent, a cornerstone of identity is lost. Rules upon which one previously relied no longer operate. The speech, the language that previously confirmed one's status, now denies it. Where harmony could be achieved in interaction, now only dissonance emerges. One faces alienation from one's social circle, without access to any original community in which to take refuge. One becomes estranged from elements of one's own psyche, sensing one really is still the person one always was, yet that someone unfamiliar has intruded.

EJC encapsulates the feeling thus: 'I went through this door; when I came through it the next morning it was not me . . . Where did I go to? It's not me, you know, it's somebody else . . . People ask me where I come from. I say S. They say, I never heard anyone in S talk like that before. I think: that's right. I come from here, but I don't come from here any more. Where do I come from, where did I go to?' (Miller et al. 2006a: 406).

The search for the old or new self can take on poignant dimensions. Tiffany Roberts contemplated moving from the US to the UK. Sharon (not her real name) set off on a forlorn quest to find a village in Poland where she believed the inhabitants must speak as people now perceived her, a place in which she would finally feel at home again. Joan treasured a recording made before the onset of FAS. On it she could hear her old self, the true self she struggled to find again, and the interviewer addressed her by her name. For her this confirmed she really did exist; it reassured her that she would find herself again in the face of the distressing fact that people now always misnamed her Shona on account of how she pronounced 'Joan' in her new accent.

For the person with FAS the benign and malign reactions of others represent denials of his or her self. With time it may be easiest to give up trying to explain 'it's not a real foreign accent, it's because of a stroke'. Typically such declarations meet with disbelief. People may believe individuals can develop a stutter, lose their voices or badly slur their words because of illness. Acquiring a foreign accent seems just too bizarre, especially if the accent has no association with anywhere the speaker ever lived or with anyone he or she ever knew. In the face of this, individuals may withdraw or simply acquiesce to peoples' notions of where they are from (Charmaz 2002). Some start to invent a story of how they came to live in those parts. Ken (a pseudonym) even found himself adopting the hand gestures to accompany his new 'Italian' accent.

7. Conclusion

Thomas Mann's fictional character Tonio Kröger (Mann 1903) famously lamented that he stood between two worlds yet was at home in neither. He was struggling to reconcile an existence as an artist in a material world, and to resolve the tensions between introversion and extroversion, and opulence and austerity. Kröger's predicament could, *mutatis mutandis*, be equally applied to the majority of people with FAS. They are caught between different existences, different identities, yet are at home in none. They have a neurological disorder but few, if any, acknowledge this. They have a genuine organic speech disorder, a diagnosis often denied to them. They have a new accent, but clearly do not fit when placed alongside people with 'authentic' accents. Alienation from community and self leaves them stranded in time (they have lost elements of their past and of the person they had built themselves up to be) and space (people take them to be from somewhere they are not, and their own communities no longer recognise them as part of their group). Yet they have no way back to their old selves, no original communities in which to seek asylum, no affirmation of their new selves except in terms of 'foreigner', 'outsider', or person with psychiatric disorder. These elements, it is argued here, are what make FAS unique in terms of issues in language and identity.

This is not to claim that all people with FAS exist in a state of depersonalised anomie and reclusion. It should, though, be emphasised that without an appreciation of these dimensions of understanding and adjustment, and the impact of the condition on personal identity, one will not gain a full insight into the true nature of FAS. In understanding how linguistic identities are constructed one can also conceptualise how they are *de*structed. This chapter has sought to apply notions from the interactionist negotiation of identity to illustrate how identity is distorted or lost for people with FAS. It has also pointed to possible positive rehabilitation lessons for FAS. Examining which aspects of interaction pose the greatest challenges for the person with FAS and his or her family and applying social psychological therapies to achieve collaborative resolution of communicative issues represent a fruitful possibility in rehabilitation, especially given that direct speech therapy targeting sound modification has not proved an easy option in the support of people with FAS. This also shifts the focus from one of pathologising the speaker to one of sharing resolution with interlocutors, with restorative work required from the listener as much, if not more, than from the speaker. As people with FAS repeatedly point out, 'it's still the same me in here, you know, they just can't see'. It is the reactions of listeners that distort and deny a speaker's identity. If, through listener education about FAS and seeing beyond their prejudgements about accent, listeners can glimpse again the true speaker, then there is hope of healing much of the trauma that stems from the unfamiliar conflict between language and identity that characterises FAS.

The Identification of the Individual Through Speech

Dominic Watt

1. Introduction

Research on language and identity, including studies carried out by contributors to this book, reveals that the language choices we make are a central element of our conception of ourselves not just as members of social groups but as self-contained individuals distinct from all others. This chapter explores some of the evidence for and against this view of our own linguistic uniqueness, by looking at ways in which an individual can be identified by others through his or her speech patterns.

For reasons of space it will not be possible to give an account of other means by which linguistic identification of a person might be attempted, such as through handwriting analysis and the sophisticated stylometric techniques developed by literary scholars and forensic document analysts (see further Chaski 2005; Grant 2008). Since the aim is to identify collocations of features that are unlikely to be shared by more than a few people, the methods used to try to attribute a written text to a particular author resemble those employed in analysis of speech recordings, and in some criminal investigations both have been carried out in parallel (for example, Windsor-Lewis 1994; Ellis 1994). Our focus here, however, will henceforth be exclusively on speech.

We will firstly consider what has been called 'lay' or 'naïve' speaker identification: that is, impressionistic identification of individuals by listeners lacking specialised linguistic or phonetic training. It is a task we perform on a day-to-day basis, and it seems plausible to suppose that the cognitive mechanisms that permit the recognition of known voices are unconsciously activated whenever we are exposed to a voice we have not previously heard.

A second type is the 'technical' speaker identification used for forensic applications. Here, a speech analyst is instructed by the police or a lawyer to scrutinise a voice recording using a set of formalised procedures, usually as part of an investigation of a crime in which one or more speech recordings have been adduced as evidence. Experts have a range of analytical methods at their disposal. Among these are the International Phonetic Alphabet (IPA), which through careful listening permits detailed transcription of spoken utterances, and acoustic phonetic analysis, which is made fast and efficient by dedicated and ever more powerful speech analysis software. This combined auditory/acoustic approach has proven successful in profiling speakers in investigations as yet lacking a suspect, and in cases in which comparisons are made of an incriminating speech sample with reference recordings of a known individual.

Thirdly, there now exist automatic speaker recognition (ASR) and speaker verification systems reliable enough to be used for gatekeeping applications, for example to verify the identity of callers to telephone banking operations by matching utterances to voice samples held in a database. ASR software is also used in surveillance and criminal investigations by police forces and intelligence agencies, who may wish to attempt to match an incriminating recording with a speech sample from a known individual.

These approaches to speaker identification depend upon the notion that it is legitimate to associate a particular voice with a specific person. Common sense might dismiss this as a truism but, as we shall see, we should exercise caution when making assumptions about the uniqueness of individual voices, and the existence of unique 'idiolects'. We must also be wary of overestimating our skills at identifying voices as ones we think we have heard before. In forensic contexts an uncritical reliance on these assumptions has been, and in many jurisdictions still can be, literally a matter of life and death.

Nevertheless, we should not dismiss our capabilities as listeners too casually, as in many ways they are impressively sophisticated, whether or not the listener has had prior formal training. We turn first to look at aspects of the identification of individual speakers through their speech by 'lay' listeners.

2. Informal speaker identification

Almost everyone reading this book will have had the experience of answering the telephone and recognising the voice of the caller, perhaps after only one or two syllables. We can perform this task fairly well even in the absence of any nonlinguistic information about the talker, and in spite of the degradation of the acoustic signal imposed by the limited bandwidth (c. 300–3,500Hz) of the telephone line. It is not difficult to elicit anecdotal examples of cases in which people have recognised voices they have not heard for substantial periods of time: the voice in question might be that of the presenter of a television programme forgotten since childhood, say, or that of a schoolmate with whom contact had been lost for decades. Even if we cannot immediately name the person we think is talking, we may feel absolutely certain that the voice is known to us.

This suggests that we store detailed information about the voices of individuals we encounter throughout our lives (Meudell et al. 1980; Hollien and Schwartz 2001), just as we store information about aspects of people's appearance, such as details of faces, hairstyles and clothing (for example, Mäntylä 1997; Burgess and Weaver 2003; Yarmey 2004). Not surprisingly, the amount of attention paid to the heard speech on the part of the listener appears to affect the accuracy of subsequent speaker recognition, as does whether the listener actively participated in a conversation or was a passive eavesdropper, conditions which predict better and worse performance respectively (Hammersley and Read 1985). The amount of exposure a listener has had to a voice is obviously crucial too; it constitutes, of course, much of the difference between novel and familiar voices. Not surprisingly, novel voices that are heard for longer are more reliably identified afterwards (Pollack et al. 1954). Numerous experimental studies, beginning in the 1930s with

McGehee's research on the effects of delay on voice identification accuracy (McGehee 1937; Yarmey et al. 2008), also demonstrate a fairly rapid decline after initial exposure in our ability to pick a previously heard but unfamiliar voice out of a line-up of voices selected for their similarity to the target voice.

However, the fact that we can internalise a representation of a voice such that a novel talker relatively quickly becomes familiar suggests that our capacities here are quite highly developed. There is a ring of plausibility to Hollien's hypothesis that the ability to associate voices with individual in-group members and potential rivals or enemies evolved as a survival strategy in early *Homo sapiens* (Hollien 2002: 17). Research on other species indicating that birds, cetaceans and even amphibians can identify conspecific individuals through their vocalisations (for example, Clark et al. 2006) shows that humans are not unique in this regard. The number of individual voices we may retain memory traces of is still unknown, however. It is probably unsafe to assume that because our memory capacity for faces seems to run into the thousands (Dudai 1997; Quiroga et al. 2005) our memory for voices is necessarily equally well developed, but the latter seems likely to extend to at least three figures. Given that some estimates of the typical size of an individual's social network fall in the 100–300 range (for example, McCarty et al. 2001; Hill and Dunbar 2003), and that it is not improbable that that individual would stand a fair chance of correctly identifying a substantial proportion of network members by their speech, we can start to hypothesise in a principled way what a working minimum might be. In view of what is expected of audiences for TV and more particularly radio shows themed around impersonation of celebrities and politicians (see Eriksson, this volume), we need not restrict ourselves to considering just individuals known personally to the listener. Further research will help to resolve this question.

2.1 Sources of individual variation

So what sorts of features make voices different from each other? Some variation is attributable to differences in anatomy – the dimensions of the oropharynx, dentition, palatal arch curvature, vocal fold thickness, and so on. Others are related to vocal tract function. An example is the degree of vocal fold adduction during phonation: incomplete closure yields a breathy or whispery voice quality, for instance (Laver 1980). Habitual failure to lower the velum so as to admit airflow into the nasal cavity, giving the voice a denasalised 'adenoidal' quality, is another. The anatomical structure of an individual's vocal tract is essentially fixed in early adulthood, although foreign objects (orthodontic braces, piercings to the tongue or uvula, and so on) may sometimes be fixed into the vocal tract, and with ageing certain significant morphological changes take place (J.M. Beck 1999). Ossification of the laryngeal cartilages and tooth loss are examples. Some vocal characteristics may be pathological in origin – the harsh irregular phonation nicknamed 'smoker's voice' may be symptomatic of permanent damage to the vocal folds caused by tobacco smoke, and lisps, stammers and other dysfluencies may stem from problems with motor control of the speech organs (see Miller, this volume). The involuntariness of certain articulatory habits and settings is, however, not always easy to judge. Some may be entirely idiosyncratic and not subject to the speaker's control, while others may be part of the mosaic of phonetic features that makes up a regional or social accent (for example, Stuart-Smith 1999; Coadou and Rougab 2007). It may be the case that the phonetic distinctiveness of a person's speech derives from a mixture of features not normally found in combination in a single individual, perhaps as a result of extended residence in different areas (see further Nolan 1983, 1993; and for other relevant discussion, Remez forthcoming).

Given the degrees of freedom involved in speech production, and therefore the huge number of possible combinations of segmental and prosodic features available to speakers, it is not at all surprising that speech patterns can (at least potentially) vary down to the idiolectal level. And this is before we consider non-phonological (grammatical and lexical) resources speakers exploit for communicative and identity-marking purposes. Studies of identical twins by Nolan and Oh (1996) and Johnson and Azara (2000) indicate that despite these individuals having vocal tracts as nearly alike as two vocal tracts can conceivably be, as well as having had closely comparable parental input and social and educational backgrounds in the majority of cases, they still exhibit differences in speech production. Although they might result from such anatomical differences as do exist, these discrepancies encourage the conclusion that even within the bounds imposed by anatomy, physiology, dialect background, and so forth, individuals can still exercise a degree of choice over how they speak.

2.2 Limitations in informal speaker recognition

For all our often impressive skills in correctly identifying speakers by their voices, these abilities are anything but infallible. Many readers will no doubt have been in the embarrassing situation of phoning a friend, family member or colleague and being mistaken in thinking that the intended person has answered, when in fact the answerer was someone else. We know rather little about how untrained listeners gauge the similarity of two voices – whatever analysis takes place must typically be fairly automatic and well below the level of conscious awareness – but errors of this sort presumably arise when there is a sufficiently close match between the vocal characteristics of the person talking and the listener's stored representation of the voice of the call's intended target. This would usually necessitate a degree of consistency in the acoustic cues to the talker's perceived sex (probably based principally on voice pitch), and in terms of his or her broad accent and voice quality characteristics, relative to those of the target individual. We can at times even get the sex of the speaker wrong, which is less surprising than it sounds given that the ranges of average fundamental frequency (the physical correlate of pitch) for men's and women's voices overlap to a considerable degree (Künzel 1989).

In other cases we may fail to recognise the voice of someone who is well known to us. This might be expected where the signal quality is degraded by extraneous noise (if a call is made from a moving vehicle, say), or because of distortion brought about for technical reasons (for example, through loss of signal strength). Also, an individual's voice characteristics can vary markedly in line with factors such as health, fatigue, intoxication, or emotional state (Nolan 2005). We may fail to recognise a familiar voice if the speech is shouted, as demonstrated experimentally by Blatchford and Foulkes (2006), and voices with which we have previously been familiarised can be hard to identify if purposefully disguised, such as by whispering (Hollien et al. 1982; Masthoff 1996; Künzel 2000).

Accurate attribution of a voice sample to a known individual may even be difficult in near-optimal conditions. Peter Ladefoged admits that when presented with a series of good-quality recordings of a mixture of talkers of varying levels of familiarity he failed to recognise the voice of his own mother saying *hello* and a longer sentence; only when she had finished reading a 30-second passage did he suggest that the talker was 'possibly' his mother (Ladefoged and Ladefoged 1980: 49). McClelland (2008) reports comparably poor performances in a study she carried out among members of her own family. Similarly, Foulkes and Barron (2000) found that among a tightly knit network of ten young British men reliable attribution of eight- to ten-second speech samples to the appropriate peer-group members was surprisingly variable. Misattributions of the speech of out–group 'foils' to network members also occurred, and in one case a participant failed even to recognise his own voice. The last of these findings is probably a consequence of the fact that perception of one's own voice is mediated by sound transmission through the bones of the skull as well as through the air, so that we do not hear ourselves as others hear us.

An earwitness's age appears to relate to the reliability of his or her identifications. Listeners between the ages of 16 and 40 were found by Clifford et al. (1981) to perform better in speaker identification tasks than older (40+) listeners, while Mann et al. (1979) reported that only those children in their sample over 10 years of age could identify speakers at adult-like levels of accuracy. These findings have clear implications in forensically relevant scenarios involving child witnesses, whose testimony must in any case be treated with particular caution (Parker et al. 2006).

The correlation between identification accuracy and listeners' confidence ratings – that is, how sure they feel about their judgements of whether a voice has been heard previously – has repeatedly been found to be alarmingly weak (for example, Philippon et al. 2007). Indeed, when witnesses are instructed to describe a voice verbally before being asked to identify the target voice in a voice parade, the accuracy of their judgements is impaired, despite their confidence ratings remaining unaffected (Perfect et al. 2002). This decline in performance is attributed to what is known as the 'verbal overshadowing' effect (see also Cook and Wilding 2001; Vanags et al. 2005). In light of these findings there is merit in considering carefully whether, when taking statements from earwitnesses to a crime, police officers should avoid asking for a description of the perpetrator's voice because the witness's memory of the voice may be compromised as a result. The risk would then be that the earwitness might fail to identify the wrongdoer when exposed to his or her voice in a voice parade, or worse, to 'recognise' an innocent foil speaker. If, on the other hand, police have not yet identified a suspect and the earwitness's description of the perpetrator's voice could lead to an arrest being made, there is little alternative but to elicit a verbal description. The methods used by police forces in the UK and elsewhere to obtain earwitness descriptions of voices in general appear rather *ad hoc* (with some exceptions, such as the detailed interview protocol developed for use in the Netherlands), and research on how best to gather relevant information from witnesses while minimising the influence of overshadowing is urgently needed. Comprehensive summaries of existing literature on earwitness reliability may be found in Bull and Clifford (1984), Broeders and Rietveld (1995) and Kerstholt et al. (2004).

2.3 Somatic impairment and speaker identification

It seems clear from both informal observations and experimental evidence that individuals vary widely in their ability to identify people solely by their voices. In rare cases, this ability is severely impaired or altogether absent. This condition, known as phonagnosia, is normally acquired through damage to the right cerebral hemisphere resulting from stroke or other injury (Van Lancker et al. 1988). However, the first reported case of developmental phonagnosia came to light only in 2008 (Garrido et al. 2009). KH, an otherwise normal 60-year-old woman, has extreme difficulty recognising voices, including her daughter's. Surprisingly, KH had had a successful management consultancy career even though she had avoided answering the telephone unless the caller had specified a time in advance. Garrido and her colleagues assessed KH's skills in recognising the voices of celebrities, identifying emotional information in speech samples, general speech perception and processing of non-speech sounds. They conclude that because KH exhibited no sensory or cognitive impairments except in her ability to assign names to the celebrity voice samples she heard, those areas of the brain which handle memory for individual voices must be neurologically distinct from those responsible for more general speech processing tasks.

A particularly well-developed faculty for recognising individual voices has been anecdotally claimed for blind listeners. The assumption, it appears, is that the lack of one sense is compensated for by another, which then becomes unusually acute. Research on the topic has failed to demonstrate that visually impaired listeners have any advantage over normally sighted individuals, however. Although Bull et al. (1983) found that blind subjects outperformed sighted ones in a series of voice identification tests, more recent research refutes their results. Eladd et al. (1998) simulated a robbery witnessed by three groups of listeners: voice identification experts, totally blind people and untrained control listeners with normal vision. The listeners then tried to identify which voice among a line-up of foil voices was the one they had heard during the robbery. Correct identification was most accurate among the voice experts, and the blind listeners performed no better than did the untrained sighted listeners. Contradictory results in this area have apparently not deterred Belgium's federal police service from recruiting a unit of blind officers because they are thought to be more skilled than sighted analysts at discriminating voices and determining place of origin by accent in recordings of criminal activity or of the speech of suspects (Macaskill 2008).

It should be noted, however, that trained listeners of the sort enlisted by Eladd's group do not necessarily perform very much better than untrained ones in speaker identification tasks. Shirt (1984) compared the performance of phonetically naïve subjects with that of twenty volunteer phoneticians in a set of tests in which both groups listened to the same materials. The phoneticians' average accuracy scores were in many cases not markedly higher than those of the untrained subjects, although the former group's individual scores tended to be more consistent with one another. It could be concluded from her results that extensive training in phonetics does not automatically make one a better judge of voice similarity. We should remember, however, that Shirt's study lacked forensic realism – her voice samples were very short, for instance, and she did not distinguish between types of error, some of which were made for valid phonetic reasons.

Experts of course do not have to rely exclusively on their ears, and the instrumental aids to analysis that are available to contemporary forensic phoneticians are more developed than they were when Shirt conducted her study. The results of a collaborative exercise reported by Cambier-Langeveld (2007) make encouraging reading, in that while the experts who participated in the mock speaker comparison case made use of a wide assortment of methods (fully automatic, semi-automatic, and auditory-acoustic) and had varied linguistic backgrounds and levels of casework experience, the number of correct judgements greatly exceeded the number of incorrect ones.

There is now also greater control over how forensic speech science is practised, at least in Europe and North America, than was the case until quite recently. In part this has come about through the foundation in 1991 of the International Association for Forensic Phonetics and Acoustics (IAFPA), a principal aim of which is to develop and enforce standards and best practice among those working in the field. In the following section we consider some of the methods analysts apply in casework involving samples of recorded speech.

3. Technical speaker identification

The majority of work undertaken by forensic speech analysts, at least in the UK, is of two main types: speaker profiling and speaker comparison. Profiling is carried out when no suspect has yet been identified, as for example when recordings of anonymous phone calls from kidnappers or bomb hoaxers are produced. Its purpose is to narrow down the population of possible suspects by identifying linguistic features associated with certain geographical and social groups, and any unusual pronunciations that may be attributable to exceptional anatomical or pathological characteristics.

Ellis's (1994) study of the 'confession' recorded by an individual claiming to be the serial killer 'The Yorkshire Ripper' is a well-known example of speaker profiling. The speaker on the tape was obviously accentually from north-eastern England, but through careful listening and consultation of published sources on accent variation Ellis identified features such as (h)-dropping in the word *having*, a diphthongal /uː/ vowel, and the use of [ai] in *strike*, that would place the talker's origin more specifically in the city of Sunderland. Next, comparison of the recording against reference samples from other Sunderland males narrowed down the speaker's likely provenance to the northern suburbs of Southwick and Castletown. The correctness of Ellis's accent profile of 'Wearside Jack', whose confession turned out to be a hoax, was confirmed in 2005 after the arrest of John Humble, a man who had grown up just one mile from Castletown, and who readily confessed to having prepared the hoax tape more than twenty years earlier (French et al. 2007). Humble's speech was still remarkably similar to that on the tape, in spite of the effects of age and alcohol abuse.

Speaker comparison, as the name implies, is based upon close comparison of two speech samples with a view to estimating the likelihood that the samples were produced by the same person. The expert's task is to look for points of similarity and difference between the voice of the speaker in the 'questioned' or 'disputed' sample and that of a speaker whose identity is known. The disputed sample could have been made covertly by the police, or seized as evidence, for example from a video camera or an answerphone belonging to a suspect. Or it might have been made incidentally, for example by a bystander who used a mobile phone to record an assault on a third party. The 'known sample' is typically a recording of a suspect in police custody, but it may also be a recording of a telephone call (say, to a bank) in which the caller's identity is not in question.

In the UK, and in many other jurisdictions around the world, an analysis procedure based on a combined auditory-acoustic method is most frequently used. Repeated and careful listening to samples is undertaken alongside detailed instrumental scrutiny of digitised copies using dedicated acoustic phonetic software. As a first step, transcriptions of a range of segmental (vowel and consonant) features and notes on observations of the prosodic characteristics of the samples (intonation, rhythm, tempo, voice quality) are made using IPA symbols and other specialised notation. Any other relevant linguistic information – hesitation markers, dysfluencies, nonstandard grammar, unusual lexis such as dialect words or slang terms, and so forth – is also noted, as it may be of evidential value.

Acoustic properties of the samples are then measured. Software packages such as *Praat* (Boersma and Weenink 2009) allow extraction of statistics relating to the fundamental frequency of a talker's voice (mean, range, standard deviation), and measurements of features such as vowel formants and voice onset times of stop consonants are also generally straightforward if the recorded material is of adequate quality. The speaker-discriminant potential of vowel formant trajectories is currently being assessed by groups in the UK and Australia (McDougall and Nolan 2007; Morrison 2008), and the relative stability of formants over extended stretches of speech is also considered to have particular value in forensic speaker identification (Nolan and Grigoras 2005). Speech articulation rate can be expressed in syllables per second (Jessen 2007) and rhythmic properties can be quantified using indices such as the Pairwise Variability Index (Low et al. 2001). Voice quality variations may be related to characteristic patterns in the harmonic spectrum (Gobl and Ní Chasaide 1992; Nolan 2005), though as yet the forensic tools for impressionistic labelling and acoustic measurement of this particular aspect of the speaker's voice are comparatively underdeveloped. This is perhaps surprising considering that experts are frequently presented with speech samples which are segmentally very similar but markedly divergent in terms of voice quality.

As time goes on it is becoming increasingly common for recordings to be subjected to automated analysis by machine only, and indeed in some continental European jurisdictions the method is preferred. For this task, programs like *Loquendo ASR* (www. loquendo.com) and *BATVOX* (www.agnitio.es) have been developed. Impressively high accuracy rates are claimed for these packages by their manufacturers. Speaker verification systems are becoming more commonly used for other applications – for example in computing, banking and building-access security systems – and there are proposals to include speech samples as part of the biometric data stored on individuals by government security agencies (Woodward et al. 2003). Voice data retained for security purposes is the only form of biometric information not directly related to measurements of visible features of the human body, but the currency of the popular term 'voiceprint' encourages the misperception that individuals possess vocal profiles that are at some level as immutable as physical attributes like fingerprints or facial features.

It may come as a surprise to some readers that at present, in spite of the aforementioned technological developments and the research that underpins them, we know of no one speech feature – analogous to a fingerprint – that can be used to single out an individual from a sample of sociolinguistically comparable speakers. Just as the presence of a particular pronunciation in a person's speech (say, a dentalised 'lisped' /s/ and /z/, or the use of labiodental [ʋ] for /r/) may contribute to the distinctiveness of his or her voice, so too may the absence of a feature. It may be the case, for instance, that on the basis of what is typically heard in the social or regional accent of the speaker one would expect to observe features which in fact do not occur, or are found only sporadically. An example might be the absence of linking and intrusive /r/ in phrases like *you're about* or *pizza instead* in the speech of a talker using an accent in which (like most non-rhotic British accents of English) the majority pattern is to produce an overt rhotic consonant at the word boundary. Especially problematic is the fact that the envelope of variability defining a single person's speech ('intraspeaker variation') will almost certainly overlap with those of other speakers ('interspeaker variation'). This must be taken into account when assessing whether the differences we inevitably observe between two samples are likely to indicate that the samples were spoken by two different talkers or the same one. That is, are the differences sufficient in nature and in number to allow us to rule out the possibility that they arose as a result of intraspeaker variability – which can in some cases be on quite a considerable scale – and thereby to eliminate the known suspect as the talker in the disputed sample?

If we consider multiple phonological features in combination we can generally identify what makes Speaker A's voice different from the other voices in our sample, but it does not follow that we can then say with any certainty that Speaker A is linguistically unique among the population at large. The number of speakers who may share that same set of features is unknown. For this reason, any judgement we make about the degree of correspondence between two speech samples not known in advance to have been produced by the same person should, where feasible, be cast in terms of the likelihood ratio (LR) of the Evidence. The evidence is the observed difference(s) between the suspect and offender speech samples. The LR is then the probability of these differences assuming the prosecution hypothesis (same talker) is correct, relative to the probability of the differences assuming that the defence hypothesis (different talkers) is correct (Rose 2006). Where it is not possible to express an opinion in this way – which is in reality almost always, because in most cases we lack population statistics on the distribution of speech features even in well-described languages like English – the use of likelihood statistics should be avoided altogether. The position statement published by a working group of UK-based forensic speech scientists in 2007 (see http://www.forensic-speech-science.info) recommends instead that the expert's decisions be expressed in terms of the *consistency* and *distinctiveness* of samples. If analysts find similarities between two samples that, in their opinion, are sufficient to satisfy them that the samples are consistent with one another – that is, they could have been produced by the same talker – the question then becomes one of how distinctive the combination of features heard in both samples is in the context of the wider population. At the low end of the distinctiveness scale we have 'not distinctive' (the samples are consistent but there are no features of special note) while at the high end is 'exceptionally distinctive', a label used when 'the possibility of this combination of features being shared by other speakers is considered to be remote'.

A good deal of ongoing research aims to identify speech parameters which would help forensic experts to link recordings to individual talkers more reliably than is presently possible. It is true that significant advances in this area have been made in recent years, and we should not devalue the methods currently used given the success with which they have often been applied in criminal investigations. However, analysts are duty-bound to inform legal professionals, jurors and the general public of the limitations of these methods, an obligation necessitated further by the so-called 'CSI effect', whereby laypeople's expectations are raised to unrealistic levels by the misleading portrayal of forensic speech analysis on television and in film (Schweitzer and Saks 2007). This misconception stems in part from the notion that because human listeners can identify individuals by voice the task must be one that machines can do at least as easily, and probably very much faster and more accurately. After all, modern computers are, by any standards, capable of some extremely impressive feats. As we saw in section 2, however, human listeners are in fact not as good as we might like to believe at speaker recognition, and even the best machines available are at present unable to accomplish what we see them do in the movies. As yet they cannot cope sufficiently well with factors such as channel mismatch (telephone speech versus recordings made in quiet conditions, for example), differences in voice quality and pitch brought about by emotional state or by the Lombard background-noise-compensation reflex (Hirson et al. 1995), and other intraspeaker variability exhibited by talkers in forensically realistic situations.

4. Conclusions

As should be clear from the brief overview presented in this chapter, it is prudent given our current state of knowledge to approach the idea of a one-to-one mapping between individual people and voices with some scepticism. It would be true to say that at a general level people do have distinct voices – professional impersonators make a living on this basis, and an underlying assumption made by forensic speech analysts and computer programmers working on ASR and speaker verification is that although there is always a chance that two people will share precisely the same vocal characteristics, the odds of this actually occurring in the scenarios of central concern to professionals in these areas are typically very slim.

Nevertheless, the experimental work on earwitnessing and memory for voices, which shows that we are often not especially good at identifying even familiar voices – including our own – compels caution. Consistency in the methods used to elicit statements about perpetrators' voice characteristics from victims and witnesses is lacking virtually everywhere at present, it seems, and the extent to which verbal overshadowing may influence the quality of earwitness evidence is still largely unknown. Further research should be done on the latter before attempting to address the former. There is also much to do in terms of convincing laypeople, police officers and legal professionals of the non-existence of the 'voiceprint', despite what is claimed by some software manufacturers and reinforced by unrealistic representations of forensic speech science in the popular media.

It should be pointed out, lest these observations strike the reader as reasons for alarm or pessimism, that while the field of forensic speech analysis is still relatively young it is rapidly maturing into a branch of forensic science that bears comparison with areas more firmly established in public consciousness, such as fingerprinting, DNA profiling, toxicology or ballistics. Considerable levels of research effort and resources are being committed internationally to improving and standardising procedures and analytical methods in forensic speech science, and tighter controls over who is permitted to practise it and to present expert evidence in law courts are being imposed in many countries. Qualms about levels of governmental surveillance of private citizens of the sort voiced recently by the British House of Lords (2009) certainly give grounds for serious concern. But we can at least weigh any curtailment of personal freedoms that new intelligence-gathering measures may entail against the knowledge that improved, more reliable speaker identification methods will result in fewer errors of impunity and wrongful convictions, and a greater number of correct decisions pertaining to the identities of individuals recorded or overheard committing an offence.

8

The Disguised Voice: Imitating Accents or Speech Styles and Impersonating Individuals

Anders Eriksson

1. Introduction

For obvious reasons forensic speech science is precisely about language and identities, albeit in a relatively restricted domain. Its goal is often to associate a given speech sample with a specific individual (see Watt, this volume). Another aspect is speaker profiling, where the task is to isolate a specific group of individuals sharing certain properties – dialect, speech style, foreign accent – but not necessarily a single individual. I describe below how language, dialect and accent affect speaker recognition, and how manipulating these factors by various types of disguise also affects recognition. I consider several types of disguise, but particularly imitation and impersonation.

Webster's dictionary (www.m-w.com) defines the word 'impersonate' as 'to assume or act the character of'. But impersonation may also be seen as a special case of another, related concept – 'imitation'. Imitation is a much wider concept denoting the act of copying or reproducing something. Consulting Webster again, the definition most relevant in the present context is 'the assumption of behavior observed in other individuals'.

There is no sharp borderline between these two concepts, but in analysing different aspects of imitation we may make fruitful use of the different aspects of imitation emphasised by the above two definitions. In this chapter, 'imitation' will denote the wider concept encompassing all types of behavioural mimicry including impersonation, but I restrict the meaning of the latter to cases where the target of the imitation is the vocal behaviour of a specific individual. Typical cases of impersonation would then be the copying of the speech style and habits of well-known political figures, often for entertainment purposes. When the behaviour is shared by a group of individuals, like regional dialects or foreign accents, I will prefer the more general term 'imitation'. Viewed from the behavioural angle, it is obvious that imitation is also much the more common and basic of the two types of behaviour. For example, in the acquisition of language by infants, imitation plays a crucial role.

2. How common is disguise in forensic cases?

The occurrence of voice disguise is apparently not very common. Künzel reports that 'over the last two decades, between 15 and 20 per cent of the annual cases dealt with at the BKA [*Bundeskriminalamt*, German Federal Criminal Bureau] (speaker identification section) exhibited at least one kind of disguise' (Künzel 2000: 149). Masthoff records that 'less than 5 per cent of the cases worked on at the University of Trier during the last seven years involved voice disguise' (Masthoff 1996: 161) and JP French Associates (UK) estimates that approximately one case in forty involves some form of disguise (Clark and Foulkes 2007: 198). The occurrence of disguise depends, however, on the type of crime: 'Abductions, extortions, sexual harassment and hoax calls are affected most frequently, and in this order' (Künzel 2000: 150). The BKA reports an overall occurrence of 52 per cent in cases where the offender may have expected to be recorded (Masthoff 1996: 160), and Figueiredo and Britto (1996: 168) report that disguise is 'very common' in Brazilian kidnapping cases.

3. What are the most common types of disguise observed in forensic cases?

Voice disguise may cause serious problems for speaker identification. If sophisticated electronic manipulations were used, like vocoders or communicating via speech synthesis (Clark and Foulkes 2007), speaker identification would be extremely difficult and in many cases virtually impossible. This type of disguise is rare, however. During a seven-year period of forensic casework undertaken at the University of Trier, less than 1 per cent of the cases involved electronic manipulations (Masthoff 1996: 161), while Gfroerer (1994) reported the use of electronic devices in 10 per cent of cases. Künzel remarks that electronic manipulations have been used 'very rarely' but that 'In the last few years . . . "borrowing" someone else's voice and editing such speech material on a computer for the playback of pre-fabricated messages has created a major problem' (Künzel 2000: 149). But the majority of cases involve voice disguise of a rather unsophisticated nature. Based on his BKA experience, Künzel reports that 'falsetto, pertinent creaky voice, whispering, faking a foreign accent and pinching one's nose' are the most common types. In a study by Masthoff (1996) undergraduate students were told to read a message in a disguised voice. They were not instructed to choose any particular type of disguise, but could freely choose whatever disguise they felt appropriate. It transpired that the preferred types were generally the same as those found by Künzel in real-life cases. Most of the chosen disguises (35 per cent) were phonation-level disguises (whisper or raised/lowered pitch). Articulation-level disguises (dialect mimicry, foreign accent, and so on) were used in 20 per cent of cases. The remaining disguises were combinations of these two types.

4. Effects of disguise on aural speaker recognition

Although the preferred types of disguise are, as we saw above, mostly of a rather unsophisticated nature, disguise may nevertheless have a considerable detrimental effect on speaker identification. Reich and Duke (1979) recorded forty speakers talking in their normal voices and in five guises: imitating a 70–80-year-old speaker, severely hoarse voice, hypernasal voice, extremely slow speaking rate, and freely-chosen disguise. Twenty-four native listeners and six linguistically-trained listeners served as subjects. All disguise types resulted in fewer correct identifications, with hypernasality producing the greatest effect. Interestingly, the freely chosen disguises produced almost as many errors, but we are not told what types of disguises were chosen.

The effect of whisper, one of the commoner types of disguise, on speaker recognition has been studied by Orchard and Yarmey (1995). In their study, participants heard a mock perpetrator speak for thirty seconds or eight minutes. Two days later the participants returned and were presented with a six-person line-up. Their task was to identify among the line-up speakers the individual they had previously heard. Several factors were studied in this experiment, but the relevant aspect here is the fact that the perpetrator's speech in the initial presentation was either phonated or whispered. In the subsequent task, those listeners who had heard the whispered version were presented with either a phonated or a whispered voice line-up. Throughout the various other combinations of factors, those who had heard the perpetrator's whispered voice and were presented with a phonated line-up produced fewer correct identifications.

Figueiredo and Britto (1996) have studied how restricting jaw movement by firmly grasping a pencil (or some other object) between the front teeth can serve as a method of voice disguise. This type of disguise is reportedly often found in Brazilian kidnapping cases when the perpetrators make telephone calls they suspect will be recorded. To study the acoustic effects, the authors recorded three male subjects speaking in their natural voices and with jaw movement restricted by biting a pencil. One effect of restricting jaw movement was an alteration of vowel timbre. The subjects' vowel spaces were decreased by lowering high vowels and raising low vowels. Perceptually, this may obscure important dialectal cues for certain varieties of Brazilian Portuguese, and emphasise others. Lowering high-back vowels, for example, is typical of southern dialects, and a disguise which has this effect might erroneously point in that direction. Biting a pencil also affected consonants; [s] is retracted to [ʃ], as in some southeastern accents, particularly that of Rio de Janeiro. Interestingly, this observation was confirmed in an interview with a criminal who said he used this disguise to sound like someone from Rio.

As mentioned above, phonation-level disguises (whisper or raised/lowered pitch) are commonly chosen. Change in pitch (fundamental frequency, F0) is one such type of disguise. With respect to what kind of modification a speaker chooses, the pattern seems reasonably consistent. According to Künzel (2000: 150), 'speakers with higher-than-average F0 tend to increase their F0 levels' while 'speakers with lower-than-average F0 prefer to disguise their voices by lowering F0 even more and often end up with permanently creaky voice'. If F0 is raised beyond a certain point, a change in vocal register occurs. The resulting voice quality is usually referred to as falsetto.

There also seems to be a sex difference with respect to the use of pitch modifications: Künzel observes that 'females are generally more reluctant to make drastic changes to their fundamental frequency patterns' (Künzel 2000: 150). A change in fundamental frequency of the voice source makes speaker recognition more difficult, a fact observed as early as the 1930s by McGehee (1937), who demonstrated experimentally that correct recognition fell from 80 per cent to 63 per cent as a function of F0 changes. Similar results have been found by others. Wagner and Köster (1999) let twenty listeners listen to familiar speakers talking in their normal voices or in falsetto. Their task was to name the speaker. Recognition rate for the undisguised voices was 97 per cent, but it fell to only 4 per cent for the disguised voices.

If F0 is drastically lowered, for instance halved, a change in voice quality called creak or 'vocal fry' results. This occurs routinely in normal speech, particularly towards the ends of phrases where subglottal pressure (the driving force of vocal fold vibration) tends to reduce. If applied consistently, vocal creak may be used as a disguise, thereby hindering voice recognition. In a study by Hirson and Duckworth (1995) ten male subjects were recorded speaking in their normal voices and imitating creaky voice phonation. In a subsequent perception test, naïve listeners and trained phoneticians were tested to see whether creak had any effect on speaker recognition. It emerged that creaky voice considerably reduced the proportion of correct identifications in both groups (93 per cent v. 51 per cent and 99 per cent v. 73 per cent, respectively).

The aforementioned voice source manipulations may be seen as imitations of speech styles. A perpetrator may imitate a speaker with an unusually high-pitched voice or a constantly creaky voice to make recognition of his or her normal voice more difficult.

5. Effects of disguise on automatic speaker recognition

There are at present no automatic methods that can handle disguise efficiently. The task is more complicated than one might initially think. Rodman and Powell (2000) identify the following steps in an automatic process: (1) determine that a voice has been disguised; (2) determine the method of disguise; (3) perform computer speaker identification despite the disguise.

The first step, determining that a voice has been disguised, is often possible for human listeners to do reliably. Reich (1981) used samples of forty males recorded speaking in their normal undisguised voices as well as using a freely chosen form of disguise. Two panels of listeners – phonetically naïve listeners and a group of professional speech and hearing scientists – were asked to classify the speech as natural or disguised. Both groups reached a disguise detection accuracy of around 90 per cent. But whereas determining whether a voice has been disguised is often a fairly easy task for human listeners, there are currently no correspondingly reliable methods for doing so in automatic systems. Attaining this would require large, varied databases of disguised speech and models trained to distinguish between the two categories. No such systems exist today. A first step in that direction would be to create a database comprised of talkers recorded speaking undisguised and using at least a set of the commonest types of disguises. Such a database could then be used to determine the type of disguise used in a particular case, and to design models capable of handling the particular type found. But such work is, as far as I am aware, only just beginning.

6. Effects of foreign language on speaker recognition

In forensic investigations the analyst is sometimes faced with the task of analysing speech material in a language which is not his or her native language, and an important question is then how far this may affect the accuracy of the speaker identification task. Several studies have addressed this question.

Thompson (1987) recorded six bilingual male students speaking English, Spanish, and English with a strong Spanish accent. The messages were presented to monolingual English-speaking listeners. One week later the same subjects were asked to identify the speaker they had previously heard in a six-person line-up in the same language or accent as the initial message. Voices were best recognised when speaking English, and worst when speaking Spanish. Identification accuracy was intermediate for the accent condition.

Goggin et al. (1991) also showed that in voice identification language familiarity has a central role. Monolingual English and German speakers recognised voices better in their native languages. For English and Spanish bilinguals, however, language had no demonstrable effect: they identified speakers of either language equally well.

Schiller and Köster (1996) used recordings of six native German speakers to test speaker recognition among Americans with no knowledge of German, Americans who knew some German, and native German speakers. Subjects with no knowledge of German made significantly more identification errors than the other subjects. Those who knew some German performed about as well as native German speakers. Köster and Schiller (1997) replicated the experiment using Spanish and Chinese listeners, and found that Spanish and Chinese listeners familiar with German showed better recognition rates than Spanish and Chinese listeners with no knowledge of German, whereas the former set performed measurably worse than the German and English listeners with a knowledge of German.

The results of these studies are thus in reasonable agreement that listeners with no knowledge of a language perform worse than listeners with some knowledge of it, or native speakers. In two of the studies, listeners with some knowledge of the language performed as well as native speakers. It should be noted, however, that the similarity between the tested language and the listener's native language may also play a role.

7. Effects of foreign language imitation on speaker recognition

One might think that what was said above about the effect of foreign language on speaker recognition must also apply to foreign language imitation. But this is not necessarily the case. Foreign language imitation may be used for at least two reasons: to conceal one's own voice, or to pretend that the language used is the speaker's native language. As is discussed in section 11, an imitated dialect does not have to be particularly convincing in order to efficiently mask the speaker's native variety. Is the same true of foreign language imitation? Or is it more difficult to hide one's own language background when speaking a foreign language than when speaking a dialect of one's own language? If so, what methods are available to detect the native language behind the disguise? This might be crucially important in the case of a terrorist threat, for example, where a language other than the native language of the perpetrator is used to misdirect attention. Surprisingly little has been done in this area of forensic speech science. An interesting study, tangentially relevant, is that of Simo Bobda et al. (1999). It focuses on language analysis of asylum seekers using English as the medium of communication, but with phonological and other influences from other languages. The authors argue that 'the identification of the region and even the country of origin of the subject, is possible, from phonetic/phonological, sociolinguistic, socio-cultural and other clues' (Simo Bobda et al. 1999: 300). The bottom-line for this section has to be, however, that much more research is needed to better understand these issues.

8. Effects of foreign accent on speaker recognition

The influence of foreign accents or foreign languages on speaker identification has been investigated in several studies. It is generally found that a foreign accent makes identification more difficult, but the difference is often small and not always present. In McGehee's (1937) experimental work mentioned above, an investigation of the influence of foreign accent formed a substudy which tested the recognition of a speaker of English with a German accent. No difference in recognition rate was found. 'An unfamiliar foreign (German) voice was recognized by approximately the same percentage of auditors as an unfamiliar American voice when each occurred under similar conditions' (McGehee 1937: 269).

Other studies contradict these results, however. Doty (1998) recorded native speakers of English from the US and England, and speakers of English as a foreign language from France and Belize, reading English sentences. With native speakers of English as listeners, the recognition rate for other native speakers was dramatically higher than for foreign-accented speakers.

Goldstein et al.'s (1981) results fall somewhere in between. 'With relatively long speech samples, accented voices were no more difficult to recognize than were unaccented voices; reducing the speech sample duration decreased recognition memory for accented and unaccented voices, but the reduction was greater for accented voices' (Goldstein et al. 1981: 217).

The results from different experiments are thus somewhat ambiguous. There is a tendency for accented voices to be less well recognised, although the difference is often small. It is also highly likely that experienced professionals such as linguists recognise accented voices better than lay listeners do.

9. Effects of foreign accent imitation on speaker recognition

The results of a case study by Rogers (1998) are worth mentioning here. The case involves a threat call in Cantonese-accented English to an office in Toronto. A suspect was arrested and interviewed, and the interview recording was compared to the recorded threat call. When Rogers analysed the recordings he found the suspect's accent was considerably stronger than the accent of the speaker in the incriminating call. Rogers consequently concluded that the suspect was not the caller. 'The theoretical point underlying the conclusion is that non-native speakers can imitate a stronger accent than they normally use, but not a weaker accent' (Rogers 1998: 203).

Another crucial question concerns how well listeners can distinguish authentic accents from imitated ones. Neuhauser and Simpson (2007) recorded native German speakers imitating French and American English accents in German, and native speakers of French and American English speaking German. Native German-speaking listeners were then asked to indicate whether the accent was authentic or imitated, and to name the accents they recognised. Somewhat surprisingly, whereas listeners could correctly identify imitated accents, they did not very successfully identify *authentic* accents. The authors offer the explanation that 'native German speakers and listeners seem to be in strong agreement about the stereotypical phonetic patterns which they consider characterise a particular foreign accent' (Neuhauser and Simpson 2007: 1808).

Similar results were obtained by Torstensson et al. (2004), for whom native Swedish speakers imitated Swedish spoken with a British English accent. Torstensson et al. do not describe the imitations as stereotypical (although they might well have been), but they too stress the similarities between imitators: 'It, thus, appears possible that speakers of Swedish form a cognitive prototype for accents that are to a high degree similar between individuals' (Torstensson et al. 2004: 276).

10. Effects of dialect on speaker recognition

Dialect is, for good reasons, an important piece of information in speaker profiling (see Moosmüller 1997). If the talker speaks a dialect with relatively few speakers and the telephone call may be traced to an area where a different dialect is spoken, the number of possible perpetrators can sometimes be narrowed down to only a handful. But also when comparing a disputed recording with a known one, dialect can be an important factor in determining if the speakers in the recordings are the same person (Shuy 1990: 206–7). In voice line-up confrontations it is important that the dialect of the suspect matches rather closely with that of the foils used in the line-up. Dialect is a strong identity cue (see section 11) and if some speaker stands out as having a different dialect it may make the whole confrontation invalid (Shuy 1990: 199–200). It is a reasonable assumption that dialect may influence speaker recognition in general in similar ways to foreign accent (see section 9), but the present author is unaware of any study examining this in detail. It should also be pointed out that the linguistic competence of the listener may play a significant role.

11. Effects of dialect imitation on speaker recognition

Tate (1979) investigated the ability of linguistically untrained listeners to distinguish a genuine southern US dialect from an imitated one used as disguise. One group of imitators were trained actors and the other group were untrained impostors. Ten untrained speakers of a southern dialect acted as auditors. They could distinguish a fake dialect from a genuine one in most cases. Interestingly, the trained actors did not succeed significantly better at imitating the dialect than the untrained impostors did. It should also be mentioned that as many as 34 per cent of the imitations were accepted as genuine.

For Markham's (1999) study, eight Swedish speakers were recorded speaking their own native dialects and three freely chosen imitations of other dialects. A panel of eight judges listened to recordings of the dialect imitations and tried to determine the target dialect, to judge the samples' naturalness, and to detect the imitator's native dialect. As Markham observes, the effectiveness of dialect imitation as voice disguise depends not on the imitator succeeding in convincingly imitating a given dialect, but on how well the imitation obscures the speaker's native dialect. Markham's data indicate that for eight of the twenty-four dialect imitations, the imitator is completely successful in concealing his/her native dialect without doing a very convincing job of the dialect imitation as such.

Dialect may be such a strong identity factor that we tend to let it obscure other factors like voice characteristics. In particular, we do not normally expect speakers to be perfectly bidialectal. At least one study lends support to this assumption. Sjöström et al. (2006)

used a bidialectal speaker in a series of voice recognition experiments. In line-up tests with four foils, the speaker was equally well recognised when heard and tested in either of the two dialects. But when first heard speaking in one dialect and then tested for recognition in a line-up where he spoke in the other, recognition fell to chance level. The authors suggest a 'possible reason for the results is that when making judgments about a person's identity, dialect as an attribute is strong and has a higher priority than other features' (Sjöström et al. 2006: 115). If so, a dialect imitation which succeeds in that it obscures the speaker's own dialectal identity, but is not good enough to sound genuine, would have a less adverse effect on voice recognition in a comparable line-up situation. This possibility has, however, not been investigated, as far as I am aware.

12. Acoustic analyses of impersonation

Impersonations performed by professional artists are mostly meant for entertainment purposes. They may usually be seen as caricatures, exaggerating some characteristic traits in a well-known public figure's speech. These types are interesting in their own right. One may ask, for example, what makes such impersonations so efficient even though they are often not particularly accurate copies of the target speech. Here, however, we will deal not with this type of impersonation, but with the type of impersonation of particular interest in forensics, namely where the impersonator aims to produce a maximally accurate copy of a specific individual's speech. The criteria by which to evaluate the success of such impersonations are of two types: the extent to which the impersonator succeeds in deceiving critical listeners who are well acquainted with the target speaker's voice, and how close the impersonator can get to certain acoustic targets, defined by the target voice. The acoustic targets most often considered are fundamental frequency level, formant frequencies and speech rate. Prosodic targets like word stress, sentence accent, focal accent and sentence-type intonation (such as question intonation) are also often considered.

Intuitively, one would suggest that F0 level would be the easiest target to match, assuming it is physically possible. We continually use F0 modulations to signal prosodic information and are thus well equipped to change the frequency to meet different targets. Several studies of impersonation confirm these expectations. Eriksson and Wretling (1997) recruited a professional impersonator who aimed at mimicking three well-known Swedish public figures as closely as possible. The target material consisted of approximately thirty-second excerpts of uninterrupted speech by the three individuals recorded from radio or TV shows. The impersonator had practised his impersonations for some time in his home studio prior to the recordings. Two versions were recorded for each target: the impersonation and the same text spoken in the impersonator's normal voice. These recordings were then analysed and compared to the target recordings. In all three impersonations, the F0 of the imitated speech was closer to the target than to the impersonator's natural speech. Zetterholm (2003), using a different impersonator and a different target, observed the same tendency. In her study, the prosody – the speech melody of selected portions of the three recordings (target, impersonation and natural speech) – was compared. In these cases the impersonator succeeded quite well in mimicking the target.

Formant frequencies are the phonetician's way of describing voice timbre. The basic timbre of a given voice is determined by the size and proportions of the vocal tract, and just as a musical instrument receives its specific timbre as a function of size and shape, so does the voice. But whereas the timbre of many instruments is static, we as speakers may adjust timbre somewhat by modifying the configuration of the vocal tract. This is what we do to produce different vowels, for example. It should therefore be possible for a skilled impersonator to approach the timbre (of the vowels in particular) of a specific target voice, at least to some extent. Results from the aforementioned studies confirm this assumption. In Eriksson and Wretling's study this was the case for two of the three impersonations, while Zetterholm's impersonator also managed to approach the target vowels, but only approximately.

Results compatible with these findings have been obtained in studies of impersonation in languages other than Swedish. Schlichter (1996) analysed impersonations of two French public figures. Average F0 levels are not specified, but Schlichter reports that prosodic contours came close to the targets in many cases. Vowel formant frequencies also approached those of the targets in most, but not all, cases. Endres et al.'s (1971) study of impersonation in German may also be mentioned. They recorded two German impersonators imitating five different speakers. Both impersonators managed to change F0 levels and vowel formants, but not always in the direction of the targets. It should be mentioned, however, that the texts of the targets and the imitations differed, meaning that the compared vowels did not necessarily occur in identical contexts. This must have influenced the results, but based on the published data it is not possible to say how, or how much.

We may thus conclude that it is possible for a skilled impersonator to approximate a target speaker's F0 levels/contours and vowel timbre, but in the reported cases this was done imperfectly and with varying success. We should also note that in all the studies reported above the impersonator and the targets were males. Owing to male/female differences in average vocal tract size it should generally not be possible for a male impersonator to mimic the timbre of a female speaker, or vice versa, but this has not, to the author's knowledge, been studied.

It is known from studies of sequential motor patterns in domains other than speech (typing, for example – see Shaffer 1978; Terzulo and Viviani 1980) that highly automated speech behaviour tends to be quite rigid in a given individual. Since speech must be considered an example of such automated motor activity, it seems probable that timing patterns in speech should also be fairly stable within a speaker. This hypothesis was tested in the Eriksson and Wretling study. It turned out that the deviations from the time course of the target were almost identical in the imitation and the natural rendition. That is, the impersonation did not succeed in approaching the temporal organisation of the target to any appreciable extent.

Zetterholm (2003) also addressed this question, but her data did not support the assumption of speaker-specific and essentially rigid timing patterns. The question thus remains open to a degree, and more research is needed to resolve the contradictions.

13. Effects of impersonation on aural speaker recognition

In a series of experiments Schlichting and Sullivan (1997) studied the effect of including impersonations of a familiar speaker in a voice recognition line-up. They used recordings of a well-known Swedish politician and impersonations of his speech by professional and amateur impersonators. The professional imitator's normal voice was also used. Among other things it was found that listeners could reliably distinguish between the real voice and the imitated voice when both were presented in the same sample. One result the present author finds particularly interesting is that when the impersonator's natural voice was present in the line-up along with the impersonation and the target voice, the recognition of the target was high, but when the natural voice of the impersonator was absent, the answers were almost equally divided between the target and the impersonation for the more successful of the two impersonations. The authors suggest that when the impersonator's 'natural voice was present the listeners may have been able to notice a similarity between his natural voice and the imitation' (Schlichting and Sullivan 1997: 159). This observation is important. It demonstrates that, under certain circumstances, it is quite easy to fool an unsuspecting witness, but if the witness is provided with more information suggesting a greater variety of possible choices, it may improve voice recognition.

In section 11 of this chapter we learned from Sjöström et al.'s (2006) study that a bidialectal speaker may be perfectly able to escape recognition if the witness heard the voice in one dialect and the suspect appears in the line-up speaking a different dialect. But the findings on impersonation described above suggest that the results might differ if the witness has reason to suspect that the dialect heard is just one of several possible dialects in the perpetrator's repertoire. Awareness that voice quality and dialect are not necessarily inseparable might help the witness. There is no evidence available to support this idea, but it would not be difficult to design an experiment to investigate the influence of variation in expectations on speaker identification in cases where suspected bidialectality or impersonation is present.

14. Effects of impersonation in voice-based security systems

Our knowledge of impersonation and security systems is based almost entirely on experimental studies. There are at least two possible explanations for this: such attacks are very rare or non-existent, and owners of such systems are as reluctant to go public about attempts at fraud as banks are about credit card scams. This lack of relevant real-life cases means that this section will have to deal exclusively with experimental studies.

Blomberg et al. (2004) let a professional impersonator practise impersonations of two target speakers using scores from an automatic verification system as feedback. The target speakers were chosen by comparing between the verification scores of the impersonator's natural voice and each of the twenty-two speakers in the system's database. The speaker whose voice most closely resembled the impersonator's voice was chosen as one of the targets, and one voice from the middle of the range of verification scores as the other. The impersonator succeeded in approximating both targets to a considerable degree after training. Whether the scores came below threshold level for the verification system is not mentioned, however.

A follow-up study (Zetterholm et al. 2004) using these same data compared the results from a perception test where subjects made similarity judgements of voice samples. The results showed little agreement, however, between verification scores and perception results. The reason for this discrepancy, according to the authors, was that the 'prosodic features, which seemed important to human listeners, are not explicitly used by the system' (Zetterholm et al. 2004: 397), but they do not carry the comparison any further than that.

15. Summary

In this chapter we have seen how various types of disguise may affect both the recognition of a speaker by voice and discrimination between unfamiliar speakers. We have also seen how naturally occurring variation like foreign language, dialect or accent may influence recognition and discrimination in similar ways. One may perhaps say that some of the individual properties in the voice may be obscured by other factors. When voice disguise is used, it is important to remember that in most cases the purpose is to conceal identity. And if imitation is used as disguise, it is necessary to separate how successfully the imitation achieves its goal as an imitation from how well it serves the purpose of obscuring the personal characteristics of the speaker. In sum, we may thus say that the perception of the identity of a speaker depends on a whole range of both naturally occurring factors like dialect and familiarity with the spoken language, and various ways of disguising one's identity via manipulations like imitation and impersonation.

Part III
Groups and Communities

9

The Authentic Speaker and the Speech Community[1]

Nikolas Coupland

1. The authenticity debate: the elephant in the room

The debate to which this section title refers was crystallised at a meeting of the annual North American conference on language variation and change in 2002.[2] Penelope Eckert set the scene on this debate by describing (with clear irony) 'the authentic speaker' as the 'spontaneous speaker of pure vernacular . . . the dialectological poster child' (Eckert 2003: 393). Eckert's point was that sociolinguistics, and particularly its variationist wing, had worked with a set of tacit assumptions about authenticity which at that time were ripe for critical reconsideration. Authenticity was 'an elephant in the room' – something significant, perhaps embarrassing, that no one was talking about. In Eckert's image the authentic speaker, if such a person could be found, would be someone that variationists would revere and iconise, because he or she had the core attributes they wanted all their informants to have.

What Eckert foregrounded in part was the tension, as it has emerged in sociolinguistics generally, between static and dynamic conceptions of language, because, she argued, 'authenticity implies stasis – the "real" peasant is just like the peasant that came before' (Eckert 2003: 393). That is, it is sometimes convenient for sociolinguists to assume that members of a social group can be studied as if they are all the same, equally authentic members of the social group as the sociolinguist defines it. Eckert referred to several limitations here. One is what we could call *the politics of normative authentication*, if we are tempted to orient to some people as being more authentic exemplars of social groups than others – for example, if vernacular-speaking men are treated as defining the vernacular norm of a city or region. A second limitation, linked to the first, simply has to do with the observable facts of linguistic variation. We have come to expect individual members of a regional or social group to vary, both linguistically and socially, in predictable but also in less predictable ways. In illustration Eckert raised the thorny issue of age differences, and the variationist assumption (underlying the 'apparent time' method of studying language change) that adult speech is more or less 'fixed', when in fact this assumption may not be fully borne out in studies of language use across the lifespan. (And to that extent, normative assumptions about the 'inflexibility' of older people's speech are ideologically questionable.) A third limitation emerges when we broaden the debate into more funda-mental considerations of structure versus agency in sociolinguistics. To what extent is it tenable to think of language use as being constrained by people's (authentic) member-ship of social groups (what Eckert called 'ingrained behavior'), as opposed to the social construction of personal, relational and social meanings in discourse?

The structure–agency debate cannot be resolved in favour of one side as opposed to the other. Under the weight of argument and evidence from qualitative linguistic anthropol-ogy, various versions of discourse and conversation analysis, and social constructionism generally, it is impossible to ignore the role of speaker agency in the use or deployment of sociolinguistic variation in particular social situations. Sociolinguistics has taken on a constructionist stance across most of its major paradigms (Coupland and Jaworski 2009). Ethnographic studies of 'dialect in use' have become well established, often under the heading of 'style' or 'styling' research (for example, Kiesling 1998; Bucholtz 1999a, b; Schilling-Estes 2004; see Coupland 2007 for an overview and theoretical account of a 'resource and deployment' approach to dialect style). Yet such studies add to rather than detract from the canonical, survey-based, structuralist approach to sociolinguistic varia-tion and change (Labov 2001), notwithstanding some important epistemological tensions. Eckert (2003) took this conciliatory line too. One good reason for an inclusive perspective is that we have to ask how sociolinguistic resources for stylistic creativity are constituted; where do they come from? The answer is in broad indexical patterns of co-variation between linguistic styles and social contexts of use.[3] Indexical resources are orderly or structural, in the sense that speakers can draw from a template of known, generalised associations between linguistic styles and social meanings. These are the resources that they have at their disposal, to creatively re-enact or rework established indexical rela-tionships in their talk, and to make sense of other people's performances. Structure and agency feed each other in stylistic practice.

The relevance of authenticity to sociolinguistics does not, however, start and end with the structure–agency debate. It certainly does not resolve itself into the observation that canonical variationism has over-invested in authenticity (which, from a more contempo-rary perspective, is the case) while speaker-agency approaches have 'solved the problem of authenticity'. It is probably in relation to the concept of *speech community* that authen-ticity and the idea of authentic speakerhood have most needed to be clarified, and I take up the link between authenticity and community in sociolinguistics in the next section. But in a following section I shall try to provide a more open account of authenticity and language, as a preface to a brief summary, in the final section, of an empirical case study where these issues are pertinent. I introduce the case study as a way of demonstrating (as other researchers have also argued) that authenticity can sometimes be a major motivating factor for sociolinguistic analysis, rather than a silence-inducing elephant.

2. Authenticity and community in sociolinguistics

The concept of *speech community* has a long and chequered history in sociolinguistics. It was one of the discipline's early cornerstones, much debated by Dell Hymes, John Gumperz, William Labov and others (for a review of the history of the concept, see Rampton 1998, 2009). Speech community became established as a core concept before it achieved a lasting, consensual definition, and in fact it has never achieved this. Its most enduring meaning is simply in referring to a site of sociolinguistic inquiry and a targeted group of speakers. Feagin (2002) has been able to write about 'entering the community' as the basic empirical procedure in sociolinguistic research, without considering any particular criteria against which 'community' might need to be precisely defined. In variationist practice, as Feagin says, the researcher selects a 'community' (treated as a self-evident, pre-existing social structure) and selects 'speakers' within it, then proceeds to observe language use (with a minimum of intrusiveness, in deference to the well-known observer's paradox). Most critical debate around the notion of speech community has in fact focused on what 'speech' might signify in this connection, while taking the concept of 'community' for granted.

In a thorough historical review of definitions of speech community, Patrick (2002) launches a robust defence of Labov's approach, despite pointing to its enormous diffuseness in sociolinguistic applications.[4] Urban and rural localities, large and small, whole ethnic or gender groups, but also highly local ones, have been treated as speech communities, to the extent that Patrick concedes that it is a concept that is 'evidently fraught with difficulties' (Patrick 2002: 576). In the past, evolving sociolinguistic definitions sometimes emphasised formal linguistic similarity as a criterion for recognising a speech community, but 'people speaking the same way', even in a relatively abstract sense, always seemed to defeat the main goal of variationism, which has been to show structured diversity. More pervasively and persuasively, there was an appeal to (a) participation in a system of structured linguistic variation (the idea that people in an urban enclave fit into a sociolinguistic system that, at least in an abstract sense, binds them together), and (b) the existence of shared interpretive norms about language use (the idea that people who speak differently in the same enclave at least share an understanding of what it means to use particular varieties of language in the system). These are the criteria defended by Labov. Although they offer some principled basis for linking the term 'speech' to some concept of social structure, they make few demands on the specific concept of community. Patrick argues that the litany of hostile reactions to the Labovian model of speech community, including the now-common view articulated by Milroy and Milroy (1998) that the model inappropriately presumes a social consensus about social class, for the most part miss the point. He makes it clear that Labov's conceptualisation of speech community is *not even a social one*. He quotes Labov saying that sociolinguists need to 'avoid any error which would arise in assuming that a group of people who speak alike is a fundamental unit of social behavior' (Labov 1994: 4–5; Patrick 2002: 585). So in the social dimension, structured linguistic variation and shared speech norms apart, we are left, once again, with speech community being treated as any site of sociolinguistic engagement where some pre-defined but weakly theorised social group has been identified – this is *community-as-demography*, the weakest interpretation of community.

What is most striking about this conception of community is how it cuts away most aspects of subjectivity; there is no requirement for a criterion of felt communality of any significant sort. Yet if we look outside sociolinguistics, we find that community is most commonly defined in subjective terms. It is associated with social and moral *values*, such as trust, solidarity, mutuality, and so on, as well as with more material and pragmatic considerations of people occupying a defined space and taking part in conjoined activity. In an influential sociological treatment, Cohen wrote that 'people construct community symbolically, making it a resource and repository of meaning, and a referent of their identity' (Cohen 1985: 118). Quite similarly, and in an influential empirical project, Putnam (2000) documented the social (and health) benefits of what he called 'social capital', seen as established norms of friendship, reciprocity and trustworthiness working through communities. As we shall see, there are in fact serious challenges from social theory to the assumption that this is how people *actually* experience their lives together nowadays, and there is an argument that community in Cohen and Putnam's senses is becoming untenable. But it is already interesting to point to a serious disjunction between their *community-as-value* approach and the socially thin model that has dominated variationist sociolinguistics.

As regards authenticity, contrary to Eckert's arguments above, we could say that there is *no* significant presumption of authentic membership in Labovian research on speech communities, because membership is not conceived in *any* social or psycho-social sense other than demographic. Authentic membership could mean nothing more than meeting the formalised criteria for participating in a defined sample of informants – typically being residents of a certain locale and having lived there for a specified period of time.[5] As we noted above, in the canonical variationist approach to speech community the only aspect of social consensus to be investigated is the degree of participation in normative style-shifting (and particularly using 'more standard' ways of speaking under 'more formal' conditions). Identity also has no place in the canonical account, despite the fact that it is commonly associated with the subjectivity of community in sociological treatments (see the Cohen quote, above).[6] Descriptive and quite strictly linguistic priorities dominate, and it is for reasons like these that Figueroa observed that Labov's version of sociolinguistics is not an interdisciplinary one; it is a realist orientation to the dispersion of linguistic forms (Figueroa 1994: 70). From an interdisciplinary (anthropological linguistic) perspective, Duranti (1997: 82) favours abandoning the concept of speech community altogether, and it would be fair to say that we have learned relatively little about the sociology and anthropology of community from variationist studies, whose priorities have lain elsewhere.

The argument that sociolinguistics *should* engage with community-as-value has, however, been persuasively made, along with the argument that we need to understand the role of language and social interaction in the construction and maintenance of community in this sense. In such a project we could argue that research must be sensitive to (at least):

(a) the local dynamics of socio-cultural organisation in providing a basis for community;
(b) the subjective experience of communal participation;
(c) the linguistic/discursive means by which a valued sense of community is achieved; and
(d) the subjective and perhaps moral outcomes of community participation.

Considerations (a) and (b) are at the heart of *community of practice* perspectives in sociolinguistics, heavily influenced by the theoretical discussion in Eckert and McConnell-Ginet (1992) and Eckert's empirical research on phonological innovations among style-groups in the vicinity of a Detroit school (Eckert 2000). In a review, Meyerhoff explains that the communities of practice concept firstly 'describes an analytical domain' (for the sociolinguistic study of variation), and that it is 'crucially . . . defined in terms of the members' subjective experience of the boundaries between their community and other communities' (Meyerhoff 2002: 526). Three criteria must be satisfied, she explains, in identifying a community of practice: (i) mutual engagement by members (whether harmonious or conflictual); (ii) the sharing of some jointly negotiated enterprise (of a relatively specific nature); and (iii) the existence of a members' shared repertoire (linguistic or otherwise).

A detailed discussion is beyond my scope here (see further Moore, this volume). But it might be relevant to ask whether establishing a community of practice as 'an analytical domain' does not perpetuate too much of the structural realism of Labov's speech community. What 'is' or 'is not' (pre-defined to be) a community of practice is, strictly speaking, irrelevant within a theory of practice (Bourdieu [1972] 1977). In such a theory, practice not demography is the starting point. Practice is what shapes (among other social phenomena) different experiences of community, and to that extent the phrase 'community of practice' is tautological. In purely practical terms it is of course difficult to avoid predetermining a research site and presupposing how people within it might act as community members, but the issue is not trivial. Community of practice approaches sometimes perpetuate the socio-structural ambitions of survey research, for example in seeking out sub-groups within a 'community' in order to compare and contrast their speech correlates. The interpretive emphasis in Eckert's and others' research is certainly on the *emergence* of identities and of new linguistic forms in the context of social and (non-linguistic) stylistic innovations, sometimes in very local respects. Even so, the correlational, variationist approach that Eckert pursues in aspects of her (2000) study, and that most of the studies reviewed by Meyerhoff also take, arguably limits our appreciation of the role of language use in the achievement of community (consideration (c) above), and indeed of what particular sense of community is achieved (consideration (d)).

A lot depends on how 'mutual engagement' (Meyerhoff's first criterion) is analysed, and the ethnographic methods favoured by community of practice researchers are ideally suited to exposing processes and trajectories of engagement. We often get rich accounts of the practices around which group members coalesce (such as 'cruising' in Eckert's Detroit research; the use of makeup and dress-styles in Mendoza-Denton's (2008) study of Latina youth-gangs) and of how leaders emerge and carry forward innovations in the styling of appearance and outlook as well as speech. Following Bergvall (1999), Meyerhoff considers whether community of practice perspectives will tend to be brought to bear particularly on adolescent and school-based groups (and this has been the main tendency in research so far), where style innovation and the remaking of social identities have special salience and affordances. Meyerhoff says this needn't be the case, although the concepts of authenticity and community are likely to play out in distinctive ways in school-student contexts. Schools are, for example, fields of social practice and identity experimentation that are relatively disconnected from the neighbourhoods that they serve; school-student communities inevitably have shorter histories, identity formations may be less durable, and so on.

Membership and negotiation of style groups at school are clearly powerful classificatory processes. But there may be further work to be done in understanding whether and how linguistic innovation, or linguistic styling generally, impinges on young people's more general experience of relationships and community, bearing in mind Labov's caution that shared ways of speaking might have no social reflex at all. For example, do young people equate core linguistic membership of a community of practice, or being a stylistic innovator within it, with specific community-linked values and authenticities, and how can we establish this? Can the community of practice paradigm model community-as-value in the social class environments *outside* schools and those settings where community of practice research was instituted? Similar questions can be raised in relation to *social network* analysis, notwithstanding Lesley Milroy's argument that social networks are 'personal communities which provide a meaningful framework for solving the problem of daily life' (Milroy 2002: 550). Social network research refined the sociolinguistic account of language maintenance and change within working-class communities, but it has relied on statistical indicators of network strength (*community-as-association*, then) rather than seeing community as subjectively constructed in practice networks.

The concepts of social network and community of practice have been enormously facilitative in advancing our understanding of dialect change. They have certainly shifted sociolinguistic engagement with 'community' towards an appreciation of community-as-value, but we could argue that they have also tended to hold on to conceptions of community-as-demography and community-as-association. As Rampton (2006: 15) points out, community of practice research has tended not to look beyond the bounds of the particular communities under investigation, and this has made it difficult to bridge between local and more global (socio-economic, historical, cultural) processes.

3. Authenticity, language, community and social change

In other places (Coupland 2001b, 2003) I have suggested that authenticity points above all to a *value* system, much as we have been discussing it here, and specifically a value system that, where it exists, is able to anchor personal, social and cultural identities. The values that we associate with authenticity can be specified in terms of:

(a) *ontology* – authentic things being felt to have a particular depth of reality;
(b) *historicity* – authentic things being perceived to be durable and sometimes timeless;
(c) *systemic coherence* – authenticity as a matter of 'making sense' and imposing order; and
(d) *consensus* – authenticity resulting from some social process of authentication accepted by a group.

Sociolinguists have sometimes approached language and community in precisely these terms, for example in Fishman's passionate Herderian account of language, nation and ethnicity (1989/1997). Fishman defines ethnicity here, with a distinctive language at its symbolic heart, as 'collective, intergenerational cultural continuity', a matter of 'fundamental essence', which can be 'creative and healing' (authenticating, in fact) as well as 'irrational' and 'disruptive' (Fishman 1989/1997: 330–4). Non-linguists do indeed sometimes represent their own community and linguistic allegiances in these terms, perhaps most predictably when they are at some remove from their cultural centres or under circumstances of threat or endangerment (see, for example, Bishop et al. 2003).

This view of linguistic and cultural authenticity, however, tends to meet with critical resistance nowadays, often expressed in relation to the concept of *essentialism* (for example, Bucholtz 2003). Sociolinguistic essentialising is considered to be a problem or at best a naïvety. Bucholtz writes that 'essentialism is the position that the attributes and behavior of socially defined groups can be determined and explained by reference to cultural and/or biological characteristics believed to be inherent to the group . . . The idea of authenticity gains its force from essentialism' (Bucholtz 2003: 400). Bucholtz endorses a shift towards more reflexive ideological critique within sociolinguistics, where essentialism can be recognised and laid to rest. Authentication as a discursive process, rather than authenticity as a claimed or experienced quality of language or culture, can then be taken up analytically as one dimension of a set of intersubjective 'tactics', through which people can make claims about their own or others' statuses as authentic or inauthentic members of social groups. Indeed, it is increasingly common to find sociolinguistic analyses couched in terms of the discursive construction of authenticity and inauthenticity (for example, Coupland 2001c; Sweetland 2002; Chun 2004; Sebba 2007; Shenk 2007; Johnstone and Kiesling 2008). At a more macro-level, Heller (2010) shows how languages can be commodified in the New Economy, for example in call-centre work, and promoted for their perceived authenticity value, when older, community-linked values help sell products and services.

There are clearly countless ways in which authenticity and inauthenticity can be ascribed to people, selves or others, or withheld from them, or put to work in the service of local interests. These are sociolinguistically important processes (see further Bucholtz and Hall, this volume). The political critique of essentialism took shape when it was recognised that there were broad tendencies, including academic ones, to 'other' socio-cultural groups by homogenising them (inappropriately attributing qualities of authentic membership, as in Bucholtz's argument but also in Eckert's remarks, above) or by treating them as peripheral (inappropriately withholding authentic membership from them, for example, Said 1978; Riggins 1997; Coupland 2000). Authentication practices can certainly have profound political consequences as well as, on other occasions, being framed as verbal play or some other mode of talk where category membership is invoked. But there is a crucial distinction to be made between identity as representation and identity as felt subjectivity, and an over-zealous project of outlawing essentialism, and the shift into *only* discursive treatments of authentication tactics, risks trivialising deeply held subjective convictions and allegiances (cf. Rampton 2006: 233–6).

When constructionist approaches to authenticity are overplayed, there can in fact be *an essentialising of relativity*, implying that any subjective sense of 'essential' belonging (like that described by Fishman, above), or even a sense of affiliation to a particular social category, is impossible or somehow illegitimate. While strongly defending a sociolinguistics of practice, Rampton (2006: 233) discusses how practice perspectives generally might tend to 'empty out' the meaning of social class, for example, and this echoes concerns colleagues and I have expressed in our research on language, ageing and identity. From his own research on school students' vocal dramatising of social class voices, Rampton concludes that class in fact reaches quite deeply into the 'psycho-social imaginings' of the young people he studies. However, social class provides a repertoire of styles that allow kids to achieve very local interactional outcomes, rather than being a framework that limits their lives and language (see further Rampton, this volume).

There has often been an academic market in cynicism, and the ideology of anti-essentialism can easily brand any intellectual engagement with authenticity-as-value, and therefore community-as-value, as being 'romantic' or 'romanticising'. Rampton (2009) agrees with Pratt (1987) and Bernstein (1996) that early sociolinguistics sustained a current of romanticism, in which the idea of speech community might have played a part. Rampton points to how sociolinguistics tended to value working-class people and language as having inherent validity, which of course was an ideological stance in opposition to establishment validation of 'standard' varieties (Coupland 2003). But I would press for a more nuanced orientation to sociolinguistic romanticising, and authenticity. Many sociolinguists will have been struck by the cultural and personal values seemingly embodied in informants' lives and language, particularly when ethnolinguistic distinctiveness is under pressure. This is usually a conflicted perception, complicated at least in part by the disjunction between the institutional and class position held by the researcher and the so-called 'lay' position of informants. Romanticism is an apt term for interpreting social distance as value, when academics 'look out at' social groups and attribute values to their identities and practices that might not be fully warranted or perceived outside of academic frames of reference.

Yet most of us appeal to the values I earlier associated with authenticity in making social judgements of various sorts, even in our academic practices; criteria such as consensual worth and historicity are ones we do have some faith in. It would be perverse to rule them out in relation to language or community, particularly when we have evidence of such values mattering to the people we orient to in research terms. There is the problem that what we usually have available to us as evidence is, once again, representations and performances of authenticity (for example, narratives of cultural continuity and distinctiveness). But it is too cynical to believe that authenticities are 'purely discursive', particularly when the act of dismissing authenticity has material consequences. In a sociolinguistic context, Eira and Stebbins (2008), for example, discuss competing authenticity claims made in relation to endangered languages and communities. They are adamant that, for language planning and preservation initiatives, it is essential that *some* principled criteria for linguistic authenticity have to be agreed, case by case. If, for example, we want to intervene to try to support migrant groups whose linguistic and cultural heritage is being stripped away, Eira and Stebbins say we have to make judgements about what can and should count as linguistically and culturally authentic for those groups. This is a long way from the facile assumption that triggered a reassessment of language and authenticity – that all vernacular language use in its 'natural' setting within 'the speech community' is authentic.

Behind this debate, at least as it relates to 'the West' and to globalising culture, there is the question of whether social life *can* any longer involve authentic experience. Rampton (2006) points to social changes and discourses linked to globalisation and late-modernity that have undermined consolidated notions of social structure, and notions of community and authenticity as part of that shift. Beck (1992, 1999) has formulated a vision of late-modernity as a 'risk society' where the certainties and comforts we associate with community are generally unattainable, and where 'the individual is . . . removed from traditional commitments and support relationships, but exchanges them for the constraints of existence in the labor market and as a consumer, with the standardizations and controls they contain' (Beck 1992: 131). Bauman (2000, 2001) similarly argues that we confront a social world of personal disengagement from elusive support systems, in a socially 'liquid modernity'. In late-modernity he sees 'the celebration of socially and morally unaccountable individualization' (Bauman 2000: 200; see also Beck and Beck-Gernsheim 2002). Under these circumstances, community tends to become a nostalgic (cf. 'romantic') or an aspirational concept, when 'common cause' (class, citizenship, the family, and so on) is 'unmade' in the conditions of consumerist and heavily individualist late-modern life. Rampton (2009) speculates that a late-modern sociolinguistics is the analysis of 'life without community'.

However far and fast we want to run with these apocalyptic conceptions of contemporary life, there are plenty of reasons here, beyond those we considered earlier in the chapter, to argue that older sociolinguistic models of speech community are outdated. It seems ironic that cities or city-districts were the earliest environments to be labelled speech communities, when cities today are typically multicultural meeting places subsuming complex and fluid social networks, sometimes organised on shifting ethnic as well as socio–economic principles. Cities, we might also add, are often experienced as lonely rather than communal spaces. Gumperz (1996) points out that new inter-culturalities are tending to undermine old structural assumptions about both culture and community. A modern urban geographical space is not culturally uniform, but it is liable to sediment out new cultural norms and boundaries, which may cut across language code distinctions – Gumperz discusses the experiences of South Asians in Britain. It is also true that some of the strongest communities – strongest in the sense of promoting communitarian values – have tended to be fractured in changes linked to de-industrialisation (in Britain, particularly in the last two decades). This is the backdrop to the case study I shall now introduce, which I am interpreting as an initiative to refashion community-as-value in the South Wales Valleys, where much-vaunted earlier communitarian values are seriously threatened by poverty, unemployment, health problems and out-migration.

4. Local radio, community-as-value and cultural validation

I would like to end this theoretical discussion with a speculative, preliminary analysis of a particular broadcasting phenomenon in contemporary Wales. *The Chris Needs Show*, sometimes referred to as 'the friendly garden show', is a late-night music and chat show broadcast in English on (national) BBC Radio Wales. Its presenter, Chris Needs, won an award as 'best UK regional radio presenter in 1996 and an MBE (Member of the [Order of the] British Empire) for services to broadcasting and charity work in 2005. The show's format centres on 'putting people in the garden', thereby creating a virtual 'community' of, currently, more than 40,000 listeners who Chris refers to as 'flowers'. I am interested in what sort of community is being constructed here, and in how mediated community plays off against other social formations. Can the garden constitute community-as-value, and might it even support a sense of authentic community membership? If so, how are these values worked up sociolinguistically? What might this case suggest about the affordances of community in late-modernity?

Notwithstanding the problems of definition I referred to earlier, the Chris Needs garden can reasonably be called a community of practice. Callers phone in and, on the first occasion of calling, Chris allocates them individual identification numbers, confirming their membership. Garden members sometimes meet non-virtually, for example at charity events and live broadcasting events organised by Chris. Many members call the show repeatedly, getting into intimate and disclosive chat, sometimes about personal problems and crises, sometimes about thoroughly mundane matters in their lives. But this is a community centred on Chris Needs himself. His complex media persona is, in turn, constructed around his celebrity – achieved via the show, but also through his other public appearances and functions. This is a form of celebrity premised on ordinariness, as celebrated in Chris's published autobiography (Needs 2001). On air and in print Chris is disclosive about his own health problems, his ambitions and frustrations, his gay relationship, his love of shoes, bling (gaudy jewellery), disco and soul music from the 1970s and 1980s. Other recurrent themes in his talk are Spanish holidays, his two grocery shops in the Valleys village of Cwmafan (shops which used to be run by his mother), his day-to-day life and likes, and so on. Openness and personal vulnerability clearly provide one basis for celebrity status in the 'intimate distance' design of some contemporary media. We can briefly look at one sequence from the show, extract 1.[7]

Extract 1

Caller Sue Griffiths has been congratulating Chris on getting his MBE at Buckingham Palace.

Sue   oh wonderful wonderful experience
Chris   and they put this clip on you see when you go in and you have like
          glass of water or squash or whatever like ((you want))
                                                             [   ]
Sue   yes
Chris   and they put this clip with a hook . and it's . there for Her Majesty
          to . put the medal on you know
Sue   oh right everything
Chris   yes
Sue   everything correct yeah
                                        [
Chris   oh oh it was stunning . stunningly run
Sue   yes
Chris   oh and (breathy voice) see inside the palace we went to we went
          all around there different places in there
Sue   wow
Chris   it was phenomenal
                                  [
Sue   I bet it was
                                  [
Chris   oh::
Sue   I bet it was
Chris   it was-
Sue   well thoroughly deserved Chris
Chris   it was the business . it was . er the business
Sue   feeling tired now?
Chris   yeah little bit . I'm alright though
Sue   come down to earth yet?

Chris	er no
Sue	no no
Chris	(coyly) I'm staying where I am for a little bit
Sue	(laughs) did many people go up from the garden to see you?

Chris has been giving a lengthy account of how overawed he was when he collected his MBE award from the Queen, how gorgeous the Palace was, and how tiring the day was, and these themes are picked up in the extract. Chris's account constructs him as unsophisticated and perhaps childlike in his reactions: *they put this clip on you see when you go in; we went all around there different places in there*; drinking squash (fruit cordial) is child- and perhaps working-class-marked, and so on. Chris's remark *it was . er the business* gives a brief glimpse of his propensity to shift into stylised utterance, voicing personas other than the one we take to be his own. In the current instance we get a feeling of 'smart talk' or 'smooth talk' being momentarily inserted into Chris's account. Chris's voicings stand out because the baseline indexicalities of his own and most callers' voices are South Wales Valleys, which provides a vocal semiotic of 'ordinariness'. Chris's stylisations therefore create the effect of *confirming* ordinariness and localness, because managing ephemeral personas that are 'knowingly false' (Coupland 2001c, 2007) acts as counterpoint to the underlying vernacular.

Valleys voice in the extract is marked in schwa-like tokens of Received Pronunciation (RP) [ʌ] (for example in *wonderful, come*), [iw] for RP [juː] (*you*), [oː] monophthongs for RP [əʊ] (for example, *oh, go*) and [eː] monophthongs for RP [eɪ] (*places*), open short [a] for RP [æ] (for example *and, Majesty*), centralised onset of RP [aɪ] and [aʊ] (for example *like, right; around, down*), the idiosyncratic south Walian use of schwa in *want*, /h/-dropping in *have*, alveolar 'ng' (for example *everything, stunning*). Other indexical features include south Walian intonation, but also discursive stances likely to be associated with either powerlessness (Chris's passivity in the process of being given his award, *they put this clip on you*) or deference (*Her Majesty* rather than 'the Queen') or self-protectiveness and self-diminution (*staying where I am for a little bit*).

It is necessary to engage with the data over many broadcast hours of *The Chris Needs Show* and over time to appreciate how callers are socialised and socialise themselves into Chris's and the garden's themes and values. In the extract we see Sue congratulating and commending Chris on his award, but also scaffolding his narrative and endorsing his affective stances. Chris's interaction with callers often focuses on his own personal agenda in this way, which is of course unusual in radio phone-in talk. When Chris invites comment from callers about their own lives – with personal troubles being a major theme – callers' accounts often match those that Chris has already told. A longer analysis would be needed to reveal the range of ways in which Chris's ordinary celebrity is mapped onto the large and growing circle of listener-flowers in this way, and it is the mechanism through which this mediated value-community is worked up discursively. If we bear in mind the wider social and historical context in which the show operates, we might already begin to see what values are in question.

Valleys voice bears indexicalities of place and social class of the sort that often leads sociolinguists to describe such varieties and their speakers as 'stigmatised'. The Valleys today are in fact among the most socio-economically deprived regions of the UK (Osmond and Mugaseth 2004). Yet the Valleys were an international icon of working-class community achievement and resilience through the nineteenth and early twentieth centuries. Socialist historians and critics (Smith 1999; G. Williams 1985; R. Williams 2003) celebrate the cultural vitality of the Valleys before deindustrialisation, where communitarianism and authenticity (personal and cultural) were key themes. I believe we can find significance in the Chris Needs data partly in the continuity between industrial and post-industrial Valleys experience, and partly in the (more obvious) disjunctions between the past and the present. I would finally like to consider the possibility that *The Chris Needs Show* provides a public footing of sorts for coming to terms with social change.

Several of the key values indexed in the show have cultural resonances with Valleys life, past as well as present. The show creates opportunities for the disclosure of personal hardship, and to do this in a participation framework that is simultaneously intimate and public. It creates quasi-therapeutic frames for the negotiation of coping, exactly as Chris does in his own movement between stories of personal incompetence or vulnerability and his extravagant indulging in rather dated popular culture. Participants do appear to seek social support and sometimes to genuinely find it through these exchanges, and there are echoes here of the principles of self-help and self-improvement that were strongly in evidence in early twentieth-century mining communities. In more general terms *The Chris Needs Show* helps to give the Valleys a degree of prominence in the public sphere, in a political and cultural climate where the Valleys tend to be sequestered as a zone of deprivation. The show in many ways exposes and validates the Valleys and their problems.

Voice adds an important dimension to this exposure. The last thirty years have seen a gradual relaxation of the ideological proscription of regional Welsh English voices in the mass media, although Valleys voice is still rare outside of drama and vox pop genres. Valleys speech has many indexical referents, and they include traditional manual work-based masculinity and the associated 'strong, silent but resilient' stereotype. But the rapidity and scale of deindustrialisation in the Valleys has cut Valleys voice adrift from this dimension of its traditional meaning. Work–centred community experience in the Valleys is acknowledged to have been radically fractured, and social change has been far too swift to be matched by linguistic change of any comparable extent. The social meaning of Valleys voice has therefore, at least for men, become decentred, socially disembedded and deauthenticated. What does *The Chris Needs Show* pitch into this semiotic space?

In his own baseline persona, as a camp, self-presenting gay male, Chris Needs diverges radically from the image of the silent, strong, resilient, heterosexual Valleys working man. Chris, the ordinary celebrity, complicates and destabilises some key parts of the indexical meaning of Valleys speech. Traditionally positive valencies are refuted by Chris's talkativeness (he is after all a radio DJ) and self-projected vulnerability. So is the dominant semiotic simply 'disadvantaged' or 'common', or could it somehow have started to incorporate 'cool' and 'consumerist abandon'? Chris presents his audience with the conundrum that a Valleys male can actually embrace bling, disco, sun-worshipping and camp, even while his show displays and addresses the social problems that beset the Valleys. The role of vocal stylisation here requires much closer attention, because stylisation is often able to heighten reflexivity around social semiosis, bring conflicting identities and realities into contact with each other and make them available for reassessment.

The speculation that I would like to carry forward into that longer analysis is that *The Chris Needs Show* gives us an instance of discursive practice functioning simultaneously to *create* community-as-value and to critically *deconstruct* and *reformat* the social footings on which community is based. In his self-presentation Chris deauthenticates himself relative to old certainties of class and gender, but proposes new criteria that might be more valid in the shifted social circumstances of Valleys life in the twenty-first century. It is the focusing potential of the mass media that allows a single individual to function as a prototype and, paradoxically enough, to constitute community largely through individual action. If we are indeed living in a late-modern world of increasing individualisation, public intimacy and mediated community, *The Chris Needs Show* would appear to be a highly contemporary manifestation of it. The Valleys context undoubtedly shows how economic restructuring linked to globalisation can ruthlessly sweep away the orderly social structures and values of class and gender to which language variation and social identification were once intimately linked. *The Chris Needs Show* also illustrates how, from the ashes of detraditionalisation and sociolinguistic deauthentication, new forms of community-as-value can arise, in surprising ways.

Notes

1. I am very grateful to Peter Garrett, Adam Jaworski, Carmen Llamas, Peter Patrick and Dominic Watt for helpful comments on an earlier version of this text.
2. The panel in question was titled 'Elephants in the room', convened by Penelope Eckert at NWAV31 at Stanford University. The papers presented there were subsequently published in *Journal of Sociolinguistics*, referenced here as Eckert (2003), Bucholtz (2003) and Coupland (2003).
3. This idea is familiar in the sociolinguistics of style, for example in Bell's claim (2001) that stylistic variation draws from and is enabled by indexical relationships at the level of social group variation (see also Coupland 2007, Chapter 2). Hastings and Manning (2004) extend this approach by theorising a relationship between identity and alterity in spoken discourse. Following Goffman, they suggest that speakers animate various figures in their talk, ranging from 'natural figures', which are performances of 'one's authentic self', through to 'mockeries', when people voice stereotyped others.
4. Peter Patrick points out, in his very helpful review of an earlier draft of this chapter, that variationists' use of the speech community concept served their own purposes well at the levels of methodology and analysis while it was less successful at the level of explaining and interpreting language variation and change. He also argues that the variationist model of speech community was empirically valid, in the sense that groups labelled 'speech communities' have tended to show a vigorous and significant pattern of unity in terms of patterns of variation and/or shared evaluative norms.
5. There are sociolinguistic studies which can give us at least some empirical purchase on authenticity in this simple distributional sense, such as attitudinal studies that ask whether supposedly representative members of particular localities can be recognised as coming from those localities on the basis of their speech characteristics. If people within the same communities cannot do this regularly, we might doubt the assumption that people are ever 'perceptually authentic' members of their 'communities'. Findings tend to be mixed. For example, Garrett et al. (2003) found that secondary school teachers produced rates of between 28% and 68% for the 'correct' recognition of young speakers of six different accent varieties of English in Wales, while school students' rates ranged between 21% and 42%.

6. Variationists have sometimes been quite hostile to explanations centred on 'identity'. One striking example is Trudgill's (2008) claim that identity was 'irrelevant' in the development of colonial varieties of European languages. In his article Trudgill argues against 'jump[ing] to conclusions based on notions of identity' and he cites Labov's view that 'as always, it is good practice to consider first the simpler and more mechanical view that social structure affects linguistic output through changes in frequency of interaction' (Trudgill 2008: 251; Labov 2001: 506). Trudgill's stance was thought to merit close critical examination (see Coupland 2008 and the other responses to Trudgill's article in *Language in Society* 37).

7. In the extract, overlapping speech is marked by square brackets, brief pauses are marked by dots, and underlining represents heavy syllable or word stress. Single round brackets enclose my own notes about nonverbal behaviour or delivery style; double round brackets enclose stretches of talk that are unclear.

10

Two Languages, Two Identities?

Norma Mendoza-Denton and Dana Osborne

1. Introduction

Despite the fact that bi-/multilingualism is the most common linguistic condition of societies, and although no state is exclusively monolingual (Thomason and Kaufman 1988), academic and popular accounts of bi-/multilingualism have struggled with monolingualist biases. From the earliest (modern) academic descriptions of bilingual individuals, we find narratives such as the following:

> White Thunder, a man around 40, speaks less English than Menomini, and that is a strong indictment, for his Menomini is atrocious. His vocabulary is small, his inflections are often barbarous, he constructs sentences of a few threadbare models. He may be said to speak no language tolerably (Bloomfield 1927: 395).

The charge and spectre of speaking 'no language' similarly follows us into the present, with horrified accounts from journalists who occasionally write exposés on 'alingual' migrant children in American classrooms. The following is from a *Washington Post* article on immigrant four-year-olds in a Head Start class in Montgomery County, one of the United States' richest jurisdictions: 'When a . . . boy flung dirt on others with his shovel, or when some wanted to put worms in a bucket, the children had no words in any language. They filled the air with inarticulate grunts and cries of "Heeeey" (Schulte 2002). The same story, this time entitled 'Alingual education: young victims of mass immigration', was picked up shortly afterwards in the *National Review* (Krikorian 2002). The US does not have a monopoly on bilingualism panics, nor is population movement the only cause of such panics. In 2008, a family court in Wales heard an English expert witness testify that Welsh-medium classes would cause retardation in some children and could not stimulate a child to the same level as English medium education (Shipton 2008). This testimony remained unchallenged and caused a shift in custody arrangements for the child at the centre of the trial. Widespread social reaction followed, including from Wales' First Minister, who instructed the Ministry of Justice to conduct an investigation.

Against this prickly political background, research on bilingualism seems a Sisyphean task. Research retreads paths already worn, continually 'proving' that bilingualism and linguistic diversity in general are not deficits (Labov 1982; Romaine 1995; Zentella 1997; Smitherman and Baugh 2002), that bilingualism in itself will not tear polities asunder, but bureaucracy is much more likely to do so (Fishman 1991), and demonstrating that bi- and multilinguals have cognitive flexibility and facilitation of various tasks because of using two or more languages (Gardner-Chloros 1991; Sommer 2004; Kroll and de Groot 2005).

The present chapter reviews the literature on bilingualism and identity, taking a necessarily restricted scope dealing primarily with sociolinguistic and linguistic anthropological approaches. We restrict the concentration of our coverage to bilingualism literature from the last thirty years, and we cannot for reasons of space include detailed discussion of psycholinguistic approaches, structural approaches to codeswitching, bilingual education, language policy, endangered languages, or language revitalisation, despite their importance (see instead Romaine 1995; Mendoza-Denton 1999; Muysken 2000; Li Wei 2007). We acknowledge the postcolonial condition by focusing on power relations, and attempt to fill some gaps by treating lesser-known linguistic situations and integrating linguistic anthropology. We primarily attend to semiotic and performative approaches to bilingualism and identity, and the overarching question we seek to answer may be framed as: how far can and do speakers strategically mobilise one language or another to achieve desired social and political effects?

2. Linking bilingualism and political economy

Discussion, analysis and policy designed to address issues of bilingualism are intimately connected to political economy. Heller points out that the 'common sense' understanding of bilingualism is implicitly predicated on the 'coexistence of two linguistic systems' (Heller 2007: 1), but the story becomes complicated when considering the political environment contributing to what is seen as bilingualism. For Heller, the assumption that distinct linguistic systems exist allows for the reification of languages, rather than allowing us to see that language policy and classification are media through which social and political ends crystallise. The very project of defining 'bilingual' as a category ultimately serves to normalise the monoglot standard, and historically this has helped bolster the status of nation-states as bounded and fully controlled entities (Heller 2007: 4–5; Woolard 1999; see also Bucholtz and Hall 2004a on the fallacy of bounded identity). Examining the processes that contribute to the constitution of contemporary nation-states concerned with issues of bilingualism against the practices of the individual actors who enact bilingualism helps us understand how the nation's ideological concerns are reflected and reified in the everyday practices of speakers (and policymakers). This perspective, informed by Bourdieu [1972](1978), contributes to a theorisation of the bilingual that is shaped in a complex way by macro-sociological and micro-interactionist factors.

Moyer and Rojo (2007) point out that in many contexts state-run institutions such as schools magnify the implications and consequences of bilingualism because of their homogenising role (see also Coronado Suzán 1999 for literature on indigenous Mexico). In the case of Madrid, Spain, policies and procedures designed to grapple with language heterogeneity reinforce societal norms privileging the dominance of Castilian Spanish.

This is accomplished through erasure of other languages by denying their speakers social capital and resources; in a sense, they are incomplete citizens. 'Rather than considering them an asset, [other] languages (Arabic, etc.) are considered an obstacle to integration. This is demonstrated by the fact that educational actions and resources are directed preferentially to ensuring the teaching of the monolingual norm' (Moyer and Rojo 2007: 145). In addition to implicit policies, ideological structures that moralise about the language's usefulness, classifying some languages and consequently their speakers as outmoded or not fully able to participate in civic activity, deny speakers total citizenship (143). In the case of Spain, full citizenship is achieved by fulfilling normative expectations, so that 'students who own a valued resource (namely, knowledge of the language of classroom instruction) because of their social and regional origin, are considered normal participants who are legitimate in the social space of the school' (148). Being a partial citizen not only has ideological implications but also material ones, where access to healthcare, government and the economy affect more than the ego. Linguistic competencies in themselves provide access to resources. As Bourdieu writes, language is tied intimately to power:

> The linguistic relation of power is never defined solely on the relation between the linguistic competences present. And the weight of different agents depends on their symbolic capital, i.e. on the recognition, institutionalized or not, that they receive from a group. (Bourdieu 1984: 72)

The material consequences of bilingualism in the global economy may have subtle manifestations, as in the case described by Heller (2005). It is within the shifting state of the new globalised economic conditions that workers in Montreal are 'stuck in the transition' as the world becomes increasingly interconnected through processes of globalisation. In examining the case of Canadian language workers (translators, mediators), Heller articulates the role of language produced as a commodity, pointing out that within the framework of the globalised economy 'we used to sell our physical labour; now we sell our intellectual and communicative labour, both as a skill and as a cultural artefact' (Heller 2005: 5). According to da Silva et al.:

> contrary to what one might expect given Canada's 'linguistic duality', inherited from its 'founding people' (the English and French), it is multilingualism and not just bilingualism that is valued and commodified. This value, however, is not institutionalized because Canada remains 'officially' bilingual and 'unofficially' multilingual – a linguistic reality the state refuses to recognize for fear of discrediting its nationalist roots. (da Silva et al. 2007: 188)

3. Social contexts of language choice and codeswitching

There have been two basic approaches to understanding the social contexts of language choice and codeswitching (the alternation/insertion of two or more varieties within the speech/sign stream). Auer and Di Luzio (1992) and Li Wei (1998) characterise them as the 'brought-along meaning' and the 'brought-about meaning' approaches. We will use these distinctions to organise some classical and more contemporary approaches to the problem.

3.1 'Brought-along meaning' and the variability of identity

'Brought-along meaning' approaches view identity construction as primarily indexical: Language X indexes an identity as an X-er, whereas the identity of a Y-er is achieved by speaking Y-ish (adapted from Fishman 1965). In these cases, social meaning is 'brought along' with the language being spoken in the interaction. Ferguson's classical conception of diglossia (1991) defines two complementary languages: the 'high' language, H, of education, literature, writing and formal oral communication, and the 'low' language, L, used for informal oral purposes. This framework assumes direct and indirect indexicality (Ochs 1993) for a given language choice. To illustrate what is meant by H and L languages with a concrete example: in Morocco, a complex history of language contact between Berber, Hebrew, Spanish, French and Arabic speakers (Chetrit 1994, 2000), alongside a history of Judaism, Islam and Spanish and French colonialism, has led to a situation where there are several dominant and subordinated languages, all with complex indexicalities. Widespread codeswitching occurs despite ideologies of language purity accompanying the spread of Islam in Africa and the Middle East (McIntosh 2002; Haeri 2003). Simply considering Arabic in Morocco, one can speak of (i) urban Moroccan Arabic varieties, (ii) rural Moroccan Arabic varieties, (iii) Hassaniya Arabic, a regional variety spoken in the south, (iv) Judaeo-Arabic of the remaining Moroccan Jewish population, (v) the standardised Modern Standard Arabic (*Fuṣḥā*) that is widely understood in the Middle East and taught in schools along with French (Boum 2008), and (vi) Classical, Qur'ānic Arabic. According to Ennaji, the direction of codeswitching is determined by social class:

> Upper class people code switch *from* French *to* urban Arabic, but rarely to Berber or rural Arabic because these are outside their geographic and social domains. Likewise, middle class people tend to switch *from* urban Arabic *to* French, rural Arabic, or Berber. As for the working class, they tend to codeswitch more frequently as they get into contact with the middle class, the upper class and the business area. (Ennaji 2005: 145)

Because of their prestige and involvement in the school system, French, urban Arabic and *Fuṣḥā* are H languages, while Berber, rural Arabic, Judaeo-Arabic, and Hassaniya are L languages. It's important to remember here that one person or situation's L might be another's H. But the indexicality doesn't stop there. Classical and Standard Arabic, with their associations with literacy, politics and religion, are symbolic of masculinity (Sadiqi 2003; Ennaji 2005; see also Haeri 1991 for similarities with Cairene Arabic). In contrast, Berber becomes indexically associated with female domains (Hoffman 2008), partly because there is almost no historical association between Berber and literacy (Berber-medium education has until recently been suppressed), which has highlighted Berber's L status as a minoritised, home-domain, rural language spoken by 'large populations of rural and illiterate women . . . However, this does not entail that Berber men do not speak their mother tongue; it only entails that they speak it less frequently than women' (Ennaji 2005: 146). In this situation, men have greater social and geographical mobility than women, and Berber has acquired gendered associations alongside these gendered usage patterns. The particular social history of this region has produced the alignment of an ethnicised, classed, spatialised gendered identity (Berber, rural, female) with a specific linguistic variety.

Another example of an analysis using an indexical approach is Gal's classic study in Oberwart, Austria (Gal 1978, 1979). The shift from Hungarian to German in Austria was phrased as the answer to the question 'why can't Hungarian-speaking peasant men get wives?' The answer is because in the communities where the ethnography was done, Hungarian was the L language, linked to family, tradition, the elders and farming. German, on the other hand, was the H language, envisioned as the one indexing youth, modernity and progress. German use was understood by prospective marriage partners as producing the possibility of a life away from the hardships of farming, but unlike the Moroccan case, it is the women in Austria who were aligned with the H over the L. This variability in the alignment of identities with linguistic choices highlights one of the most important aspects of current understandings of bilingual situations: the indexical link between a particular language and a particular identity cannot be taken for granted. Gendered identities may align with dominant or subordinated varieties, depending on socio-historical factors, rendering suspicious such universalising statements as 'women are conservative (or linguistically insecure, or prestige-seeking), and will always be on the forefront of language standardization' (see discussions in Labov 1991; Eckert 1990; Cheshire and Gardner-Chloros 1998; Mendoza-Denton 2004). Unique and particular historical conditions tie fluid and locally relevant identity categories to particular con-figurations of language use (Mendoza-Denton 2002; Bucholtz and Hall 2004a). Social categories such as women signers in Ireland (LeMaster 2006), Tuntun-speaking black-smiths in Burkina Faso (Bangali 2002), and estate-class workers in Guyana (Rickford 1986) create divisions that are deeply felt at the level of language ideology and linguistic usage.

Blom and Gumperz's (1972) idea of *situational shifting* involves code selection accord-ing to the situation and 'assumes a direct relationship between language and the social situation [involving] clear changes in the participants' definition of each others' rights and obligations' (Blom and Gumperz 1972: 424). In Oberwart, as documented by Gal, a situational language shift to using German in the doctor's office or with a government bureaucrat was a widely held community norm. *Metaphorical shifting*, on the other hand, is not related to a change in situation *per se*, but would be indexically linked to the varieties concerned. It would be switching into German *as though one were speaking to a doctor*, and indexing the social meanings that are available in those situations.

Consider the following example of metaphorical switching. This excerpt comes from an interview conducted in 1994 by Norma Mendoza-Denton with two teenage Latina girls ('Cristy' and 'Pilar') from the San Francisco Bay Area while conducting research on language, youth and gangs (see Mendoza-Denton 2008 for background on this research). Norma, Cristy and Pilar are all bilingual Spanish-English speakers and routine codeswitchers. Cristy and Pilar are 13 and 15 years old respectively, and they attend the same school and the same Catholic church. The interview situation doesn't change – the three participants remain the same throughout the interaction, with no other interlocu-tors present – but when Cristy talks about her mother, voicing her speech and opinions, she uses reported speech in Spanish. Voicing involves 'encounters in which individuals establish forms of footing and alignment with voices indexed by speech with social types of persons, real or imagined, whose voices they take them to be' (Agha 2005: 38). Voicing is not a neutral phenomenon, but is loaded with value and indexical significance as both the speaker and the hearer(s) orient themselves in positions relative to the voice.

Example 1: Topic/metaphorical switching:

1 Cristy: My parents said that if I got married to a guy and he treated me bad,
2   **me pegaba o algo,**
             if he hit me or something,
3   that I couldn't go back home . . .
4 Pilar: You know, I mean,
5   if you make a mistake, what –
6   you're going to have to pay for your mistake?
7   I don't believe that, you know,
8   if you got married,
9   and your husband is beating you,
10   I'm sorry, but leave him!
11   I mean, **nomás por no estar pecando** or whatever, how can you . . .
             just so you won't be in sin
12 Cristy: **O nomás porque,** you know,
             Or just because, you know,
             porque tus padres te enseñaron a seguir eso . . .
             your parents taught you to follow that . . .
13   doesn't mean **que te tienes que estar ahí.**
             that you have to stay.

In this example, Cristy switches into Spanish when voicing her Spanish-speaking parents' admonitions to remain in an abusive relationship for the sake of preserving the marriage. Pilar positions herself relative to that voicing by invoking, through an intonationally exaggerated codeswitch (underlined) a popular phrasing of religious ideology, 'por no estar pecando/so you won't be in sin', an ideology emanating from older members of the community and the church. Together, in mutual, sequential positioning, Pilar and Cristy use Spanish not only to invoke, but to effectively distance themselves from their elders and the Catholic church. It is important to note that not only persons experiencing or encountering the voice align with it in certain ways, but the individual invoking the voice also (dis)aligns with it. Hill points out that 'the voice system interacts with prosodic structure; prosodic strategies, particularly intonation, are important to development and a prosodic interruption, the break through the narrative voice of an "intonational shadow"' (Hill 1995: 109). It is this 'intonational shadow' that functions in a micro-context for understanding the discursive implications of voicing and its eventual enregisterment as stereotypically indexing social 'types' of persons. In Cristy and Pilar's case, the 'intonational shadow' itself indexes a social type – the older, traditional, church-going woman who would not leave her husband despite abuse. According to Silverstein (2003: 202),

> interactional happenings are social-actional 'events' of interpretable cultural meanings only to the degree they 'instantiate' – indexically invoke – macro-sociological partitions of social place, in terms of which cultural values can thus be said to be indexically 'articulated'. This connection of identity with value manifests itself in the micro-contextual order to be sure, where perspectival

interests are played out; but it really constitutes a universe of cultural imagination. (Silverstein 2003: 202)

A further point to be made about Pilar and Cristy's example is that the conversation starts in English, with temporary switches and insertions in Spanish. In terms of Myers-Scotton's rational-actor Markedness Model (Myers-Scotton 1983, 1988, 1993a, b), English is the unmarked, ongoing, *matrix language* and Spanish is the *embedded language*. That is to say, the conversation proceeds ordinarily in English until one of the speakers – a rational actor – switches to Spanish in order to highlight the 'rights and obligations set' associated with Spanish. There can only be one matrix language at a time, and a change to it signals a change in the dynamics of the conversation. In later formulations of the model, Myers-Scotton allowed that codeswitching itself might be the neutral (unmarked) frame, invoking two rights-and-obligations (RO) sets, but the core of her model assumes mutually exclusive possibilities, the binary choice between which gives rise to meaning. Such an approach offers a marked contrast to dialogic, Bakhtinian approaches such as that of Woolard (1999), which explores simultaneity rather than binarism. Just as we may understand Pilar and Cristy's Spanish and English alternations as rational-actor choices, one may also theorise them as hybridity, 'the mixing, within a single concrete utterance, of two or more different linguistic consciousnesses' (Bakhtin 1981: 429).

3.2 Brought-about meaning, performativity and the crafting of identity

Auer's second category of approaches to social motivation in language choice is that of 'brought-about meaning' (Auer and Di Luzio 1992; Li Wei 1998). Inspired by a turn toward Conversation Analysis, social meaning was understood as an interactive (brought-about) accomplishment rather than a calculation of rewards or a given from the prior community linkages (Auer 1984). This type of approach was prefigured at least as far back as Valdes (1981), where it was the *fact* of a codeswitch, not its direction, that was found to be symbolically significant, and which served to both aggravate and mitigate requests. In other words, the switch itself was an interactional resource, functioning by virtue of having built up a contrast with the previous turn, and thus only interpretable in the sequential context. And yet one can also observe a contrast and tension obtained by *not* switching. Francom (2009) documents an unusual case of lack of accommodation in a Mexican *panadería* (bread shop) in Tucson, Arizona. Despite pervasive bilingualism and the fact that both the bread shop worker and customer were bilingual Latinos, the service interaction unfolded with the worker speaking only Spanish and the customer only in English. They understood each other perfectly, but simply did not switch over the course of ten turns at talk. The lack of switching produced such an effect that a co-worker took a turn in English in the middle of the interaction to address/accommodate the customer. When interviewed later, the co-worker remarked that the use of English by Latinos in the shop could produce the effect of lack of solidarity (Francom 2009: 13–14). If the *expectation* is of Spanish usage by Latinos in the bread shop, then lack of switching and accommodation are themselves interactional events.

Viewing the interpretation of social meaning strictly as an interactional accomplishment is a significant departure from a conventionally associative 'brought-along meaning' approach. In the first place, it requires that analysts dispense with their interpretive categories of what they think the languages may index and commit themselves to locally relevant interpretations demonstrating how speakers orient to the identity categories (Auer and Di Luzio 1992; Li Wei 1998; Gafaranga 2007; see Mendoza-Denton 2002 for a similar strand of developments in ethnographic sociolinguistics). New identity categories may well be emergent in codeswitching, and not just with an additive function that codeswitching as a matrix language would have us posit: a new, brought-about meaning is not just the addition of two rights-and-obligations sets. Returning to the Moroccan situation above, we expand on an example given by Ennaji (2005): when two Moroccan doctors switch from Moroccan Standard Arabic to French in talking about medical terminology, and then produce a joking aside in rural Moroccan Arabic, they produce and perform for each other both cosmopolitan and local identities – privileged enough to switch to French when needed, and down-home enough to not speak French all the time; transnational and educated, yet local and authentic. Bentahila and Davies (2002) claim that pervasive French-Arabic switching in Morocco and Algeria produces a new indexicality among raï (north African popular music) performers and ties them simultaneously to global and local by the very order and nature of the switches in the songs. So strong is this local association that lyrics of the songs must be 'uncodeswitched' (delocalised) to be marketed in the Gulf States. And yet the brought-about approaches have structural consequences too. In a related article, Davies and Bentahila (2008) analyse the poetic and structural functions of these switches, where, as in natural conversation, switch patterns highlight semantic opposition or similarities, provide emphasis, and achieve various types of parallelism. According to Li Wei, codeswitching 'can help the speaker restart a conversation at the end of an interactive episode, or to change conversational direction; it also helps participants to keep track of the main 'drift' of the interaction by mapping out complex nested structural patterns in the conversation' (Li Wei 1998: 169).

An example of an interactional codeswitch comes from the work of Quintos-Pozos (2006) on Mexican Sign Language (MSL)/American Sign Language (ASL) bilingualism. In this excerpt, three bilingual ASL–MSL participants are talking about cooking. The reiterative switch from ASL to MSL is noted in bold type.

> Participant 1: point-middle finger TOMATO (.) **TOMATE** ADD-INGREDIENTS MIX gesture: 'thumbs-up'
>
> Gloss: '(. . . and then you take) tomatoes (.) **tomatoes** and you add them to the other ingredients and mix everything together. It's great.' (Quintos-Pozos 2006: 183)

Because of the delay between the first ASL item and the MSL switch, as well as eyegaze gestures towards the two other participants, this switch in its context was interpreted as emphasis or accommodation to the other interlocutors who were both frequent users of MSL. A reiterative switch with an interactional function of emphasis does not signal a distinctive, symbolic value, as would be the case under an approach such as the markedness model. And yet we (and others, notably Gafaranga 2007) cannot emphasise enough that the two approaches are not incompatible, and indeed *must* be applied simultaneously if we are to capture the complex performative effects of voicing and stylisation in codeswitching and language choice. How else can we capture the resolute ambiguity of a

Catalan comedian whose utterances build up bilingual tension by being *bivalent*, not identifiable as either Castilian Spanish or Catalan (Woolard 1999)? A notion of bilingualism-in-action brings to the forefront two primary interrelated ideas: the idea of choice as a category in itself, and choice within a larger system of tension.

4. Circulations: passing, mock languages, blends

When two or more languages are available as part of the community repertoire, they exist in the community choice space as potential resources from which to draw in both production and interpretation. Indexical approaches allow us to attempt identification of the various intonational/prosodic/lexical 'shadows' (Hill 2005), using evidence of patterning and recurrence in the community to tie them to potential social types (Butler 1993; Rampton 1995; Silverstein 2003; Bucholtz and Hall 2004a), while brought-about meaning approaches alert us to the sequential dynamics that produce hybridity and new indexicalities. With any of these microcontextual situations comes the mobilisation of larger situations of sociality, political situations, and ideologies of belonging and not belonging, which give an utterance, informed by the situated politics of bilingualism, a life of its own.

Orcutt-Gachiri (2008), in her study of Kenyan language shift, identifies a kind of language policing that fixates on correcting and ridiculing a practice called *shrubbing*, whereby the pronunciation of English words is influenced by interference from indigenous Kenyan languages. But shrubbing is not just English–Kenyan language interference, since bilingual foreigners by definition can't do shrubbing (but it is said that the Americans do *twenging*). As Orcutt-Gachiri explains:

> For Kenyans, ridicule of shrubbing seeks to constitute the hierarchy of languages and people in Kenya, creating an elite class of Kenyans who participate linguistically and economically in the upper echelons of Kenyan life. The people who benefit from making fun of shrubbing, therefore, are Kenyans who do not speak indigenous languages, because they are less likely to shrub than Kenyans who learned English as a second language in school and may have a heavier accent. In Kenya, only the urban wealthy, a very small group, grow up speaking English as a first language, so this reinforces existing class distinctions, as well. (Orcutt-Gachiri 2008: 7)

The contested in-betweenness of shrubbing appears at both the discursive and metadiscursive levels. It is not only in face-to-face contexts that Kenyans police shrubbing; there are newspaper columns inviting readers to send in shrubs that they have witnessed, thus sending into wider circulation ideologies based on essentialist stereotypes of 'types of persons' who shrub. Linking these iconic types to the linguistic detail of specific performative moments is one of the aims of our project (see especially Mendoza-Denton 2008, Chapter 7).

We close with the example of Osborne (2008), who instrumentally analysed Hill's (1995) 'intonational shadows', the prosodic traces of other voices present in a single speaker's production. While conducting fieldwork with middle-aged Mexican-American Angelenos, Osborne recorded Ana, who had moved from East Los Angeles to a more affluent suburb when she was about 12 years old. Caught in the tension between Anglo-assimilation and Mexican-national rhetoric, Ana carved a linguistic niche in perform-ance through the modulation of voices in monolingual English speech. Ana's contested positionality is indexed through her performances, in which she strategically 'voices' the social personae in metrical contrast to the ambient discourse to calibrate and signal her stance and identity in relation to them. Osborne's study shows that a series of measureable paralinguistic features such as pitch and utterance duration differ from normal speech in the performance of 'Mexicano' and 'White' voices. On average, 'Mexicano' performances exhibited slightly longer duration times than the 'normal' voice, and 'White' perform-ances exhibited greater pitch variation. These performances carry with them pragmatic force, are socially salient, and are the realisation of identity work, formulating a register as understood by Agha (2007). Registers carry with them a pragmatic force of signs (in this case a specific performance) derived from the socio-historical contexts in which they are embedded. The implications of the social and personal impacts of strategic perform-ances of Mexicano and White voices in natural conversation underscore the performative quality of a bilingual person's experience.

In socially salient realisations of identity work in multilingual interactions, speakers use pitch, duration, gestures, bivalency, ambiguity and presence and absence of switch-ing. Bi- and multilinguals take advantage of the contrasts created by switches in code, or by the mere expectation of switches. The next task of research is to trace more thor-oughly the connections between political economies, their indexical relationships with social types and personae, and the specific linguistic deployments of these personae in voicings.

11

Communities of Practice and Peripherality

Emma Moore

1. Introduction

Despite being acknowledged as a useful addition to our sociolinguistic toolbox (Gee 2005; Meyerhoff 2005), the Community of Practice (CofP) has been criticised for its incomplete treatment of peripherality (Davies 2005). This is curious, given that Eckert and McConnell-Ginet's (1992) paper introducing the CofP to sociolinguistics presented it as a way to access the locally constructed gender identities of speakers. In urging socio-linguists to look beyond hegemonic sex-class-based aggregations, Eckert and McConnell-Ginet effectively called for research on all kinds of speakers, including those who might previously have been classified as 'non-typical'. Hence, 'peripherality' has always been a central concern of the CofP approach.

In the light of this observation, this chapter will re-examine the notion of peripherality in sociolinguistics, focusing specifically upon its role in CofP research. Using a CofP case study it will be argued that, despite criticisms to the contrary, the CofP approach does more than simply *handle* peripherality, it also makes maximal use of the concept to provide insights into the understanding of sociolinguistic meaning.

2. The place of the CofP in sociolinguistics

How any model handles a concept is determined by the work the model is intended to do. Much of the work in sociolinguistics – what Trudgill (1978: 12) provocatively calls 'socio-linguistics proper' – is concerned with documenting social differences in the advance of sound change. Research of this kind examines large samples of data for changes in usage, the goal being to document the distribution of linguistic variation and analyse its linguistic constraints. As Eckert (2003: 392) has observed, this kind of work requires us to generalise about populations because, without simplification, it would not be possible to track patterns of language use across time in a statistically reliable way.

However, as Labov (2001: 325) acknowledges, once our interests go beyond the progress of language change – when we seek explanations for the transmission of observed changes (Labov's concern), or wish to explore the social meaning of language patterns in a community – we need to look beyond the generalisations of survey data. Analysing any group or population as an 'autonomous system' prevents us from explaining how the function of language changes within that community (Bucholtz 2003: 209). Change – whether in the meaning of a stable feature, or in the levels of a feature's usage – is normally generated by some kind of social shift. To explain such shifts, we must look at the sites where a community's social and linguistic style is being constructed, questioned and evaluated.

The CofP is a concept intended to capture the sites in which relations within and between different social groups are negotiated. It also offers a way to keep a check on the social categories employed by sociolinguists. CofP research starts with ethnography – that is, systematic study and observation of a given population and its practices. Unlike survey-style research, which tends to correlate predetermined social categories with linguistic features, CofP research makes no *a priori* assumptions about which social aggregations are noteworthy. Rather, it seeks evidence of significant sociolinguistic engagement in the course of sustained fieldwork. CofPs are the social groups uncovered in this type of ethnographic endeavour. They comprise clusters of individuals *mutually engaged* in a *joint enterprise* – an enterprise resulting in the construction of a *shared repertoire* of social and linguistic resources (cf. Wenger 1998: 73–83 for discussion).

3. Peripheral and marginal members in sociolinguistics

Because CofP research starts by considering the population as a whole, researchers are forced to see everyone in a given context, rather than seeking out particular kinds of speakers at the expense of others. In this sense, any single CofP must be viewed as part of a 'system of distinction' (Irvine 2001: 23–4); that is, alongside, and in relation to, other CofPs. This makes it difficult to see any individual speaker as peripheral in any absolute way. While speakers may be peripheral to a given CofP, it is unlikely that such a designation accurately depicts their whole identity.

In writing about Black English Vernacular (BEV), Labov (1972) discussed speakers peripheral to Black vernacular culture who were labelled 'Lames' by central members of that culture. Labov was concerned with ensuring the accurate depiction of BEV, and there were clear educational implications to his research, particularly in ensuring that BEV was perceived as a systematic form of English rather than a substandard form of the language. His observation that Lames '[f]ell short as informants' (Labov 1972: 288) referred to their inadequacies as informants of a clearly defined BEV.

However, it is important to remember that the perspective that sees Lames as inadequate informants is one where a particular vernacular culture is brought sharply into focus, while the social contexts surrounding it are left blurred. If one's goals were slightly different – say, if one wanted to explore the social meaning of BEV features or consider the adoption or transmission of BEV features beyond prototypical contexts – then Lames might well be valuable informants. After all, by engaging variably with BEV features, they are perfectly placed to inform us about how features are adapted and redeployed for sociolinguistic effect.

In this sense, as with much sociolinguistic work, Labov's study is skewed. As Bucholtz observes, how one interprets a context depends very much upon 'where one is standing' (Bucholtz 1999b: 220). While Lames may not have been central members of the BEV community studied by Labov, he provides evidence that they may well have been members of other communities. For instance, when talking about the 'Vacation Day Camp' members (which included 'intermediates' and 'Lames'), Labov observed that 'some boys reported membership in named groups that we were not familiar with' (Labov 1972b: 262). If the study had sought out practice-based aggregates, rather than focusing upon a predetermined 'central group and its culture' (Labov 1972b: 258–9), it is possible that other groups would have been identified and, indeed, that some Lames would have been found to be key members of these alternative groups. It is also possible that some of the members of the BEV culture studied by Labov would have been found to be peripheral members of these different CofPs.

Labov himself alludes to the fact that Lames are much more than inbetweeners falling between the BEV system and the white nonstandard English system. In stating that their relationship with Standard English (SE) 'does not necessarily imply that Lames are modelling their behaviour directly on the white nonstandard speakers, but rather that their interaction with SE patterns brings them from a point farther away from SE to roughly the same distance as members of the white vernacular culture' (Labov 1972b: 271), he implies that, while Lames and white nonstandard English speakers may seem similar in their use of certain features, these features do not necessarily 'mean' the same for the two different groups. If we're interested in the social meanings of features (that is, how language variables enter into the repertoires of different groups and what they mean), there is obvious merit in studying groups like the Lames *on their own terms* rather than simply viewing them as derivative of the community characterised by 'central' BEV speakers.

This discussion of Labov's work is not intended to critique the BEV study *per se* (we should only judge a study in relation to its goals, and the goals of this study were to investigate BEV), but to highlight problems surrounding the notion of peripherality when applied to the legitimacy of social aggregates. Without CofP research, sociolinguists are always in danger of viewing informants from a unitary perspective, instead of seeing them as members of a wider system of distinction, where meanings shift according to where one is standing. If we want to make claims about the social meaning of linguistic variation then we should (at least occasionally) check how the social world operates 'on the ground'. Otherwise, we are in constant danger of reproducing stereotypes and marginalising communities who may be interesting when viewed on their own terms (Hall 2003b). Many recent CofP studies provide coherent examples of how one's understanding of linguistic variation and its meaning can shift dramatically when the researcher assumes a less conventional viewpoint. Key works include Eckert's (1989; 2000) study of 'Jocks' and 'Burnouts' in Detroit, which interrogates class- and gender-based categorisations; Bucholtz's (1999) study of nerds, which demonstrates a CofP engaged in a positive process of identity construction quite different from that of their high school peers; Moore's (2003) study of high school students in Greater Manchester, which examines local instantiations of female identities; Rose's (2006) study of senior citizens in Wisconsin, which considers elderly identity styles; and Mendoza-Denton's (2008) study of gang girls in California, which re-evaluates ethnic categorisations (see also Mullany, this volume).

4. Peripheral members of CofPs

Seeing each social aggregate as operating within a system of distinction, rather than as an isolated social unit, is key to understanding peripherality and its role in variation. We are all members of multiple CofPs – core members of some and peripheral members of others – and it is the complexity of these social memberships that facilitates variation and change. While acknowledging that CofP research provides a better view of this social reality, Davies (2005) critiques the CofP approach for inadequately characterising types of CofP membership. In particular, Davies argues that the distinction between core and peripheral members leads to an analytic problem with respect to brokering of change. She observes that brokering must occur on the boundaries of communities, but that those on a CofP's periphery are unlikely to have the status to ratify group-wide innovations (Davies 2005: 574). 'Peripherality' here, then, refers to the status of one or more individuals relative to a community, rather than the status of a whole group of individuals (such as the 'Lames') relative to a hegemonic aggregate.

If one views CofPs as bounded in the kind of hierarchy assumed by Davies (a top-down allocation of power, with a clearly delineated and controlling centre), it is indeed hard to imagine how change filters in from the periphery. But the reality is that CofPs and CofP memberships are fluid, and hierarchy is not inevitably a corollary of community. Nor is it necessarily linked straightforwardly to the allocation of power or control. CofPs may have a number of different structures which may interact in complicated or unexpected ways with other CofPs. Davies' critique stems partly from concerns about the distinction between the concepts 'peripheral' and 'marginal', which she argues are not clearly differentiated in the CofP literature (2005: 565). While Wenger (1998: 164–72) clearly states that the two differ in whether or not an individual's overall involvement in a CofP is dominated by participation (the peripheral member) or non-participation (the marginal member), it is true that it is difficult to deduce from this (mainly theoretical) account how types of participation are to be evaluated. Nonetheless, subsequent accounts of actual CofP studies and theoretical elucidations (Eckert and McConnell-Ginet 2007; Eckert and Wenger 2005; Moore 2006) have clarified the distinction by stressing the difference between activity and practice. Peripheral participants are not core members of a CofP, but they nonetheless engage in and contribute to some of the *practices* of the CofP and, in doing so, can potentially affect the overall CofP style. Marginal participants are involved in the same *activity* as CofP members, but not in an 'engaged' way. An example is a school netball team whose members socialise beyond sporting events, thereby constructing a repertoire of practices including ways to tell jokes, to dress, or to discuss attraction to the opposite sex. The team's wing attack is also a member of the school choir and, consequently, her need to attend choir events means that she does not make as many social events as some of the other girls. She is still a key team member who, when she can, thoroughly engages in the team's social scene. On the other hand, a substitute player, who only plays when someone is sick or injured, attends practice just once a fortnight and socialises with her teammates only at formal team events. Accordingly, the wing attack is a peripheral participant of the netball CofP, whereas the substitute is a marginal participant. This is because the ability to affect the practices of a CofP (in particular, the ability to affect the way in which activity is undertaken or the meaning of resources utilised) is determined by the *quality* of one's engagement, not just by one's presence in the same locale or at the same activity as CofP members. As Eckert and Wenger observe, '[l]egitimacy in any community of practice involves not just having access to knowledge necessary for "getting it right", but being at the table at which "what is right" is continually negotiated' (Eckert and Wenger 2005: 583). The wing attack is peripheral because she makes it to the negotiation table relatively frequently and engages, whereas the substitute is marginal because she remains something of a disengaged bystander.

Viewed this way, we can easily see how different CofP members contribute to socio-linguistic processes in ways which correlate with what other researchers have discovered about the role individuals play in sociolinguistic change (see further Stuart-Smith and Timmins, this volume). For instance, Labov (2001: 356) observes that leaders of linguistic change tend to be central members of a given social aggregation, who simultaneously have a wide range of social connections. Such people may be core members of CofP X, peripheral members of CofP Y, and thus engaged in both communities, able to broker links between them, and to facilitate change. However, what the CofP approach adds to previous models used to describe innovation and change is that it provides a better overview of these intersecting memberships. As Labov (2001: 364) observes in his study of a Philadelphia network, traditional sociolinguistic studies tend to limit themselves to one network at a time (or in the case of Milroy (1980), to separate networks that are not interrelated), and thus do not provide the larger view necessary to observe the dynamics which facilitate a change. Because CofP studies search for social aggregations and explain the sociolinguistic practice of these aggregations by virtue of their relationships with other CofPs, they are able to observe the multiple or fluid memberships any one individual may have within an extended community. In this sense, they are more likely to capture the interactional moments which reveal the roles speakers play in facilitating change in linguistic practice.

5. Case study: Tag question usage at Midlan High

The following case study provides an example of a change in practice alongside an analysis of the status of the CofP members who facilitated it. The data are taken from my study of a high school in the north-west of England, Midlan High, the fieldwork for which took place between June 2000 and February 2002. During this time, I engaged in participant observation with a group of approximately forty girls who were in Year 8 (aged 12–13) when I began the research and in Year 10 (aged 14–15) when I completed the fieldwork. CofP membership was analysed on the basis of the following practices: who an individual associated with, what activities she engaged in, her orientation to her peers and her surroundings, her personal style and appearance, and her own and other's assessments of their group memberships. My ethnographic observations were corroborated by questionnaires administered to elicit information on social practices. The linguistic data derive from recordings in which the girls would discuss recent events, activities and relationships.

The groups I will focus on here are the *Populars* and the *Townies*, two CofPs with complex and interrelated trajectories. If we simplify how kids engage in school on a pro-school to anti-school continuum (as is typical of school ethnographies; see for instance Willis 1977), the Populars could be described as anti-school in their attitude and in elements of their conduct (for example, swearing, being insolent to staff, and flouting rules by, for instance, wearing inappropriate clothing). They hung around in large, reasonably close-knit groups, both at and outside school. They dressed in sporty clothes carrying designer labels, engaged in various degrees of unsanctioned behaviour such as smoking and drinking, and were some of the first girls in their year to have boyfriends. Towards

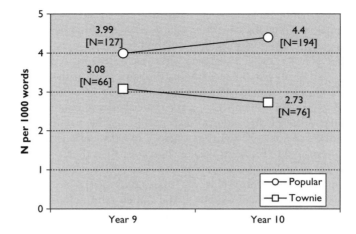

Figure 11.1 Average tag question use over time among Popular and Townie CofPs at Midlan High.

the end of Year 9, a small subsection of Populars began to participate in more extreme social activities – not just smoking and drinking, but also drug-taking; not just having boyfriends, but engaging in sexual activity with older boys from outside school; not just flouting school clothing rules, but wearing lots of gold jewellery and make-up. Over time, such rebellious activities resulted in these girls being reified as a separate CofP: the Townies.

Elsewhere (Moore 2004) I have documented how the shifts in social practice between the Popular and Townie CofPs were accompanied by shifts in linguistic practice. In this chapter, I focus on one linguistic practice: the styling of tag questions. Figure 11.1 shows tag question usage over the two years of data collection. An independent samples t-test showed no significant difference in the tag frequencies for the Populars and the Townies in Year 9. While the difference was still below significance for the Year 10 data, it was closer to significance than the Year 9 data, and the magnitude of the differences in the means in Year 9 was small (mean difference = 0.12, 95% CI: −3.15 to 3.39; η^2 = 0.06), whereas the magnitude of the differences in the means in Year 10 was moderate-to-large (mean difference = 2.30, 95% CI:−1.89 to 6.48; η^2 = 0.13), indicating CofP-correlated differences in tagging behaviour over time.

These CofP differences are not very strongly significant, but as Coupland (2007: 49–53) has pointed out, simply counting a variant's frequency does not tell us everything about how that variant functions in a community's discourse. In further work (Moore and Podesva, in preparation), significant qualitative differences in how these two groups used tag questions according to topic, grammar and phonetic design have been uncovered. Whereas the Populars' prototypical tag occurred in talk about their own group or other groups, predominantly with *me* or *she* as subject, and with moderately nonstandard grammar and phonetic design (*h*-dropping, *t*-glottalisation and some *t*-deletion), the Townies' prototypical tag occurred much less frequently in talk about groups other than their own, had much higher rates of *he* as subject and a more consistently nonstandard design (higher rates of nonstandard grammar, almost categorical *h*-dropping and high rates of *t*-deletion). These (statistically significant) patterns suggest that differences in tag use were not limited to the frequency of tag questions, but also included the ways in which tags were styled in the wider linguistic repertoires of each CofP.

To explain these differences in tagging style, we need to look to the relationships between CofPs members at the time the Popular group separated out into the Townies and the residual Popular members. The connection between the two CofPs meant that certain girls found themselves to be core members of one CofP and peripheral to the other. This situation was complicated further when friendships were compromised by shifting loyalties. Two girls caught up in this scenario were Kim and Amanda.

On starting high school, these girls were good friends squarely situated at the core of the Popular CofP. Their friendship persisted, although by Year 10 it was much less close than it had been in Year 7 (the first year of high school). Kim reported that the shift in friendship correlated with changes in Amanda's social practice. Kim's lack of participation in Amanda's new endeavours (which included hanging around with older boys and taking illicit substances) was governed by the three factors Eckert and Wenger (1993) identify as necessary to ensure active participation in the learning and development of a social style: motivation, access and opportunity.

Like other core Popular girls, Kim attended dance classes which restricted her *opportunities* to interact with the Townie girls. This, combined with parental constraints placed on *access* to the group (resulting from her mother's negative evaluation of the Townie CofP) and Kim's reluctance to transgress parental authority, resulted in Kim's lack of *motivation* to engage in the Townies' social enterprise. While the Townie girls initially encouraged Kim to participate in their new rebellious activities, sustained engagement in these activities would have come at a cost for Kim, who valued conflicting forms of engagement *and* the relationship with her mother. Consequently, Kim voluntarily hung out with the Townies less and less, and the Townies' invitations to her reduced too. The result was Kim's marginal participation in the Townie CofP, maintained only by her history with Amanda (and the fact that these two girls continued to spend time together in school) and her occasional attendance at an activity shared by the Townie girls. Metaphorically speaking, Kim assumed the status of the marginal netball team substitute of the earlier example.

A similar, but less extreme, process occurred with regard to Amanda's Popular membership. While some Popular girls found her engagement in the Townie CofP difficult to reconcile with Popular practice, her relationship with Kim and the fact that she remained on good terms with many Popular girls permitted Amanda to maintain peripheral Popular membership nonetheless. She would frequently and actively participate in Popular activities where they did not conflict with Townie engagement. For instance, if other Townie girls weren't around at lunchtime, Amanda would take the opportunity to hang out with the Popular girls. Her willingness to access Popular activities and her motivation to maintain friendships with Popular girls (many of whom reciprocally named Amanda as a friend) allowed her to assume a status in the Popular CofP akin to that of the wing attack in the earlier netball CofP example.

The complexity of Kim's and Amanda's relationships was reflected in their linguistic practice. Figure 11.2 gives Kim's and Amanda's tag question usage relative to the Popular and Townie CofPs. This figure shows that, while both Kim's and Amanda's usage patterns with that of their core CofPs, both girls have unusually high rates of use relative

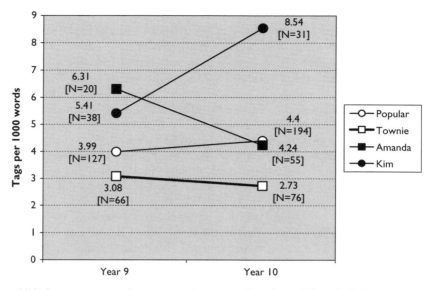

Figure 11.2 Average tag question use over time among Popular and Townie CofPs, and scores for two speakers who participate in both CofPs.

to their peers. To understand these patterns, it is necessary to think about the way that tag questions function. Moore and Podesva (in preparation) revealed that most Midlan High tags were turn-final and received much more agreement than disagreement. Such a discourse shape supports Hudson's (1975) view of tag questions as *conducive* forms (given that it's easier to agree with an established turn-final proposition than it is to construct dissent against it).[1]

It is unsurprising, then, that Kim and Amanda have high individual tagging rates given the utility of tag questions. In an extended analysis of tag questions in the wider Midlan High community, Moore and Podesva (in preparation) discovered that Popular tag questions are distinct from those of other CofPs by virtue of their regulatory function. Popular tags most commonly occur in gossip scenarios, where the tags apportion value to Populars, conducing agreement around girls' positions relative to each other and to other school CofPs. Alternatively, Townie tags occur most frequently in past action narratives, where they primarily serve to conduce agreement around intra-group dynamics and status in countercultural communities outside the school. We argue that the Popular style of tag questions follows in large part from the shifting relations between the Popular and Townie CofPs. Whereas, historically, Populars were the rebellious CofP in the school, the extremes of Townie practice robbed them of this reification, leaving the Popular girls to negotiate a new kind of 'cool' identity. Tag questions, used in a regulatory and evaluative manner, may well have assisted the Populars' embodiment of this kind of persona. Positioned on the border of these two communities, where differences are at their most salient, Kim and Amanda may have had much to gain from engaging in this style of tag question usage.

However, Figure 11.2 shows that while Amanda's tagging has declined in Year 10, Kim's use has risen. Although Kim had the highest tag use of any girl in the Midlan

High sample by Year 10, other Popular girls were producing similar tagging rates by Year 10. Concurrent with this rise in tag usage, another social change was occurring: increasingly, girls started to talk to me about the 'Smoothies'. Popular girls saw Smoothies as 'nicer people' (58A:414), who 'dress nicer' (58A:428), and are 'better looking than scallies [a synonym for Townies]' (58A:429). To the Townies, Smoothies were 'poofs' [effeminate, soft] (40B:1020), who 'look after themselves' (40B:1026) and 'dress up' (40B:1031).

The individuals identified as Smoothies had all been previously identified as Populars. In extracts (1) and (2) the Townie girls discuss Smoothies:

(1)
Ellie   Kim tries fit-, like .. fitting in and stuff and .. But she'll always – it's like with different groups .. She dunt (= doesn't) really listen to what everyone – she's – she dunt care about what we care – like what, um – people who she hangs about with ..

EM   Yeah.

Ellie   she's more bothered about the Smoothie crew.

(59A: 222–6)

(2)
Meg   Yeah, Annabel come over in registration this morning. She went, 'I hate Cindy, Paula and Tina.' I think she's got summat (= something) on her – a chip on her shoulder because it was her birthday last week and Cindy bought summat for Paula yesterday for her birthday, but

[not for her.]

Amanda   [She bought her a -] some flowers.   [You don't buy a girl [[flowers at 14 – well, 15.]]]

EM   [(Laughs)]

Meg   [[I know .. And -]]] And, er, Annabel said, 'They're like the little, erm, Smoothie crew of our Year and all, them lot.'

(55: 896–909)

The dark grey lines in Figure 11.3 show the tag question usage for three of the girls identified as Smoothies by the Townie girls. These are compared with the Townie girls (dotted black lines) and the remaining Popular girls (light grey lines). A one-way between-group ANOVA assessing the impact of Smoothie categorisation on tag question frequency in Year 10 revealed a significant difference between Townies, Smoothies and the remaining Populars: $F (2, 9) = 11.63$, $p = 0.03$. Post-hoc comparisons using the Tukey HSD test indicated that the mean score for the Smoothies ($M = 8.13$, $SD = 0.76$) was significantly different from both the remaining Populars' ($M = 2.94$, $SD = 1.95$) and the Townies' ($M = 2.38$, $SD = 1.62$) mean scores.

It is unsurprising that we get the emergence of a new social group at this time, given the need to re-evaluate Popular identity in the light of Townie emergence. Smoothie status (the 'niceness' of which is juxtaposed with the 'roughness' of the Townies) provides a clearly oppositional identity style. 'Smoothness' may well be embedded in the

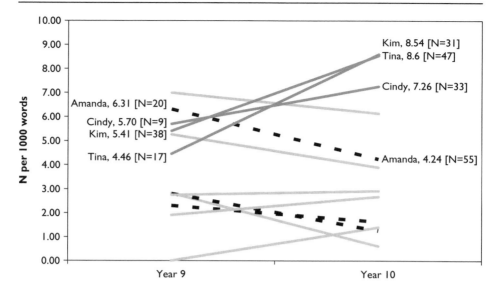

Figure 11.3 Tag question usage over time for members of one emerging CofP (Smoothie = dark grey), and two established CofPs (Townie = dotted black; and remaining Popular = light grey).

linguistic style of the Smoothies too. If we accept that tags are conducive forms, Figure 11.3 suggests that the Smoothies are the conducive group *par excellence*.

These data suggest that tag question usage was clearly affected by shifting social relations at Midlan High. Furthermore, it is apparent that individuals with memberships on the borders of the original Popular and the new Townie communities (Kim and Amanda) offered lines of communication which facilitated this sociolinguistic shift. As Rose and Sharma (2002: 15) observe, speakers who bridge the space between communities have the potential to broker the emergence of new stylistic endeavours. It is likely that Kim's marginal participation in the Townie CofP made her more aware of identity issues than her Popular peers, whose distance from the new CofP made it impinge less dramatically upon their sense of self (cf. Wenger's [1998: 164] discussion of the importance of contact with other ways of being). Nonetheless, Kim's core status as a Popular, alongside Amanda's peripheral engagement with the Popular CofP, may have caused the concern with status to infiltrate Popular discourse more widely (extract 2 offers evidence to substantiate this), causing both the Populars' tag question style and the frequency of tagging we see among the emerging Smoothies in Figure 11.3.

This discussion suggests that the linguistic shift we see at Midlan High relies upon Kim's marginal Townie participation and Amanda's peripheral Popular participation. To understand and explain the variation in tag question use it is not sufficient to see the Populars and Townies as two separate social groups with clearly delineated borders. We must view them as parts of a wider social system within which all community borders are fuzzy, prone to overlap and vulnerable to change. Because CofP research starts by observing a population, it forces researchers to see everyone in a given context, making us better able to appreciate the nature and quality of group overlap. This ability to see and monitor the periphery provides a clearer perception of the social processes which facilitate change.

6. Conclusion

Using a CofP approach to analyse Midlan High not only allows us to see subtle differences in language use, exposing the function, fluidity and flexibility of linguistic resources such as tag questions, it also allows us to see how subtle differences in language use are brokered by those who inhabit peripheral space.

As discussed in the introduction, the CofP approach has been criticised for an incomplete treatment of peripherality. However, as this chapter has demonstrated, it is not that CofP research inadequately deals with peripherality, it is rather that the picture it provides is not as orderly as that provided by other societal models used in sociolinguistics. It's hardly surprising that some find messy categorisations less satisfying than those which neatly demarcate groups, characteristics or linguistic behaviours. However, social life *is* messy and speakers' memberships shift depending upon the specific contexts in which they are engaged. Calls for the CofP to model peripherality more rigidly are based upon an idealised view of community. Clearly, a certain amount of idealisation can be helpful – without it we cannot even begin unravelling the social life of language. However, sociolinguistics already has several structural models providing an overview of language variation and change. The utility of CofP research lies in its capacity to unpack this structural representation. As Eckert and Wenger (2005: 588) observe, imposing a predefined structure on CofP research robs it of its utility as an exploratory framework. CofP research is a means to evaluate the validity of social structures, not a means to reproduce them.

Peripherality is something that happens to all of us depending upon where we are and in what we happen to be engaged. It is an inevitable part of social interaction for all speakers. If we are to understand this phenomenon we need to see our informants as three-dimensional members of multiple communities – simultaneously peripheral, core and marginal, depending upon the perspective from which they are viewed. While it is often desirable to work with a snapshot of a community, we must remember that taking a snapshot requires us to stand in a particular place and focus upon a unitary view. There are some questions in sociolinguistics which cannot be answered in this manner. Ethnography, qualitative insights, CofPs and peripheral speakers have a place in sociolinguistics. As this chapter has demonstrated, when it comes to explaining local sociolinguistic processes or exploring the social meaning of linguistic resources, peripheral speakers (and, indeed, peripheral techniques) must become central.

Note

1. I deliberately avoid the term 'facilitative'. The assignment of this function to tag questions in the language and gender literature (for instance Holmes 1995) implies altruism and positive politeness on the speaker's part, but speakers can be conducive for reasons other than these.

12

Crossing Into Class: Language, Ethnicities and Class Sensibility in England

Ben Rampton

1. Introduction

In recent work on young people's speech in a multi-ethnic, multi-lingual inner-London secondary school in the late 1990s (Rampton 2006), I found a pervasive sensitivity to the traditional semiotics of British social class. Their parents might be foreign-born, at home they might speak another language, and the hot political topics might be sexuality, ethnicity and race. But the English of these youngsters showed the same vernacular-standard style-shifting that UK variationists have been reporting for more than thirty years, and about once or twice an hour, their vivid stylisations of 'posh' and Cockney conjured an imagery of inhibited snobs and oversexed low-lifes that stretches back several centuries. The school population might be mixed, mobile and located in a late-modern global city, but the voices they stylised most frequently implied contrasts – high/low, mind/body, reason/emotion – with deep roots in British class structure.

This sociolinguistic testimony to the power of class provides the background for a line into the relationship between migration, ethnicity, class and peer-group interaction I shall pursue in this chapter. From the 1980s to the early 1990s I studied language crossing, a set of practices that involved white and Asian adolescents using Caribbean Creole, black and white kids using Panjabi, and all three doing Indian English. In my analyses at the time, I mostly concentrated on crossing as a reworking of ethnic identities and affiliations, but having witnessed class meanings signalled so conspicuously by adolescents in another multi-ethnic school ten years later, it is worth looking back to see if there are signs of this insistent class consciousness in the crossing data. Amid all those instances of black and white kids talking Panjabi, and Asians and Anglos using Creole, can we see class 'determination' in minority ethnic language crossing, taking 'determination' to mean 'setting limits and exerting pressure' rather than 'predicting' or 'totally controlling' (Williams 1977)? My conclusion will be 'yes'. Through language crossing, my informants had developed a set of conventionalised interactional procedures that enabled them to reconcile and rework their ethnic differences within broadly shared experience of a working-class position in British society.

Of course, as well as requiring substantiation in what follows, this conclusion depends on what exactly is meant by 'class', and so this needs to be clarified at the outset. My understanding of class draws on the classic work of Raymond Williams and Edward Thompson, and connects with the more recent 'return' to class analysis led by scholars like Skeggs (1997, 2004), Savage (2007) and Reay (1998) (see Rampton 2006: Ch. 6). In a country with a long history of stratification like Britain's, 'class' embraces a huge range of economic, material and cultural processes, covering social differences in main source of income, family background, place of residence, cultural tastes and political affiliations (cf. Bradley 1996: 46). So, first, if our interest is in language and class, we need to consider not just economic position but also class consciousness, class formation, the 'meaning' of social class – a single indicator like parental occupation isn't sufficient. Second, we need an account like Thompson's, focusing on how class identities are produced in cultural activity:

> [p]olitics is often about exactly this – how will class happen, where will the line be drawn? And the drawing of [the line] is not . . . a matter of the . . . volition of 'it' (the class), but the outcome of political and cultural skills. To reduce class to an identity is to forget exactly where *agency* lies, not in class but in [people].
> (Thompson 1978: 295–6)

Here, 'class' is a sensed social difference that people and groups produce in interaction, and there is struggle and negotiation around exactly who's up, who's down, who's in, who's out, and where the lines are drawn. These differences aren't created from nothing, of course, and material and cultural inequalities are often highly intractable. Even so, human agency plays an important part in class processes, so when analysts see people in better/worse or higher/lower positions, it is vital to look for the cultural practices that accomplish this.

Taking all this on board in a reinterpretation of the data on language crossing, there are five empirical dimensions I shall consider:

1. the historical, demographic and economic features of the site I studied, drawing on demography and survey research;
2. my informants' 'folk' representation of the social distribution of language crossing;
3. the representation of Creole, Panjabi and Indian English in British institutions (dominant, countercultural and partially independent);
4. the evaluations and cultural imagery evoked in adolescent language crossing;
5. the acts and activities that supported crossing practices.[1]

I shall begin by briefly summarising the first of these.

2. An historical and demographic background of wealth and status stratification

My research in the 1980s followed about sixty white, black and Asian adolescents (roughly two-thirds male, one-third female) in playgrounds and youth clubs in one neighbourhood of Stoneford (not its real name), a market town in the south Midlands of England with population of approximately 100,000 (Rampton 2005: 37–44). The town had a long history of labour in-migration, first from elsewhere in the UK, and then in successive waves after

1945, from eastern Europe, then Italy, the Caribbean, India and Pakistan, and finally, after 1972, from Bangladesh and East Africa. There were post-war difficulties recruiting indigenous workers to low-paid manual jobs in the local heavy industries, and migrants provided 'replacement labour'. Racial discrimination in housing, employment and local government was well-documented in the town, and in 1976, 'Ashmead' – the neighbourhood where my research was sited – accounted for two-thirds of the town's 'high stress' housing. During the 1960s, the threat of major road redevelopment led to substantial white Anglo migration out of Ashmead, and the depreciation of house values provided opportunities for the town's ethnic minorities to make their first house purchases. They moved into Ashmead from run-down lodging houses in the town centre, where incoming groups traditionally found their first accommodation. By 1971, almost 40 per cent of Ashmead residents had been born overseas, and in 1984, 75 per cent of children at the local state middle school were black and Asian minority ethnic, with 20 per cent white Anglo. In the town at large, there were strongly negative perceptions of Ashmead – local kids knew that the neighbourhood had a(n unwarranted) reputation for crime, and they joked about visitors needing a passport. Italian families, who nearly all sent their children to a local Catholic school, were now starting to move out of the smarter parts of Ashmead into other areas, and in smaller numbers, so did some Indian families. So overall there was significant ethnic stratification in housing, employment and education, with European migrants better positioned and Bangladeshis, the newest arrivals, generally doing worst.

How far and in what ways were these patterns of ethnicity and socio-economic inequality reflected in my informants' ideas about language crossing?

3. Socio-economic stratification and local accounts of crossing's inter-ethnic distribution

Language crossing was widely noted and very often accepted in the neighbourhood, and informants had much to say about its inter-ethnic dynamics and significance in interview. Beyond that, crossing itself figured as something of a local emblem, signifying the difference between Ashmead's mixed adolescent community and the wider Stoneford population. This was evident in their ideas about the kinds of people who *wouldn't* do language crossing. These non-crossing others, it emerged, weren't just placed at a distance on some kind of horizontal mosaic of group differences – rather, they were vertically placed at either end of a bipolar hierarchy of wealth and status, with my informants locating their own normality in the intervening middle ground. On the one hand, up above, there was the picture of 'posh wimpies', who lived in wealthier districts outside Ashmead, had attended different middle schools, occupied higher curriculum sets, dressed badly, stuck to themselves, and were capable of only the most laughably feeble gang-style activities:

> 'gorra' – white man . . . always call the people who didn't go to [our school] gorras, yet I'm white myself . . . cos we reckon they're a bit you know upper class (most of them) . . . the gorra gang. (Peter, in Rampton 2005: 62)

At the other end, down below, were Bangladeshis, residing in the poorest parts of town, linguistically incompetent, lodged in low sets or the English language unit, unsociable, sexually aberrant and unfashionably dressed.

These local stereotypes weren't particularly accurate – for example, some of the Bangladeshis engaged in exactly the same kinds of crossing as Ashmead 'normals' – and the feelings provoked by these images weren't straightforward either. Nevertheless, two broader points are clear. First, although my informants and I all initially attended to language crossing as an intricate reworking of ethnic boundaries, they also described this boundary work as the activity of young people occupying a particular position within a wider hierarchy of wealth and status. Second, these folk representations of hierarchy matched quite well with 'objective' social science descriptions of the migration and socio-economic stratification in Stoneford.

Further links between ethnicity and class emerge if we turn to young people's interethnic use and evaluation of the *specific* varieties typically involved in language crossing.

4. Social class in the multi-ethnic speech economy

4.1 Creole as a working-class British vernacular

In line with perceptions reported by researchers in other areas (Hewitt 1986; Harris 2006), Creole was widely seen as cool, tough and good to use. It was associated with assertiveness, verbal resourcefulness, competence in heterosexual relations, and opposition to authority. It was scarcely represented at all in the official school curriculum, and it occupied a dominant position in popular music and performance youth culture. Particularly among Asian informants, Creole was also often reported as part of their general local linguistic inheritance. Using Creole forms was something 'we been doing . . . for a long time' and unlike the situation reported by Hewitt, it didn't depend on particularly close involvement with black friends. Instead, it was something boys acquired from black female classmates, from other Asian friends, older brothers and the media, and indeed Asian boys' use of certain kinds of Creole language was also quite widely accepted by local black kids.

These associations start to place Creole close to local nonstandard English, and when Asian and Anglo parents corrected nonstandard forms in their children's speech, the home defence of 'proper English' was sometimes said to focus on the intrusion of Creole tense forms, question tags and swear words (Rampton 2005: 135–6). When Ian, a 15-year-old white boy, explained how his American cousins were disappointed by his English, again it was Creole he invoked:

> They think we speak really upper class English in England . . . they say that Englishmen has got such beautiful voices, and they express themselves so well . . . ((*shifting into an approximation to Creole:*)) 'eh what you talkin' abaat, wha' you chattin' about, you raas klaat', and they don't like it! They thought I was going to be posher.

In fact, this broad functional equivalence of Creole and traditional nonstandard British speech was celebrated much more widely during the 1980s in a record called 'Cockney Translation' produced by the black British MC ['Master of Ceremonies'] Smiley Culture (see Gilroy 1987; Hebdige 1987; Jones 1988).

I elaborate on this in the next section, but it is first worth bringing in another variety in the local adolescent inter-ethnic repertoire – Asian English.

4.2 Class consciousness in polarised evaluations of Creole and Asian English

When discussing Asians speaking non-proficient English as a second language, young-sters with Panjabi backgrounds generally reported mixed feelings. If relatives didn't speak English very well, they tended to be sympathetic, supportive and/or sometimes angrily defensive, but in the peer-group, accented L2 English was typically associated with Bangladeshis. As already indicated, Bangladeshis were a stigmatised group, asso-ciated with a remedial curriculum and regarded as youth-culturally incompetent. The phrases kids used to typify Asian English – 'jolly good', 'very very good', 'excuse me please', 'I no understanding English' – projected a ridiculously deferential, polite and uncomprehending persona, and this matched a wider set of racist representations in TV comedy, reproducing nineteenth-century British imperial stereotypes of the 'pliable, plastic . . . receptive . . . [and] servile' *babu* (Yule and Burnell (1886) 1985: 44).

So broadly speaking, Creole and Asian English signalled a rather different set of orientations – whereas one represented verbal quick-wittedness and an excess of demean-our over deference, the other stood for bumbling dysfluency and a surfeit of deference. Kids were also much more attracted to the former than the latter, and this was evident in crossing practices themselves in at least two ways.

First, Creole crossing was much more frequent. In my corpus of field observations, interviews and more than 100 hours of radio-mic recordings, I identified more than 250 episodes where there was a clear Creole influence in the speech of whites and Asians, compared with about 120 exchanges involving Stylised Asian English [SAE], and 68 episodes with black and white uses of Panjabi.

Second, to use Bakhtin's terms (1984: 193), the 'double-voicing' involved in crossing into Creole was usually 'uni-directional'. It lent emphasis to evaluations that synchro-nised with the positions and identities that the crossers maintained in their ordinary speech, and consistent with this, Creole was often hard to disentangle from their ordinary vernacular (Rampton 2005). In contrast, stylisations of Asian English tended to be 'vari-directional', projecting a clear boundary between the speaker and the voice being used. Consistent with this, SAE was often used as what Goffman calls a 'say-for' (1986: 535) – a voice not being claimed as part of the speaker's own identity but one that was relevant to the identity of the person being addressed or targeted critically. The contrast could be seen, for example, in the way that each related to male–female relations. There wasn't much vulgarity in Asian English utterances, and when relations with the opposite sex were in question, SAE implied hesitation or ineptitude. In contrast, a lot of sexual terms figured in Creole crossing, and it tended to conjure the prospects of successful sexual engagement (*'gewaan* Bruce *gewaan*! Bruce's got two girls!'; 'Micky's goin' out with Laura' – *'aah* go*'aan* Laura') (Rampton 2005: 216).

In previous work, I proposed that in the context of migration, these two varieties formed an important symbolic contrast. Creole symbolised an excitement and an excel-lence in youth culture that many adolescents aspired to, and it was even referred to as 'future language', while Asian English represented a stage of historical transition that most adolescents felt they were leaving behind, consistently symbolising distance from the main currents of adolescent life. So in the contrast between these two varieties in the local inter-ethnic repertoire, there was a sense of the trajectory associated with migration, with Asian youngsters inhabiting local Englishes much more fully than their parents and other newcomers, and also developing an alignment with black British culture.

Actually, though, there is more to be said about the symbolism of the Creole/Asian English contrast, and this brings social class more fully into the picture. As noted earlier, I found in my study of social class in London that when kids adopted exaggerated 'posh' and Cockney they reproduced quite a clear set of high/low, mind/body and reason/ emotion contrasts, with posh invoking the first term in each of these pairs and Cockney indexing the second. This replays a binary framework that can be described as 'hege-monic' in scope and influence, stretching across a range of fields in class societies, and Bourdieu, for example, talks of 'dualistic taxonomies which structure the social world according to the categories of high and low . . . refined and coarse . . . distinguished and vulgar . . . well-mannered and sloppy' (Bourdieu 1991: 93). This dualistic idiom, says Cohen, was generated 'from within certain strategic discourses in British class society, [and] from the very outset [it was] applied across a range of sites of domination, both to the indigenous lower orders and ethnic minority settlers as well as to colonial populations overseas' (Cohen 1988: 63). Section 4.1 pointed to my informants' sense of Creole's prox-imity to nonstandard working-class varieties of English, and Creole can be located on the low side of this traditional class semiotic. As many have noted, popular culture on the low side of the binary has been continually replenished by the traditions and practices associ-ated with Creole and black music, and this vitality was very appealing to Ashmead kids, imaging a powerful set of positive values counter-posed to respectability and education.

But equally important, Asian English can be seen as oriented to the high side of this class binary. English is a prestige variety in the Indian sub-continent, and informants with relatives there saw their own varieties as rather inferior:

> In India right, the people that I've seen that talk English . . . talk strict English, you know. Here, this is more of a slangish way . . . the English that people talk round here you know, they're not really talkin' proper English . . . if you go India right . . . they say it clear, in the proper words.
>
> My cousin come [over from India] . . . he's got a degree and everything, he speaks good English, but he didn't used to speak in English with us though, cos they sort of speak perfect English, innit. We sort of speak a bit slang, sort of innit – like we would say 'innit' and all that. He was scared we might laugh at this perfect sort of English . . . the good solid English that they teach 'em.

Transposed to the UK, however, adolescents in Ashmead depicted this orientation to the high, proper and polite as absurd, its aspirations hopelessly marred by foreignness (Blommaert 2005: Ch. 4).

Combining these observations, we can say that Ashmead kids simultaneously posi-tioned themselves within *two* major social processes when their accounts and crossing practices articulated the contrast between Creole and Asian English. They not only situ-ated themselves at an endpoint in the migratory transition from outside into Britain, but then also once inside, they aligned themselves with values more associated with the lower than the higher classes.

Something similar to these images of ethnicity and class was circulating much more widely. In the UK at the time, Asians were often stereotyped as compliant newcomers, ineptly oriented to bourgeois success, while African-Caribbeans were portrayed as troublemakers, ensconced in the working class and adept only in sports and entertainment (Cohen 1972; Rampton 1983; Hewitt 1986; Gilroy and Lawrence 1988; Jones 1988). At this point, however, it is essential to introduce a major qualification which will still allow us to speak of 'class determination' in Williams' sense, but which prevents any inference that we are witnessing here the unconstrained reproduction of dominant ideologies.

4.3 Ethnolinguistic creativity within non-elite class practices

It is vital not to neglect the significance of local friendship as a space for the negotiation of different and/or independent sociolinguistic evaluations, and this was most obvious in Panjabi's inter-ethnic currency. Although it was starting to make itself felt both in education and the media, Panjabi had nothing like the wider public profile of Creole and Indian English, and its relative freedom from association with powerful external agencies correlated with much less complex and conflicted accounts of Panjabi crossing in interview. White and black uses of Panjabi were generally seen as just ordinary or funny – 'if they're our friends, we teach them it'.

It is also important to recognise that the practices, situations and social relations which fostered inter-ethnic Panjabi displayed the non- and indeed anti-elite alignments characteristic of a particular class niche. Yes, you might extend your linguistic repertoire in language crossing, but you didn't use dictionaries and grammar books. Panjabi was beginning to be taught at school but nobody white or black attended, and hardly any of my informants said they'd be interested, even in principle. In reality, the lexicon of cross-ethnic peer-group Panjabi consisted of nouns referring to body parts, bodily functions, animals, ethnic groups and kin, as well as verbs to do with sex, violence and ingestion. And in the two situations where most crossers got interested in Panjabi, the ethos was broadly anti-establishment. First, Panjabi was quite useful for excluding teachers and other white adults, and second, it had entered playground language and lore, figuring in incrimination traps, jocular abuse and chasing games. Obviously, with all three varieties – Panjabi, Creole and Asian English – there were interactional intricacies linked to their distinctive symbolic loadings. But broadly speaking, in the cross-ethnic spread of these three varieties, opposition to authority and the activities and codes of conduct characteristic of playground recreation figured centrally, and here minority varieties had a *use-value* that was partly independent of the (positive and negative) exchange-values they accreted in their uptake in external institutions (Skeggs 2004).

4.4 Restraint in the reception of dominant ideological valuations of other-ethnic speech varieties

In fact, there was also another way that, in their local peer relations, kids refrained from embracing the commodification of ethnic languages entailed in dominant ideologies. Youngsters avoided crossing with particular ethnic others in quite consistent ways, and it seemed to be a sensitivity to potential contamination by public representations that led white and black kids to avoid using Asian English with Panjabi peers, and deterred Anglos from using Creole with African Caribbeans. In view of the parodic and remedial images of Asian English projected in the media and education, you didn't address Asian English to Panjabi friends because they'd think it was mockery, and you generally avoided Creole with black peers because you didn't want to be seen to be expropriating a widely valued popular resource. Indeed with Panjabi, it was precisely at the point where *bhangra* started attracting wider interest and prestige that whites and blacks stepped back. At the time of my fieldwork, *bhangra* music was becoming popular and getting noticed, and it was in this context that Asian kids talked negatively about white interest, that a lot of male cross-ers lost interest, and that white girls only participated with the personal authorisation afforded by (actual or potential) romance with Asian boys. Certainly, kids were alert and potentially susceptible to the sharply different degrees of distinction that ethnic varieties accrued through their representation within powerful cultural agencies like the media and education. But the multi-ethnic peer-group could often monitor the non-inheritors of a particular variety and make sure they didn't succumb too far to temptation. In this way, the peer-group can be seen as a social space that actively mediated dominant ideologies of class and race, and that didn't absorb or reproduce them without qualification.

5. Summary

I showed earlier that adolescent ideas about the distribution of language crossing located it in a space between higher and lower groups in a wealth and status hierarchy that loosely reflected the demographics of class and race in Stoneford at that time. I then looked inside the particular niche these kids felt they occupied. Here too, their valuations of individual ethnic varieties bore the stamp of a hegemonic stratifying binary with a long pedigree in the English class system, although with Creole and Asian, this binary had acquired ethnic inflections and showed sensitivity to migration as well. These valuations were massively amplified in major institutions, and through these, all three varieties acquired a significance and value beyond the control of the local peer-group. Through the popular performance arts, Creole had global countercultural prestige; Panjabi was starting to look in the same direction; and through its positioning and representation at school and in the media, Asian English was stigmatised. At the same time, however, beyond these high-profile sites of cultural production, the stratifying class binary was not completely over-powering, and aspects of the perception of inter-ethnic Panjabi pointed to local peer culture as a source of partly independent valuation. Indeed, it seemed to be a variety's valuation within national and international institutions that made ethnolinguistic owner-ship rights a sensitive issue, but here too kids displayed habits of avoidance that at least partially interrupted the stratification dictated from outside.

That said, two major caveats apply. First, the focus has been on a specific set of collec-tive perceptions and conventional practices and we cannot extrapolate from these to the attitudes, aspirations and trajectories of individuals. Yes, as a group, my informants were structurally positioned as working class, and their crossings were embedded in popular rather than elite practices and pastimes. But they also engaged in many other practices which haven't been considered, and in fact my data collection was explicitly biased towards recreation. It is very possible – indeed highly likely – that when, say, they settled down to work in lessons, many kids could put aside the stances and alignments displayed in crossing – the attraction to Creole's street credibility, the pleasures of Panjabi abuse, the mockery of Asian English deference. All these might well be sectioned off as just 'having a laugh', messing around with friends.

Second, my analysis has concentrated on *cross*- and *inter*-ethnic practices. Inside minority ethnic networks, the linguistic forms, social functions and symbolic meanings of Creole, Panjabi and Asian English were no doubt often much more complex and extensive, elaborated in a range of inter-generational and diasporic relations that remained largely opaque to other-ethnic peers.

The overall effect of these two caveats is to underline that this is a sociolinguistic analysis of ethnicity and class targeted on a very specific set of inter-ethnic practices, although that now facilitates the formulation of my main claim:

> in language crossing, Ashmead youngsters developed a set of conventionalised interactional procedures that enabled them to reconcile and rework their ethnic differences within broadly shared experience of a working-class position in British society. Race and ethnicity were big and controversial issues in media, education and public discourse generally, but in language crossing, kids had found and affirmed enough common ground in the problems, pleasures and expectations of working-class adolescent life to navigate or renegotiate the significance, risks and opportunities of ethnic otherness. Through language crossing, adolescents refigured ethnicities within the dynamics of British social class (partly changing this in the process, of course).

6. Conclusion

Although I conducted the research on language crossing in the 1980s, there are areas and networks in England today where crossing remains a significant part of the 'complex experiential chemistry of "race", class and gender' (Gilroy 1987: 19). Admittedly, in the London secondary school I studied in the 1990s (Central High), class was more explicitly thematised in exaggerated stylisations of posh and Cockney, and these were much more frequent than minority language crossing. But minority language crossing certainly wasn't unknown, and when it occurred it displayed some of the same class imprint evidenced in Ashmead.

When white and Asian youngsters used Creole from time to time at Central High, it generally carried the same connotations of popular cultural vitality (see also Harris 2006), and a very broad functional equivalence to Cockney could be seen when they were both used for the same types of speech act (Rampton 2006: 298–300). Asian (or Indian) English didn't have as significant a local presence as in Ashmead, but there were a lot of migrant and refugee newcomers in the school, and their peers engaged in broadly comparable processes of sociolinguistic status deflation when they stylised English foreigner talk to project a very non-cool, school-enthusiastic persona oriented to the high and polite. When, for example, the teacher mentioned standard English, Rafiq altered his voice quality and used an exaggerated rise-fall to declare 'oh that's very (good)', and it was a mock foreign voice that Simon used for: 'I finished, I go onto my new matrix'. Comparably, Joanne used foreigner talk in 'oh no no no, theese a bad thing to do', as did Hanif when addressing Zainab – a very keen student who came to the school as a refugee speaking very little English – with 'Zainab, why you laughing, you very happy today'.

Abroad, the global prestige of English might have encouraged you to see your acquisition of the language as an upward move, but among classmates here and now, that was strictly comical (Blommaert 2005). So although Central High differed from Ashmead in many ethnic and migratory specifics, in their local recontextualisations of varieties with transnational origins and currency, there was a class sensibility similar to Ashmead's. Creole, along with hip-hop Black Englishes, was valorised, and school-oriented second language learners were devalued.

In my 2006 study, I used the data on stylised posh and Cockney to challenge claims about the 'demise of class'. Sociologists may have suggested that young people 'are especially responsive to . . . the cultural changes discerned by post-modernists' and are thus most likely to be affected by 'the decline of class awareness' (Bradley 1996: 77; Surridge 2007). But here, in the heart of a global city where these changes might be felt most sharply, youngsters were putting on posh and Cockney voices on average once every forty-five minutes. The effect of the present chapter is to intensify this challenge, drawing in the data on language crossing. Yes, as at Central High, there was little explicit discussion about social class in Ashmead, and race, ethnicity, gender and sexuality were all more controversial. But class-related processes were still formative, 'setting limits and exerting pressure', even on a set of practices that (a) thematised a social dimension often considered to have displaced class in significance (i.e. ethnicity/race), and that then also (b) scrambled it up, destabilising dominant modernist assumptions about identity inheritance. Posh, Cockney, Creole, Panjabi and Asian English certainly did differ in their individual associations and affordances. But they were all still an integral part of the daily round of ordinary urban adolescent life, and in putting them together like this, the dynamics of British social class can be recognised in all of these expressive practices. In minority language crossing, social class may not have been foregrounded as it was in the stylisation of posh and Cockney. But it was still a major element in the position from which kids spoke when they put on other-ethnic voices, and it was their inter-ethnically shared experience of positioning within the British working class that gave crossing much of its shape, intelligibility, currency and resonance.

Note

1. There are, however, at least two flaws in what follows: (i) I rely on re-reading what I myself wrote about language crossing, rather than revisiting the empirical materials themselves. And one effect of this has been (ii) to tilt the account towards classed *masculinities*. Quite a full picture of gender differentiation in the *inter-ethnic* dynamics of language crossing is presented in Rampton (1995), but for the interpretation of class dynamics, the book allows a clearer view of boys' sensibilities than girls'.

13

Ethnicity, Religion and Practices: Adolescents in the East End of London

Sue Fox

1. Introduction

According to *Census 2001* data, there are 283,063 Bangladeshis living in the United Kingdom. Of these, 65,553 live in Tower Hamlets (see Figure 13.1), a borough in the East End of London, where the group constitutes over one third of the total borough population and represents the largest group of Bangladeshis living in an area outside of Bangladesh. The formation of this well-established Muslim community began in the early part of the twentieth century, but it was the 1970s and 1980s that saw the largest influx of immigrants to the area, and since then their number has continued to grow. The Bangladeshis are predominantly a young population, with the second and third London-born generations constituting around one half of the community. This raises the issue of competing identities, particularly among younger community members: they are members of a religious community, but also speakers of a regional variety who thereby ally themselves with the rest of the local, non-Muslim population. This chapter sets out to explore how Bangladeshi adolescents construe themselves in terms of ethnicity and religion, as well as within the broader geographical region in which they live.

2. The geographical variety

The geographical variety referred to here is one associated with the 'traditional' East End of London (Fox 2007), the heartland of the variety commonly known as Cockney. This is the area confined to the present day Tower Hamlets, the borough directly to the east of the City of London.

Among other features, the variety is characterised by the diphthong-shifted quality of the vowels of the FLEECE, FACE, PRICE and CHOICE lexical sets (Wells 1982), as shown below:

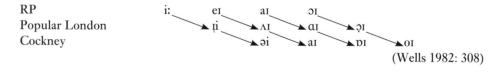

(Wells 1982: 308)

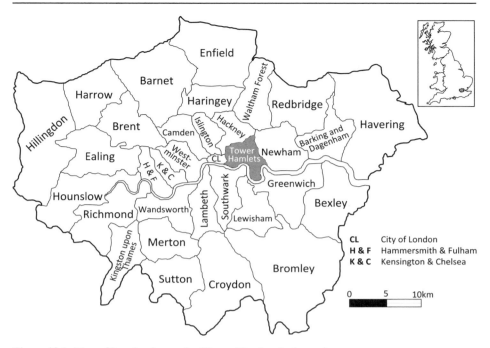

Figure 13.1 Map of London boroughs. Tower Hamlets is shown in grey.

In effect, the overall pattern for the fronting-closing diphthongs in London is generally perceived to be a counter-clockwise shift from Received Pronunciation (RP) forms. The discussion below will focus on the PRICE and FACE vowels.

Until recently there were very few sociolinguistic studies of London, but those that there were confirmed that the variants found for these vowels aligned to the above pattern. For example, Sivertsen (1960), Beaken (1971), Tollfree (1999) and Peys (2001) all found examples in their data of the PRICE vowel having fully back onsets and examples of the FACE vowel having more open onsets than RP. Data from the *Survey of English Dialects* (Orton and Tilling 1969/71) provide further examples. However, recent studies (Fox 2007; Kerswill et al. 2008) have documented ongoing vowel change among London adolescents.

Fox (2007) is a study of language use among 39 Bangladeshi, white and mixed-race adolescents in Tower Hamlets. The adolescents were aged between 12 and 17 years old and were either born in London or had settled there by the age of three. All had similar socio-economic backgrounds, loosely termed as working class. The study adopted an ethnographic approach to data collection, with fieldwork taking place over a period of nine months at a youth club held during the evening in the local area. The young people who attended the youth club were drawn from the local and neighbouring areas, but it was not attended by Bangladeshi girls. This is explained by the fact that adolescent Muslims are not encouraged to interact socially in mixed-sex settings. The data presented here come from ethnographic interviews conducted during that period. Auditory analysis reveals the use of variants for both the PRICE and FACE vowels which have not previously been documented for this variety. These are shown in Figures 13.2 and 13.3.

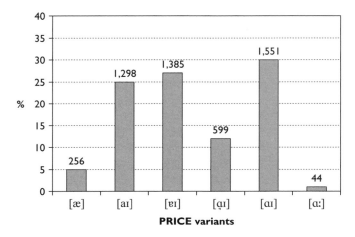

Figure 13.2 Distribution of variants of the PRICE vowel among East London adolescents (Ns above each column; total N = 5,133).

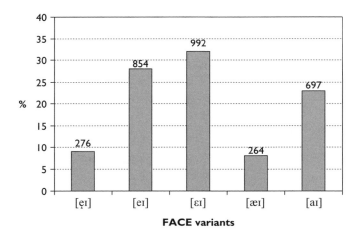

Figure 13.3 Distribution of variants of the FACE vowel among East London adolescents (Ns above each column; total N = 3,083).

For PRICE the previously unreported variants are [æ], [aɪ] and [ɐɪ]. The first variant is, as the transcription suggests, a monophthong similar to the TRAP vowel in RP. The second variant has an onset close in quality to that of RP PRICE, but is a narrower diph-thong with an offglide closer to [ɛ]. The third of these variants has a first element which is slightly more raised than that of [aɪ]. The overall use of these variants accounts for 57 per cent (N = 5,133) of the realisations of this vowel.

The undocumented variants of FACE are [e̞ɪ], [eɪ] and [ɛɪ]. The first of these has a closer onset than does the RP equivalent and is at times almost monophthongal, overlapping phonetically with the RP KIT vowel. The variant [eɪ] has a slightly more open onset than the preceding variant but is again a much narrower diphthong than the typical RP realisation of FACE. [ɛɪ] has previously been identified as a London variant (Wells 1982; Hudson and Holloway 1977), though these sources talk of a variant closer to [ʌɪ], with a more open, central onset. The [ɛɪ] variant described here has a front onset slightly lower than [e] but higher than [æ]. It is also a narrow diphthong, one of the most striking features of these newer variants, the overall use of which accounts for 69 per cent (N = 3,083) of realisations.

Closer analysis revealed that the newer variants were mainly used by the Bangladeshi boys. Of the total number of PRICE tokens, they used one of the three variants [æ], [aɪ] and [ɐɪ] 93 per cent of the time, with only 7 per cent use of the remaining traditional Cockney variants. For FACE their use of one of the three variants [e̞ɪ], [eɪ] and [ɛɪ] was almost categorical, at 99 per cent. Overall, then, they had not adopted the variants associated with the regional variety. Given that the adolescents in this study were born in the area or had settled there at a very young age, we must seek an explanation for why they do not use the regional variety. Although it may be tempting to assume that they are performing their linguistic difference as a way of signalling their membership of an ethnic or religious community, it is important also to consider the social and historic context in which this community emerged in Tower Hamlets.

3. The social and historic context

The period after the Second World War was a time of social upheaval for the East End of London. During the war, planners had worked on the postwar reconstruction of Britain. The *County of London Plan* (Abercrombie and Forshaw 1943) contained detailed plans for the East End. The aim was to provide four acres (1.62 hectares) of open space per 1,000 citizens in order to considerably reduce housing density, although open spaces were generally scarce. The main solution to providing this space was to decentralise the population to estates outside London and to New Town developments built specifically for this purpose. Between 1951 and 1981 the population of Tower Hamlets fell from 230,000 to 140,000, and the East End was left with an ageing population because most people of working age had left (Forman 1989: 14).

At the same time as working-class East End families were systematically being removed from their homes and relocated to out-of-London housing, the London Docks were also closing down. London, then the largest port in the world, started to close its docks in 1967, and by 1981 operations had completely ceased, causing thousands of job losses and a rapid decline of the docklands area. Those dependent on the docks for employment were forced to move further east to the only remaining open docks at Tilbury, Essex, or face unemployment in an area with little else to offer. The area occupied by the docks, approximately 8.5 square miles, lay redundant while planners tried to deal with the issue of what was to be done with the land. The result of their decisions has been one of the most rapid social, economic and physical transformations of any area in Britain. Tower Hamlets is now home to the Canary Wharf Development, described as a 'city within the City' (Bird 1993: 120), and a far cry from its working-class roots (see Fox 2007 for further discussion).

It was in this context, then, during the same period as decentralisation and the decline then regeneration of the dock area were taking place, that the traditional East End started to receive an influx of Bangladeshi immigrants. Although there had been a small Bangladeshi presence in the area before this time – around 150 to 200 people from Bangladesh (then East

Bengal) lived in London in 1939 – it was in the 1970s and 1980s that their number increased substantially. Of course, the East End of London had always been a 'point of arrival' (Bermant 1975) for immigrant groups (such as the Huguenots, the Irish and the Jews) but I would argue that the Bangladeshi settlement has deeper roots than previous groups.

After the Second World War people from former British colonies were encouraged to come to Britain to mitigate the labour shortage, and at the end of the 1950s around two to three thousand mainly male migrant workers from Bangladesh arrived in London. By 1962 the community was around 5,000 strong (Adams 1987: 64). Most came from the north-eastern region of Sylhet. The 'myth of return' (Anwar 1979) persisted among the Sylhet Bangladeshis for a long time. They considered themselves migrant workers with the intention of returning to Bangladesh to buy land and build better houses, thereby raising their social status in Bangladesh; they 'did not intend to enter into British society and become acculturated' (Anwar 1979: 21). Until 1970, only 2–3 per cent of the Sylhet men had their families in the UK. However, changes in immigration law and civil unrest between what was then West Pakistan (now Pakistan) and East Pakistan (now Bangladesh) led to families joining the men in London.

The arrival of these families caused acute housing problems. The women and children could not fit into the accommodation the men had been living in, so the majority of families moved into council tenements intended for demolition. Pockets of the area very quickly became Bangladeshi strongholds. By the 1981 Census, Tower Hamlets contained the largest group of Bangladeshis in the UK, and the largest group of Bangladeshis outside Bangladesh. By 1984, 46 per cent of all live births in Tower Hamlets were to Bangladeshi mothers (Forman 1989: 36).

Although immigration is no longer at the same levels as it was in the 1970s and 1980s the Bangladeshi population has continued to grow, for two reasons. First, mixed marriages are very uncommon; second, arranged marriages are still practised, so it is reasonably common for the bride or groom of a newly married couple to be brought to the UK from Bangladesh after the marriage. This means that there is always a steady stream of 'first generation' immigrants. But even with zero immigration the population would still increase, as birth rates among Bangladeshi women are higher than those in the general UK population. In 1993, they were five times higher (Choudhury 1993: 227). Today, the Bangladeshis represent over 33 per cent of the total population in Tower Hamlets, and 57 per cent of all school-aged children in the borough are of Bangladeshi origin.

These historical facts may shed light on why the London-born British Bangladeshis have not adopted the local vernacular. Most accounts would seem to predict that immigrant offspring acquire local indigenous native-like phonology. Chambers (2002) refers to this phenomenon as the 'Ethan experience', after the son of eastern European immigrants in Toronto. Ethan was born and raised in Toronto and, like many immigrant offspring, acquired the accent of his native-born classmates rather than the foreign-accented features of his parents. Chambers attributes this to an innate filter operating below the level of consciousness, which filters out foreign-accented features (Chambers 2002: 122). The assumption underlying this principle is that the offspring of immigrants are surrounded by native-born classmates and that they acquire the indigenous accent of their peers. The Bangladeshi children were, however, not surrounded by peers with indigenous accents but instead found themselves among peers from backgrounds similar to their own.

The men who arrived in the early period of immigration did not acquire English to any great extent. They came as migrant workers with the intention of resettling in Bangladesh with their wives and families. As a consequence of this intention to return home, the community in London became very insular, and the men did not want, or need, to integrate with the local community. The community quickly became self-sufficient, with curry shops and other businesses selling provisions opening up and catering almost exclusively to the Bangladeshi community. As they were run by the Bangladeshi men themselves, it was not necessary to learn English in these early years for them to function in the local community. When the women and families later joined the men, the women maintained their cultural tradition of not going out of the family home. They were rarely seen in public; it was the men who would be seen doing the shopping and going to work. As the Bangladeshi community grew, there was no need for the women to learn English because their home language, Sylheti, could easily be maintained within the community. There are still many first-generation immigrants, particularly women, who do not speak English, and Sylheti continues to be the language of the home, at least among the older members of the families.

For the majority of the families the first real exposure to English was through the children when they went to school, but the local schools quickly filled with predominantly Bangladeshi children who were then only exposed to the input from their teachers and not to the local vernacular spoken by indigenous families. Even today, many second-generation Bangladeshis do not formally learn English until they go to school. For many in the first generation of immigrants, then, learning English was not a priority, and for those who did learn, it was generally learned either from members of their own community who had been settled in the area for longer, or within a more formal educational institution. Few would have had sufficient interaction outside of the Bangladeshi group to have learned it from the indigenous community. As with most first-generation immigrants, the English they speak is a heavily-accented second-language variety, which for most second- and third-generation immigrants, I would argue, has become the target, rather than the indigenous Cockney. The Bangladeshis have additionally often been regarded as an insular group that interacts relatively little with other groups in the area. In such situations, where interaction is primarily among in-group members rather than with native speakers of the local target language variety, the original contact-induced changes or innovations tend to get preserved (Winford 2003: 245). What appears to have emerged from the Tower Hamlets context is a new variety of English, probably influenced by Sylheti at least in terms of its phonology, which is now spoken by the majority of people in the area.

It is tempting to say, then, that this variety is an ethnolect and that its speakers are marked as being of Bangladeshi origin. However, this is not quite the case. Firstly, speakers from other ethnic backgrounds are also using these variants (Fox 2007; Kerswill et al. 2008), and secondly, there is variation among the Bangladeshis themselves.

4. Bangladeshi variation and the role of religion as social practice

Fox (2007) shows that the variants discussed have, to some extent, also been adopted by the white and mixed-race adolescents in the Tower Hamlets study, and that friendship networks and social practices seem to play a key role in the diffusion of innovative features. The same factors are shown to be significant in the spread of innovations in other

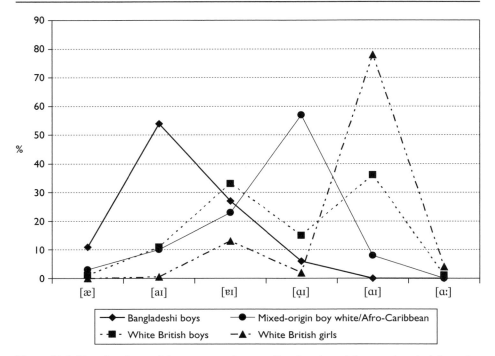

Figure 13.4 Use of variants of the PRICE vowel among East London adolescents by ethnicity and gender.

parts of London (Kerswill et al. 2008). Figures 13.4 and 13.5 show the distributions (in Tower Hamlets) of the PRICE and FACE vowels according to ethnicity and gender. For both vowels, it can be seen that the white and mixed-race boys use variants closer to those used by the Bangladeshi boys than to those used by the white girls in the study who, in the main, continue to use variants associated with the area's traditional dialect. These usage patterns are apparently directly related to friendship networks and the amount of social interaction between the different groups.

As this was an ethnographic study spanning a period of nine months of participant observation alongside data collection from ethnographic interviews, the friendship networks could be established with reasonable accuracy. The participants were not just asked about their friends and the degree of engagement with other members of the youth club; these networks were also observed at close hand and confirmed by the researcher. Figure 13.6 is a visual representation of the friendship groups formed by the participants in the study.

Each small numbered circle in the sociogram in Figure 13.6 represents an individual speaker, and the larger circles are the friendship groups. If a speaker claimed, and was observed, to have a 'best friend' a line joins those individual speakers (girls only), and the lines joining the different groups depict the fact that there was some interaction between members of one group and members of the adjoining group. As previously mentioned, the girls did not use the innovative variants, which would seem to be directly linked to the

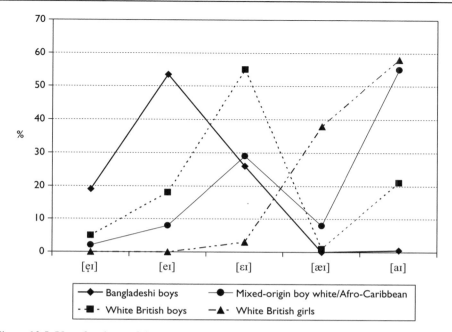

Figure 13.5 Use of variants of the FACE vowel among East London adolescents by ethnicity and gender.

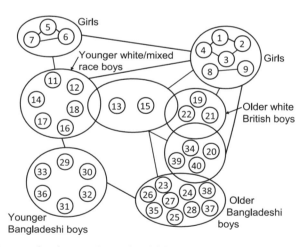

Figure 13.6 Sociogram showing youth members' friendship groups.

fact that they had little, if any, interaction with the Bangladeshi boys. Furthermore, these girls stated that they did not have any Bangladeshi friends away from the youth club, and all attended schools without large numbers of Bangladeshi students.

Among the boys, however, particularly the older ones (aged 15–17), there was much more social interaction between the different ethnic groups. The younger Bangladeshi boys (aged 12–14) were perhaps the closest-knit and most self-contained group. Although they happily interacted with the other boys during club activities such as pool and table tennis, they maintained social and spatial distance at other times. All but one of these speakers went either to one of two predominantly Bangladeshi local authority schools – a single-sex boys' school and another co-educational school – or to an all-boys Islamic school with a comparably high proportion of Bangladeshi students.

Two boys at the local authority schools also attended a local Sunday Islamic school. It seems, therefore, that these boys spent most of their time (their school hours and a large proportion of the weekend) among their Bangladeshi peers, and that there were also strong cultural and religious ties. They had a much more committed attitude to school life than many of the other youth club members, which may explain some of their more conservative practices within the youth club. This suggests, therefore, that we should take wider social network factors into consideration in our analysis of language variation. It was this group who used the extremely fronted PRICE variants and the raised variants of FACE most frequently.

Among the older boys there was much more social interaction between the Bangladeshis and the white Anglo group. The organised youth club activities were still popular, but many social practices among these groups were conducted in the street outside the club premises, and hanging about in the street seemed to involve more social mixing between the different groups. Many (but not all) of these boys were or had been involved in drug-related practices, driving stolen mopeds around the streets, under-age car-driving and involvement in youth gangs.

Most Bangladeshi boys in the older group had attended schools with very high proportions of Bangladeshi students. However, of the nine speakers in the main older Bangladeshi cluster, six had left school and were unemployed. They often expressed negative attitudes towards their school experiences. Because these boys were not in school or employment, they spent time together during the day, mixing with some of the older white boys who were also out of school or unemployed. The other two Bangladeshi boys in the study, speakers 39 and 40, had both left school at 15, having been expelled. Both were unemployed and had been involved in crime. These two speakers were also key intermediaries between the older white boys and the older Bangladeshi boys, seemingly being accepted equally by both groups and playing leadership roles in each.

Given the amount of social mixing between the two older groups and the similarities of their social practices, it is perhaps not surprising that there are also linguistic similarities. The analysis of the PRICE variable showed that the older white boys do not use the broadest form associated with Cockney English ([ɑːɪ]) at all, and although some boys in this group use the [ɑɪ] variant, they do so less often than do the younger white Anglo and mixed-race boys. The commonest variant is [ɐɪ], which has a more centralised, raised onset and may sometimes be near-monophthongal, though some older white boys are also using the fronter variants [aɪ] and [æ]. Some of the older Bangladeshi boys also use these fronted variants (the most commonly-used variants among the younger Bangladeshi boys) but, as with the older white Anglo boys, the most frequent variant appears to be [ɐɪ]. Some Bangladeshis also use (albeit to a much lesser degree) the more traditional London variants [ɑɪ] and [ɑɪ].

The FACE variable shows a similar pattern. Some of the older white boys do not use the traditional London variants [æɪ] and [aɪ] at all, and have instead adopted the raised variants [ɛɪ] or [eɪ], the pronunciations also most frequently used by the Bangladeshi boys. Unlike the PRICE variable, there is very little use of the traditional London variants among the Bangladeshi boys, although there is still some variation within the Bangladeshi group.

It seems, then, that the social practices of these adolescents correlate with the phonetic variants they use. However, as suggested above it may not suffice to consider language use in this single setting to account for the variation. We are seeing only one facet of their lives and, as Eckert and Wenger note, 'identity is constructed in the negotiation of participation in multiple communities of practice' (2005: 585). The results cannot be explained by considering the friendship groups within the youth club alone, and are better informed when account is taken of such factors as the schools attended by the adolescents and their orientation to, for example, cultural, religious and kinship ties. In the above discussion of language use among the younger group of Bangladeshi boys, it was suggested that their attendance at and involvement in their predominantly Bangladeshi schools might be greater influences on their language use than is their involvement with other adolescents in the youth club. Another factor may be their alignment to or disengagement with religion: some of the Bangladeshi boys often prioritised their Muslim identities over their Bengali culture. I consider next whether religion may play a role in influencing language use.

In this part of the analysis I compare the results for ten Bangladeshi boys. Five of these speakers explicitly aligned themselves with Islamic teachings:

Speaker 6:   If you've got your religion that's all I need . . . I've got my religion I don't need my culture . . . so yeah culture ain't that much to me.

These speakers would often refer to their religion when asked about aspects of their social behaviour. When asked whether he would ever have a white girlfriend, one boy replied 'not really . . . my religion wouldn't accept that . . . that's difficult with my religion'. Two of the five boys went to an Islamic school at weekends, and one boy received his full-time education at such a school. This group is labelled as having a 'strong Muslim identity'.

The other five boys did not explicitly reject their Muslim identity, but much could be inferred from comments they made and the social practices they engaged in. In discussing Bengali Muslims in the East End, Glynn (2002) points to the growing polarity between drug culture and Islam. The five boys in this sample had all been involved in drug-taking, and all spoke of being arrested for driving offences. At least one of them had a non-Muslim girlfriend. This group is labelled as having a 'weak Muslim identity'.

The results for the PRICE vowel (N = 1370) are shown in Figure 13.7.

As previously discussed, the most frequent PRICE variant among both Bangladeshi and non-Bangladeshi boys who engaged in a lot of inter-ethnic social interaction was [ɐɪ]. These speakers were shown to participate in social practices associated with a 'street' subculture. It is perhaps unsurprising, then, that the results shown in Figure 13.7 reveal that [ɐɪ] is the variant most frequently used by boys with a weak Muslim identity. These speakers are also all members of the older Bangladeshi boys group. The range of [ɐɪ] usage for the five individuals in this group was between 21 per cent (13/61 tokens) and 65 per cent (95/135).

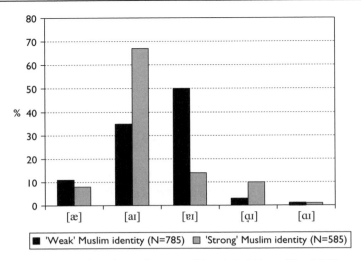

Figure 13.7 Use of PRICE variants by a sub-group of Bangladeshi boys (N = 1,370).

Four of the 'strong Muslim identity' boys were members of the older group of Bangladeshi boys, and one was from the younger group. The [ɐɪ] results for these five boys show it being used overall only 14 per cent of the time. On the face of it, it would seem that professing religious belief exerts some influence over language use. However, looking at the group's results by individual reveals that [ɐɪ] use for four of the boys ranged between 1 per cent (1/70 tokens) and 7 per cent (5/69). However, the fifth (older) boy in this group used it 46 per cent of the time (66/144 tokens) and his results matched more closely those for 'weak Muslim identity' boys. In fact, although this boy had made statements such as 'if you've got your religion that's all I need' and 'I take my religion more than my culture' his actions often contradicted his sentiments about his faith. He admitted that he had been a member of a gang, and although he claimed that 'now everyone's like realised that kind of stuff don't work . . . territory . . . gangs . . . everyone's like growing up' he was frequently observed in the company of those boys who hung about on the street, and at weekends, by his own admission, was often involved in 'breaking into cars you're doing this you're doing that . . . you're hot-wiring and joy-riding . . . and stuff like that cos there's nothing to do'. It would seem, then, that rather than indicating that certain variants are associated with connotations of religious affiliation, these results suggest that particular variants have become socially meaningful (Labov 1963; Eckert 2000) in other ways. The use of [ɐɪ] is perhaps associated with a group of people who engage in social practices related to street culture, regardless of their ethnic background.

Let us turn, lastly, to the results for the FACE vowel (N = 858).

Figure 13.8 shows the FACE variants to be much more evenly distributed among the two sub-groups. In fact, it is the 'strong Muslim identity' group which uses more [ɛɪ], the variant preferred by the non-Bangladeshi boys. In this case, we cannot make any observations about religion and language use.

Taken overall, these results would seem to indicate that there is no direct correlation between a person's professed religious beliefs and the variants that he/she uses. Perhaps,

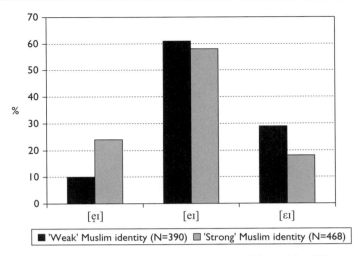

Figure 13.8 Use of FACE variants by a sub-group of Bangladeshi boys (N = 858).

though, there is an indirect link: it seems clear that those adhering to a strict lifestyle in a scriptural sense are less likely to engage in street activities such as drug-taking and other crime-related social practices. If the social meaning attached to certain variants denotes that a speaker is a member of a subculture associated with these street-related social practices, then it seems likely that speakers not wishing to be aligned with that subculture will avoid using those variants.

5. Conclusion

It has been shown here that, in general, the Bangladeshis have not adopted the traditional local Cockney variety, and that a possible explanation for this is the unique social and historical context in which the community came to, and settled in, London. The fact that they arrived at a time when most of the indigenous community was moving out to the suburbs and beyond, together with the fact that the first immigrants came as migrant workers with the intention of returning to Bangladesh, meant that they interacted very little with the indigenous population. As a result, a variety of English has emerged among the Bangladeshis which is influenced, particularly in its phonology, by the community native language, Sylheti. The London Bangladeshis have always lived in close proximity to each other, and because of the sparseness of interaction between this community and speakers of the native target language it is this Sylheti-influenced variety which has been passed to second and subsequent generations.

Qualitative analysis shows also that the Bangladeshi adolescents do not see themselves as Cockneys – when asked, none of the Bangladeshi participants related to a Cockney identity. The following comments were typical:

Speaker 40:   'I don't class myself . . . I'm not Cockney'
Speaker 39:   'Cockney doesn't really come across nowadays amongst us'

There is, however, some polarity among Bangladeshi adolescents, who are split between those with friendship groups consisting mainly of other Bangladeshis, and those who interact frequently with non-Bangladeshis and are involved in a more street-related subculture. The engagement with social practices relating to drugs, car crime and generally anti-social behaviour correlates with the levels of usage of those variants of the PRICE and FACE vowels which are used most frequently – that is, [ɐɪ] and [ɛɪ] respectively – and perhaps even determines the variants' use, if they have these potent social meanings attached to them. The fact that non-Bangladeshi boys, particularly those who interact heavily with the Bangladeshi boys and engage in the same social practices, are also beginning to adopt the [ɐɪ] and [ɛɪ] variants (which are dissimilar to the traditional variants recorded for the regional variety) would seem to provide further evidence of this.

In rejecting the [ɐɪ] and [ɛɪ] variants, and distancing themselves by using variants differing from the traditional Cockney variants, the Bangladeshis may well be prioritising their Muslim identity. Equally, however, they may be emphasising their alienation from a Cockney identity. Doubtless, there are elements of both involved in the complex construction of identity for these adolescents, who endeavour to negotiate their multiple identities in different contexts and settings. Perhaps what this discussion highlights is that issues of identity cannot be generalised, and that the intricate weave of interdependent factors underlying them must be unravelled for each unique community and possibly for each of its individual members. The complexity of the situation is probably best summed up in one young man's own words:

> Speaker 40:   'like I wouldn't really base myself on Cockney . . . I'm just straightforward . . . straight English . . . straight Bengali boy that's it'.

14

Variation and Identity in African-American English

Erik R. Thomas and Alicia Beckford Wassink

1. Introduction

Much writing bearing on language and identity, whether directly or indirectly, has focused on ethnic identities, national identities and language attitudes, reflecting listeners' attitudes towards speakers of shared or other linguistic identities. With respect to the particular case of African-American English (hereafter AAE), writings have focused on a range of applied issues, for example the abilities and attitudes of AAE-speaking youths in vernacular settings (Labov 1972c; Alim and Baugh 2007), students (Perry and Delpit 1997; Richardson 2003, 2006), and non-black populations using AAE by 'crossing' (Ash and Myhill 1986; Rampton 1999). This literature stands alongside a wealth of descriptive writing on the linguistic structure of AAE, and the adjunct debate regarding the validity of regarding it as a dialect based upon its internal structural system (cf. the comprehensive bibliography in Rickford et al. 2004).

Much of the scholarly focus on AAE has centred on the difficult task of providing much-needed information about the linguistic structure of AAE to as broad an audience as possible (see Rickford and Rickford 2000; Wassink and Curzan 2004) to mitigate misunderstandings about the structure or 'logic' (Labov 1972c) of AAE. Wolfram (1998) was among the first to outline the ideological roots of several of the most fundamental and widespread misconceptions about AAE, suggesting that dissemination of information about its linguistic structure was complicated by a layering of beliefs about AAE's origins, the capabilities of bilingual or bilectal speakers, and dialect diversity more generally. This complex layering of ideologies has impeded the take-up of supposedly 'neutral' structural information about language, and has made it equally difficult for scholars to justify turning their attention to identity construction in a range of types of AAE speakers. Because of the ways that use of AAE carries implications for educational attainment and for addressing inequities in social mobility and civic life, scholars have seen greatest urgency in addressing links particularly between AAE and social matters in youth, male, and at-risk populations, to the exclusion of other types of speakers and issues (Alim and Baugh 2007).

As a variety, AAE can be said to have norms which cut across region and social class, although individual speakers may not use all the variants that comprise these norms.

However, despite the existence of such norms, AAE does exhibit regional variation, and knowledge of such differences is necessary for a fuller understanding of AAE as a variety. Furthermore, a nuanced appreciation of the construction of identity and identity-work is necessary when examining variation in AAE. We need an understanding of the language/ identity nexus that goes beyond monolithic assumptions regarding the ethnicity of AAE speakers. That is, there is no simple one-to-one relation between African-American ethnicity and use of AAE, and neither is there such a relation between a particular set of linguistic forms and being 'African American'. This chapter presents first a description of AAE and some of the regional variation observed in the variety to date, before turning to a consideration of the identity-making and -marking functions of the variety.

2. Regional variation in AAE

The Uniformity Controversy (Thomas 2007) revolves around the question of how much regional variation AAE exhibits. AAE certainly shows social differentiation (for example, Wolfram 1969, 2007), but its degree of regional differentiation is less well understood. A common assumption is that AAE possesses a set of national speech norms to which African Americans aspire. That is, 'sounding Black' is supposed to be a key identity factor among African Americans. Fordham and Ogbu (1986), in fact, describe a stigma among African Americans against 'acting white'. This leads us to question whether regional differentiation in AAE should always be understood as the degree to which AAE assimilates to local European-American English (hereafter EAE) dialects or whether AAE shows regional differentiations that are independent of EAE. The complexity of the issue would caution against assuming that AAE is perfectly uniform everywhere, but also against the supposition that AAE lacks any norms.

2.1 Overview of AAE variables

Research on AAE has shown a grossly uneven division in terms of the variables examined. A great deal of attention has been paid to certain morphosyntactic variables such as copula deletion (for instance 'we working right now'), invariant habitual *be* ('we be working all the time'), 3rd person singular -*s* absence ('she get on my nerves'), possessive -'*s* absence ('I get on people nerves') and *ain't* in place of *didn't* ('I ain't see him yesterday'). Certain consonantal variables have attracted considerable research, especially consonant cluster simplification (such as [ɹɪs] for *wrist* or *risk*) and non-rhoticity (for example, *here* pronounced [hiə]), and to a lesser extent several others, such as (th)-stopping and -fronting – the replacement of historical /θ/ by [t] or [f], and /ð/ by [d] – and loss of final nasals, as in *man* pronounced [mæ̃]. Several vowel variables have received sporadic attention, particularly recently. Intonation has been the object of occasional study and a few specialists have examined lexical variation or pragmatic constraints, but voice quality has been almost completely ignored, aside from a handful of studies of fundamental frequency (F0) (for example Hudson and Holbrook 1981; Walton and Orlikoff 1994).

Finally, folk vocabulary has received some attention from dialect geographers. For example, Pederson et al. (1986–92) noted that terms which are strongly associated with the Mississippi River delta, such as *lagniappe* 'something extra', *cush* or *cush-cush* 'mush' and *bayou* 'backwater, stream', occur in both African-American and European-American speech there, but not elsewhere.

2.2 Morphosyntactic variation in AAE

An ironic outcome of the work on AAE is that the most extensively studied variables, those involving morphosyntactic and consonantal variation, are among those for which information on regional variation is hardest to find. The great early studies of AAE, which basically studied African-American *Vernacular* English (AAVE), were conducted in widely separated locations: Labov et al. (1968) in New York City (see also Labov 1972c), Wolfram (1969) in Detroit, and Fasold (1972) in Washington DC. These studies focused on describing targeted variables and (when applicable) their semantic significance, identifying the phonological constraints on them, and determining their social distributions. They avoided geographical issues. Those differences that did appear between the studies were attributed – no doubt accurately – to differences in methodology. In the early work, the pervasive assumption was that AAE was geographically uniform and that the main divisions fell along social class, gender and perhaps generational lines.

Subsequent research in a variety of locations (for example Guy 1980; Baugh 1983; Sommer 1986; Bailey and Maynor 1987; Rickford et al. 1991; Wolfram and Thomas 2002) has not turned up much unassailable evidence for geographical differentiation in the core morphosyntactic or consonantal features of AAE. In fact, authors often point out how similar their findings are to those from other study sites. When differences did appear, they did not necessarily correlate with geography. One possible geographical difference is that Butters and Nix (1986) found slightly lower rates of 3rd person singular -*s* absence in Wilmington than Wolfram (1969) recorded in Detroit. Quantitative differences rather than qualitative ones seem likely to be the extent of geographical differences for many variables associated with AAE. A possible exception is one particular meaning of the *be done* construction, the 'habitual resultant state', which Green (2002: 64) suggests is more common in some regions than others, but she gives only anecdotal support for the suggestion.

Nevertheless, a few studies of morphosyntactic variation have found that African Americans in certain parts of the South show some local features that are apparently absent in other parts of the South, and which Northern African Americans have apparently lost. Hazen (2000) notes the occurrence in a rural county in the North Carolina Piedmont of the past tense copula form *wan't*, as in 'he wan't there yesterday'. Atwood (1953) had earlier reported this form in European-American speech of Virginia and the Carolinas. Another feature is levelled *weren't*, as in 'he weren't there yesterday'. Wolfram and Thomas (2002) find it among older African Americans and among European Americans of all ages in a coastal North Carolina county, though younger African Americans there have nearly abandoned it. A third such feature is the locative use of *to*, as in 'he's over *to* the store' instead of 'he's over *at* the store'. Nichols (1986) reports this form from coastal South Carolina, as do Carpenter (2004) and Vadnais (2006) from various parts of eastern North Carolina, where it was diminishing across generations. Like *wan't* and levelled *weren't*, locative *to* occurs in the speech of older European Americans in the same areas where African Americans use it. African-American accommodation to regional morphosyntactic variants outside the South has received minimal attention.

2.3 Consonantal variation in AAE

Among consonantal variables, two are said to show geographical variation in AAE. One is a particular form of consonant cluster simplification. Reduction of /ks/ to [k], as in *six* [sɪk] and *box* [bɑk], is reported by Fasold and Wolfram (1970) to be more frequent in Southern AAE than in Northern AAE. The other is non-rhoticity. As a whole, AAE tends to be less rhotic than EAE in a given locality, but there is considerable variation among regions. The most common pattern in AAE is rhoticity in stressed, syllabic positions, such as in *turn*, *work*, *first* and *stir*, and non-rhoticity elsewhere. Intervocalic contexts, as in *sorry*, may be non-rhotic as well, though less often and more among lower social levels. Rhoticity increases with social level and is also commoner in certain parts of the US. Within the South, African Americans in areas with small African-American populations and traditionally rhotic EAE, such as the southern Appalachians and the Pamlico Sound region of North Carolina, are often quite rhotic (Wolfram and Thomas 2002). Outside the South, African Americans in some urban areas have become strongly rhotic. Known examples are Columbus, Ohio (Thomas 1989/1993) and Davenport, Iowa (Hinton and Pollock 2000). On the other hand, in some parts of the Deep South (that is, from South Carolina to Louisiana) and up the Mississippi Valley, African Americans may be non-rhotic even in stressed, syllabic positions. Williamson (1968), the *Linguistic Atlas of the Gulf States* (LAGS; Pederson et al. 1986–92), and Wroblewski et al. (2007) have noted the persistence in AAE of the [əɪ] diphthong in checked syllables, as in *turn*, *work* and *first*. [əɪ] formerly predominated in some Southern states in both AAE and EAE but has nearly died out in EAE. Non-rhoticity in stressed, syllabic contexts occurs at low levels in some Northern cities (Labov et al. 1968; Wolfram 1969).

Other consonantal features are good candidates for regional variation. For example, some African Americans from the South produce words such as *shrimp* with initial [ʃw ~ sw]. It seems plausible that this variant is less common among African Americans in the North, though at present there is no evidence either way.

2.4 Vowel variation in AAE

Although relatively little attention has been paid to vowel variation in AAE, it has yielded the most extensive evidence for regional differentiation in the variety. It should be emphasised that AAE shows some vocalic commonalities nearly everywhere. As discussed in Thomas and Bailey (1998) and Thomas (2001, 2007), in a given community African Americans tend to show less fronting of the GOOSE, GOAT and MOUTH vowels than do European Americans (the names henceforth used for vowels follow the conventions developed by Wells [1982], with one addition, PRIZE, that has been used by other subsequent authors). AAE speakers also frequently exhibit raising of the TRAP vowel and resist merging the LOT and THOUGHT vowels, often by fronting LOT somewhat and raising THOUGHT. Like Southern European Americans, they generally merge the KIT and DRESS vowels before nasals, as in *tin* and *ten*, they usually weaken the glide of the PRIZE vowel, and they often round the nucleus of START. Within the South, however, they are much less likely than European Americans to weaken the glide of PRICE/PRIZE when it falls before a voiceless consonant, as in *price*; their glide weakening is mostly limited to contexts before a voiced consonant, as in *prize*, or word-finally, as in *pry*. They have largely retained these Southern variants after establishing African-American communities outside the South (for example, Ash and Myhill 1986 on Philadelphia; Edwards 1997 on Detroit; Gordon 2000 on Gary, Indiana). Becker and Coggshall (2008), however, find that African Americans in New York have lost the *tin/ten* merger while retaining some glide weakening of PRIZE.

Nevertheless, the commonalities still allow plenty of room for variation, including geographical variation. In large part, the variations occur in two distinct settings. One is in traditional, rural Southern communities where residents have generally lived for many generations, often somewhat isolated in the past from other areas. The other occurs mostly outside the South, where African Americans have come into contact with non-Southern European Americans. Studies have revealed vocalic variation in local African-American communities in both settings. In addition, a third possible setting is in Southern urban areas, many of which did not become major cities until the twentieth century or at least until the late nineteenth century. Many Southern cities thus resemble Northern cities in that most of their African-American population did not arrive until the twentieth century.

In rural Southern communities, African Americans frequently share numerous vowel variants with neighbouring European Americans. The *tin/ten* merger, glide weakening of words such as *prize* and *pry*, and rounding of the START vowel, as noted above, are widespread in both AAE and Southern EAE. Local Southern variants have also seeped across ethnic boundaries. Wolfram and Thomas (2002) found fronting of the GOAT vowel in a community along the Pamlico Sound in eastern North Carolina among both ethnicities and all age groups. Older speakers of both ethnicities shared three other local variants: fronting of the MOUTH glide, backing of the PRICE nucleus, and lowering of the SQUARE nucleus. More recently, Childs et al. (2007) have documented that African Americans in the mountains of western North Carolina share glide weakening of the PRICE vowel before voiceless consonants with European Americans in that region. In rural southern Louisiana, Wroblewski et al. (2007) found a different set of variants shared by local African Americans and European Americans. Besides variable retention of the [əɪ] diphthong in words such as *first*, both groups also showed raising of the FACE vowel so that it was barely differentiated from the FLEECE vowel. In addition, some speakers showed a merger of the DRESS and TRAP vowels before nasals, so that *ten* and *tan* were homophonous.

Outside the South, several studies have examined African-American vowels in the cities of the Great Lakes region. Here the focus has been on the degree to which African Americans accommodate to the Northern Cities Shift (NCS; see Gordon 2004), a series of vowel shifts that occurs in European-American speech of the region, and in the status of glide weakening of PRIZE. The NCS consists of raising and ingliding or downgliding of the TRAP vowel, fronting of LOT, lowering of THOUGHT, backing of STRUT, and lowering and/or backing of DRESS and KIT. Deser (1990) and Jones and Preston (forthcoming) both examined TRAP raising, and Jones and Preston also the fronting of LOT, in Michigan (Deser in Detroit and Jones and Preston in Lansing). Deser found a weak correlation between TRAP raising and whether a speaker was judged to sound more Detroit-like, as opposed to more Southern-like. Jones and Preston found a good deal of TRAP raising but little LOT fronting in Lansing, which they interpreted as selective accommodation to the NCS. These results suggest that TRAP raising might represent a regional feature of AAE in the Great Lakes area. However, Deser was unaware, and Jones and Preston acknowledged only in a footnote, that TRAP raising is actually widespread in AAE. A difference exists between AAE raising and NCS raising that could be examined in this region. The AAE raising leaves the vowel monophthongal, while fully developed forms of the NCS raising render it ingliding or downgliding. This difference contradicts the stereotypical expectation for most vowels to glide more in the South – the source of AAE (see further section 3) – than in the North. However, within the South, the gliding tendencies seem to be stronger in European-American speech than in African-American speech.

Glide weakening of PRIZE has garnered some attention in studies of the Great Lakes region. Purnell (2008) finds loss of PRIZE glide weakening in Milwaukee. Deser (1990) reports a tendency in Detroit for younger African Americans to exhibit stronger PRICE/PRIZE glides than older speakers, suggesting a North/South divergence for this variable. However, Anderson (2002), using younger Detroiters than Deser's informants, finds that young African Americans had actually extended glide weakening of PRICE/PRIZE to contexts before voiceless consonants, which also represents divergence from Southern AAE norms. They apparently did so as a result of contact with Appalachian European Americans in Detroit. Edwards (1997) finds that middle-class African Americans in Detroit show fuller PRICE/PRIZE glides than working-class African Americans, suggesting class-based divergence from Southern AAE norms.

Anderson (2002) finds another trend among Detroit African Americans that contradicts tendencies noted for Southern AAE (Thomas and Bailey 1998; Thomas 2001). This trend is a fronting of the GOOSE vowel. The same trend is joined by fronting of the GOAT vowel – which occurs among European Americans in the Midland areas that lie south of the Great Lakes region but not in the Great Lakes area itself – in some Midland cities, particularly in Columbus, Ohio (Thomas 1989/1993; Durian et al. 2007). Even though African Americans in Columbus do not front GOAT or GOOSE quite as much as European Americans there, they still front them more than African Americans in many parts of the South or on the East Coast. Eberhardt (2008) reports that African Americans in Pittsburgh, another Midland city, have also adopted moderate GOAT fronting, and Bloomquist (2008) finds the same shift in AAE of the Susquehanna Valley in Pennsylvania. In the Southern city of Memphis, Tennessee, Fridland and Bartlett (2006) similarly find some fronting of the GOOSE, FOOT and GOAT vowels among African Americans, though not quite as much for GOOSE and GOAT as European Americans there exhibit. Comparison of GOAT and GOOSE realisations for African Americans in Thomas (2001) and those in these subsequent studies shows considerable variation in AAE, much of it apparently related to accommodation to local European-American dialects.

Research on Southern cities has yielded further possibilities for regional variation. The Southern Shift (Labov 1994) is a set of vowel shifts widespread in Southern EAE. It involves, among other things, the fronting of the GOOSE and GOAT vowels mentioned earlier, and a series of shifts among the front vowels such that the nuclei of FACE and DRESS switch places (making the FACE nucleus lower than the DRESS nucleus) and the nuclei of the FLEECE and KIT vowels sometimes also switch positions. Mild forms of the FACE/DRESS interchange have been found in AAE both in Memphis (Fridland 2003) and in a suburb of Atlanta (Andres and Votta 2007), and undoubtedly occur elsewhere – in fact, some of the African Americans in Thomas (2001) show such a pattern. This pattern differs from that found in some other areas, such as southern Louisiana (Wroblewski et al. 2007) and Milwaukee (Purnell 2008), where both local EAE and local AAE lack lowering of the FACE nucleus.

3. AAE and identities

Beyond the issue of regional difference, a further complication in understanding variation in AAE use regards the question of just *who* uses AAE. Ash and Myhill (1986) found, for an ethnically mixed sample of Philadelphia speakers (including African, Puerto Rican and European Americans), that African Americans and Puerto Ricans in their sample used AAE at comparable levels. The authors examined the use of ten linguistic variables considered to be core features of AAE, including: final -*n* deletion, PRICE-monophthongisation (where deletion in prevoiceless contexts was found to be less frequent than deletion in prevoiced contexts among Puerto Ricans, just as it was for African Americans in Ash and Myhill's sample), indefinite article *a/an* alternation, 3rd person singular -*s* absence, habitual *be*, possessive '*s* absence, use of *ain't*, and a small set of shared AAE lexical items. They further found that EAE speakers with predominantly African-American social networks also used AAE norms, although at lower levels than their African-American counterparts. In fact, the grammatical variables studied were used much less frequently than the AAE phonological variables by both European Americans with predominantly African-American networks and African Americans with predominantly European-American networks. Edwards (1992) reported a similar finding for a sample of African Americans residing in Detroit who varied in the ethnic composition of their social networks. These studies make it very clear that (i) African Americans vary in the use of AAE forms, (ii) other ethnic groups may align themselves with AAE speakers in their use of AAE forms, (iii) social network composition impacts on the use of AAE, including for African Americans, and (iv) the identity work accomplished by use of AAE forms in non-African-American groups is an issue in need of continued research (Rampton 1999).

Although the issue of who uses AAE is a complex one, the variety must still be understood as a means of accomplishing identity work in important ways for African-American speakers. For example, the ways that speakers vary in the use of AAE in style-shifting is still poorly understood. When we move away from the simplistic understanding that AAE use indexes only ethnicity to focus on some of the ways AAE may be used in different interactional settings, we stand to improve our knowledge of how speakers use it to index a range of social meanings.

Researchers have described at length the sociolinguistic settings in which AAE forms are used. Interested readers are referred particularly to Rickford (1999), Rickford and Rickford (2000) and Poplack and Tagliamonte (2001). More relevant to the present discussion is that AAE arose within a colonial context in the Southern US, becoming hegemonically positioned relative to a superposed standard. Such a standard language, according to Silverstein, 'is hegemonic in the sense that it constitutes the ideologically-neutral top and center of all variability' (1995: 22; see also Silverstein 2003). With AAE relegated to a position of linguistic subordination, it has, across American history, been strongly stigmatised: claimed to have no grammar, to be no more than a corrupt version of mainstream American English, somehow a deliberate attempt on the part of speakers to escape proper English, and often regarded by both out-group and in-group members as useless for social advancement. However, its use persists, situated within complex, multi-valued language attitude systems which show it, though stigmatised, to have significant (social) value. Several authors have explored the persistence of stigmatised varieties, finding that it is possible for speakers to positively value multiple linguistic varieties simultaneously, affording some varieties overt prestige while attributing covert prestige to others (see for example Ryan 1979; Rickford and Traugott 1985; Wassink 1999). Overt prestige is typically accorded to varieties that are valued openly and publicly, in both in- and out-group contexts; that is, varieties that are associated with upward social mobility and education. Covert prestige is the value accorded to language varieties that are viewed as expressing shared history, cultural values, authenticity and, often, shared struggle. This type of prestige tends to be verbally expressed in in-group contexts only. Linguists also study how speakers exhibit conversational codeswitching between a stigmatised and a standard variety, in response to complex situations where in-group and out-group identity roles are expressed, judged as appropriate or inappropriate, and contested. Further research on the use of AAE as a fluid in-group marker in codeswitching contexts will shed light on AAE's potential as a stylistic resource.

4. Conclusions

It seems clear that AAE has some commonalities or norms that are widespread, even though individual speakers may not use all the variants that comprise the norms. However, AAE is not uniform, either socially (as numerous studies have demonstrated since the 1960s), or geographically, as recent research has begun to show. The evidence so far of geographical variation is fragmentary. The reasons for this are that studies of morphosyntactic and consonantal variation have mostly been concerned with other issues and have not looked for geographical variation, and that studies of many other variables, especially prosodic and pragmatic ones, are too poorly developed to provide information on geographical variation. Most of the currently available information on geographical variation in AAE is derived from vowel studies, both of Southern rural forms and of newer urban forms, from dialectological studies of traditional Southern lexicon, and from a few studies of local morphosyntactic variables. In all cases, the geographical variations are closely linked to local or regional variations in European-American speech. Geographical variation interacts with social class such that middle-class African Americans or sometimes – as in Detroit (Anderson 2002) and in rural Southern communities – working-class African Americans may accommodate to local EAE norms more if they have more contact with European Americans. So far, it is unclear whether the regional variation that appears in AAE is independent of regional variation in EAE (or other ethnic varieties such as Mexican-American English). A possible exception is regional AAE slang, though with slang regional distribution is often ephemeral as terms spread rapidly through various forms of contact. At any rate, one obvious conclusion is that in the future AAE specialists will need to devote more attention to regional variation in AAE and the related question of its dependence on EAE variation.

As was outlined above, much of the literature about AAE has been focused on describing a single sociolect, as if AAE were monolithic. Researchers have struggled to identify a set of core linguistic features that constitute the variety, with recent research proposing metrics to enable objective measurement of use of dialect norms to support a range of types of research (for example, Craig and Washington's 2006 Dialect Density Measure). Linguists know that social, geographical and historical separation over time contribute to differentiation between linguistic varieties (in other words, dialect formation; Wolfram and Schilling-Estes 1998). In much the same way, since AAE is not monolithic, we might expect variation between speakers who come from a range of regional and social backgrounds.

AAE has always existed in spaces of contested identity. Schieffelin and Doucet (1998: 286) say that it is known to laypeople that at sites where identity is contested, choosing what gets said, written, or transcribed is about multiplicities of images choosing among competing conceptualisations. Who black people are, who they are not, what they may do, what they may not do, what they can do (capabilities), what they cannot do, have been controversial and polarising sites of contestation since the first Africans came to the United States. Such questions remain the subject of vigorous ongoing debate.

15

Language, Embodiment and the 'Third Sex'

Lal Zimman and Kira Hall

1. Introduction

Groups whose gender identities and enactments fall outside of socio-cultural norms for women and men are often described by both scholars and the groups' members as constituting a 'third gender' or 'third sex'. This chapter discusses the utility of this categorisation (which we will hereafter refer to as *third sex*) for the study of language, gender and sexuality. We begin by acknowledging the problematic nature of this terminology as established by critiques levelled against its use within the history of anthropological scholarship. However, we maintain that careful deployment of the concept can be theoretically illuminating when providing ethnographic accounts of gender-variant communities who themselves articulate their subjectivity through the idea of 'thirdness'. Most notably, the way this term refocuses the analytic lens on biological sex – an issue feminist scholars have often subordinated to their interest in the social construction of gender – highlights how sexual embodiment, no less than gender, is constructed in culturally and historically specific ways. Our purpose here is to demonstrate the importance of the body in shaping the relationship between language and identity among gender-variant groups.

Attention to the body is crucial for understanding gender variance because it is very often the combination of apparently incongruous social and biological gender cues – such as feminine dress on a male body – that is seen to distinguish a group from gender-normative women and men. Furthermore, many gender-variant communities engage in transformative bodily practices that mark their gender difference physically, such as the use of hormones, silicone injections, or any number of surgical procedures ranging from traditional forms of castration to modern medicine's genital reconstruction surgery. For members of these groups, a deviant body is often simultaneously a reflection of identity and self-determination, and a source of marginalisation (cf. Stryker 1994, 2006, 2008; Sullivan 2006). Yet we argue that the body serves not only as a crucial variable that often explains or correlates with sociolinguistic phenomena, as Borba and Ostermann's (2007) analysis of Brazilian *travesti* recently suggested, but is itself a product of linguistic practice. In other words, bodies do not derive their meanings from a pre-linguistic natural order, but are imbued with meaning through discourse.

To demonstrate the import of the body for language and identity research, we outline two approaches to language and embodiment that build on our research among gender-variant communities: transsexual men in the US, and *hijras* in India. This is not to suggest that the groups are at all similar in socio-cultural terms, nor do we wish to advocate the categorisation of either as a third sex (whatever that would mean). Rather, we present their communicative practices to call attention to the way in which biological sex is as much a product of everyday interaction as is social gender. As groups whose embodiment is marked as deviant within their respective cultural contexts, transsexual men and hijras both use language to subvert dominant ideologies surrounding their bodies, and thus reclaim more control over the meanings ascribed to them. The highly contestable nature of these individuals' identities reveals the processes through which normative and non-normative bodies alike are implicated in the construction of gender.

The first approach to language and embodiment we address, inspired by poststructuralist feminist characterisations of sex as discursively constructed, focuses on how language is implicated in creating the categories of 'male' and 'female' bodies. We illustrate this perspective with an analysis of how transsexual men in an online community negotiate the gendered meanings ascribed to their genitals. The first author's research in this area reveals how members of this marginalised group contest and reconstruct sex through linguistic practice to accomplish the social needs of the community. The second approach draws on the growing body of linguistic literature that views language as inextricably tied to gesture and other aspects of embodiment. Taking a socio-cultural perspective on gesture, Hall's work with the hijras of India demonstrates how group members assert their positionality as 'neither man nor woman' through the use of a distinctive hand clap. Together, these examples reveal that the relationship between language and the body is a recursive one, with language shaping conceptualisations of the body, and embodied action functioning as an integral part of language.

2. (How) should we use the concept of a 'third sex'?

The last three decades of scholarship on sexual and gender alterity has focused principally on groups whose existence is seen to undermine fundamental assumptions about gender long associated with Western society and scholarship. When feminist theorists in the 1970s and 1980s started to challenge the naturalisation of gender by showing how masculinity and femininity are socially constructed, cultural anthropologists began to question the same dichotomy by demonstrating how gender and the related category of sexuality are often pluralistically constructed in non-Western cultures. The anthropological interest during this period in gender and sexual alterity – what Rubin acknowledges as 'the exotica in which anthropologists delight' (1975: 165) – was certainly not new. But the research of earlier anthropologists was suddenly validated by a new feminist agenda inspired by social constructionist theory, leading to a resurfacing of anthropological studies on the cultural existence of third sex and non-heterosexual categories that were interpreted as defying European and North American organisations of gender: for example, gender-variant groups among the Nigerian Igbo (Amadiume 1987), the *xanith* in Oman (Wikan 1982), the *berdache* in Native America (Whitehead 1981; Williams 1986; Roscoe 1991, 1998; Lang 1998), the *mahu* in Tahiti (Levy 1973), and the hijra in India (Nanda 1985, 1990). The burgeoning field of gay and lesbian studies added impetus to such research, particularly as scholars sought to critique homophobia and heterosexism through reference to the cultural possibility of more liberating systems of gender and sexuality. The resulting body of research employing a third sex framework thus served not only to increase the scholarly visibility of non-binaristic gender systems, but also to feed theoretical discussions regarding the value of such systems. The essays included in Herdt's (1993a) edited volume *Third Sex, Third Gender*, for example, are essentially a challenge to the assumed naturalness of binary gender systems, an approach made clear in the book's subtitle: *Beyond Sexual Dimorphism in Culture and History*.

The concept of transsexuality entered the anthropological literature through these same discussions, but often as a means of underscoring the comparative gender fluidity associated with three-gender cultures. Nanda (1990), for example, in her groundbreaking ethnography of the hijras of India, discusses the cultural position of Western transsexuals as inferior to that of hijras, asserting that the designation *trans-* itself betrays that 'we view an intermediate sex or gender category as nothing other than transitional; it cannot be, in our culture, a permanent possibility' (Nanda 1990: 123). Scholars from diverse fields have overwhelmingly focused on transsexuals as enacting normative, as opposed to subversive, femininity and masculinity, creating a theoretical role for the transsexual as the ultimate gender conformist. The literature thus produces a reductive picture of transsexuality, leading to its easy appropriation as the theoretical whipping boy for a rigidly unimaginative gender binary.

Given the widespread usage of the third sex framework during the final three decades of the twentieth century to describe a range of identities across cultures, it is not surprising that several scholars working with gender-variant communities have since questioned the usefulness of this categorisation. Most significantly, the emphasis on non-western-third-sex groups whose existence is acknowledged or institutionalised to some degree by the larger society has led to the misguided assumption that these populations are less marginalised than their Western counterparts, leading to skewed representations of the cultural value placed on alternative gender identities (see Hall 1995, 1997; Herdt 1993b). Similarly, scholarly discussions of third sex categories may inadvertently work to reify the 'normalcy' of first and second gender categories. Towle and Morgan (2002) pursue this critique, arguing that accounts of third sex groups 'might imply – wrongly, in our view – that "first" and "second" [male and female] categories are inviolable and unproblematic, at least for the purposes of exploring gender variability' (Towle and Morgan 2002: 484–5). Stryker (2004, 2008) makes a similar argument against the broadening of the transgender category to include all forms of 'gender trouble'. In a three-gender system, anyone whose expression of gender falls outside of normative expressions of masculinity or femininity within a given culture can be methodologically relegated to a third (or occasionally fourth) group, leaving only gender-normative individuals in the male and female categories. Finally, research on third sex categories often encourages conflation of many different forms of non-normative gender expression into a single group, while leaving other forms of gender diversity invisible. In her work on the *kotis* of India, a transgender group that distinguishes itself from the better-researched hijras, Hall (2005) argues that queer theory's uptake of poststructuralism, spearheaded by Butler's (1990, 1993) concept of gender performativity, has led a new generation of scholars to focus on the subversive potential of third sex groups like the hijras as a theoretical trope, thereby overlooking the existence of other, less visible gender-variant groups. In short, the use of terminology like *third sex* can create the illusion of three homogeneous groups – male, female and other – rather than facilitating subtler understanding of diversity both between and within groups.

Nevertheless, a third sex category can be a useful analytic tool, particularly in so far as it reflects group members' self-understanding and/or the image of the group promoted by more powerful factions of society; both criteria hold for the hijras. Yet we must not lose sight of the diversity and contestability of gender and sex ideologies, even among people sharing common identities. The question of whether Western transsexuals and other transgender people should be understood as a third sex illustrates the difficulty of making these determinations. A number of sexologists researching transgenderism (for example Bockting 1997; Diamond 2003) together with transgender authors (notably Bornstein 1994, 2006 [1994]; Wilchins 1997; Feinberg 2006 [1992]) have recently argued that characterising transgender identities as a kind of third sex distinct from male and female categories empowers transgender people personally and politically. Echoing earlier anthropologists' work on third sex systems, these authors emphasise the oppressive nature of the gender binary and argue, as Bornstein has claimed, that '[t]he correct target for any successful transsexual rebellion would be the gender system itself' (2006 [1994]: 242). Bornstein goes so far as to explicitly align her-/himself with second-wave feminists like Raymond (1979), who argued that transsexuals are agents of the patriarchy, writing that s/he 'agree[s with these scholars] that hiding and not proclaiming one's transsexual status is an unworthy stance' (Bornstein 2006 [1994]: 239). As Towle and Morgan (2002) show, Bornstein's stance exemplifies a larger trend among many transgender authors of appropriating the 'transgender native in the form of [their] assumed primordial ancestors' (Towle and Morgan 2002: 478), or rather, of viewing indigenous gender-variant identities as the forebears of a universal transgender experience. Other transgender scholars have strongly disagreed with this perspective. While recognising that there ought to be room for people who do in fact identify outside of the male/female binary, Serano (2007) argues that indiscriminately grouping all transgender people into a third sex – even those who identify strictly as women or men – casts transgender identities as illegitimate and denies transgender people the right to name themselves (see also Namaste 1996; Stryker 2008). It is thus unclear whether transgender people should be discussed as a third sex, particularly given the dissent that exists among members of this group on the issue.

Similar contestation surrounds the status of hijras in urban centres like Delhi. While hijras claim a long history dating at least from the time of the mediaeval Mughal empire, many educated English-speaking Indians have now embraced gay and lesbian identities associated with the processes of globalisation, rejecting traditional cross-gender practices as lower-class forms of homosexuality. The non-governmental organisation (NGO) that Hall's (2005) recent work focuses on serves as a community centre for queer Indians, and while hijras have never been explicitly barred, its policy against cross-dressing at the time of Hall's field research prevented hijras from participating in the organisation. Hijras were required to wear men's clothing just like the gay-identified men and effeminate men known as kotis, suggesting that the NGO's administrators see hijras not as members of a third sex but as men whose gender presentation is inappropriately feminine. The influence of globalisation and HIV/AIDS activism in sparking this rapid and dramatic shift in queer Indian society underscores the constant flux of gender categories, including something as fundamental as whether there are three genders or two.

Socio-cultural linguists who have worked with gender-variant communities have been sensitive to these problems and have maintained critical perspectives in their engagement with the third sex concept. For example, Hall (2005) describes how hijras exploit the widespread ideology that they are members of a third sex, born without genitals, to create a distinction between themselves and kotis, a group that engages in similar sartorial practices, particularly when doing what they call 'hijra-acting'. Because kotis generally do not engage in genital modification practices and pride themselves in being sexually licentious (an image that the already marginalised hijras do not want to be associated with, at least publicly), the embodied difference between hijras and kotis is discursively invoked as proof of their distinctiveness. While hijras characterise anatomically male cross-dressing groups like the kotis as 'fake hijras', kotis spend much of their hijra-acting performances mocking the hijras' self-representation as penisless ascetics. Hall's description of the ideological workings behind hijras' claim to third sex status draws attention to the body by focusing on thirdness not as a theoretical construct, but as an everyday notion that emerges as part of the ethnographic encounter.

More commonly, however, socio-cultural linguists have understandably refrained from engaging with the third sex concept, given the baggage it entails – for example Barrett (1995, 1999) on African-American drag queens; Besnier (2003, 2007) on Tongan *fakaleiti*; Gaudio (1997, 2005, 2007) on the *'yan daudu* of Hausaland, Nigeria; and Kulick (1997) on Brazilian travestis. Yet we propose that the concept of third sex, because of its now canonical association with biology, suggests an alternative understanding of the body with the potential to reveal important connections between embodiment and social actors' ongoing negotiation of gender identity. We additionally argue that incorporating embodiment into socio-cultural analyses of language and gender can reveal understudied dimensions of both identity and linguistic practice. Indeed, the lack of attention to the body in studies of language and gender variance leads Borba and Ostermann (2007) to argue that biological sex demands closer sociolinguistic scrutiny because of its crucial role in defining gender-variant groups as outside of the normative gender binary. The authors present rich ethnographic background on the somatic practices of Portuguese-speaking travestis, and demonstrate how these individuals' choice of grammatical gender relates to their embodiment. For instance, travestis often use masculine grammatical forms when referring to past selves that preceded the feminising use of hormones and silicone injections. However, by taking a conventional view of gender as socially constructed and sex as biologically given, Borba and Ostermann overlook how travestis' bodies do not just influence linguistic practice, but are in fact constructed through and constituted by language. In the following section, we discuss Zimman's (2008, in preparation) research among transsexuals in an online community to show how gendered meanings of bodies can be rewritten to accomplish the needs of the community.

3. The discursive construction of sex

In the early 1990s, poststructuralist feminist scholars began to reject the traditional second-wave 'coat rack' model of sex as the natural, biological antecedent to the social construction of gender (see especially Butler 1993 and Nicholson 1994; for a linguistic perspective, see Bing and Bergvall 1996 and McElhinny 2002). Instead, they argued that sex, like gender, is socially constructed within specific historical and socio-cultural contexts. As an illustration, Nicholson (1994) draws on Laqueur's (1990) history of the medicalisation of sex, wherein Laqueur demonstrates that the dichotomy between male and female bodies is a relatively recent development even in the West. According to Laqueur, it was not until the eighteenth century that men and women were seen as having categorically different physiologies. Previously, women were ideologically positioned as underdeveloped men, a fact reflected linguistically by the absence of unique names for body parts now seen as 'female' (such as ovaries, which were conceptualised as undescended testicles). Yet Western non-dualistic configurations of sex are certainly not limited to this historical moment; such systems also presently exist, where they compete, albeit in a marginalised capacity, with the dominant male/female binary. We consider here how socio-cultural linguists can contribute to the poststructuralist argument that sex is discursively achieved. Drawing on Zimman's (2008, in preparation) analysis of talk about the body in one community of English-speaking transsexual men, we argue that the empirical methodologies employed in sociolinguistics, linguistic anthropology and socially-oriented discourse analysis are highly amenable to an exploration of how linguistic practices produce both dominant and subordinate conceptualisations of sex.

Transsexual men are individuals who were assigned a female gender role at birth and raised as girls, but who in adulthood identify as men and often employ medical technology to masculinise their bodies. The data presented in this section were collected in 2007 as part of ongoing participant observation in a popular internet community for transsexual men and others on the female-to-male transgender spectrum. Community members use the online forum to discuss a range of transgender issues, circulate information and provide support to those experiencing difficult emotions. Because of the significance of embodiment for transsexuals, the body is a recurring topic among this group, and negotiating how transsexual men's physiologies should be talked about is commonplace. These discussions are particularly interesting for socio-cultural linguistic analysis because of the great importance this group places on the use of appropriate language when talking about transsexuality, and the heatedness of occasional disagreements.

Understanding how transsexual men talk about their own and each others' bodies requires some additional background information. Female-to-male transsexuals are understudied relative to their male-to-female counterparts, and consequently the practices that distinguish these groups often go unremarked in the transsexuality literature. One significant difference for our purposes here is the fact that transsexual men are considerably less likely to undergo genital surgery than transsexual women. Female-to-male genital reconstruction is perceived by many community members as producing unsatisfactory results, while costing up to US$100,000 for the most complex procedures. The use of testosterone therapy, which creates a typical male hormonal balance by replacing oestrogen and progesterone with androgens, is thus the most viable medical intervention for most transsexual men. Such therapy is highly effective in producing many of the corporeal cues associated with masculinity, among them body and facial hair, a drop in vocal pitch, and an increase in muscle mass coupled with the redistribution of fat from areas like the hips and thighs to the abdomen. The result in terms of gender semiotics is that many transsexual men are socially recognised as men, even though they have what most people would consider female genitalia. However, many transsexual men who use testosterone therapy object to the notion that their bodies are in any way female. Instead of consenting to the dominant ideology that having a vagina makes a person female-bodied, these individuals destabilise the boundaries between male and female embodiment through a subversion of the semantics of words for gendered body parts, particularly ones referring to genitals.

While one of the most salient practices among transsexual men talking about their own and each others' bodies involves the coining of new expressions, such as *bonus hole* or *front hole* to refer to the vagina, our focus here is on their more subtle reworking of traditional genital terms. This takes place by disrupting the semantic link that ordinarily exists between genitals and biological sex. Conventional dictionary definitions of *vagina* and *penis* describe the body part in question in terms of physical structure ('the passage that connects the vulva to the cervix') or function ('the organ of copulation and urinary excretion'), but also biological sex (the vagina is a female body part while the penis is a male one). Transsexual speakers contest the connection between the physiological and gendered elements of these definitions and thus subvert the idea that having a penis necessarily makes a body male, while having a vagina makes a body female. In strategically aligning themselves with either traditionally masculine or traditionally feminine genital terminology – an alignment that shifts depending on the circumstances of talk – speakers can accomplish different kinds of social work fulfilling this particular community's needs.

The commonest tactic employed in communities of transsexual men is to align with vernacular terminology ordinarily used for male genitals, such as *dick* or *cock*. By using these words in reference to their own bodies, speakers challenge the physiological definition of the term as an organ for penetration or urination. Instead, they embrace the gendered meaning of *dick* as a term referring to men's genitals and apply it to their own physiology, eschewing dominant scientific categorisations of their genitals as biologically female. To legitimate this move, transsexual men draw on their own set of scientific discourses emphasising similarities between the penis and the clitoris. That is, while popular opinion categorises them as separate and distinct organs, biologists and sexologists (as well as lexicographers) have long recognised that penises and clitorises are analogous in that they develop from the same embryonic tissue. Furthermore, the medical realities of intersex conditions in Europe and North America, where genitalia seen to be 'ambiguous' are arbitrarily classified as either a small penis or a large clitoris (Kessler 1990; Chase 1998), illustrate the continuum between 'female' and 'male' body parts.

Because testosterone causes clitoral enlargement, transsexual men's genitals can easily be framed as falling on a clitoris/penis continuum. Example (1), taken from a posting in the online community under discussion, illustrates this framing, when a member seeks feedback regarding the timeline of the changes brought about by testosterone ('T'):

(1)   Hey, so I've been on T for 6 months now. It's mostly going pretty much as expected . . . lotsa hair, random bursts of "must hump the furniture now", voice dropping, all that good stuff.

        But . . . ZERO on the dick growing!

        Everyone I've talked to says they had noticeable cock magnification very soon after starting T, so . . . what the hell? It's crazy . . . I didn't think I was going to care if it grew much or not, and I don't really . . . but seriously, six months and it's the same ol' teeny weenie.

> Did anyone else's take a really long time to grow, or not ever start growing at all?

Lamenting that testosterone has not yet provided the expected genital growth, this speaker uses the terms *dick* and *cock* to reference his own (purportedly female) genitalia. Through the self-referential use of phrases like 'the dick growing' and 'cock magnification', he reframes the primary difference between his own physiology and that of non-transsexual men as one of size, not gender. The semantic fuzziness thereby created decouples the specific corporeal characteristics of the penis from the masculinity entailed by words like *dick*. Furthermore, blurring the line between clitorises and penises functions to destabilise the boundary between male and female bodies.

The way transsexual men talk about their genitalia creates what Bucholtz and Hall (2004b) call *adequation*, or 'sufficient similarity', between transsexual men's bodies and normatively male bodies. The tactic thus linguistically enacts the more general ideology promoted by community members that there is no significant difference between transsexual men and men who were raised as boys. Although members of this community rarely, if ever, make the overt claim that sex is socially constructed (in contrast to gender, which members typically describe as a construction), the practice of using the same vocabulary to talk about penises and clitorises breaks down the naturalisation of sex in two ways: first, by suggesting that a clear line may not exist between female and male bodies, and second, by implying that social gender identity in a sense determines sex, rather than vice versa. Thus, we can view this subversive reshaping of genital terms as accomplishing one of the primary projects of many transsexual communities: to place self-identification at the core of legitimate and authentic gender.

The second tactic community members employ when talking about transsexual bodies is the de-feminisation of terminology normatively associated with female embodiment. Use of any kind of 'female' language in reference to community members is marked within this community, such that in certain contexts it elicits scorn or even outrage. However, transsexual men do sometimes use terms like *vagina* and even vernacular words like *cunt* to refer to their own and each others' bodies. Speakers can accomplish this move without undermining community members' identity as men by marking these lexical items as masculine. For instance, one community member posted the question 'I'm not the only one that is filled with immense hatred over his vagina, am I?' By using the masculine pronoun *his* rather than *my* to modify *vagina*, the speaker makes it clear that he is talking about the problems faced by *men*, not women, who have 'immense hatred' of their vaginas. He thus reinforces the group's core belief that no matter how a transsexual man feels about his body, he is still a man. A related tactic involves the resignification of vernacular terms like *pussy* and *cunt* as male. The use of apparently oxymoronic compounds like *boycunt*, *man-pussy* and the self-consciously comical blend *mangina* similarly questions the assumed correlation between biology and gender (see Zimman in preparation).

Transsexual men thus navigate choices between male and female genital terminology, including both vernacular and more medical options, without allowing their linguistic choices to undermine their identity as men. The words these speakers use to refer to their genitals facilitate the social work speakers engage in, whether it involves requesting medical information, providing or asking for support during times of distress and sadness, or promoting transsexual men's bodies as sites of sexual pleasure. However, the fundamental work this community is engaged in is asserting the legitimacy of transsexual men's self-identification as men. The tactical claiming of 'male' terminology in reference to body parts viewed as female, alongside the refashioning of 'female' terminology as male, works to construct transsexual men as male-bodied, or at the very least, *not* female-bodied.

4. Gesture

The second approach to language and embodiment that could enhance the study of gender-variant communities focuses on gesture, which language and gender researchers have only recently begun to incorporate into their analyses (for example, Goodwin 2006; Mendoza-Denton 2008). Previous language-oriented work on gesture, much of it written from a conversation analysis standpoint, addresses the role of gesture in facilitating the interactional management and organisation of discourse, particularly with respect to conversational turn-allocation (Fox 1999; Goodwin 1986; Lerner 2003), quoted speech (Sidnell 2006) and the management of co-constructed talk (Hayashi 2003). These studies consider varied forms of embodiment, among them pointing (Goodwin 2003), the torque of the upper body (Schegloff 1998) and gaze (Sidnell 2006; Streeck 1993), so potentially represent useful starting points for deeper consideration not only of how gestures demonstrate socially driven variation, but also of how the body itself is a crucial site for the linguistic enactment of identity. This holds especially when those identities depend on specific forms of embodiment, as is true for gender-variant individuals.

Other work on gesture has framed it as the product or reflection of a particular language or society (Kendon 1997, 2004; McNeill 1997; Haviland 2004). Kendon's (1997) review of research on gesture is written in this vein: he presents a number of cross-linguistic and cross-cultural differences in how and to what degree speakers use gesture. For example, he presents differences in gesticulation that mirror the structure of the gesturers' native languages, such as the use of absolute versus relative coordinate systems. He also discusses the evolution of gestural systems as a product of cultural and historical developments in a given society: 'In a city such as Naples, the particular combination of climatic conditions, built environment, social structure, and economy that have come to prevail there over more than two millennia has created communication circumstances in which gesture would be particularly valuable' (Kendon 1997: 117). The usefulness of this type of macro-perspective for the study of language and identity is unclear, particularly since it assumes that people sharing a language or culture will produce and interpret gesture in similar ways. Yet Kendon's point that gesture and speech are coordinated and 'must therefore be regarded as two aspects of a single process' (Kendon 1997: 111) is potentially illuminating for the sociolinguistic analysis of gesture, because it challenges researchers studying the discursive production of gender to consider the contribution gesture makes to the process. Furthermore, reviews of research on the relationship between culture and gesture suggest promising directions for more particularist perspectives on gesture and identity. As Kendon (1997) and Haviland (2004) point out, ideologies about gesture, because they vary across cultural groups, potentially shape the way that bodies are managed and deployed as communicative resources. Dominant ideologies about socially appropriate enactments of gesture in any given culture can also carry gender-specific norms, often, for instance, requiring more restraint from women with respect to physical expressiveness (see, for example, Rossini 2004). Significantly for our purposes, these ideologies can be exploited by social actors occupying liminal and marginalised gender positions as part of a broader semiotic toolkit (cf. Hall 2003a).

Linguists interested in the fundamental inseparability of gesture and spoken language have, somewhat predictably, characterised gesture's primary role as enhancing or punctuating the semantics of an utterance; in Kendon's own words, '[s]peakers often employ gesture in such a way as to make something that is being said more precise or complete' (Kendon 2000: 51). Thus, a speaker recounting the children's story *Little Red Riding Hood*, to borrow Kendon's (1997) example, might produce an axe-swinging gesture in conjunction with the word *slice* in an utterance such as the following: 'And he took his hatchet and with a mighty sweep *sliced* the wolf's stomach open.' Speech and gesture are here coordinated as part of a single communicative event. The swinging movement of the speaker's arm contributes visual data enhancing the semantics of the utterance by specifying the instrument used for the slicing action. Yet we contend that gesture contributes not just to an utterance's semantic meaning, but also to its social meaning. That is, just as the use of spoken language situates speaker and hearer in a complex matrix of social positions – a process exemplified in earlier discussion by transsexual men's deployment of both 'male' and 'female' genital terms – gesture too is a crucial component of the communicative practices through which identities are constructed.

A prime example of this kind of function in gesture can be found among Hindi-speaking hijras in Varanasi, researched by Hall in the early 1990s for a long-term project investigating language, sexuality and globalisation in northern India. Hijras in this northern city (and indeed throughout much of India) use a distinctive hand clap produced with palms flat and fingers spread wide. Widely recognised as unique to hijras, this clap constitutes an important index of identity because it functions to situate users as 'neither man nor woman'. That is, while hijras' aesthetic conduct is feminine (they wear clothes, jewellery and makeup traditionally associated with Indian women), their behavioural conduct, which includes sexually crude speech and this loud clap, calls this representation into question. Because 'extreme' cursing and clapping are ideologically positioned in dominant Indian discourses as unfeminine and inappropriate for women, at least in unmarked everyday middle-class contexts (cf. Raheja and Gold 1994), the hijras' emphatic use of them in highly public domains helps distinguish hijra identity from that of both women and men.

The hijras' use of clapping and sexual insult ironically also instantiates their ongoing self-construction as religious ascetics. This self-designation is contingent upon the claim that they are a people 'born without genitals' and hence lacking in the sexual desire associated with normative men and women. Although the claim of biologically determined asexuality is undermined by the fact that many hijras undergo penectomy and castration (performed by in-house hijra surgeons) and also engage in various kinds of sex work, it nevertheless works to authorise their societal role as performers of ritualistic fertility blessings. In short, because the hijras exist outside normative structures of sexual kinship they have earned the mystique of having power over procreation. Their use of loud claps and highly sexualised insults in the context of a ritualised birth celebration thus calls attention to their embodied alterity, particularly as these behaviours appear to contradict their self-positioning as ascetics. Indeed, Indian journalists have sought to explain this apparent contradiction by appealing to popular psychology, arguing that the hijras' penchant for clapping and sexual insult is compensatory for sexual deficiency. Yet the hijras' employment of these claps reflects much greater social complexity: in addition to underscoring their identity as hijras, the claps also convey information about how to manage non-hijra listeners. In brief, the hijras' claps constitute a small-scale semiotic system involving a number of different forms conveying specific interactional meanings, among them the *ḍeḍh tālī* 'one-and-a-half clap' and *ādhī tālī* 'half clap' (see Hall 1997).

As one of the most salient markers of hijra identity, the hijra clap is also a primary index appropriated by groups parodying hijra behaviour. For instance, the Delhi kotis who are the subject of Hall's (2005) research make exaggerated use of the clap during hijra-acting to mock the hijras' self-portrayal as ascetics born with neither genitals nor sexual desire. Many kotis have spent significant time within hijra communities and thus use this performance genre to display insider knowledge regarding the 'truth' of the hijras' sexuality, spoofing their public claims to sexual purity. As men who forefront their attraction to other men as a key part of their identity, yet remain situated in normative family structures, kotis parody hijras' rejection of the procreative kinship system that underlies mainstream Indian society. With their wives and children, kotis remain untainted by one of the hijras' primary sources of stigma, even if the kotis are generally assumed to be hijras when publicly engaged in this parodic practice. Partly for this reason, kotis self-identify over and against hijras as *cauthī nasal* 'fourth breed', a term highlighting kotis' ability to move between the identities of the first three sexes: they are alternatively men (in their relationships with their wives and children), women (as the sexually passive partners of their boyfriends), and hijras (as cross-dressing hijra impersonators).

The following example from Hall (2005) illustrates how the hijra clap is incorporated into koti identity construction. After a long day's work at the NGO, the kotis gather to perform as hijras for their middle-class gay and lesbian colleagues. Because cross-dressing is prohibited at the office, kotis have few material resources with which to construct a hijra image; on this night, a long red scarf and an illicit dash of makeup stand metonymically for the feminine aesthetics associated with the hijra community. Yet because kotis also engage in cross-dressing practices that are distinct from what they define as 'hijra-acting', these gender props do not by themselves serve as boundary markers for the performance frame. Rather, it is a series of loud, flat-palmed claps that signal the breakthrough into hijra-acting (Hymes 1975), when Mani, taking on the role of hijra guru, calls forth her disciples. Claps are indicated in the transcription by asterisks.

Roles
Mani: Hijra guru
Sanni: Great-grandmother hijra of new bride
Balli: New hijra bride/daughter-in-law/disciple

1	Mani:	**cal merī naī navelī bahū,	M:	**Come my brand-new bride,
2		yahã pe baiṭh beṭā,		sit here child.
3		rajdhānī mẽ āī hai.		You've come to the capitol.
4	Sanni:	acchā celā kar use mere nām pe:::	S:	Good, make her a disciple in my name!
5	Mani:	jī::yo:::	M:	Live long!

6 Sanni:	surīle ke parpoṭī celā:::	S:	Great granddaughter disciple of the sweet-voiced one!
7 Mani:	are khān*dān bara:::	M:	Hey it's a big *family!
8 Sanni:	are mere (gharõ) kā celā:::	S:	Hey disciple of my clan!
9 Mani:	are *kis kā parpotī *celā re beṭā::	M:	Hey *whose granddaughter *disciple are you, child?
10 Sanni:	*merā aur *kisī kā ((laughs))	S:	*Mine, *who else's? ((laughs))
11 Mani:	*are parpotī terā:::*	M:	*Hey your great granddaughter*!
12	[are *khāndān baṛā pūrā:::		[Hey the *family is so big and full!
13 Balli:	[(xxx)	B:	[(xxx)
14 Sanni:	acchā merī pãcõ (ālī) aur terī	S:	Yeah, I got everything desired
15	to kaccī kar dī ((laughs))		but you've been put to shame! ((laughs))
16 Mani:	are gul*bār, gul*bār, gul*bār.	M:	Hey Flow*er, Flow*er, Flow*er!

In this excerpt the claps serve to accentuate precisely what differentiates kotis from hijras: kinship. Whereas kotis integrate into the extended families so fundamental to Indian society, hijras have created an alternative system of asexual kinship paralleling normative heterosexual kinship structures. In brief, the guru assumes the role of mother-in-law to her disciples, who enter the community as daughters-in-law in the symbolic form of newlywed brides. Since these daughters later become gurus with their own disciples, hijras can increase their family structures both vertically and horizontally. It is this scenario the kotis are parodying in the above example, as Mani and Sanni brag competitively about the size of their respective hijra families. The concentrated use of claps in this opening scene, even for the clap-happy kotis (thirteen claps in twenty-four seconds), works to highlight this essential difference, indirectly establishing kotis, through the reflexive processes of parody, as an entirely different 'breed'.

5. Conclusion

In this chapter, we have argued that the marginalised embodiment of gender-variant individuals compels consideration of the import of the body for the discursive construction of identity. The examples taken from our research among transsexual men and hijras suggest a discursive relationship between language and embodiment. On the one hand, language shapes our understanding of the human body and its meanings. In the transsexual men's online community, biological sex is linguistically reconstructed to better suit a marginalised community's needs. On the other, language is also an embodied undertaking in that it collaborates with gesture as part of a broader communicative act. In the hijra community, the deployment of flat-palmed claps marks the hijras as external to the normative gender binary. For the hijras who offer fertility blessings, and the kotis who parody them, gesture helps to accomplish identity-work, even distinguishing a self-identified 'third sex' from their 'fourth-breed' imitators.

Our goal has thus been to illustrate that the meanings ascribed to different forms of embodiment – including their interpretation as female, male or something else entirely – are themselves the product of linguistic practice. Because gender-variant social actors experience non-normative corporeality, the status of their bodies is especially prone to contestation, and thus becomes a key site for the negotiation of group members' identities. This process is not unique to gender-variant people, as future research in this vein will undoubtedly show. Yet the embodied alterity of groups such as transsexual men and hijras creates a greater degree of transparency regarding these negotiations, thereby revealing the potential significance of the body to any social interaction.

16

Gendered Identities in the Professional Workplace: Negotiating the Glass Ceiling

Louise Mullany

1. Introduction

The sociolinguistic study of gender identities within professional workplaces has become a burgeoning area of research in recent years. Investigators in a variety of global locations have examined the complex process through which interactants in particular groups and communities negotiate their gender identities at work. Recent examples include Holmes' (2006) work in New Zealand, Schnurr (forthcoming) in Hong Kong, Martín Rojo and Gómez Esteban (2005) in Spain, Yieke (2005) in Kenya, Ostermann (2003) in Brazil, Mullany (2007) and Baxter (2008) in Britain, and Kendall (2004) in the US. This expansion of research interest is inextricably interlinked with the 'rapid increase in numbers of women in the workplace worldwide' which has taken place in the last four decades (Barrett and Davidson 2006: 1).

The growth of scholarship in gender and the professions can be witnessed across the humanities and social sciences. A key unifying factor is the aim of examining gender inequalities. One of the most significant and widespread problems is the persistence of the 'glass ceiling' (Morrison et al. 1987), the metaphorical, transparent barrier preventing women in professional occupations from reaching the higher echelons of power. The impenetrability of the 'glass' ceiling has recently led to some commentators (Johnson 2006; Wahlin 2007; *Equality and Human Rights Commission* 2008) to redefine it as a 'concrete' ceiling. The 2008 *Equality and Human Rights Commission* statistics in Britain show a marked decrease in the number of women reaching positions of power in the professions. The Commission's current projections are that it will take another seventy-three years for women to be equally represented in the boardroom in the FTSE 100 companies.[1] The report also highlights that women from ethnic minorities are disadvantaged the most. While only 11 per cent of directorships in FTSE 100 companies are occupied by women, less than 1 per cent (0.7 per cent) are women who belong to ethnic minorities.

Sociolinguistic investigations of gender identities in the professional workplace have set out to examine the role that language can play in maintaining and reproducing gender inequalities. The importance of an overarching political goal to conducting research on language and identities has long been an aim of sociolinguistics (see Labov 1982). Cameron reiterates her long-standing belief that language and gender studies should be politically motivated, highlighting the discipline's responsibility 'to contribute to the wider struggle against unjust and oppressive gender relations, by revealing and challenging the ideological propositions which support and naturalize those relations' (Cameron 2007: 16). In this chapter I attempt to contribute to this effort by revealing and challenging 'ideological propositions' which 'support and naturalize' gendered relations and thus perpetuate gender inequalities in professional workplaces. The role that sociolinguistic investigations can play in the broader aim of attempting to bring about gender equality will be examined by analysing data taken from ethnographic studies of two businesses based in England, where women managers are actively trying to break through the glass, or concretised, ceiling.

2. Theorising gender(ed) identities

It is crucially important to acknowledge that gender should be viewed alongside other features of our social identities, including class, age and ethnicity, as well as the enactment of professional identities and roles. However, I firmly believe that gender is omni-relevant and ever-present in every interaction (Eckert and McConnell-Ginet 2003; Holmes 2005). Our gender identities are thus constantly being performed when we interact with one another.

Since the mid-1990s, gender identities have been conceptualised as fluid, negotiated and dynamic, following broader trends in linguistic anthropology, social psychology and sociolinguistics (de Fina, forthcoming). The empirical data in this study will be examined from an integrated theoretical perspective which combines three distinct yet complementary notions: performativity (Butler 1990, 2004), the Foucauldian-influenced concept of 'gendered discourses' (Sunderland 2004), and the notion of indexicality (Ochs 1992).

2.1 Identities and performativity

Recent language and gender studies have aimed to problematise the binary oppositions of sexes, genders and sexualities (see further Zimman and Hall, this volume). Butler famously argues that gender is something that we *do* as opposed to something that we are or have: gender is a 'doing, an incessant activity performed'. Her perspective emphasises a point crucial for sociolinguistic investigations of groups and communities, that gender identity construction emerges during interaction with others: 'one does not "do" one's gender alone. One is always "doing" with or for another' (Butler 2004: 1).

Butler has been criticised for placing too much emphasis on individual agency, leading to the (mis)reading that individuals are free to say/do anything, thus neglecting the crucial role played by powerful societal structures in governing sociolinguistic speech styles. However, Butler has always made reference to a 'rigid regulatory frame' which governs behaviour (Butler 1990: 33). Drawing on Foucault, she highlights how regulation operates as 'a mode of *discipline* and *surveillance* within late modern forms of power . . . [regulation] is bound up in a process of *normalization*' as it 'relies on categories that render individuals socially interchangeable with one another' (Butler 2004: 55, emphasis in original). The gender norms of the rigid regulatory frame 'operate by requiring the embodiment of certain ideals of femininity and masculinity' (Butler 1993: 231–2). The rigid regulatory frame can be elaborated through integration with the frameworks of gendered discourses and indexicality.

2.2 Gendered discourses and indexicality

In coining 'gendered discourses', Sunderland argues that the term 'gendered' clearly signals that gender 'already is part of the "thing"' which it describes (Sunderland 2004: 20). 'Discourses' in this sense are defined following the macro-definition of 'practices that systematically form the objects of which they speak' (Foucault 1972: 49). When defined in this manner, 'discourses' can be seen as '*carrying* ideology' (Sunderland 2004: 6, emphasis in original). This approach to conceptualising discourses is, to quote Heller, 'obviously linked to the notion of ideology, in so far as ideologies are understood as means of structuring and orienting domains of activity, and therefore inform discursive production and content'(Heller 2001: 120). Integrating this model of gendered discourses with performativity enables researchers to focus upon the systems which regulate gendered norms and govern our judgements and evaluations of one another through analyses of discursive content and production.

According to Sunderland (2004: 52–5), one crucial overarching discourse is the 'gender differences discourse' – an all-encompassing discourse governing gendered norms and notions of appropriate gendered behaviour: '[i]t is a significant "lens" for the way people view reality, *difference* being for most people what gender is all about. Once its "common-sense" status has been contested, "Gender differences" can be *seen* as such' (Sunderland 2004: 52, emphasis in original). It successfully operates upon the widely accepted view that women and men are inherently different due to biological differences that exist between them. From a sociolinguistic perspective, within the overarching 'gender differences discourse' there is the persistence of the inaccurate, scientifically unproven and stereotypical view, perpetuated by the mass media and popular culture publications, that owing to differences in biological hardwiring men and women speak in intrinsically different ways over and above what can be ascribed to basic anatomical factors (Cameron 2003, 2007).

In contrast, a gendered discourses approach enables masculinities and femininities to be viewed as non-binary, pluralised concepts. Nevertheless, a dominant hegemonic discourse of heterosexual femininity as well as one of heterosexual masculinity (Sauntson 2008: 276) can be identified, where hegemony is broadly defined as 'people's compliance in their own oppression' (Mills 1997: 30). These discourses can be viewed as being contained within the overarching gender differences discourse, working to regulate Butler's aforementioned 'ideals' of femininity and masculinity.

The analytical usefulness of the Foucauldian-influenced notion of dominant gendered discourses has been utilised across disciplines investigating the complexities of gender identities within the workplace, including sociology (Fitzsimons 2002). Fitzsimons classifies the 'hegemonic discourse of femininity' with the identity categories of emotionality, maternity, deviousness, slyness, untrustworthiness and bitchiness (Fitzsimons 2002: 152). In contrast, the 'hegemonic discourse of masculinity' is characterised by rationality, competitiveness, power, emotional control and independence (2002: 103). Her typologies identify men in the public sphere, in professional occupations, whereas women are identified either within the private sphere as mothers/carers, or if in the public sphere, within caring professions.

Our performances of gender identities are assessed and encoded through these hegemonic discourses. It is thus important to emphasise that, as they are hegemonic, they are not all-encompassing and controlling. They rely on consent and can be challenged. Resistant, alternative and competing discourses including feminist discourses do emerge (Coates 1997). However, such resistance may come at a price. For example, if women stray beyond the boundaries of expectation for acceptable 'feminine' language use, they may be subject to negative evaluation and viewed as deviant or aberrant for breaking gendered norms and expectations (Lakoff 2003). The theoretical framework of indexicality helps to elucidate this perspective further.

Ochs (1992) argues that a model for language and gender analysis should be composed of direct indexical relations and indirect indexical relations. Direct indexicality refers to referential lexical items where gender is directly encoded, such as 'boy'/'girl'. Indirect indexicality, which is far more frequent, refers to particular ways of speaking which come to be indexicalised with specific gendered meanings, and thus we can talk of encoded *gendered* speech styles. Early language and gender studies which searched for gender differences can be re-interpreted through the indexicality perspective. The majority of these studies found that women were more indirect, co-operative and collaborative than men in their interactional speech styles (see Holmes 2006 for a detailed summary). Instead of simply dismissing these findings as overgeneralisations, we can reinterpret them as ideological expectations governed by the 'rigid regulatory frame' of the gender differences discourse. Early work thus provides 'an analytic window that constructed and constrained women's linguistic stage, offering a set of features that operated stereotypically and en masse to help index "woman"' (Queen 2004: 291–2).

Furthermore, it is important to highlight that these ideological expectations of women's language are also raced, classed and sexualised. Queen argues that Lakoff's (1975) descriptors of women's speech styles commented 'just as strongly on racial, social-class and sexual-identity stereotypes as they did on gender' (2004: 292), with Lakoff presenting a trope of white, middle-class, Western (presumably) heterosexual linguistic features. Thus, earlier findings give evidence of gendered expectations, norms and conventions, which hold that the speech norms stereotypically associated with white, middle-class, heterosexual women are the most powerful, hegemonic discourse styles for *all* women to follow – that is, the speech style imbued with the most linguistic and cultural capital in Western societies (Bourdieu 1991).

In summary, indexicality represents a fruitful way forward for sociolinguistic language and gender studies as it shifts the focus from debates about 'when' gender may be relevant in analysis to focus instead upon '*how* gender is relevant' (McElhinny 2003: 35). It also acknowledges that gender stereotypes ideologically prescribe gendered behaviour, thus presenting a clear rationale to explain why interactional speech styles are deemed to be more appropriate for some speakers but not for others.

In contrast to early work, findings influenced by the indexicality approach have found that women managers utilise a wide-range of different linguistic styles, characterised as a 'wide-verbal repertoire' (Holmes 2006; Marra et al. 2006). Studies have also found that women and men managers use a range of similar strategies to perform their gender and professional leadership identities in a way entirely appropriate to their status and role (Mullany 2007). Marra et al. (2006: 244) have utilised the communities of practice (CofP) approach (see also Moore, this volume; Coupland, this volume) to enhance understandings of speech styles in specific workplaces, arguing that workplaces can be categorised on a continuum ranging from 'more feminine' to 'more masculine' CofPs.

However, while empirical evidence has shown that the speech styles women and men managers perform may be remarkably similar, the crucial point is that they may not be evaluated and assessed in the same manner, thus highlighting how gender ideologies affect how we evaluate one another. Marra et al. (2006) draw attention to the fact that exactly the same linguistic strategies can be evaluated very differently depending upon whether they are spoken by a woman or a man, with women often being subject to stigmatisation and negative evaluation. As McConnell-Ginet (2000) comments, men and women in the professions expect different things from each other and evaluate one another very differently, often leading to women being undervalued while men are overvalued.

2.3 The search for legitimate identities

In the field of Organisational Studies, Alvesson and Billing (1997) comment that among the most crucial problems women face in the professions is how to perform acceptable, legitimate social identities. They argue that, while the 'modern career woman' has now become an acceptable identity category, it is crucial for women managers not to deviate far from the traditional view of hegemonic femininity associated with 'sexual attractiveness' and 'family orientation' (Alvesson and Billing 1997: 98).

In analysing the identity performances of women trying to break through the glass ceiling, I am particularly interested in examining if there is any evidence of the performance of the identity categories from Kanter's (1977) ground-breaking sociological work on identity role categorisations. Kanter introduced a range of gender identities which she perceived to be developing at the time for women managers within organisations. She defined these identity categories as minority roles which could develop further as more women entered organisations.

The first category, the 'mother role', clearly falls under the dominant hegemonic discourse of femininity, representing women managers as caring and nurturing, qualities displayed through facilitative, cooperative and thus stereotypically feminine speech styles. In contrast, the 'iron maiden' is characterised instead by the performance of masculine speech styles, thus according with the dominant norms of hegemonic masculinity. Attempting to fulfil both these roles can result in women being subject to what can be considered a double bind.

The category of 'seductress' describes a woman who has strayed too far beyond the discoursal boundary of acceptable hegemonic femininity. She has gone from being harmless and sexually attractive to using her sexuality as a manipulative tool against men. She is thus subject to negative evaluation, risking 'the debasement of the whore' (Kanter 1977: 234). She may be forced to leave the workplace. The 'pet' arguably occupies more of a transitional category, showing some movement away from traditional femininity, with women being included in humour and seen as 'one of the boys'. However, while these women are seen as fun, they are not perceived as equals.

3. Data and methodology

Previous sociolinguistic language and gender researchers have drawn quite extensively upon the notion of indirect indexicality to investigate the performance of gendered identities in professional workplaces (Holmes 2005, 2006; Mullany 2007; Schnurr forthcoming).

In this chapter I will broaden the analytical focus of indexicality by exploring the multiplicity of identity performances in the professional workplace through an examination of both direct indexicality and indirect indexicality gained via a multi-method ethnographic approach.

A focus upon direct indexicality is popular within certain circles of conversation analysis. Such analysts argue that only by analysing instances of direct indexicality, 'where speakers use explicit gender references' (Stokoe and Smithson 2001: 275), can researchers be certain that gender is relevant to an interaction. From this analytical perspective, highlighting lexical terms which directly indexicalise gender is not enough in itself – there also needs to be evidence that interactants then focus upon gender in the subsequent interaction (Stokoe and Smithson 2001: 275; Stokoe 2008). In contrast, I believe that both indirect and direct indexicality can be integrated to analyse language and gender.[2] In addition to examining indirect indexicality through gendered speech styles, it will be fruitful to analyse instances of direct gender indexicality, where referential gender categories are directly foregrounded and become the topic of interaction in interview data, thus providing a useful technique to assess participants' own direct conceptualisations of gender identity categories.

The analysis focuses upon the identity performances of three women managers: Amy, from a retail organisation, and Kate and Becky from a manufacturing company. These participants are selected as they are all actively trying to break through the glass ceiling, as well as being united by the fact that they all work in the area of sales. Sales positions in both companies are heavily male-dominated, and they are the first women within their respective organisations to break through the company's managerial structure in this particular domain. Kate and Becky are aged 31 and Amy is 38. None of them has children. Amy occupies an upper-middle-management post, while Kate and Becky are middle managers. Amy will break through the glass ceiling if she can gain promotion to the next level. Kate and Becky have two more managerial levels to go before they can enter the boardroom. Focusing upon their identity performances should provide an insight into how they align themselves with particular gender identity categories within their respective workplaces. Examining women at different stages on the career progression ladder but from similar sales occupations should give an interesting perspective on perceptions of career progression at different managerial stages in these organisations. Unlike Kate and Becky, Amy has a team of people working for her, and meeting data were recorded where she could be witnessed directly enacting her leadership roles. I will thus analyse both meeting and interview data to study Amy's identity performance.

I will focus upon interview data extracts where interviewees use narratives which include directly indexicalised gender terms to perform either their own identities autobiographically or to construct the identities of their colleagues. The use of interviews as a research method to elicit narratives of identity performance is a long-standing technique in sociolinguistics, and it is well documented that narrative 'plays a key role in the construction of gender' (Thornborrow and Coates 2005: 8). Furthermore, Holmes and Marra point out that 'narrative analysis clearly offers researchers an additional source of insight into the ideological significance of the way people talk at work' (2005: 212), aptly illustrating the complexities of social identity performance in the workplace. A detailed rationale for methodology and data elicitation techniques can be found in Mullany (2006, 2007).

4. Analysis

4.1 Flower fairy little girlie versus the business woman

The analysis commences with a focus upon Amy talking about the development of her professional career. Her narrative performance of identity is particularly revealing if we view her representation of businesses from the perspective of Marra et al.'s (2006) masculine–feminine workplace continuum. Amy categorises the company she previously worked for as follows (directly indexicalised gender phrases are highlighted in bold):

> *Extract 1*
> I went into **a very soft feminine environment** . . . there were the company shop visits which were 'come on **girlies**' you know 'nicey nicey nice' . . . but then you'd go to a franchise meeting talking about slashing costs and you can't be **flower fairy little girlie** you've got to be **the business woman** . . . I'd had enough after three years and left . . .

Amy identifies the workplace as a 'very soft feminine environment' and then uses the directly indexicalised term 'girlie' in a pejorative form, with a series of diminutives to signal her dissociation and dissatisfaction with this gendered identity category. She negatively evaluates this 'feminine' culture. Her identity performance clearly indicates that she does not value a 'feminine' approach to sales and that she perceives this to be an insufficient way to enact managerial identity. She dichotomises the highly negative, diminutive identity category of 'flower fairy little girlie' with 'the business woman', the alternative category with which she clearly identifies herself. As part of her use of reported dialogue as a narrative technique, the terminology she uses to critique this 'soft feminine' managerial approach directly echoes a feature of Lakoff's (1975) women's language. Arguably Amy constructs 'nicey nicey nice', not as a direct report of speech that actually took place but as a summary of a 'fantasy' dialogue to encapsulate all that is wrong with these 'soft feminine' styles. Amy clearly rejects a more 'feminine' CofP workplace, positioning this in direct opposition to what she would expect for success in sales.

4.2 The 'iron maiden' and the 'mother role'

In a detailed study of Amy's interactional speech styles in two CofPs there is evidence of her using 'a wide-verbal-repertoire' (see Mullany 2007: 169–76), and the majority of strategies she uses to enact her authority are cooperative, aligning her with her current workplace culture. However, there are instances where Amy uses strategies stereotypically associated with masculine speech styles with subordinates:

> *Extract 2*
> *Amy is discussing company 'forfeits' that teams are given if they fill out rotas incorrectly*
> Amy: When I got them in {departmental name} I gave

> them back to the managers (.) who'd let me down
> so they ended up doing the forfeits (smile voice))
> so be warned
> ((laughter from all subordinates))

Amy: Don't do it
Mary: hh. (-)

Amy issues a direct warning using the performative speech act, mitigated only by a 'smile voice', followed by a direct directive. The next example, taken from the same departmental CofP meeting, conversely demonstrates Amy drawing upon a range of stereotypically feminine speech styles:

Extract 3
Amy: Anything Eddie?
Eddie: No not today
Amy: No
          ((laughter from many))
Amy: How are you feeling?
Eddie: Alright yeah I've been round with Bobbie this morning
Amy: Good (-) okay (-) Kirsty?
Kirsty: Nothing
Amy: Yeah you're feeling okay?
Kirsty: Yeah
Amy: Erm I was just gonna say what you just need to remember
          is there's all of us (.) so if there's anything just shout up you know

Kirsty and Eddie are new members of Amy's CofP, and this is their first departmental meeting. Amy ensures all team members have the opportunity to take the conversational floor at the end of her meetings. When asking Eddie she follows this with the question 'How are you feeling?' and then does the same with Kirsty. She goes on to emphasise, using hedges and minimisers ('just', 'you know'), that if they need anything they can approach any team member. Amy thus performs stereotypical feminine speech strategies here and there is evidence of the 'mother role'. She can clearly be seen as caring for the emotional well-being of her subordinates. In interview, she explicitly comments that she sees part of her role as having to 'nurture' subordinates.

Nevertheless, Amy experiences a range of negative evaluations from subordinates, status equals and superiors, men and women alike, which was evident from the moment I began the ethnographic data collection. She was described as 'bossy', 'bombastic' and 'dragon-like'. She is referred to via a whole range of negative identity categories, including 'tyrant', in numerous interviews. Another subordinate commented that 'she's quite abrupt you know as a woman'. There is clear evidence of Amy being subject to the aforementioned double bind for using interactional strategies outside of the stereotypical gendered expectation. The negative evaluation she experiences can be classified as part of the identity category of 'iron maiden'. Amy herself acknowledges that she uses 'masculine' speech features, aligning herself in direct opposition to the identity category which she characterises as a 'typical female manager':

Extract 4
Amy: I talk and act more like **a man** . . . I'm not your **typical female manager**
. . . some people find my (-) erm directness difficult (.)

4.3 'Northern lasses'

The first example of direct indexicality from interview data with Kate and Becky occurs
when they are talking about their own perceptions of the sales field:

Extract 5
Becky: it's more difficult being a **woman** in sales and I think
especially in our trade there's not many **female account managers**
within the company trade in fact we were the first
(.) it tends to be **a lad thing** . . . you've got to be (-) **one of
the lads** like Northern and stuff like that so (-) there's
definitely erm a difference in it . . . I think if we were **men** in
this role if I'm totally honest if we were **men** in this role we'd
have more of a mark on the business that we do (.)
Kate: and a bit more respect
Becky: yeah definitely
Kate: The other thing that we've both got is that we're both
Northern lasses so we do get a lot of like gags I mean everybody
knows that they can be very open with us but sometimes I don't think
it always works to our best advantage even though I mean there are
a lot of people that are from like wealthy backgrounds or could have
been aren't there and we are just like **dead normal girls**

Becky initially highlights the problem of a lack of female managers in sales, and then
directly identifies their profession as 'a lad thing'. One identity category that they collectively construct is 'northerners'. Becky evaluates their regional identities positively,
giving them strength to succeed in selling products. By having a regional accent they can
perform being 'one of the lads' when they are in the field with customers (cf. Trudgill's
1974 notion of covert prestige). Kate builds upon this, using the regionalised gendered
variant 'Northern lasses' to characterise their combined gendered and regional identities.
She also draws attention to another positive, derived from a long-standing stereotype of
'Northerners' in England speaking their minds and being 'open' and 'honest'.

However, despite these perceived advantages associated with their regional Northern
identities, they both argue that they are not taken as seriously as men are when it comes
to making 'a mark on the business' and gaining 'respect'. Arguably, there is evidence of
the 'pet' identity here, particularly when Kate states that they are the subject of 'a lot
of gags' (jokes) – as mentioned above, in Kanter's 'pet' category women are perceived
as fun but are not taken as seriously as their male counterparts. Furthermore, Kate
also presents this display of regional identity as disadvantageous when communicating
within the company, as a number of colleagues are from 'wealthy backgrounds' and thus
by implication do not speak with regionalised accents/dialects in workplace interactions (confirmed by my ethnographic observations). Kate uses the direct indexicalised

category 'dead normal girls' as a positive in-group identity marker for her and Becky, but also as a category that marks them out as different from those from a higher social class grouping.

4.4. 'Seductresses' and 'career women'

There is evidence of Kate and Becky receiving negative evaluation from male colleagues, not as a result of any performance of their regional identities, but instead through perceived performances of their sexual identities. According to David, their status equal:

> *Extract 6*
> David: Two **female account managers** here are not slow to use the combi-
>   nation of will and gender to good effect when they can see an opportu-
>   nity to do so and that's usually in the direction of **a male person** get
>   what they want I've no doubt about it

This is a prototypical example of the construction of the 'seductress' identity, with David negatively evaluating Kate and Becky for their perceived attempts to manipulate male superiors. Extract 6 thus illustrates that within the 'career woman' category the perform-ance of sexual identities is precariously balanced. As far as David is concerned, Becky and Kate have overstepped the mark by trying to make career progression based upon what he later calls 'sexual wiles' versus his 'skill'. There is evidence here, arguably, of a perceived threat to dominant hegemonic masculinity and the traditional norms of the sales domain as a result of the combined gender and sexual identity performances of Kate and Becky, as constructed by David.

Finally, in Extract 7 Kate tells a narrative about what kind of 'identity' category a female superior informed her she could legitimately occupy:

> *Extract 7*
> Kate: I remember going out for a meal it was the first meal for the {xxx}
>   Committee [and] the {job title} director was there and there
> Louise: [mm]
> Kate: was a few people there and I remember her saying 'you you don't want
>   kids you'll be **a career woman**' and I said 'no actually I do want kids'
>   and it was quite ((puts on a mocking voice)) 'no no you can't' ((laughs))
>   no I CAN'T have them

The director whose speech Kate presents is one of only two women to break through the glass ceiling in this organisation. Alvesson and Billing's (1997) legitimate identity cat-egory of 'career woman' is explicitly referenced through the directly indexicalised term, but Kate reports how she was told that she cannot occupy the identities of both a career woman and a mother. In interview this director explicitly stated her belief that she herself was able to break through the glass ceiling precisely because she did not have children. In interview, Kate and Becky express both a wish to have children and their frustration at having to openly deny such desires.

5. Discussion

The analysis of gender identity categories in relation to three women managers attempting to break through the glass ceiling has been very revealing. The women can all be viewed as performing a range of different gender identities, including the full range of categories initially identified by Kanter (1977). Despite the different gender identities that Amy performs, she is negatively evaluated and subject to the double bind for going against gendered norms and expectations. Whilst Amy perceives herself to be a good manager, she is not an effective leader in the sense defined by Marra et al., who state that one has to ensure a balance between 'getting the work done and keeping people happy' (2006: 256). Nonetheless, a few months after recording officially finished Amy did break through the glass ceiling within this organisation, though she had to take a promotion over 300 miles away, something that she argued was only achievable as she was single and without children.

As Butler points out, gender intersects with 'racial, class, ethnic, sexual and regional modalities of discursively constructed identities' (1999: 6). Examination of Kate and Becky's narrative performances of gender identities has enabled important observations to be made regarding the complex and multilayered nature of identity performances. In Kate and Becky's case, a key aspect of their self-reported social identities, in conjunction with gender, was regionality and, additionally (if only by its conflation with 'Northernness'), social class. Sexualised identities also emerged as another salient identity category when Kate and Becky's identities were being reflected upon by a male colleague. These findings highlight the importance of attempting to account for the full complexity of identities in future work, and also emphasise the importance of ensuring that women from different social class, regional and ethnic backgrounds are investigated. This may result in researching not just the professions but a range of different workplaces, as in, for example, recent work on low-paid, menial positions in call centres (Cameron 2003; Hultgren 2008) and factories (Holmes and Stubbe 2003).

6. Conclusion

A multitude of issues has been raised in this sociolinguistic examination of gendered identities and the glass ceiling. Coming back to the original aim, it is hoped that these findings have gone some way towards revealing and challenging ideological propositions that are preventing women from breaking though the glass – or concrete – ceiling. The one manager in my study who did manage to achieve this was very unpopular and needed to be able to relocate to somewhere more than 300 miles away. The issues of flexibility, work–home balance and childcare are particularly salient, and they reflect the major concern expressed in the Equality and Human Rights Commission (2008) report, that the decision to have children still seriously derails women's careers.

Overall, the findings of this chapter appear to raise more problems than solutions in terms of the negotiation of the glass ceiling. However, it is hoped that raising awareness of gendered speech norms and gendered discourses maintained by gender ideologies can contribute towards helping individuals unpick prejudices and negative stereotypes. By integrating an investigation of sociolinguistic speech styles with a consideration of broader gendered discourses through performativity and indexicality, it is clear that it is not just sociolinguistic attitudes, prejudices and judgements, but also a range of broader social/ political issues, that need to be addressed if workplace equality is ever to be achieved. An interdisciplinary approach to future academic work, drawing much further upon the disciplines touched upon in this chapter, could help sociolinguists move further towards the overarching political goal of bringing about gender equality and seeing women from a range of different ethnic, class and regional backgrounds breaking through the glass, or concrete, ceiling.

Notes

1. FTSE 100 stands for the 100 companies which make up the *Financial Times Stock Exchange* Index. These companies are the largest on the London Stock Exchange and the index is utilised most frequently by governmental organisations when compiling workplace statistics in Britain.
2. I have recently argued that lexical terms which directly index gender are excellent lexical tools to utilise as starting points to develop multilayered analyses of language, gender and indexicality in larger sets of business corpora, enabling quantitative techniques from corpus linguistics to be combined with qualitative analysis (Mullany 2008).

Part IV
Regions and Nations

17

Supralocal Regional Dialect Levelling

David Britain

1. Introduction

'Regional dialect levelling' or 'supralocalisation' are terms referring to the process by which, as a result of mobility and dialect contact, linguistic variants with a wider socio-spatial currency become more widespread at the expense of more localised forms. A classic example of this phenomenon is the ascendance, in Newcastle in the north-east of England, of the glottal stop [ʔ], a nonstandard, geographically and socially widespread supralocal variant of (t), at the expense of both the much more localised north-eastern 'glottal-reinforced' variant [ʔt] and the standard variant [t] (see, for example, Milroy et al. 1994a). Figure 17.1 shows results for the glottal stop and glottally reinforced variants across apparent time pooled from two studies, one of 5- and 10-year-old children and the other of younger and older adults.

Important for our discussion here is to note the rise across apparent time in the use of the supralocal [ʔ] and the fall across apparent time in the use of the local [ʔt]. We can also note that the supralocal form is in the ascendancy most obviously among middle-class women, and the local form has persisted most among men. These studies make it clear that the standard variant [t] plays relatively little role in the ongoing changes to (t) in this community.

Remarking upon the similarities of their findings in Newcastle with those in Cardiff and the Wirral (Mees 1987; Newbrook 1986), Milroy et al. (1994a: 352) conclude that 'the glottal stop – the variant favoured by females – has become supralocal and apparently quite generalized in its distribution in contemporary British English'. The patterns of change highlighted in this example have been replicated in many different communities: for example, Vandekerckhove (2005) in Belgium; Røyneland (2009) in Norway; Hernández-Campoy and Villena-Ponsoda (2009) in Spain; Hornsby (2009) in France; Christen (1997) in German-speaking Switzerland; Cornelissen (1999) in Germany, Al-Wer (1997) in the Arab world; and Altendorf (2003), Britain (2005), Przedlacka (2002), Torgersen and Kerswill (2004) and Watt (1998, 2002; Watt and Milroy 1999) in England.

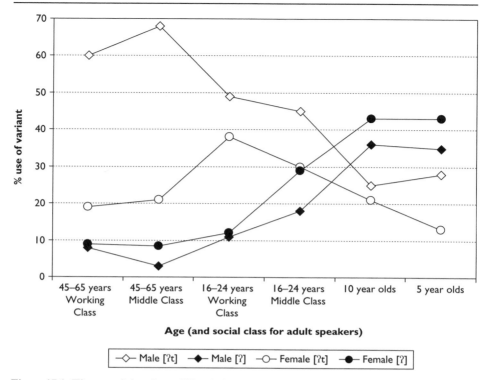

Figure 17.1 The use of glottal stop [ʔ] and glottally reinforced [ʔt] variants of (t) in Newcastle. The data for this graph are drawn from Milroy et al. (1994a) and Docherty et al. (1997).

2. Deconstructing supralocal regional dialect levelling

2.1 Levelling

Levelling is a widely used term in dialectology to denote the process by which, over time, a reduction in the number of variants[1] of the same variable occurs. It is used in two distinct contexts. In, for example, studies of verbal morphology, 'levelling' is often used to describe analogical developments leading to a reduction of forms within a paradigm. For example, Schilling-Estes and Wolfram (1994: 284–5) examine how in Ocracoke, North Carolina, speakers are gradually adopting *was* ('was levelling') as the form of past BE in affirmative contexts, irrespective of person and number (cf. Standard: *was* and *were*) – and in negative contexts they are adopting *weren't* ('were/n't levelling') (cf. Standard: *wasn't* and *weren't*). Here, one form is spreading across the person/number paradigm at the expense of other forms normally used in other parts of the system – this process is sometimes also labelled 'simplification' as it reduces paradigmatic redundancy in the grammar (for example Mühlhäusler 1980; Trudgill 1986).

More commonly, 'levelling' is used to show how, in dialect contact situations (such as in the aftermath of colonial migrations, or in recently established New Towns), one variant emerges victorious from the mixing of many different dialect variants of the same variable. For example, Prompapakorn (2005) analysed the consequences of dialect contact in Ban Khlong Sathon (BKS) in north-east Thailand, a town established in the 1960s originally to rehouse people from around the country following the establishment of National Parks to protect vulnerable rainforest. Prompapakorn recorded representatives of the settler generation and their descendants to examine the consequences of contact. One variable examined was the use of [r], [l] or [h] in words such as /rian/ 'study', variably realised as [rian], [lian] and [hian]. [r] is the standard variant, [l] the variant used in central Thailand, including Bangkok and the area surrounding BKS itself, and [h] the form most frequent in the Isan region near the border with Laos, though all areas use [l] to some extent. As expected, Prompapakorn found [l] to predominate in her data, but also that over time the other variants gradually disappeared from the community. [h], for example, represented 31 per cent of all tokens among the settlers from Isan, but only 2 per cent among their grandchildren. [h] and [r] had, then, been levelled away in favour of the majority [l]. As we will see, this form of levelling is the most relevant in the supralocal contexts under discussion here.

One question which has arisen in the context of levelling is how far we can predict the forms that will prevail in such contact situations. It is very often the case that *majority variants* in the contact community will level away all others (regardless of whether that majority form is a standard form or stigmatised). A case has also been put forward suggesting a role for (i) markedness – all other things being equal, unmarked forms survive at the expense of marked forms; (ii) a role for social/regional stereotyping (forms which do *not* have strong social/regional connotations are likely to be successful); and (iii) a (controversial) role for 'perceptual salience' (see Trudgill 1986; Kerswill and Williams 2002). In the majority of cases of contact, of course, these issues do not arise because there is one clear majority form in the dialect mix.

Some accounts of levelling incorporate other factors. Williams and Kerswill propose the following definition: 'a process whereby differences between regional varieties are reduced, features which make varieties distinctive disappear, and *new features emerge and are adopted by speakers over a wide geographical area*' (Williams and Kerswill 1999: 13, my emphasis). However, the emergence of new features and geolinguistic spread is usually classed as 'innovation diffusion' rather than 'levelling', as the outcome of 'levelling' is the victory of a pre-existing form, rather than the emergence of a new one (see Trudgill 1986, for example). The inclusion of innovation diffusion in the definition of supralocalisation could be seen as problematic, however, since many of the (especially consonantal) innovations currently spreading, for example, across Britain have by no means operated at a regional level, but at a supra-regional, national one (see Kerswill's [2003] discussion of the diffusion of TH-fronting). It is also the case that many diffusing innovations do not have the effect of eradicating a diverse range of local forms, but simply replace one conservative form with an innovative one. In the case of TH-fronting, the arrival of [f v] represents a relatively simple replacement of the overwhelmingly dominant conservative forms [θ ð] (cf. Britain 2005: 1016). In places which had other local variants (for example Liverpool [Watson 2007] with plosive variants), the diffusion of [f v] has been hindered.

There is a sense, though, in which the rapid diffusion of innovations may well be particularly vigorous and less constrained in communities where processes of levelling have been highly active. It is often argued that in fluid, highly mobile communities of the kind that are predisposed to levelling, social networks in the local community tend to be relatively weaker than in more stable communities (see, for example, Milroy and Milroy 1985a; Trudgill 1992). Given James and Lesley Milroy's convincing argument that 'linguistic change is slow to the extent that the relevant populations are well established and bound by strong ties, whereas it is rapid to the extent that weak ties exist in populations' (Milroy and Milroy 1985a: 375), it is not surprising that in those very areas where we find mobility, levelling and supralocalisation, new changes will find fewer barriers preventing their diffusion (see also Milroy 2004).

2.2 Regions

Important, I believe, to our understanding of the geographical *scale* of the linguistic developments under discussion here is a recognition of the fact that regions are not 'pre-given bounded spaces' (Allen et al. 1998: 137) awaiting analysis, but are formed by *social practice* (see further Beal, this volume). They are, then, *processes*, subject to change as human practices change, always in a state of 'becoming' (Pred 1985: 361). Following the lead of Allen et al., then, we need to apply a 'strongly relational approach to thinking about space and place' that 'understands both space and place as constituted out of spatialized social relations – and narratives about them – which not only lay down ever-new regional geographies, but also work to reshape social and cultural identities and how they are represented' (Allen et al. 1998: 1–2). I'll argue that dialectological 'regions' are formed as individuals interact while they go about their everyday lives, free to move but constrained in that movement by institutions of capital and the state (cf. Johnston 1991: 51).

This approach forces us to recognise that space is not only physical, but also social and perceptual (Britain in press a, b). Social space is important because it highlights how past events and manipulations of space can shape future ones. And our actions (and those of capital and the state) have the potential both to trigger change or to cement past practices even further. Since the performance of routinised face-to-face interaction entails movement across time and space, so these routines build up spatialised patterns – life-paths – for individuals and communities. Routine behaviours ensure that some 'paths' are well-worn, paths around our homes, paths to work, paths to consume, leading over time and on a community scale to the emergence of 'places' and 'regions'. Viewing places and regions in this way emphasises that they are shaped by practice, that they are processes rather than objects. We produce places and regions, but they in turn provide the context – enabling as well as constraining – for that production. And of course we live in a socio-economically differentiated world, and some will have more power and resources to shape space than others (see Johnston 1991: 67–8). Allen et al. (1998: 32) argue that 'thinking a region in terms of social relations stretched out reveals, not an "area", but a complex and unbounded lattice of articulations with internal relations of power and inequality and punctured by structural exclusions' (1998: 65).

2.3 Supralocal

The view of 'regions' as 'complex and unbounded lattices of articulations' rather than sharply predefined bounded entities lends preference to the term 'supralocal' as part of the descriptor for the sociodialectological processes under discussion here. 'Supra' denotes 'above', 'beyond', 'transcending', without having to commit to a particular geographical scale – it denotes simply a higher scale – or to a perspective that forces all variables to be analysed at that same scale. 'Regional' forces us to define the scale at a particular level, and has the unhelpful connotations of *fixed* geographical space that Allen et al. (1998) are keen to contest. 'Supralocal' conveys the desired message that what is happening is at a scale higher than that of the local, *without being more precise*. It allows us to examine: processes that are taking place, say, across the still fairly narrow geographical sphere of a large town relative to individual villages within that sphere; changes across a whole county or group of counties or districts relative to one large town in those counties; and significant chunks of a whole nation-state relative to counties within it. Some variables may only show levelling at one of the lower scales, others possibly at the higher scales, but all can then rightly be classed as supralocal levelling, and examined in the context of the eradication of features with a more circumscribed geographical and social distribution.

3. Why is supralocalisation happening?

It is generally agreed that this process is a result of the increased mobility and contact characteristic of everyday life in late modernity, and an increase in the scale of people's routine day-to-day spatialities. The linguistic accommodation that takes place in face-to-face interaction, particularly when routinely sustained over long periods, can lead to the stabilisation of accommodated linguistic behaviour (Trudgill 1986; Kerswill 2002). Since one product of convergent linguistic accommodation is levelling, highly local dialect forms are often beginning to be eroded, levelled away in favour of spatially more widely distributed variants.

Since the levelling of local dialect forms is driven by contact and mobility, it has to be recognised that supralocalisation at some level is not new. Ellis, for example, over a century ago, reported that:

> There are so many causes for interference with the natural development of speech, and the population is so shifting, that it would be misleading to suppose that there was any real hereditary dialect or mode of speech . . . the enormous congeries of persons from different parts of the kingdom and from different countries, and the generality of school education, render dialect nearly impossible. (Ellis 1889: 225)

It is probably not controversial, however, to argue that the scale of mobility and contact in the past half-century may well be unprecedented.[2] Spatial practices have changed, for example in England, as a result of, amongst other reasons:

- *Increasing urbanisation*: Champion (2001: 144) shows that between 1950 and 2030, the proportion of Northern Europe's population living in urban areas is set to increase from 72.7 per cent to 88.8 per cent, but also that urbanisation levels are beginning to plateau and that these figures hide important changes in the distribution of the urban population across different sizes of settlement, with the very largest cities having shrunk over the past half century (Oswalt and Rieniets 2006). The considerable linguistic consequences of urbanisation have long been recognised: Calvet argues that 'everywhere people are rushing from the countryside to false promises of the city, to its lights, to the hope of a more lucrative job. And this convergence of migrants to the city has linguistic repercussions' (Calvet 1994: 10, my translation; see also Bortoni-Ricardo 1985; Kerswill 1994). Calvet's claims of continued urbanisation no longer hold true in many parts of northern Europe and north America, however, with demographic trends reversing:

- *Increasing counterurbanisation*: migration out of cities and large towns to places of lower population concentration. Champion (1998) demonstrates that in the UK the greatest 'beneficiary' of counterurbanisation has been the 'remote rural' and 'most remote rural' settlement categories, with London and the other metropolitan cities shedding the largest proportions of their population;

- *Increased migration*: Tolfree examines migration within the area immediately to the south and west of London, showing some areas with very high district–internal migration (for instance north and east Kent) and some with very low levels of such migration (Surrey) (Tolfree 2004: 6). The pattern for cross-district migration is very different (see Figure 17.2, pane a). It shows heavy levels of migration in the areas bordering London, but notice also the lack of migration at the supra-regional level in the western area. There is also a concentration of

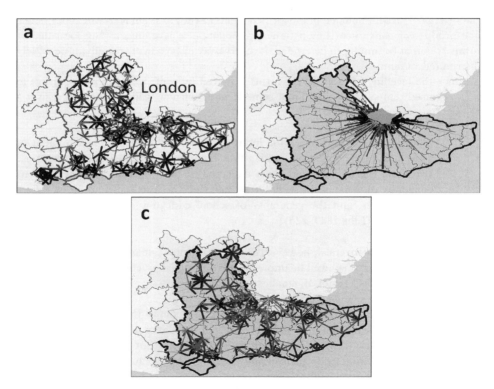

Figure 17.2 Migration and commuting patterns in South-East England. (a) Cross district migration; (b) commuting flows into London; (c) travel to work patterns. Darker arrows signify the participation of a greater proportion of the population (Tolfree 2004).

migration across the south coast. Tolfree (2004) also presents two patterns of commuting behaviour – one showing the strong pull of London for commuters (pane b) and another showing other travel-to-work patterns in the area (pane c). The distances over which people travel to work in London are markedly greater than those to other places within the region, though interdistrict commuting is nevertheless widespread (see also Green et al. 1999).

- *An expansion in uptake of higher levels of education* (in places often well away from the local speech community): In a report on widening participation in Higher Education, the UK National Audit Office (2008: 12) shows that university attendance rates have more than trebled since 1978.
- *Increases in public and private transportation*: The Department for Transport shows that: distances travelled by train increased by 55 per cent and by car by 1087 per cent between 1952 and 2007 (National Audit Office 2008: 14); the average distance travelled per person per year increased by 45 per cent between 1995 and 2006 (2008: 16) and the size of the road network increased by 32 per cent between 1952 and 2007 (2008: 125).
- *A shift from primary and secondary to tertiary sector employment as the backbone of the economy*, where 'many branches of industry have become increasingly freed from locational ties to natural resources' and 'many parts of the economy [have been given] an enormously high degree of potential mobility' (Allen et al. 1998: 141–2). Furthermore, there is a well-reported tendency for tertiary sector employment to relocate to financially more advantageous locations (Coe and Townsend 1998: 392).
- *An increase in mobile and flexible working* facilitated by transportation developments, the internet (allowing home-working, rapid connectivity from remoter rural areas, allowing businesses to relocate to financially advantageous locations, etc.), and employment legislation (for example flexibility around childcare).
- *Geographical reorientations of consumption behaviours* (shopping in out-of-town malls and hypermarkets, entertainment complexes, etc.). Findlay et al. demonstrate that recent migrants to rural areas are much more likely than longer-term residents to commute to work rather than work locally and do their shopping for milk, other food, petrol and newspapers in a town or city rather than locally (Findlay et al. 2001: 6).
- *Increasing geographical elasticity of family ties*. While the population of England increased by 9.5 per cent between 1971 and 2006, the proportion of single-person households under retirement age rose between 1971 and 2007 by 133 per cent (Self 2008: 2, 17).

There has, then, been a multitude of triggers that have made people mobile. Given these high levels of mobility – 11 per cent of the population of England and Wales moved in the *year* up to April 2001,[3] of which over a third were moves of over 10km – the levelling of distinctive highly localised dialect variants is unsurprising.

Allen et al.'s (1998) discussion of the ongoing reformation of the south-east under neoliberal economics comes to some important conclusions about 'the region' relevant to our discussion. First, they make it very clear that the 'region'-forming developments of the past half-century are extremely *unevenly distributed*. So rather than, for example, the south-east showing a rapid geo-economic homogenisation, they argue that on the contrary it became the region with the widest gap between rich and poor (Allen et al. 1998: 139), as some parts of the area were excluded from the benefits of economic growth. Second, they argue that the 'free market growth dynamics increased the separation of this part of the country from the rest', not just economically but also because 'the relative importance of the social relations linking the south-east with the rest of the country was quite considerably diminished. In part this was the result of ongoing processes of globalization and the more general effect of spatial disarticulation within local areas to which this leads' (1998: 138–9). Together these paint a picture of rapid but socially and geographically uneven developments within the region, but an increasing disengagement at the supraregional level. From the dialectological viewpoint, therefore, we must not be too hasty in nailing the coffin on intra-regional diversity, but, on the other hand, it is important (witness Watt, Llamas and Docherty's current work on the English–Scottish border[4] reported on in Llamas, this volume, and also Britain 2001) to look at the boundaries *between* regions as places where, if Allen et al (1998) are right, we may well find increasingly heightened diversity. The literature suggests a good deal of validity in their arguments.

Let's take, firstly, the idea of intra-regional diversity. It is undoubtedly the case that 'supralocalisation' is underway. One highly convincing piece of evidence supporting convergence in the south-east of England, for example, is the work of Torgersen and Kerswill (2004) examining phonological convergence between Ashford, Kent, and Reading, Berkshire, in south-east England. Here they found two quite distinct vowel systems which, over time, changed, making them considerably more alike. Ashford had to change most to achieve this, lowering the vowels in the DRESS and TRAP lexical sets (Wells 1982), backing STRUT, somewhat raising LOT and fronting FOOT and KIT (Torgersen and Kerswill 2004: 40), while Reading simply lowered STRUT, and, like Ashford, fronted FOOT (2004: 45).

But few, apart perhaps from 'Estuary English'-obsessed journalists, would claim that regional dialect levelling has eradicated *all* local diversity, or will in the future. The evidence we have reminds us not only that this is a *process* not a *fait accompli*, but also that supralocalisation can be spotted even in its relatively early stages. In the Newcastle (t) example, the supralocal glottal stop variant did not account for more than 50 per cent of the tokens for *any* of the social groups considered. Empirical studies of the south-east of England have, on the one hand, found evidence of convergence, but, nevertheless, still found considerable diversity in the extent of adoption of the convergent forms in different parts of the region. Przedlacka (2002), for example, shows that while four of the counties surrounding London appear to be dialectally converging, they are doing so to different extents, at different speeds, for different variables. Half of the variables she examined in her recordings of young speakers showed statistically significant differences between different counties, showing that while convergence may be underway, it is by no means complete or evenly distributed. She claimed, consequently, that 'the extent of geographical variation alone allows us to conclude that we are dealing with a number of distinct accents, not a single and definable variety' (Przedlacka 2002: 97). Furthermore, for some variables, she found no change across real time at all – her teenagers had levels of glottal stop use for (t) that matched Survey of English Dialects (Orton and Dieth 1962–71) speakers born a century before. Research in other south-eastern communities has found some supralocal forms being adopted, others not, and others still morphing

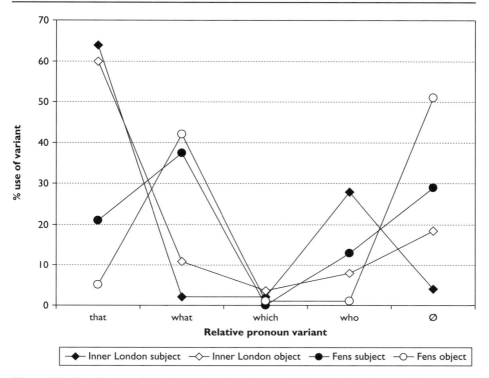

Figure 17.3 Distribution of relative markers in subject and object function in (inner) London and the Fens (from Cheshire et al. 2007).

into localised hybrid interdialect forms (Britain 2005), while an examination of relative pronoun choice contrasting London and the East Anglian Fens showed little evidence of structural similarity (Figure 17.3).

We must also not forget social diversity in supralocalisation. One consistent finding, for example, is the leading role played by women in the adoption of supralocal forms (Milroy et al. 1994b; Milroy 1999; Watt and Milroy 1999). In discussing this robust finding, Holmes argues that

> women are often the family brokers in interaction with outsiders: it is more often women than men who interact with others in shops and neighbourhood inter-actions, as well as in communications with schools, and between institutional bureaucracies and the family . . . women's social activities and jobs often involve them in interaction with a wider range of social contacts than men's (Holmes 1997: 199).

Demographic data from England also suggest that women are much more likely than men to work in (spatially fluid) 'linguistic marketplace' tertiary-sector employment (Self 2008: 51), such as sales and customer service, and are more likely than men to move home in their late teens and early twenties (Champion 2005: 94; see further Sayers 2009).

Furthermore, not everyone is equally mobile. Social inequality may well hinder mobility and consequently restrict interaction with people outside the immediate neighbourhood. Some people therefore have a greater potential to come into contact with non-locals than others, and this undoubtedly has consequences for processes such as supralocalisation. Trudgill, for example, has argued that the south-eastern supralocal dialect is a 'lower middle class' variety (Trudgill 2002: 180). We must, in sum, therefore recognise that 'the fact that social processes take place over space and in a geographically-differentiated world affects their operation' (Massey 1985: 16).

Variationist dialect boundary work in England in many ways supports Allen et al.'s view of *regional* divergence. My own work (for example Britain 2001) on the section of the TRAP–BATH boundary running through the Fens, often seen as a marker of the separation of the linguistic 'north' (where the TRAP and BATH vowels are homophonous) from the 'south' of England (where they are distinct), showed a *sharpening* of the boundary over apparent time, with the geographical distance across the transition zone becoming narrower and variability within the zone more polarised in favour of one or other of the variants.

4. Supralocalisation, attitudes and identities

This chapter concludes by looking at the rather controversial issue of the role of active identity work in bringing about the adoption of supralocal forms. It has often been stated that dialect contact produces 'neutral' outcomes as distinctive socially or regionally marked forms are levelled away (for example Mæhlum 1996; Kerswill and Williams 2000: 89). One consequence of this has been that levelled contact varieties have often been viewed by non-linguists as relatively 'standard'-like (for example Bernard 1969; Gordon 1983; Trudgill 1986). So Ellis is able to cite both Froude's view that mid-nineteenth-century Australian English was 'free from provincialism, not Americanised, of soft tone, good language and correct aspiration' (Ellis 1889: 237) as well as that of a Mr Little who claimed that the levelled dialect of Fenland Wisbech had 'very little dialect proper' (1889: 253) and that 'the fen country generally is the home of pure speech, by which I mean, of language but little differing from the ordinary literary English' (1889: 254). The question that arises about this apparent 'neutrality', and supralocalisation more generally, is the extent to which it is a relatively unmotivated product of dialect contact (Trudgill 2004, 2008) or the product of deliberate speaker choices. This neutrality, proposed in the context of supralocalisation, is driven, some argue, by a desire not to 'signal a strong or specific local affiliation' (Kerswill 2002: 198).

Watt's approach (1998, 2002) adds an extra dimension. In arguing that young Newcastle speakers are using supralocal forms of some variables to 'sound like Northerners, but modern Northerners' (Watt 1998: 7), we see a claim that there may be some positive association with a more regional identity (as a Northerner more broadly rather than as someone from Newcastle), as opposed to simply a negative reaction to local forms. Foulkes and Docherty (1999b) follow this up by suggesting that speakers have to negotiate a somewhat difficult path between not sounding too local, but also not overly disassociating themselves with the locality thereby showing apparent disloyalty (see also Kerswill 2002).

Llamas (2007b) also seeks to shed light on the agency driving supralocal changes in her investigations of change in Middlesbrough, in the north-east of England. She outlines the historical reorientation of the city – politically, socially, perceptually – from firstly looking south to Yorkshire, then north to Tyneside, and finally gaining some local political independence. The variables she examines are (p t k), which in this part of England have (at least) three variants each: standard [p t k], glottally reinforced [ʔp ʔt ʔk] often associated with Tyneside, and glottalled [ʔ] which, for (t), has a wide geographical distribution. She finds that:

- (p): [ʔp] is dominant, with higher levels found among older and younger speakers and a dip among the middle-aged, showing stereotypical stable variability (Llamas 2007b: 590);
- (t): [ʔ] has gone from being the minority variant among the old to being almost categorical among the young (2007b: 592);
- Only a minority of tokens show either of the two glottal forms of (k), with [k] dominant (2007b: 594).

Overall, speakers combine a variant largely restricted to the north-east, (p): [ʔp], with a nonstandard form widespread across the whole country (t): [ʔ], alongside a more standard-like (k): [k]. In addition, Llamas presents an analysis of comments made by her informants about their perceptions of their dialect and their area. These largely reflected the changing geographical orientations, though with little positive association at any point with Tyneside. The younger speakers, according to Llamas, demonstrate 'an increased confidence . . . in the status of Middlesbrough both in terms of its accent and in terms of it as a "place"' (2007b: 601).

How can we reconcile these somewhat different approaches? Firstly, we have to recognise that our choice of variables for analysis may lead us to different conclusions, given, as was argued earlier, it is extremely unlikely that *all* local features would ever be levelled away. Second, supralocalisation is socially differentiated: class, gender, economic activity and many more factors intermingle to ensure that regional homogeneity would be an unexpected outcome. I would argue that we should look more readily to *spatial practices*, wherein we will find differing intensities of local, supralocal and regional engagement. The geographical dispersion of our life-paths and the consequent contact with other varieties does not preclude us from still spending time moving in and around our neighbourhoods. We haven't suddenly lost all contact with the local. It is hardly surprising, then, that we adopt locally specific constellations of regional, supralocal and local forms, rather than adopting forms from one scale alone. Towns and cities are perhaps more likely to retain local dialect forms in this context, because, given the geographies of service provision, they are more 'self-sufficient' than many rural communities.

Earlier, it was proposed that 'places' and 'regions' were created through densities of routinised socially and institutionally constrained mobilities in space. Seeing space as something we interact with as we go about our daily lives enables us to be sensitive to changes in spatial orientations as a result of changes in spatial practice, to see how these practices are variable, socially differentiated and mediated by institutional forces, and to see how the intersection of our spaces with those of others can give them social meaning. We draw our spatial identities from the routinised practices we engage in in space and the ways those practices connect (or not) with those of others. In turn, these identities contribute towards the creation of contexts for subsequent spatial behaviour.

Increasingly, in late-modern Western societies, our spatial practices routinely take us further and bring us into contact with others who speak differently from us. Consequently, processes of levelling affecting some variables in our speech lead us to adopt forms with broader supralocal or regional currency. Our spatial interactions are multiscalar, however, so we are able to combine more supralocal forms with more locally focused ones too. And all of this is, of course, still passed through a complex sociolinguistic filter of diversity and differentiation.

Notes

1. As is standard in the Anglophone variationist tradition, the terms 'variant' and 'dialect' include standard variants and dialects. I do not regard standard forms as being especially forceful or dominant in the supralocalisation process *per se*. The British literature (for example, the classic example above) suggests they tend to play a role commensurate with the relatively low numbers of speakers of standard varieties in most British speech communities.
2. The nineteenth century saw rapid urbanisation as a result of triggers in industrial development. The massive population rises seen at the same time were only partly due to mobility and migration, and also linked to falling mortality rates, higher birth rates and increasing life-expectancy.
3. http://www.statistics.gov.uk/cci/nugget.asp?id=1310 (accessed 26 February 2009).
4. ESRC Grant: RES-062-23-0525; *Linguistic variation and national identities on the Scottish/English border* (see further http://www.york.ac.uk/res/aiseb).

18

Migration, National Identity and the Reallocation of Forms

Judy Dyer

1. Introduction

Over time, particularly in dialect contact situations, the indexical value or social meaning of a linguistic feature may change. This chapter describes the reallocation of linguistic forms brought about by Scottish in-migration to an English town, and examines both the linguistic patterning of a variable following migration and the possible change in its social meaning. The chapter thereby addresses David Britain's fundamental question, '[i] f feature A diffuses from place X to place Y, will feature A (i) be unchanged at Y from its state at place X and (ii) carry the same social connotations, the same values in the same places?' (Britain 2001: 46).

The testing ground here is Corby, in the English midlands. Within twenty years, Corby grew from a rural village to a medium-sized industrial town through an influx of Scottish workers to the newly constructed steel works. As a result of contact between indigenous English and incoming Scottish people, young Corby people without Scottish ancestry speak a dialect containing Scottish English features. Indeed, as the example below shows, older Corby people and outsiders perceive the young people's dialect as 'Scottish'.

> Example 1. 70-year-old Scottish-born male
> T: . . . there's children probably never been in Scotland
> J: Yeah
> T: And they'll speak broad, broad Scotch
> J: Yeah
> T: Never be – never even seen it [Scotland]
> J: Yeah
> T: Never on a map

Linguistic features of Scottish origin are not interpreted as indicative of a Scottish identity for the younger speakers in the town, however, as exemplified by the extract below:

Example 2. 17-year-old male

J: So how do you think Corby people speak then?

B: Apparently Scottish . . . Yeah and I don't speak Scottish at all you know. Do you know what I mean?

J: So you said apparently Scottish, and you said they don't sound Scottish at all

B: Well I don't

J: Why do you think you sound Scottish then? Why did you say apparently Scottish?

B: Because everyone says we speak Scottish, but we don't

J: OK, so have you ever been asked if you're from Scotland?

All: Yeah yeah yeah

This chapter considers how incoming Scottish phonological features were integrated into the new contact dialect, and if unchanged linguistically, how they are used to index both Scottish and local identities by different groups in the town – both Scottish- and English-born Corby inhabitants, and both older and younger speakers. I examine the movement of linguistic features to a new geographical location, the integration of those features into the new contact-induced dialect, and the possible change in social meaning of those features in their new context.

In the investigation, an apparent-time sample from 1998 is used alongside a later, smaller sample of teenagers' speech collected in 2006. Analysis of the changing trajectory of one phonological variable in the 1998 sample across three generations allows both apparent-time and real-time analyses. Changes in the variable's role in the linguistic system are thus charted across time, confirming the changing socio-indexical information associated with it.

2. Structural/socio-stylistic reallocation and dialect contact

As populations come into contact through in-migration, the mixing of the contributing dialects yields great linguistic variability. As a community develops, the language focuses by means of various processes. Through koinéisation the diversity of forms is reduced, with levelling of minority or marked forms which may be localised and/or stigmatised. The number of forms may also shrink through the adoption of interdialect forms that are intermediate between the two dialects. The result of koinéisation is therefore 'a historically mixed but synchronically stable dialect containing elements from different dialects that went into the mixture, as well as interdialect forms that were present in none' (Trudgill 1986: 107–8). In new-dialect formation, reallocation may also occur. Here, 'two or more variants in the dialect mix survive the leveling process, but are refunctionalized, evolving new social or linguistic functions in the new dialect' (Britain and Trudgill 1999: 245).

Britain and Trudgill (1999, 2005) classify reallocation into two types – structural reallocation and socio-stylistic reallocation. Structural, and specifically phonological, reallocation occurs when two (or more) variants in the dialect mix are retained, but function as allophones occupying distinct phonological contexts. Britain and Trudgill (2005: 188) cite Horvath and Horvath (2001) concerning the realisation of the BATH vowel (Wells 1982) in Australian English. In the UK, BATH is influenced by both geographic location and social class (Chambers 1992), with northern and lower socio-economic class speakers favouring the original /æ/, and southern and higher socio-economic class speakers using /ɑː/. However, in Australian English these variants have been reallocated according to phonological environment, with /æ/ being used before nasal clusters (for example in 'dance'), and /ɑː/ appearing elsewhere.

With socio-stylistic reallocation, both variants may be retained, but each plays a different stylistic role, one indexing a high (or formal) and the other a low (or informal) style. Domingue (1981, cited by Trudgill 1986: 110) illustrates this type of reallocation in Mauritian Bhojpuri, a new contact variety in which various regional dialects of Hindi provide high- and low-style variants. The original regional variants have therefore been reallocated to stylistic functions in Mauritius.

In terms of dialect contact, there has in recent years been an upsurge of interest in processes and products involved, including the role of identity-making and -marking functions of language in these situations (Milroy 2000; Dyer 2000, 2002; Watt 2002; Wassink and Dyer 2004; Llamas 2007b).

More recently, the role and emphasis placed on identity in language contact studies have been questioned. Trudgill's (2008) claim that identity has no relevance for new dialect formation has recently spurred much debate. Rejecting the notion that identity *per se* may be a *cause* of new dialect formation, Trudgill argues that forms found in new dialects originating from colonial contact among European settlers do not stem from a desire or need among these speakers to express a new national identity, but are rather the natural result of dialect mixing through the automaticity of accommodation. Trudgill supports an 'evolutionary' explanation for accommodation, arguing that it is an automatic or inevitable consequence of interaction, and is the main impetus behind new dialect formation. His position is not unopposed, however. Holmes and Kerswill (2008) argue that Trudgill's evidence is based entirely on pre-sixteenth-century sources, and concerns only cases of new national varieties of European languages. Trudgill himself admits that he lacks empirical evidence that identity is irrelevant in the formation of new varieties, but maintains that their emergence is explicable without recourse to identity factors. Holmes and Kerswill (2008: 275) further question why accommodation should occur at all if there is mutual comprehension, and why one party would accommodate to the other, rather than the reverse. Their answer assumes that the accommodator wishes to emulate the interlocutor in some social respect. Additionally, Holmes and Kerswill note that colonial settlers do not arrive in new territories as *tabulae rasae*. They come with attitudes, preferences and prejudices about language use. I concur with Holmes and Kerswill's contention that '[t]here is no stage in the process of new dialect formation when social factors are irrelevant' (2008: 275).

Prior to and continuing alongside this debate on identity and dialect formation is the discussion concerning the levelling of regional dialects (see further Britain, this volume) and the apparent increase in adoption of supralocal forms. Milroy (2008) suggests that socially embedded sound changes are heterogeneous and thus should be examined from different perspectives. Building on Eckert's (2003: 395) metaphor, Milroy distinguishes local or 'under-the-counter' change from supralocal or 'off-the-shelf' change. The former requires the support of local networks and interaction; the latter does not, and is more available to 'mobile or marginal individuals' (Milroy 2008: 160–1).

Regarding the general globalisation of language use, many researchers have noted that it is often accompanied by increased localisation (Meyerhoff and Niedzielski 2003: 535).

Figure 18.1 Map of Great Britain showing location of Corby. Based on Ordnance Survey map data by permission of the Ordnance Survey © Crown copyright 2001.

In a study of quotative *be like*, Macaulay (2001) found that although it is probably of US origin *be like* had been re-analysed and indigenised by the Glasgow speakers in his study. Similarly, Buchstaller (2002) discovered that the formal and functional differences in US and UK use of the same quotative show as many differences as similarities. The current study also establishes that rather than a levelled dialect forming as a result of adoption of supralocal variables, a new locally distinct dialect containing both supralocal ('off-the-shelf') and adopted contact ('under-the-counter') features has formed in Corby.

3. Historical background

Corby grew from a village of 1,500 inhabitants at the beginning of the twentieth century to the main steel-producing town in the UK, with a population of 36,000, by the 1960s. From the 1930s until the 1970s, the steel plant (owned by a Scottish company) recruited

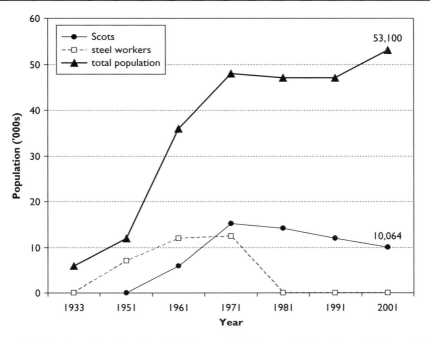

Figure 18.2 Numbers of steel workers in Corby and inhabitants claiming Scots ethnicity relative to Corby's total population (thousands) (UK National Census data, 1933–2001).

workers from closing plants in Glasgow and Lanarkshire in Scotland. The proportion of Scottish-born Corby inhabitants reached a maximum of around 30 per cent. However, in 1980 the plant closed and the migration of labour ceased.

In Corby today it is increasingly rare to hear either the English Corby village dialect, now only spoken by the oldest Corby-born inhabitants, or English as spoken in Glasgow and its surrounding areas, and by some of the earliest incomers to the town. The resulting koiné now spoken in Corby is a distinct mixture of Scottish and established and innovatory Anglo-English features, although outsiders often perceive it as a form of Scottish English. Some of the Anglo-English features are features spreading throughout the UK (see further Dyer 2000, 2002).

4. Profiles of the two samples

According to Wells (1982: 401), it is primarily vowels that distinguish 'Scottish English' from 'Anglo-English' (English with an English accent), terms which also refer to distinct phonological systems (Wells 1982; Giegerich 1992). With this in mind, speech was collected in 1998 to investigate six vocalic variables that functioned as relative indicators of Scottishness.

The sample collected in 1998 comprised the speech of twenty-seven people from three generations living in Corby. The oldest ('first') generation (aged 60–74) were divided ethnically between those born in Scotland and England, but the second (aged 40–50) and third generations (aged 14–23) were all, except one second-generation man, born in England. All third-generation speakers were Corby-born. None had college or university education, most being either blue-collar workers or factory workers. Speakers were interviewed about their lives and experiences of living in Corby. A wordlist elicited relevant phonological variables.

In 2006, a subset of data was collected from sixteen school students (14–17 years). I spent a day at the school observing three discussion-based classes from which volunteers were recruited to take part in the project. Again, a wordlist elicited relevant linguistic forms, and a questionnaire provided biographical data. Additionally, a group discussion session was conducted. Comments have been drawn from this discussion, though phonological data come from wordlist readings only. The aim of the smaller follow-up study was to undertake a real-time comparison of phonological features among the younger participants in each dataset who are comparable in that they all attended state schools in Corby and none of their parents were university graduates.

5. Change in linguistic patterning

5.1 1998 sample (apparent time)

Tokens of the vocalic variables of interest were impressionistically coded by the author and two other trained phoneticians. The variable discussed in this chapter is the merger of the vowels in Scottish English (SE) represented by the keywords GOOD and FOOD. These vowels are distinct in most dialects of Anglo-English (AE) but are merged in SE (Abercrombie 1979; Wells 1982; Aitken 1984), thus comprising the same phonological class in SE, but distinct sets in AE. In AE the vowel of the GOOD lexical set, (/ʊ/), is a short, lax, fairly back, fairly close vowel that occurs only in closed syllables, while the FOOD vowel (/uː/) is long, tense and back, and occurs in both open and closed syllables. In SE the merged variant is short and fronted /ʉ/. A further reflex of the GOOD/FOOD variable is a long fronted variant [ʏː] which appears to be an alternative incoming AE realisation for the tense vowel of the FOOD lexical set (see further Kerswill 1996; Williams and Kerswill 1999; Dyer 2000). The 1998 data for the GOOD/FOOD variable were complex and showed a shift over time. In the wordlist and conversational data, five variants were identified for the GOOD/FOOD vowels: the four variants above and [ɜuː], although only one second-generation speaker used this variant (see Table 18.1).

Three pairs of words containing the GOOD/FOOD vowels (*wool/tool, full/fool, good/food*) were used in reading style. Data were analysed for whether speakers used identical or different vowels in each pair. When merging occurred, the variant used was inevitably that associated with SE, [ʉ]. All variants used in the GOOD/FOOD lexical sets were coded in the conversational data.

Two trends emerged from the 1998 data. The first concerned the merging of the lexical sets. If no merger was occurring, the second trend entailed the individual fronting of both vowels in the GOOD/FOOD lexical sets, with the distinction between the lexical sets being maintained.

Table 18.2 presents results grouped by generation and subdivided by sex. The second and third columns from the left show counts of two of the three possible realisations for the FOOD vowel ([uː], [ʏː]) with column four showing the Scottish variant which speakers

Table 18.1 Variants of GOOD/FOOD in Corby English

Variant	Word class	Association
[ʊ]	GOOD (closed syllables)	Anglo-English (established)
[ʉ]	GOOD and FOOD (closed and open syllables)	Scottish English
[uː]	FOOD (closed and open syllables)	Anglo-English (established)
[ʏː]	FOOD	Anglo-English (innovatory)
[ɜuː]	FOOD	Anglo-English (innovatory)

either used for *both* the GOOD and FOOD sets (if they were merging the sets) or as an alternative for the GOOD vowel (while keeping the lexical sets distinct). Counts of the other possible GOOD variant, [ʊ], are shown in column five. Note that a speaker may be seen to be merging the lexical sets if there is a large number in the column showing the historically Scottish variant [ʉ] in addition to low numbers in the columns for [uː], [ʏː] and [ʊ]. The sixth column shows the number of all GOOD/FOOD vowels produced by each speaker, and the seventh the proportion of the Scottish variant [ʉ] to all the GOOD/FOOD realisations each speaker produced.

In the conversational data, merging can be seen by how distinct (or not) each speaker kept the lexical sets. If a speaker's GOOD/FOOD realisation clustered around one variant then one might assume that some merging was occurring.

In the first generation, three of four Scottish-born speakers (MS, JC and TT) consistently merged the vowels of the lexical sets in conversation, indicating that this variable may represent a fairly good indicator of Scottishness. However, only two of the four merged the vowels variably in reading style (MS and TT). One (JC) did not merge in reading, but merged consistently in conversation. This sensitivity to style in the Scottish-born speakers' data hints at the salience, and perhaps also the stigma, attached to this variable. In the first generation, some fronting of the FOOD vowel to [ʏː] by English-born speakers, and some fronting of GOOD to [ʉ] by one English-born speaker (JT), was in evidence.

In the second generation three speakers (JD, CT, TF), one of whom is Scottish-born (TF), merged the lexical sets in conversation. Other speakers (all the females and one male, JJ) fronted FOOD to [ʏː] but kept the lexical sets distinct. The SE variant [ʉ] was used only by the second-generation speakers who merged the lexical sets (JD, CT and TF). Two of the three speakers (JD and TF, the Scot who merged in conversation) also merged in reading style.

In conversation the third-generation speakers fronted both vowels, using the variant with Scottish associations [ʉ] for the GOOD set, and the innovatory variant [ʏː] for FOOD. However, in conversation all but one third-generation speaker (ClT) maintained the distinction. The one speaker who did merge consistently both in conversation and reading style was ClT. In contrast to the first generation, who tended to merge more in conversation than reading, about half of the third-generation speakers sometimes merged GOOD and FOOD in reading style.

In summary, then, two trends emerged in these data: speakers either merged the lexical sets using the Scottish variant [ʉ], or maintained the distinct lexical sets as in the AE

Table 18.2 Distribution of 'Scottish' variant [ʉ] for first, second and third generation
Corby speakers as a percentage of the total realisation of the GOOD/FOOD vowels.

			Conversation				Wordlist
	[uː]	[ʏː]	[ʉ]	[ʊ]	row total	% [ʉ]	merger?
1st GENERATION							
FEMALE							
MS (Scot)	4	0	22	0	26	85	66%
JC (Scot)	1	0	31	0	32	97	No
RT	32	9	0	11	52	0	No
JT	14	28	9	5	56	16	33%
MALE							
TT (Scot)	5	0	41	0	46	89	33%
RS (Scot)	19	0	22	7	48	46	No
RP	4	49	0	26	79	0	No
PT	6	9	0	11	26	0	No
2nd GENERATION							
FEMALE							
MF	3	31	0	16	50	0	No
KJ	3	22	0	16	41	0	No
JD	0	11	39	3	53	74	100%
CT	4	10	47	1	62	76	No
MALE							
JJ	10	18	0	10	38	0	No
DH*	25	0	0	17	42	0	No
IB	7	2	0	15	44	0	No
TF (Scot)	7	0	60	0	67	90	100%
3rd GENERATION							
FEMALE							
SB	1	18	22	0	41	54	100%
CJ	10	17	18	4	49	37	66%
SM	3	16	23	2	44	52	33%
LW	4	24	22	0	50	44	No
KF	12	16	16	13	57	28	No
MALE							
CʔT	0	0	29	0	29	100	100%
RD	0	14	34	0	48	71	66%
MB	8	0	18	5	31	60	No
AD	0	9	22	0	31	71	33%
JH	6	25	12	5	48	25	No
GS	3	16	11	5	35	31	No

* DH also produced 8 FOOD vowels as [ɜuː].

(non-merging) phonological system. When maintaining the distinction, speakers sometimes used the Scottish variant [ʉ] in GOOD as a replacement for the more conservative AE variant, [ʊ]. That is, they used a feature associated with SE but in an AE phonological system. In addition, fronting of the tense variant /uː/ to [yː], which has been reported as occurring more widely in English dialects, was evident (see Torgersen and Kerswill 2004). The third-generation data showed both kinds of trajectory – either merging the variants to [ʉ], or maintaining a distinction between the lexical sets but fronting GOOD and FOOD to [ʉ] and [yː] respectively. For our purposes here, the focus remains on the use of the Scottish variant as an exemplar of reallocation.

5.2 2006 sample

Further evidence of the GOOD/FOOD merger in the focusing of the Corby dialect was sought from comparative data in the second, smaller dataset from 2006. These data clearly show not just the continued use of the variant associated with SE, but also the fact that the merger is advancing: it is three times more frequent in the 2006 data than it was for the first-generation Scottish speakers in 1998 (see Table 18.3).

6. Change in social meaning: a comparison of the 1998 and 2006 samples

The data presented above suggest that in the Corby dialect the GOOD/FOOD merger is advancing. This may be surprising on two counts. Firstly, the merger of these lexical sets is a feature that characterises SE – the feature has clear geographical and ethnic associations. In new dialect formation, it is unusual for features that are strongly associated with a particular geographical region to be adopted, as usually such features tend to be levelled out (Trudgill 1986: 118). Secondly, Corby people have adopted two features – the Scottish variant [ʉ], and the merger of the GOOD/FOOD lexical sets, both of which are associated with a variety of English that in certain of its forms – particularly Glasgow English – has long been stigmatised (Romaine and Reid 1983; Stuart-Smith 2008; Millar, this volume). According to Craig, for Scots '[i]t is not by our colour, of course, that we have stood to be recognized as incomplete within the British context, it is by the colour of our vowels' (1996: 12). Comments on the stigma attached specifically to the Scottish merged variant of GOOD/FOOD can be found: Aitken calls it a Scottish vulgarism, mentioning it alongside 'the notorious glottal stop' (1979: 102).

In Corby, young speakers of the new contact-induced dialect have adopted not just features of a geographically and ethnically marked dialect, but also features that are stigmatised within that dialect by Scottish speakers themselves. The fact that first-generation Scottish-born speakers appeared to avoid merging GOOD and FOOD when their attention was drawn to the feature in reading style, yet merged them in the less formal conversational style, is evidence of the latter point.

7. Socio-stylistic reallocation of 'Scottish' features in Corby

Returning to the theoretical focus of this chapter, we see in the new contact dialect that has formed in Corby that some features traditionally associated with SE are being used by the young, but as their discourse about the town testifies, the social meaning of these

Table 18.3 Percentages of merger to [ʉ] in wordlist readings of GOOD/FOOD vowels (1998 and 2006).

	1998			2006
	1st generation	2nd generation	3rd generation	14–17 years old
Male	Scottish 16.5% English 0%	25%*	40%	87%
Female	Scottish 33% English 16.5%	25%	33%	66.5%
Cohort average	16.5% (Scots 25%)	25%	36.5%	77%

* TF, the Scottish-born man

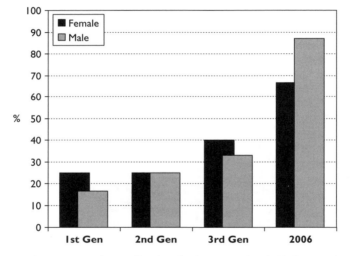

Figure 18.3 GOOD/FOOD merger in wordlist data for first, second and third generations in 1998, and 14–17 year olds in 2006.

features has been reallocated in the new dialect, so that they are not being used as a means of expressing an affiliation to the earlier Scottish settlers. The contrast between the oldest and youngest generations' commentary about the town bears this out.

For the oldest, first-generation speakers, Corby was divided along ethnic lines, with speech being seen as an instantiation of these ethnic or national differences. Many examples in the 1998 data attest to this. To cite a few, Scottish- and English-born speakers argued about whether Corby should be known as 'Little Scotland'; the Scots complained about their reception in the town by the English; the English complained that the Scots were taking over the town. Speakers also referred to the physical boundary of the railway bridge in the town between the Scottish and the English areas, with the area north of the bridge being referred to as 'Scotland'. Older speakers also frequently spoke about language use in Corby, with English people describing the Scots incomers' language as incomprehensible, and the Scots saying they had to talk 'a wee bit more posh' around the English.

One first-generation English-born speaker referring to the Scots' language remarks that 'it was like trying to listen to a foreign language'; another says 'it was a helluva job to understand them'. Interestingly, the older generation uses this conceptual frame to interpret the language of the younger generation, claiming that many of the younger generation speak 'broad Scots'.

The 1998 third-generation interview data concerning the town as a community contrast starkly with the older generation's ethnically–coloured discourse casting the Scottish/English dichotomy as part of Corby's history. Third-generation speakers frequently state that outsiders *used to* call Corby 'Little Scotland'. Younger speakers even seem perpetually surprised that people think they sound Scottish. They deny that they are Scottish, instead claiming a locally–based Corby identity. Corby speech is compared by the younger generation not to the speech of the Scots, but to the speech of people in the neighbouring town of Kettering (see Figure 18.1). 'Self' and 'other' identification categories have shifted in Corby. Just as the dialect has become focused over the generations, so has the town community itself, with younger speakers perceiving there to be more differences between themselves and people outside Corby (or foreign, non-English-speaking settlers) than with those inside the town. Ironically, while most young people do not have strong feelings about the Scottish history of the town, the third-generation speaker with the most Scottish features in his speech (CIT) jokingly refers to the Scots as 'sweaty jocks' – a term carrying negative connotations (the nickname 'Jock', equivalent to 'Jack', is used colloquially in the UK to refer to any Scottish person, more usually a male). Together, these facts give a clear indication that so-called Scottish phonological features, such as the GOOD/FOOD vowel merger and the [ʉ] variant most frequently used in the merger in Corby, have been reallocated in the new dialect and that for the younger inhabitants they index a newly constituted local identity. When using these features, speakers are perceived by local others as coming from Corby, and not from any of the surrounding villages, or Kettering.

Since the last census in 2001 Corby and its population have undergone significant change, with many more incomers arriving from various parts of Britain and from Eastern Europe. Corby feels less like a post-industrial town and more like a commuter town, with many people travelling daily to London. In 2006, a 17-year-old male student at the school where the data were collected provided an interesting insight into Corby's changing profile. His demographic characteristics alone – his parents are from Turkish-speaking Cyprus – suggest the town's ethnic composition is changing. He described his brother in the following way:

> Example 3. 17-year-old male (home language Turkish)
> F: I've got an older brother
> J: Yeah
> F: Erm he lived in Cyprus for five years before he came to here
> J: Right
> F: He refuses to be Cypriot
> J: Yeah

F:	And he refuses to be English as well
J:	Really? So what does he think he is then?
F:	Corbyish
J:	Corby?
F:	CorbyISH
J:	CorbyISH
F:	Yeah, I'm I'm uh Corbyish. That's what he says

Given the changing demographics of Corby, one wonders whether within another ten years its inhabitants, while perhaps retaining some vestiges of the Scottish history of the town in their speech, will still be able to associate the town with the Scottish steel workers who 'made the town what it is' (21-year-old male MB, 1998).

In conclusion, the Corby data offer an interesting window on the changing indexicality of linguistic variants. An apparent-time snapshot of the dialect from 1998 compared with data collected in 2006 provides insights in real time into how the dialect is changing. They suggest that Scottish features are not disappearing from the dialect but are in fact advancing, yet at the same time are losing their association (for the speakers themselves, at least) with SE. This also indicates that neither the merger itself nor the particular variant adopted, [ʉ], is stigmatised by young Corby speakers, as it was (and perhaps still is) for the older Scottish residents of the town. These data offer further understanding of the linguistic and ideological processes involved in new dialect formation. In a new context, variables are clearly able to shed previous associations and stigma and to accrue new locally relevant meaning for their speakers.

19

Shifting Borders and Shifting Regional Identities

Joan Beal

1. Shifting borders

In this chapter, I discuss the socio-psychological effects of changes in local administrative boundaries which have taken place in the UK within the last forty years. The most radical of these changes were introduced by the Local Government Act of 1972 and implemented in 1974, when a new two-tier administrative structure was introduced. This resulted in the introduction of new (shire) counties and six new metropolitan counties. Together these replaced the traditional counties which appear on older maps and which were used, for instance, by the Survey of English Dialects (Orton 1962). The result was that some counties, such as Cumberland, Westmorland and Rutland, were incorporated into new units, and many towns and districts were 'moved' from one county to another. A further Local Government Reorganisation in the 1990s introduced a number of unitary authorities in medium-sized urban areas, but it is the changes of 1974 that have, so far, had the greatest impact on the map of the UK.

One major effect of these changes has been to produce in some places a generational divide between the perceptions and regional/local identities of those who were born before about 1970 and those born after this date. To give a personal example, I was born in Warrington, Lancashire, but some of my nephews and nieces were born in Warrington, Cheshire (see Figure 19.1). Warrington has not moved, other than expanding its boundaries through development and incorporation of some neighbouring districts, but the administrative unit to which it belongs has changed. The two counties have very different images in the public consciousness: Lancashire is viewed as a blue-collar, industrial county best represented in the works of the artist L.S. Lowry, whereas Cheshire is viewed historically as agricultural and more recently as an affluent commuter belt for Manchester and Liverpool. Lancashire is perceived as northern, whilst Cheshire, at least to some, is considered a midland county (Wales 2006: 12–13). At the time of the reorganisation (1974), there was much protest from residents about being 'moved' in this way, because this distinction between Lancashire and Cheshire was locally very meaningful: the Manchester Ship Canal formed a boundary between the two counties, and, in the minds of local residents, between the 'posh' districts in Cheshire on the south bank,

Figure 19.1 Map of northern England showing locations mentioned in the text.

and the more working-class areas to the north. These protests continue to be made by pressure groups such as the Friends of Real Lancashire, who campaign for the restoration of the historical boundaries of Lancashire and the marking of these boundaries by road signs, and so forth. They encourage residents of Warrington to celebrate Lancashire Day, which has been held on 27 November every year since 1996. On 22 November 2007 the *Warrington Guardian* ran an article under the headline 'Lancashire Hot Spot', which began as follows:

> IS Warrington in Cheshire or Lancashire?
>
> Do you feel an attachment to the red rose county [Lancashire]?
>   Next Tuesday's Real Lancashire Day campaigns for the 'protection, preservation and promotion' of the true identity of the county.
>   And with the Mersey running through Warrington marking the traditional boundary of Lancashire in the south, organisers and campaigners are expecting plenty of support in the town.

The town technically stopped being in Lancashire in 1974 when changes to the administrative areas of counties saw Warrington move into Cheshire.

Chris Dawson, the chairman of the Friends of Real Lancashire, said: 'On Lancashire Day, Lancastrians wherever they are can celebrate the fact that no legislation has ever changed the boundaries of the traditional county of Lancashire'.

'Lancashire is Lancashire – from its southern boundary on the banks of the Mersey to its northern boundary on the Dusson [*sic*; 'Duddon' is meant] and west bank of Windermere.'

The rhetoric of organisations such as the Association of British Counties suggests that the historic counties remain important reference points for identity, as we see in the following extract from their homepage:

> The historic Counties of Great Britain are fundamental to our culture. Older than cathedrals, more historic than stately homes, Counties like Lincolnshire, Cornwall, Middlesex, Anglesey and Fife are basic to our life. Their names belong to the ground we tread. They are an indelible part of our history. They are important cultural entities. They are sources of identity and affection to many people. (www.abcounties.co.uk)

However, such research as has been conducted indicates that younger people do not necessarily share this allegiance to the historic counties, except perhaps in the context of sports such as cricket, which are organised on a county basis. Indeed, some of the historic counties, such as Westmorland, may well be unknown to younger people, who would be more familiar with terms such as 'Cumbria' or even 'the Lake District'. In the following sections, I discuss the ways in which the shifting of administrative boundaries in the UK, and more specifically in England, has altered the local identities of residents and has also affected both the perception and the production of local accents and dialects.

2. Perception of dialect areas

Traditional dialect studies in England have tended to use the historic counties as units of description: the Survey of English Dialects allocated numbers to survey locations on this basis and the volumes of its *Basic Materials* are organised according to groups of these counties. Thus Volume I covers 'the six Northern counties and the Isle of Man' (Orton and Halliday 1962). The six counties referred to here are Cumberland, Westmorland, Northumberland, County Durham, Lancashire and Yorkshire (see Figure 19.1). The lack of correspondence between these and the present-day divisions can lead to problems for scholars attempting to discuss changes in the varieties of English used in these areas. Explaining her decision to use the 'old' county names in her history of northern English, Katie Wales summarises the changes in county boundaries between 1974 and 1996:

> [I]n the mid-1990s there is Cumberland and Westmorland merged to form Cumbria; Tyne and Wear carved out of the south of Northumberland and the north of Durham; and around the Tees estuary Hartlepool, Stockton-on-

Tees, Redcar and Cleveland and Middlesbrough, reflecting dramatic growth in these towns. Only the East Riding of Yorkshire keeps its ancient name, since it refused to be abolished; North and West Yorkshire remain in essence, but South Yorkshire now joins them, thus making four 'ridings' instead of three, in defiance of etymology. (Wales 2006: 14–15)

Early works on dialectology, such as Joseph Wright's *English Dialect Dictionary* (1896–1905) likewise used the counties as units of reference, and many of the individual dialect glossaries printed under the auspices of the English Dialect Society purported to describe 'the dialect' of specific counties. Examples are Heslop's (1892) *Northumberland Words*, Parish's (1875) *Dictionary of the Sussex Dialect*, and Holland's (1886) *Glossary of Words used in the County of Chester*. Most of the dialect societies which exist today likewise take their titles from the historic counties: examples are the Yorkshire Dialect Society (though there is also an East Riding Dialect Society); the Lancashire Dialect Society; the Northumbrian Language Society and the Friends of the Norfolk Dialect. Some of these societies have a long history: the Yorkshire Dialect Society, for instance, was founded in 1897, but others have been set up more recently in response to perceived threats posed to traditional dialects. Thus the homepage of the Northumbrian Language Society tells us that 'the decline in the use of Northumbrian words & pronunciations has been marked over the last century – so, the Northumbrian Language Society was formed in 1983' (http://www.northumbriana.org.uk/langsoc/about.htm), and the Friends of the Norfolk Dialect was 'formed in 1999 to conserve and record Norfolk's priceless linguistic and cultural heritage' (http://www.norfolkdialect.com).

The dialect societies can perhaps be seen as analogous to the county groups in the Association of British Counties in that members of both are interested in preserving what they see as important aspects of local heritage and identity. However, results from perceptual studies carried out in England indicate that the dialects which are perceived as distinctive today are not those identified with counties, but the urban dialects of the major cities and conurbations.

Chris Montgomery (2006) conducted a perceptual study of northern English dialects. One method he used was to present participants with a blank map of England and then ask them to write the names of any dialects of which they were aware on the areas in which they were spoken. Participants were mostly aged 18–20 and lived in three 'northern' towns or cities: Carlisle in the north-west, Hull in the north-east, and Crewe in Cheshire, a county that we have already discussed as being considered by many to be in the mid-lands (Figure 19.1). There was a good deal of consensus as to the dialects named, as can be seen in Table 19.1 below. The 'top three' were always Geordie (Newcastle), Scouse (Liverpool) and Brummie (Birmingham), with Cockney (London) fourth or fifth and Manchester fifth or sixth. The only county to be named by all participants was Yorkshire. Given the discussion in section 1 about changes in the boundaries of Lancashire, it is interesting to see that only the participants from Carlisle in Cumbria, a county contiguous with present-day (and historic) Lancashire, named this dialect, and even here only a small number (8/98) did so. Elsewhere, Montgomery (forthcoming) demonstrates that, in a composite made up of participants' individual perceptual maps, Lancashire has shrunk to a size corresponding to that of the present county, and, by contrast, the perceptual space taken up by 'Manchester' and 'Liverpool' is vast. This suggests that, with the exception

Table 19.1 The ten most frequently identified dialect areas by survey location (from Montgomery 2006: 196).

Carlisle (n=98)		Crewe (n=85)		Hull (n=93)	
Area	*Number*	*Area*	*Number*	*Area*	*Number*
Geordie	52 (53.1%)	Scouse	67 (78.8%)	Scouse	44 (47.3%)
Scouse	48 (49%)	Geordie	61 (71.8%)	Geordie	43 (46.2%)
Brummie	34 (34.7%)	Brummie	61 (71.8%)	Brummie	37 (39.8%)
Cumbria	33 (33.7%)	Cockney	46 (54.1%)	Yorkshire	33 (35.5%)
Cockney	33 (33.7%)	Manchester	33 (38.8%)	Cockney	21 (22.6%)
Manchester	26 (26.5%)	Cornwall	16 (18.8%)	Manchester	14 (15.1%)
Cornwall	10 (10.2%)	Potteries	13 (15.3%)	London	10 (9.3%)
Yorkshire	9 (9.2%)	Yorkshire	12 (14.1%)	South West	9 (9.7%)
West Country	9 (9.2%)	London	9 (10.6%)	Hull	6 (6.5%)
Lancashire	8 (8.6%)	West Country	7 (8.2%)	East Anglia	6 (6.5%)

of Yorkshire, which seems to maintain its salience and perceptual prominence, the counties (traditional or modern) of England do not serve as markers of linguistic identity for young people, being replaced by major conurbations or by larger regions such as East Anglia or the West Country.

It would be interesting to see whether older participants would give similar responses to this task, or whether the traditional county names would be more prominent. Other recent studies incorporating perceptual dialectological methods have indicated that, within conurbations, participants perceive geographical divisions which correspond to social and linguistic differences. For instance, Finnegan (forthcoming) notes a strong perception of a north-east – south-west division in Sheffield, where the former area was (and, to some extent, still is) the location of steel foundries and their workforce. There is also evidence that young people in particular increasingly perceive their local identity on a micro level in terms of postcodes, which are used in the names of gangs and sprayed as graffiti. Postcodes have been used by statisticians and human geographers to map a wide range of characteristics, such as housing, unemployment or health. One result of this is that certain postcodes have become associated with positive or negative social characteristics in the media, which could then be internalised by residents of these areas. The website of the UK Office for National Statistics (http://www.statistics.gov.uk) points out that 'postcode referencing is a straightforward approach but has a number of weaknesses relating both to the unstable nature of UK geography and also the fact that postcode boundaries do not match up to those of other geographic areas'.

Nevertheless, as they are known and used as reference points, they are growing in salience, and should perhaps be taken into consideration by sociolinguists in the UK.

3. Consequences for language variation and change

We have seen in the above sections that the geography of the UK is, as the Office for National Statistics website puts it, 'unstable' and that changes in administrative boundaries since 1974 have been reflected in corresponding shifts in regional identity, especially amongst younger people. Research in perceptual dialectology (Montgomery 2006, forthcoming) has also demonstrated that younger people in northern England have little awareness of dialects associated with the 'historic' counties, except for Yorkshire. The question to be addressed in this section is whether these shifts of identity and perception are mirrored by changes in actual linguistic usage. In areas where administrative reorganisation has led to a shift across a significant boundary, does the usage of older and younger people reflect this shift?

Carmen Llamas (2001, 2006, 2007b) set out to answer these questions with regard to Middlesbrough (see Figure 19.1), an urban centre which has been subject to a number of reorganisations and boundary changes since 1974. Llamas notes that Middlesbrough was a 'new town' of the Industrial Revolution, growing from a hamlet with a population of twenty-five to a town of 91,000 in the course of the nineteenth century. The heterogeneous nature of the nineteenth-century in-migration and the situation of Middlesbrough on the border of the historical counties of Durham and Yorkshire would in themselves lead to interesting issues of identity, but successive changes in administrative boundaries since 1968 have complicated matters further. Middlesbrough was historically located in the North Riding of Yorkshire but, in 1968, Teesside was created out of the conurbations on the north and south banks of the Tees. In the 1974 reorganisation, this area was included in the new county of Cleveland. Llamas goes on to explain that in 1996, the regional affiliation of Middlesbrough 'was changed again when the conurbation was once more divided in 1996 with the formation of four separate borough councils, each being regarded as a county in its own right' and thus 'within a period of approximately 30 years . . . in terms of local government, Middlesbrough has been assigned four separate political identities' (Llamas 2007b: 583).

Llamas's study was the first to employ a new method of data collection designed for a projected Survey of Regional English (SuRE), details of which can be found in Llamas (1999) and (2001). Llamas incorporated into this research design an Identification Questionnaire (IdQ) intended to elicit participants' attitudes to their dialect and to their local area. This is consistent with the language ideological approach outlined in Milroy (2004):

> An ideological analysis treats social categories as locally created by social actors and discoverable by analysis, rather than as a given. Consequently, an ideologically oriented account of language variation and change treats members of speech communities as agents, rather than as automatons caught up ineluctably in an abstract sociolinguistic system. (Milroy 2004: 7, cited in Llamas [2007b: 581])

Llamas argues that the speech community, far from being a 'given', is a 'locally created social category' which needs to be examined by sociolinguists rather than imposed on the sample. She was able to use the qualitative data elicited from the IdQ, including participants' comments about language attitudes and local/regional identity, to systematically interpret patterns of variation and change which she discovered in the linguistic data elicited from the same participants. Llamas's sample consisted of male and female speakers who self-reported as working class, from three age-groups: young (16–22), middle (32–45) and old (60–80). In her linguistic analysis, she focused on three linguistic variables known to be involved in variation and change elsewhere in the UK, the plosives (p), (t) and (k). In Tyneside, to the north of Middlesbrough, glottalised or glottally reinforced variants of all three plosives have been widely reported, while the full glottal stop realisation of (t) is widespread throughout most of the UK, especially in younger speakers' usage. Neither variant is traditionally found in the speech of Yorkshire (though the glottal variant of (t) is used by younger speakers here, as elsewhere). Since Middlesbrough is perceived as 'a place between places' (*The Sunday Times*, 5 March 2000, cited in Llamas 2007b: 580), those 'places' being Yorkshire and the North East region, it was hypothesised that use of the glottalised variants might correspond with speakers' orientation towards the North East and its most prominent city, Newcastle, while avoidance of these variants might signify an affiliation with Yorkshire.

The results of Llamas's analysis were slightly more complicated: for (p) and (k), there was an overall increase in the use of glottalised variants by younger speakers, which, according to Llamas, 'suggests a convergence of MbE [Middlesbrough English] with speech of farther north, where use of the glottalized forms was found to be higher' (2007b: 595). The increase was most dramatic in the usage of young females when contrasted with older females, and so in their case could be interpreted as 'convergence towards male speech' (2007b: 595). In the case of (t), the glottal, rather than the glottalised, variant had increased so as to be almost categorical for younger speakers of both genders. Since the glottal variant has been found to be less frequent in Tyneside English, this would appear to have the opposite motivation of diverging from the 'speech of farther north' and/or converging with the 'mainstream' UK vernacular. In order to interpret these apparently contradictory results, Llamas turned to the attitudinal information provided by the IdQ.

The first question on the IdQ is 'What accent would you say you had, and do you like it?' Llamas found that the different responses of the three age groups correlated very closely with the chronological shifts in the regional and local affiliation of Middlesbrough outlined above. Older speakers most frequently gave the response 'Yorkshire', the most frequent response from the middle-aged group was 'Teesside', and the young speakers most frequently responded with 'Middlesbrough'. Llamas concludes from this that 'speakers react to changing political boundaries of the area in which they live, and if such boundaries change, so may the way inhabitants perceive themselves' (2007b: 596). The responses to the third question 'can you recognise the accent of your home town?' revealed that younger speakers, and especially females, felt less able to distinguish the accent of Middlesbrough from that of Tyneside. In response to question 5, which asked whether participants felt Middlesbrough to be part of a 'North East' or a 'Yorkshire' region, even older speakers who self-identified as 'Yorkshire' answered 'North East'. Llamas cites one older speaker as responding: 'you're right at the top of Yorkshire, so to get it across you'd have to say North East'. Moreover, younger speakers' responses revealed what Llamas refers to as 'the irrelevance of Yorkshire to the speakers' sense of identity construction' (2007b: 598):

> It's weird even though you're the same distance, how much you don't class yourself with them [people from Yorkshire]

> It's weird when you only go two minutes down the road and you're in like North Yorkshire. No I don't consider it at all.

Since, as we have seen, Middlesbrough is widely perceived as lying 'between' Yorkshire and Newcastle, question 2 asks 'what would you think if your accent was referred to as 'Geordie' [i.e. from Newcastle] or 'Yorkshire'?' The oldest group responded that they would be offended if misidentified as 'Geordie', but expressed surprise that this could happen. One participant responded 'I'm from Yorkshire not Geordieland – they might as well call you a Frenchman instead of an Englishman' (Llamas 2007b: 598). The middle age group were more likely to prefer being misidentified as 'Geordie' to being labelled 'Yorkshire', but most of the young speakers claimed that they would be offended by being misidentified as a 'Geordie', and some expressed surprise that they might be misidentified as 'Yorkshire'. Llamas interprets this as demonstrating an increasing sense of Newcastle as a threatening out-group which challenges the identity of the Middlesbrough speakers. Derogation of Newcastle people is further demonstrated by the young speakers' answers to question 7: 'What do you consider the local football derby [match between local rivals] to be?' No Yorkshire teams were mentioned (at the time of the study, Leeds United would have been the only Yorkshire team in the same league as Middlesbrough Football Club), but games played against Newcastle United and Sunderland were considered 'derbys' (see Figure 19.1 for geographical locations).

We saw in section 1 that some groups are reluctant to accept the boundary changes resulting from local government reorganisations. Llamas's older participants expressed such views in answer to question 4: 'do you remember when the county of Teesside was formed and Middlesbrough was no longer in Yorkshire? Do you think the change made a difference?' Expressions of regret at 'leaving' Yorkshire were mainly confined to the oldest group of participants. The middle age group tended to express uncertainty about their regional identity: one participant responded 'we're not Geordie – we're not Yorkshire – we're nothing really' (Llamas 2007b: 600), while only one of sixteen young participants in the study expressed a desire to be part of Yorkshire, and some had no knowledge of any historical connection between Middlesbrough and Yorkshire. Llamas sums up the findings from the IdQ as revealing:

- Clear generational differences in linguistic orientation in Middlesbrough.
- Clear generational differences in self-image in terms of what accent speakers perceive themselves to have.
- A lack of overtly positive identification with the dominant centre of gravity of the North East, Newcastle.
- The irrelevance of Yorkshire to the identity construction of younger speakers.
- An increase in the perception of Middlesbrough as a place with its own identity.
  (Llamas 2007b: 600)

These findings correlate very closely with the results of the linguistic analysis: the increase in the young speakers' use of glottalised variants of (p) could be interpreted as representing 'a convergent linguistic trend motivated by young speakers' positive identification with varieties of the North East', but the same speakers' self-definition in terms of accent and regional/local affiliation indicates 'a shift not from Yorkshire to the North East but from Yorkshire to Middlesbrough' (Llamas 2007b: 601). Since the glottalised variant of (p) was well-established in Middlesbrough, especially among male speakers, the shift towards this variant in young female speakers could be interpreted as indexing a 'Middlesbrough' identity. Llamas concludes:

> We thus see a focusing of linguistic choices and convergence onto a Middlesbrough form, which coincides with the rise in profile of Middlesbrough as a place with its own identity in terms of local administrative boundaries and in terms of perception of its prominence on a national scale. (Llamas 2007b: 601)

Llamas goes on to interpret the increase in use of the glottal variant of (t), in line with national trends and in contrast to Tyneside usage, as consistent with the young participants' expressed desire to distinguish themselves from 'Geordies'. She also notes the convergence between male and female speech in her younger participants, and suggests that this shows evidence of the focusing of the Middlesbrough accent as it becomes more internally consistent. This in turn is 'concurrent with an increased confidence expressed by young speakers in the status of Middlesbrough both in terms of its accent and in terms of it as a "place"' (Llamas 2007b: 601). While older speakers still consider themselves as 'Yorkshire' and middle-aged ones are uncertain of their local identity, younger speakers identify with Middlesbrough as a place and index this identity in their use of phonetic variants of (p) and (t).

Llamas presents a very convincing case here for shifts in administrative boundaries leading to shifts in regional/local identity, and then to corresponding shifts in linguistic usage as variants are employed in social work to index this new identity. Her conclusions about Middlesbrough's rise to prominence as a 'place' can be further confirmed by the relatively recent appearance of a nickname for its citizens, parallel to the much older 'Geordie'. The term 'Smoggy' refers to the miasma created by Teesside's chemical industry, and like many such nicknames (referred to in folklore studies as *blason populaire*), probably originated as a derogative term used by outsiders, especially fans of Newcastle United FC. However, some citizens have adopted this nickname as a badge of pride: Katie Wales tells us that 'Teessiders, at home or abroad, can log on to www.smoggy.org.uk' (2008: 60). Thus a distinct Middlesbrough identity is acknowledged by out-group members and by citizens of Middlesbrough themselves, whether resident in the conurbation or expatriate.

4. Conclusion

The evidence presented here suggests that sociolinguists need to take further account of what the Office for National Statistics terms the 'unstable nature of UK geography', and, indeed, the unstable nature of political boundaries at all levels. The rivers and mountain ranges that once formed barriers to communication and thus coincided with the isoglosses of traditional dialectology have been bridged and crossed by roads and railways, but it would seem that the stroke of a bureaucrat's pen can have as much effect on a speaker's sense of place and identity as these innovations in transport infrastructure and communication. This is less surprising when we consider that, despite the tangible nature of topography, 'place' is a construct (see Britain, this volume; Llamas, this volume), and so there is no reason why the labels and divisions introduced by local government reorganisation would not be internalised by residents: the postcode graffiti in UK towns and cities bears witness to this. The lesson from Llamas's study is that 'place' is not a given, to be taken for granted in our research designs: what appears to be a town or city delimited by boundaries on the map may actually be several different places to different groups of speakers, whose allegiance to these 'places' may be indexed by linguistic variables.

20

Convergence and Divergence Across a National Border

Carmen Llamas

1. Introduction

One level of self-identification which may, initially, appear rather uncontentious and non-optional is that of national identity. Even though the bounded nation state as we understand it today is a relatively novel phenomenon (there were few clear territorial boundaries in mediaeval Europe, for example), the belief that political borders are fixed and necessary may be considered widely held. Further, the idea that nationality in terms of bureaucratic documentation (passports, identity cards) is not a matter for preference or debate but is determined by the fulfilment (or not) of predetermined criteria may be considered uncontroversial. However, far from being simply a matter for officialdom, national identity is an issue for which people will die (willingly or not), will kill (willingly or not), will marry, flee, voyage. It is something that can be changed, bestowed, denied. Moreover, it is something that can be relational, fluid and emergent in context.

One of the crucial ideas entailed by the concept of the state is that geographical space is delimited and bounded by political borders which are recognised by international law. This bounding not only concerns territory and sovereignty, but can also mark the limits of culture and identity. Given the strong connections between language and nation or nationality (see further Millar, this volume), the often debatable borderlands which exist at the margins of the nation are where these connections may be strongest or weakest. Using the specific example of the border separating Scotland from England, this chapter considers whether or not inhabitants of the peripheral edges of the nation have an accentuated sense of national identity and what this means for the negotiation and projection of such identity through linguistic behaviour.

2. Nations and borders

Anderson first proposed that the idea of 'nation' involves the sense of an 'imagined' community, as 'the members of even the smallest nation will never know most of their fellow-members, meet them, or even hear of them, yet in the minds of each lives the image of their communion' (Anderson 1991: 6). For Cohen also, community is a mental construct which is subjective and symbolic, but the consciousness of community is encapsulated in the perception of its boundaries. These boundaries can also be thought of as existing in the mind of the beholders, and, according to Cohen, 'the boundary may be perceived in rather different terms, not only by people on opposite sides of it, but also by people on the same side' (Cohen 1985: 12). As political borders mark the limits of state control over citizens, they may be seen as having a tangible, perceptible quality – whether they follow fences or natural boundaries – which may be less evident in symbolic boundaries. They may be said to be objective rather than subjective, and as such we may suppose there to be an absence of variation in how they are perceived. For those who live in close proximity to them, however, assuming that movement is not restricted, borders may also come to have a subjective, symbolic quality and may be perceived and evaluated rather differently not only by inhabitants on each side of the border, but also by inhabitants of the same locality.

Social scientists, historians, human geographers, political scientists and anthropologists, among others, have increasingly focused attention on political borders in order to study the changing dynamics of territory, sovereignty and identity. Beyond relations across political borders, the cultures and identities of the borderlands themselves offer much in the way of insight into human relations. Identification of the margins of borderlands can be problematic, however, and, as Donnan and Wilson state, '[t]he symbolic constructions of the boundaries to international border cultures are often extremely significant signs of regional and national identity, but yet are among the most difficult to discern' (Donnan and Wilson 1999: 43). Among the key processes that help shape the 'borderlands milieu', according to Martínez (1994: 8–14), are transnationalism and the development of a sense of political and social separateness and otherness. That is, the feeling of being culturally different from the core or majority populations in their 'national societies' can lead borderlanders to develop shared values, ideas, customs and traditions with their counterparts across the borderline.

The sense of distance from the core is of obvious relevance to the discussion of borderlands, and the theoretical paradigm of 'centre versus periphery' (introduced by Galtung in 1971) has been influential in the political science and economics literature. The model is predicated on the concentration of political, economic or social power in a core area, to the detriment of the areas of the periphery. The model of 'regionalism' describes the rise of areas outside the previously identified 'centre' and the role that the creation of links between regions and peripheral cities plays in regional development. Both models allow insight into borderland cultures and, in offering explanations for the prestige and maintenance of local norms and local (or regional) varieties in opposition to national standards, they have value for sociolinguistic studies in addition to research with a focus on political and economic relations. The processes of decentralisation allow links between areas which do not pass through a 'centre', and localities on the periphery of the traditional centre, such as border localities, may become centres of regions themselves.

Border localities, then, though physically at the margins of their nation or state, may be at the centre of their own borderland region which may straddle the political divide and may include localities in close proximity to both sides of the border. Nonetheless, in these borderland regions sharp inter-group categorisations may remain – even where there exists a border which can be crossed without any state controls on a daily basis. One key way that this differentiation may be indicated is through language use.

3. Language and borders

How language is used and how variation is stratified and exploited in borderlands has become the subject of increasing investigation. Although according to Woolhiser 'it is difficult at present to speak of "border studies" as a distinct area of research in dialectology and sociolinguistics, analogous to what has emerged [recently] in such fields as geography, sociology or anthropology' (Woolhiser 2005: 237), a growing interest in border regions as sites of particular sociolinguistic relevance has developed, and borderlands are fast becoming a burgeoning area of research.

National borders can separate standard varieties of different languages. Indeed, as a consequence of the language planning associated with the ideology of nationalism in nineteenth-century Europe, we tend to identify standard varieties with nations. However, geographical dialect continua can result in speakers across borders being mutually intelligible even though their standard varieties are not (for example, across the Dutch–German border; see Heeringa et al. 2000). Europe is seen as a region characterised by 'an exceptionally rich variety of politically segmented dialect continua' (Woolhiser 2005: 237), and a number of recent studies of localities near borders which separate two standard languages have been undertaken (see, for example, Michele de Oliveira's [2002] study of two towns in close proximity to the Spanish–Portuguese border; Kontra's [2003] survey study of the borders of Hungary with Slovakia, Ukraine, Romania, Yugoslavia, Slovenia and Austria; and Woolhiser's [2005] study of twelve villages (six on each side) along the Polish–Belarusian border, among others). Similarly, increasing numbers of studies on non-European borderlands have been undertaken (see, for example, Martínez's [2003] folk linguistic research along the Mexican–US border; Omoniyi's work on the Nigeria–Benin (2004a) and Nigeria–Cameroon (2004b) borders, among others).

The situation also arises of a political border separating varieties of the same language. The US–Canada border, for example, has 'long been a linguistic barrier of considerable influence, just as it is a cultural divider' (Chambers 2000: 118). Lexical variation has been investigated along this border by Chambers (2000), as has phonological variation (Boberg 2000). Evidence for both convergence and divergence is found and results indicate that not only do US features spread northwards, but, less commonly, Canadian features are found to spread south. The perception that forms can index national identity is clearly crucial in the dissemination of certain forms, however, and Boberg claims that '[i]n general, it seems safe to say that Canadians do not want to sound like Americans, so that when a variant is marked [+American] rather than, say, [+young] or [+trendy] it will not be readily transferred' (Boberg 2000: 23).

4. Accent and identity on the Scottish–English border

One of the most celebrated examples of the influence of a political border on linguistic behaviour is the border separating England from Scotland. The border is not the subject of conflict or dispute: on the contrary, it has remained peaceable and fixed for hundreds of years. However, from a linguistic point of view, such is its perceived importance among certain scholars that it has been claimed that 'the greatest concentration of distinctive linguistic features in the whole of the English-speaking world is to be found along the length of that Border' (Kay 1986: 22). Explanations for this situation focus on the central importance of national identities, as Aitken's explanation illustrates: '[b]ecause of the separation of the two kingdoms since early times, many of the characteristics of Scots extend only to the Border' (Aitken 1992: 895). This is seen to have had a profound effect on linguistic behaviour, and Aitken goes further to state: '[w]hat appears to be the most numerous bundle of dialect isoglosses in the English-speaking world runs along this border, effectively turning Scotland into a "dialect island" ' (1992: 895). Perhaps more surprising still, given the current context of large-scale levelling and homogenisation in British English (see further Britain, this volume), is the view that the discontinuities of linguistic features across the border are predicted to increase, and that the dialects on either side of the border look set to diverge further (Glauser 1974; Kay 1986).

The recent climate of shifting political administration and power in Scotland (with discussion of it in northern England also), and its resulting effect on the negotiation and expression of identities, may be a contributory factor in any increasing divergence. Political attitudes and identities in Scotland have changed significantly since the 1997 devolution vote (Bond and Rosie 2002; Clayton 2002), and there are signs that devolution has also influenced expressions of English identity (Tomaney 1998). Alongside large-scale political changes at the national level, questions of regional identity are similarly gaining prominence in political life (Tomaney and Ward 2001). This situation calls for investigation of both national and regional identities and the role of linguistic variation in their construction and negotiation amongst inhabitants of the border communities.

The claimed and attributed identities of inhabitants of Berwick-upon-Tweed, an English town located three miles (five kilometres) from the border between England and Scotland, have been the subject of a sociological study by Kiely et al. (2000). As with many border localities, Berwick-upon-Tweed has seen the border move around it numerous times throughout its history. It was finally incorporated into England in the late fifteenth century; however, its status in relation to Scotland is still ambiguous in many respects, and the symbols of 'banal nationalism' in the town which can be seen as flagging nationhood and which appear 'unnoticed' on public buildings (see further Billig 1995) – the depiction of the crossing of the English flag (St George's Cross) and the Scottish flag (the Saltire) – can be seen as sending somewhat mixed messages.

Kiely et al.'s sociological study of Berwick-upon-Tweed and two neighbouring communities (the Scottish coastal village of Eyemouth nine miles to the north and the English town of Alnwick about thirty miles to the south) set out with the expectation that inhabitants of Berwick-upon-Tweed would have a heightened sense of 'Englishness' given their proximity to the border where national identity may be seen to be problematic or, at least, highly salient. The study found instead that many inhabitants encountered problems with 'being national' and preferred to mobilise a strategy of localism to overcome this. Although the focus of the study was not linguistic, Kiely et al. suggest that accent is a vital identity marker (a social characteristic of an individual that he/she might present to others to support a national identity claim), and they maintain that '[h]aving what sounds to others like a Scottish accent . . . is a key reason why people from Berwick-upon-Tweed are often attributed with a Scottish nationality by others and may have their claim to being English challenged' (Kiely et al. 2000: 11). This attribution of a Scottish nationality is not emulated by those north of the border, however, as respondents from Eyemouth are reported to perceive the accent as 'Northumbrian or Geordie[1], and certainly English' (Kiely et al. 2000: 12). The inhabitants themselves appeared to side-step the question of

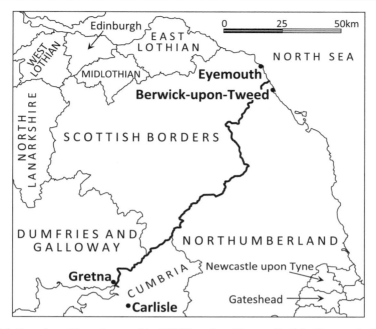

Figure 20.1 Location of four sites used in AISEB project: Gretna, Carlisle, Eyemouth, Berwick-upon-Tweed.

national identity, as they foregrounded their local identity as Berwickers. However, they also demonstrated the fluidity of the concept of national identity in their responses, as almost half (41 per cent) of the inhabitants of this English town who acted as subjects for the study described themselves as Scottish *at least some of the time*.

It seems clear from the study by Kiely et al. that national identity in border towns cannot be approached entirely from an essentialist perspective, as for many borderers national identity is not fixed, but is rather relational and emergent in context. It is also clear that as far as the attribution of national identity is concerned, linguistic behaviour is central to a categorisation. In terms of both the group identification which occurs inside the boundary and the social categorisation that occurs across it (see further Jenkins 1997: 23), the pertinent question arises of how, in the border town in question, 'doing Scottish' or 'doing English' is accomplished (for detail on linguistic accommodation in the locality, see Llamas et al. forthcoming).

In order to further this line of enquiry and to investigate empirically the extent to which language plays a role in national identity-making and -marking in this border region, the *Accents and Identity on the Scottish English Border* (AISEB) project (see further Llamas et al. 2008) examines language variation in four localities along the border (Berwick-upon-Tweed [English] and Eyemouth [Scottish] to the east, and Carlisle [English] and Gretna [Scottish] to the west) (see Figure 20.1). The study examines the extent to which discontinuities of phonological features persist across the border, whether features can be said to be indexical of 'Scottishness' or 'Englishness' and to what degree their use correlates with claims and attributions of the national identities available (Scottish, English, British, Scottish–English hybrid).

Preliminary results have focused on (r), as this particular variable, specifically in a non-prevocalic environment, is considered by some to be 'the most important feature for defining the relationships between varieties of English' (Maguire et al. 2008). Furthermore, of all phonological features, (r) is singled out by inhabitants of the border area as diagnostic of national identity most frequently when they are asked to identify features of local language associated with 'Scottish' or 'English' speech.[2]

The perception that post-vocalic (r), along with trills and possibly also taps, index a Scottish identity rather than an English one fits well with the status of (r) described in the literature. Scotland is traditionally rhotic, though non-rhoticity is increasingly reported in the larger urban centres (see further Romaine 1978; Johnston 1997; Stuart-Smith 2003). This non-rhoticity appears to be associated primarily with younger working-class male speakers. Derhotacisation of varieties of Northern England occurred considerably earlier than is reported for Scotland. By the early 1970s derhotacisation of rural Northumbrian English was already well underway (see Påhlsson 1972), and today use of coda /r/ is reported as occurring only sporadically among older people in isolated rural areas of the county such as Holy Island (Maguire 2005). With very few exceptions, then, even the most northerly Northern English varieties are now effectively non-rhotic.

Wordlist and reading passage data were analysed from younger (aged 11–22) and older (aged 56–82) male speakers from all four localities in the initial recordings for the AISEB project.[3] Variants were categorised in both VR (for example *car*, *four*) and VRC (for example *cart*, *force*) contexts into trilled forms [r ʀ], tapped/flapped forms [ɾ ɽ], central approximants [ɹ ɻ Vʲ Vⁱ], back approximants [ʁ ʕ Vˠ Vˤ], a miscellaneous category [h ɕ], and zero. For our purposes in this chapter, we are primarily interested in whether or not there is a zero realisation of coda /r/.

Figure 20.2 clearly demonstrates the marked difference between the Scottish and the English localities, with both English localities demonstrating very little use of coda /r/ and the Scottish localities showing use of a wide range of variants, but much less zero realisation on the whole. In the Scottish localities, the data also reveal a sharp east/west differentiation. We note a decreased use of coda /r/ across age in Gretna, but, surprisingly given the derhotacisation noted in urban varieties of Scotland, we find an increased use of coda /r/ in Eyemouth with the younger males overwhelmingly preferring use of the central approximants in this environment. In the English localities, although remnants of rhoticity are apparent in the older speakers of Carlisle, coda /r/ is almost nonexistent in the speech of the younger Carlisle males and all speakers in Berwick-upon-Tweed. To some extent, then, we see evidence for both the view that the accents are converging (on the west side) and that they are diverging (on the east side). In order to shed more light on these seemingly conflicting trends, insights from cognitive and affective attitudinal information gathered from speakers are considered.

Attitudinal data were elicited on how informants' identities are defined and delimited, in particular the national and regional identities they claimed (cognitive component), as well as how positively or negatively disposed towards those accents and identities speakers felt (affective component). Tables 20.1 and 20.2 illustrate how informants (represented individually by ✕) responded to questions on what accent and national identity they believed they had.

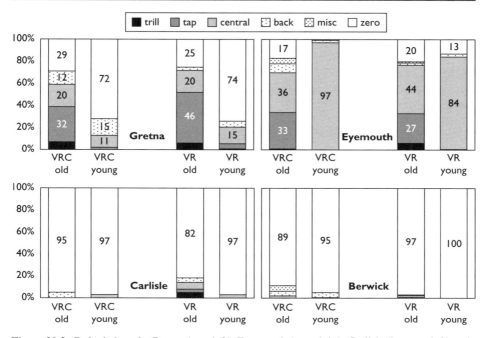

Figure 20.2 Coda /r/ use in Gretna (top, left), Eyemouth (top, right), Carlisle (bottom, left) and Berwick-upon-Tweed (bottom, right). Numbers in bars represent percentages.

Table 20.1 indicates that the cognitive attitudinal data demonstrate a similar east/ west split on the Scottish side as was found in the linguistic data, as younger speakers of Gretna believe themselves not to have Scottish accents, unlike the older speakers in Gretna and both the older and younger speakers in Eyemouth. The English localities shown in Table 20.2 appear more similar both across age and across the east/west dimension. More younger Berwickers believe themselves to be strongly English than do younger Carlisle speakers, however, though fewer Berwickers than young Carlisle speakers believe themselves to have a strongly English accent. The east appears to be a more stable divide, whereas the west appears to show that the young speakers are converging by moving towards feeling less English and less Scottish, thus mirroring the differences between use of coda /r/, which showed advergence of the young speakers on the west side but not on the east.

Table 20.3 presents the affective component of the attitudinal data. How informants (again represented by ✕) responded to questions as to how they would evaluate the accents and the national identities (Scottish or English) they claimed is placed on a cline from strongly negative to strongly positive.

The affective component of the attitudinal data again reveals differences between north and south and between east and west localities. As a general trend, informants from the Scottish localities appear to fall slightly more towards the neutral to positive side of the cline than do the English informants. What stands out in the data, however, is the fact that the most strongly positive group in terms of national identity are the younger

Table 20.1 Cognitive component of attitudinal data from Scottish speakers (O = older speakers, Y = younger speakers).

	not Scottish		mildly Scottish		strongly Scottish	
	accent	nationality	accent	nationality	accent	nationality
Gretna O			××	×	×	××
Gretna Y	××××	××		×		×
Eyemouth O				×	××××	×××
Eyemouth Y				×	××××	×××

Table 20.2 Cognitive component of attitudinal data from English speakers (O = older speakers, Y = younger speakers).

	not English		mildly English		strongly English	
	accent	nationality	accent	nationality	accent	nationality
Carlisle O			××	×	×	××
Carlisle Y		××	××	×	××	×
Berwick O			×××	×		××
Berwick Y			×××	×	×	×××

speakers from Eyemouth, all of whom responded in a strongly positive manner. These young Eyemouthers were the speakers who demonstrated not only an increased use of coda /r/ compared with the older speakers from their locality, but also the highest use of coda /r/ across the sample of speakers as a whole.

Preliminary results from the AISEB project, then, indicate that there is a clear connection between use of forms which can be said to be indexical of national identity and both a claiming of that identity and having a positive disposition towards it. The data suggest that as regards the Scottish–English border, the divide is stronger and more stable on the east side both linguistically and in terms of social categorisations. The inhabitants of the border region in question have available to them the alternative shared British identity, but this appears to be considered relevant only by younger inhabitants on the west side. Thus, in terms of use of coda /r/ and use of the available national identities, the young on the west end of the border appear to be converging, while those on the east appear to be diverging. Why this should be requires further consideration.

In terms of the east side, where the division appears more robust, as both towns are very close to the border (Berwick-upon-Tweed three miles and Eyemouth six miles), from a centre–periphery perspective we might expect inhabitants to have developed a strong association with the border region. However, Berwick-upon-Tweed is much further away from its national capital (299 miles from London) than is Eyemouth (53 miles from Edinburgh). It may be that given its distance from the national capital and the generally

Table 20.3 Affective component of attitudinal data from Scottish and English speakers (O = older speakers, Y = younger speakers).

	strongly −		mildly −		neutral		mildly +		strongly +	
	accent	nat.	accent	nat.	accent	nat.	accent	nat.	accent	nat.
Gretna O (Sco)					××			×	×	××
Gretna Y (Sco)			×		×	×××	××			×
Eyemouth O (Sco)							××	××	××	××
Eyemouth Y (Sco)					××		××			××××
Carlisle O (Eng)						×××	×××			
Carlisle Y (Eng)			×	×		×××	××		×	
Berwick O (Eng)	×					××			××	×
Berwick Y (Eng)			×	××		××	×		××	

negative attitudes revealed in interviews towards Newcastle, the centre of gravity of the North East region, Berwickers define their space by placing their town at the centre, and they define themselves primarily by using a strategy of localism as found by Kiely et al. (2000) and also in the current data.[4] Eyemouthers, on the other hand, may view themselves as Scottish first – even though they are on the peripheral edge of the nation – because being peripheral to an Edinburgh centre may be seen to carry more prestige than being peripheral to Berwick (which is a considerably larger town than Eyemouth) or Newcastle. One of the ways they may indicate their Scottishness in opposition to Berwick-upon-Tweed is through their use of the indexical feature, coda /r/.

On the west side inhabitants appear to be more non-essentialist in their approach, and not only do younger inhabitants appear to be converging and accepting their shared British identity, but they also report an awareness of the advantages of switching allegiances to enhance a situation (for example, to attract the attention of the opposite sex or to avoid conflict).

Although preliminary, these results illustrate that different strategies appear to be in operation in different localities along the border. Though the attitudinal findings tie in with the linguistic patterns uncovered so far, perceptual testing of linguistic features is necessary in order to establish their indexicality with more certainty. Such complex data as we have not only require further investigation, they also demonstrate the difficulty of generalising about borderlands. The significance of the border to the inhabitants of border localities is likely to impact on both their claimed and ascribed national identities and also on their linguistic behaviour, but each border locality has its own relationship to the border – a relationship which is the result of historical circumstance, regional affiliation, demographics, contact, core–periphery relations, and so on. Broad generalisations about inhabitants' identities and linguistic behaviour in borderlands would fail to address the complexities involved in each individual case.

5. Conclusions: the currency of identity

The Scottish–English border study used to exemplify this topic illustrates how national identity can, at times, be exploited to the benefit of the holder in a given context. If we consider the question the chapter set out to examine – whether or not inhabitants of border locations have an accentuated sense of national identity and whether they use language to project this – we see that broad generalisations of this sort appear to be problematic for locations along a single border of around 100 miles. Such generalisations, then, will certainly prove unsatisfactory for the enormous diversity of complex and ever-changing borderlands that exist today. For some inhabitants nationality may be an unchanging, essential part of their identity. This may be to do with the prestige of local choices available. For others, it clearly is not an essential part of their identity. Furthermore, speakers for whom national identity is fluid are able to exploit whichever identity they wish for social gain. This currency of identity is central, and if an identity carries prestige in a given context, it may be foregrounded, often through linguistic behaviour. This foregrounding of certain aspects of identity in a given moment is something that is available to all speakers, though having the ability to foreground one *national* identity over another while speaking the same language may be a particular fluidity shared by those inhabitants of borderlands who accept and exploit the benefits of their hybrid identity.

Notes

1. Geordie is the variety associated with the Tyneside conurbation, south of Berwick-upon-Tweed and, more specifically, with the centre of gravity of the North East England region, the city of Newcastle.
2. Informants were asked about their perception of features differentiating Scottish and English accents: rhoticity and forms of (r) were mentioned more frequently than any other linguistic feature.
3. Four younger and four older speakers from each locality were sampled, with the exception of Gretna and Carlisle, where data from three older speakers were collected.
4. The majority of informants from Berwick-upon-Tweed chose the local identity label 'Berwickers' over the national labels available, unlike informants in the other localities.

21

Language and Postcolonial Identities: An African Perspective

Tope Omoniyi

Nigeria is not a nation. It is a mere geographical expression. There are no 'Nigerians' in the same sense as there are 'English', 'Welsh', or 'French'. The word 'Nigerian' is merely a distinctive appellation to distinguish those who live within the boundaries of Nigeria and those who do not. (Awolowo 1947: 47–8)

In the beginning, there was no Nigeria. There were Ijaws, Igbos, Urhobos, Itsekiris, Yorubas, Hausas, Fulanis, Nupes, Kanuris, Ogonis, Gwaris, Katafs, Jukars, Edos, Ibibios, Efiks, Idomas, Tivs, Junkuns, Biroms, Angas, Ogojas and so on. There were Kingdoms like, Oyo, Lagos, Calabar, Brass, Itsekiri, Benin, Tiv, Borno, Sokoto Caliphate (with loose control over Kano, Ilorin, Zaria, etc.) Bonny, Opobo, etc. Prior to the British conquest of the different nations making up the present day Nigeria, these Nations were independent nation states – and communities independent of each other and of Britain. (Sagay, *Nigeria: Federalism, the Constitution and Resource Control*, http://sagay.notlong.com)

I. Introduction

The link between national identity and language is a highly political and politicised subject, perhaps more so in Africa than in Western Europe, where we can observe one-to-one correlations between nations and national languages. France and French, England and English, Finland and Finnish, Germany and German, and Norway and Norwegian illustrate this claim. I hastily add that this observation is not intended in any way to belittle the politics of minority status languages that play out in the European examples given here (see further Millar, this volume). Hastings, challenging the idea that ethnicity and nation were Western creations imposed upon Africa, says *inter alia* that 'African communities had an inherent sense of identity . . . whereby insiders were distinguished from outsiders, and that sense of identity was very closely linked with language use' (Hastings 1997: 149). Hastings goes on to argue that although it was unquestionable that the presence of missionaries and colonial officials 'affected identities quite quickly and considerably, both through administrative labelling and by privileging and stabilising certain forms of speech characteristic of one place while disregarding other varieties', it would be 'totally absurd and unhistorical' to suggest that tribal or ethnic diversities were 'an imposition upon Africa by Western interpreters' (Hastings 1997: 149). It is not part of the remit of this chapter to say whether such politics and politicisation is Africa's problem or that of those who seek to write the continent's biography and therefore have agency in this matter. However, we need to sharpen how we conceptualise identity in Africa. I believe that in that connection both of the quotations in the epigraphs at the beginning of this chapter, which emanate from two different generations of the Nigerian elite separated by some sixty years, represent critical views about postcolonial identities in Africa.

It is over a decade since Werbner and Ranger's (1996) collection of essays put the spotlight on 'how, over time, and in a plurality of contested arenas, postcolonial strategies improvise multiple shifting identities' (Werbner and Ranger 1996: 1). Their argument at the time was that it is misleading to focus on ethnicity as if it were the sole cause of Africa's crises when in fact ethnic identities are 'merely a small fraction of the many identities mobilized in the postcolonial politics of everyday life' (1996: 1). Werbner cites Hutcheon (1995: 10) in arguing that 'postcolonial' is a problematic label that is not simply construable as a temporal reference but also one signifying 'resistance and opposition, the anticolonial', a 'politicized reality'. Frankenberg and Mani (1996) argue that 'postcolonial' has varying connotations from one place to another, and illustrate their claim by citing the differences between its import in Britain where it 'signals loss of colonies, decline of empire; and the appearance on British landscapes of a significant number of people from the old colonies' on one hand, and on the other hand its 'serious calling to question of white/Western dominance by the groundswell of movements of resistance, and the emergence of struggles for collective self-determination most frequently articulated in nationalist terms' (Frankenberg and Mani 1996: 274) in the former colonies.

There is a growing body of literature in urban sociolinguistics which deliberates upon the complexities of identity construction across various social arenas in cosmopolitan settings (see for instance, Block 2005; Harris 2006; Rampton 2006; Fox, this volume). But most of these studies engage with the 'verbal coloration' that subaltern voices bring to urban communicative repertoires. In other words, their subjects include people from postcolonial backgrounds, although the context is not a postcolonial but a post-imperial context; these may be represented as opposite sides of the same coin, namely the joint colonised and coloniser contexts in which identities are differently articulated, complete with 'home and away' advantages and disadvantages respectively, to use a league football analogy.

In contemporary Africa, politics and economics have been sites for the construction and articulation of the oppositional postcolonial identities, Anglophone versus Francophone. Lusophone and Hispanophone identities belong to a lesser league considering the relatively small number of countries colonised by Portugal and Spain on the continent. The Anglophone/Francophone opposition is a consequence of the different trajectories that African populations had thrust upon them by colonial experience after the Berlin Conference of 1884/5 (Herbst 2000; Omoniyi 2004a). The fundamental difference lay in the associationist and assimilationist administrative options that British and French colonial administrators chose respectively in their colonies, which resulted either in indigenisation or appropriation in the deployment of colonial resources, including language. However, in the age of globalisation, when the nation-state framework seems to be conceding to the supra-state, and postcolonial nations are exploring strategies of reinvention in order to break completely either from the colonial yoke or from neo-colonial elite domination, we see the emergence of new sites of contestation and the articulation of multiple identities. In this chapter, I present an exploration of the postcolonial identities complex in which individuals, communities, nations and the overarching state – in this case Nigeria – constitute interconnecting and competing layers of identification.

2. Nigeria: language and identity

Across African nations the story is similar: one nation-state, many ethnonationalities and multiple languages. Some of the ethnonationalities, and their languages, are not contiguous with the established nation-state boundaries; 103 ethnic groups are partitioned by national boundaries in Africa. In other words, some languages may be present in the language profile of more than one country, thus underlining the complexity of language-based national identities. I have elected to use Nigeria, a country Afolayan (1976) describes as a 'multinationality polity', to illustrate this postcolonial African complexity.

In postcolonial contexts, there has been a tendency for language research to focus rather narrowly on the frameworks of language policy and planning, and language in education. In much of the published literature on Nigeria, the central argument that has often been made is that indigenous African languages have been displaced by former colonial languages in the 'plum and prime' functions with which any substantial social-cum-linguistic capital accruing to languages is associated. However, more recently the focus seems to be shifting to a new debate: that is, whether or not English or African Englishes are sufficiently indigenous, and to what extent they can mark national identity (see Akindele and Adegbite 2000; Omoniyi 2004a). This chapter, by virtue of its orientation, belongs in the latter category. I shall take as my entry point to the debate the fact that English has been nativised in former British colonies (see Bamgbose et al. 1995; Banjo 2000). In spite of nativisation, from both numerical and functional perspectives, these Englishes still have minority populations of mainly elite speakers in the countries in question. This characteristic raises the question of whether their statuses as 'African languages' are therefore undermined. But the fact is that numerically and functionally smaller languages do not forfeit their Africanness simply for those reasons.

Webb and Kembo-Sure (2000: 31) put Africa's languages into four linguistic families: Afro-Asiatic, Nilo-Saharan, Khoisan and Niger-Congo. Similarities abound among languages in these families. The Niger-Congo group is the largest of the families, with over 1,000 languages and 260 million speakers across sub-Saharan Africa. Most of Nigeria's languages belong in this family, with the Nilo-Saharan group accounting for the majority of the remainder. From a postcolonial perspective, most, if not all, of these languages have had contact with European colonial languages, with mutual influences in both directions. However, the differences between these indigenous languages and speakers are often highlighted and exploited to mark and validate separate group identities, especially minority ones. Igala, Oko and Yoruba are good illustrations of such exploitation of divergence and difference, with proponents of Igala and Oko claiming independent and

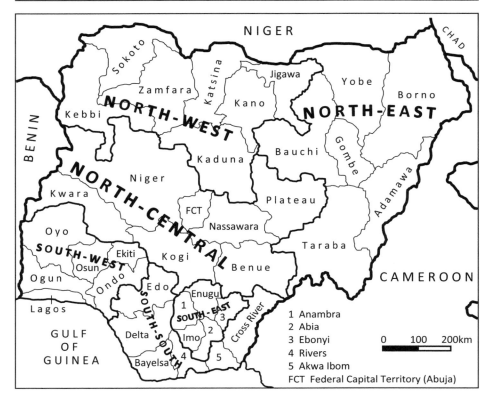

Figure 21.1 Map of Nigeria, showing state boundaries and the six geopolitical zones.

separate group identities for these languages and their speakers by stressing their divergence from the larger Yoruba group.

Although there is documentary evidence of European presence in Africa before the partition of the continent at the 1884/5 Berlin Conference, the actual formal birth of 'Nigeria' as a geopolitical entity only dates back to the British amalgamation of the Northern and Southern Protectorates in 1914. Ethnologue (www.ethnologue.com) sets the population of Nigeria at 137,253,133. It also claims that 'the number of languages listed for Nigeria is 521' of which 510 are living languages, two are second languages without mother-tongue speakers, and nine are extinct. According to Ethnologue, nine Nigerian languages – Edo, Efik, Adamawa Fulfulde, Hausa, Idoma, Igbo, Central Kanuri, Yoruba and English – are accorded national or official language status. Between them, Hausa (25 million), Igbo (18 million) and Yoruba (22 million) account for about 40 per cent of the national population. Hausa and Yoruba are also included in the language profiles of nearby countries, such as Cameroon, Niger, Ghana, Benin and Togo. In reality, with the quasi-decentralisation achieved through carving Nigeria up first into twelve states, then nineteen, then thirty-six states (see Figure 21.1), some indigenous languages have gained greater prominence within their respective states, with some of what I call the 'G4 Languages' (English, Hausa, Igbo, Yoruba) in less visible roles. For more detail on the multilingual complexity of each of the component states of the Nigerian federation, see Egbokhare (2001: 116).

3. 'Official' and 'national' language identities

It is necessary to address the distinction between 'official' and 'national' languages in interrogating the concept of national identity, as there may be slight differences in conceptualisation between contexts. 'Official language' is a functional description arrived at through status planning (again see Kaplan and Baldauf 1997). It is the setting aside of a language by government, or an institution or organisation in the case of micro-planning, for official administrative communicative purposes. In contrast, 'national language' status is assigned on the basis of aggregate attitudinal and sentimental recognition of a language as embodying and symbolising the identity of all those included in the national group (Spolsky 2004: 26). Such a language quite often has ceremonial functions, like being the medium of rendering the national anthem at important state events. In relation to this, Kloss (1968) differentiates multinational exoglossic from endoglossic African states on the basis of whether an ex-colonial language or an indigenous language is the national/official language.

According to Kloss's binary identity criterion, many African states are either exoglossic with English and/or French as sole or joint official languages (as in Nigeria, for example) or both exoglossic and endoglossic (South Africa and Kenya, for example, where indigenous languages share official language roles with former colonial languages). Awobuluyi notes that 'The 1979 Nigerian National Policy on Education . . . added 9 other indigenous languages to the curriculum for study, including: Edo, Fulfulde, Ibibio, Idoma, Igala, Ijo and Tiv' (Awobuluyi 1996: 2). Some of these have been elevated to state languages in their home states, for example, Tiv in Benue State. This is understandable, in view of the large numbers of people who speak them. In multiethnic or multiracial African states like South Africa, Zimbabwe and Nigeria, where the policy designates more than one language as having official status, what do the elected co-official African languages contribute to the character of a nation from which its identity subsequently derives?

In attempting to answer this question, we must also consider whether a genuine sense of nation and national identity can in fact be mustered without first 'disinventing' (Makoni and Pennycook 2005) the languages through which, in part, Africa and her component nation-states are constructed. The legacy of the invention that must precede such disinvention is evident in the fact that French and English, the former colonial languages, still remain the chief languages of Pan-Africanism. The analogy at nation-state level is that Nigeria and other countries of the sub-Saharan region are colonial inventions that date back to the Berlin Conference (cf. Omoniyi 2004a), and interestingly, in these countries French and English have transformed from languages of the struggle for decolonisation into languages of nationalism. That transformation has been aided by large-scale nativisation to the extent that in some cases a string of English words does not convey exactly the same meaning to people outside the community of nativisation. I shall return to this in section 5.

The argument, then, must be that nativisation may be cited as an acceptable strategy of disinvention. The completion of the process replaces the tag 'colonial language' with 'indigenous language' in respect of English.

4. Ethnic identity versus national identity

The closing years of the twentieth century in Africa produced a history that is awash with this conflict of identities. In all cases of civil strife in Africa, there is a shared official ex-colonial language that has a recognised national status, and indigenous languages which separate the populations along ethnic lines.

4.1 Ethnicity

In sub-Saharan Africa, as in many other parts of the world, ethnicity is troublesome to define. Among the numerous factors which contribute to the ethnic distinctiveness of population groups, we should in many cases take account of religion as an identity variable (see Modood 1999; Omoniyi 2006). The religion variable challenges the boundaries set by ethnicity defined in other ways, in some cases relocating these boundaries, and consequently redefining community. As in Sudan, where the war has been between the Islamic and Arabic-speaking North and the largely Christian and English-speaking South, we have seen in Nigeria a new ethnoreligious community undermine the nation. The different historical trajectories of Northern and Southern Nigeria (that is, the influence of Arabic-speaking Islamic North Africa and the Middle East on the former and English-speaking Christian missionaries on the latter) remain visible and audible in the articulated political and cultural identities of the two regions. Whereas religion became just another identity variable among the Yoruba and in the south of Nigeria in general, in the Islamic north religion became the only identity that mattered, thus drawing 'people into a single, far more universalist, community whose sole language of direct encouragement is Arabic and whose consciousness is fuelled by pilgrimage to Mecca' (Hastings 1997: 159).

By contrast, in southern Nigeria, standard forms of languages developed for use in printed text by Christian missionaries established a new sense of language community (Hastings 1997: 152). In a sense, the shared textual identity united speakers of dialectal varieties of Yoruba: Hastings notes, for instance, that the 'Yoruba Bible, with its concomitant dictionaries, grammars and readers, created a written language transcending the boundaries of spoken dialects' (1997: 159). The fact that the Yoruba did not develop into a nation-state is the consequence of European imperialism which created 'politically correct nationalisms' (1997: 159). This leads us to consider some of the key differences between Western and African conceptions of the relationship between ethnicity (including religious ties) and the process of nation-building.

4.2 Nation

The concept of nation has not been sufficiently problematised in African language research, especially in Nigeria. In much of the literature where reference has been made to nation, it has been as a loose borrowing from Western models of nationhood, in spite of the fact that the societies that gave rise to such conceptualisation are markedly different from those upon which the construct has been imposed in Africa. From an ideological point of view, it would seem that the transposition was part of an imperialist scheme of replacement. From the early history of the formation of nations, we can safely say that there is a presumption of homogeneity in the phrase 'national identity' as it was used in the political discourses of nation–states in the postindustrial world. It is also safe to say that it derives from an era in which notions of nation were woven around the myth of homogeneous language groups, as in Greece, Germany, Italy and France.

In Africa, the nation as conceptualised by the West papers over strongly held ethnonationalist emotions and the realities of ethnic loyalty and identity, which are derogatorily perceived as subnational and separatist tribal-kingdom sentiments. Thus, in part of the territory that became colonial Nigeria there had existed Yoruba and Hausa, which comprised sub-ethnic kingdoms like the Egba, Oyo and Ibadan, which waged wars against one another for supremacy and control of the larger ethnic political structure. The Ijaye wars exemplify such conflict (see Asiwaju 1976). Other political constituencies included the Igbo, Benin and Ijo kingdoms, among others.

However, it must be acknowledged that in Nigeria the struggle for independence had been largely propagated on a broad nationalist platform that recognised the nation as the sum total of its ethnic parts. In other words, there was a sense of 'peoplehood' (Wallerstein 1991: 71) already in place around language and ethnicity prior to the creation or emergence of the Nigerian nation. The National Youth Movement (NYM), established in 1938, played a leading role in negotiating Nigeria's independence. This was in spite of the fact that ethnic associations such as the Igbo Federal Union and *Egbe Omo Oduduwa* – 'Society of the Descendants of Oduduwa' (the mythical ancestor of the Yoruba-speaking peoples) – had become established as an urban phenomenon in the major cities. The fortunes of the NYM dwindled after the Second World War and it subsequently splintered along ethnic and regional lines. The Northern Peoples Congress (NPC, predominantly Hausa-Fulani and Northern), the Action Group (AG, predominantly Yoruba and Western), and the National Council of Nigerian Citizens (NCNC, predominantly Igbo and Eastern) emerged from the ashes of the NYM. This regionalisation had during the pre-independence period initially served the purpose of preserving indirect rule (Nnoli 1978: 154). Regionalisation, it may be argued, was programmed to undermine attempts at constructing nationhood, and was eventually the cause of the secession crisis which saw the deaths of millions of Igbo in the period 1966 to January 1970.

Against this general background of Nigeria's complex political history, talk of national identity is evidently contentious. Some of that contention derives from the problem of conceptualising 'nation'. Anderson (1991) and Balibar and Wallerstein (1991), among others, have contributed to the debate on nation and national identity, pointing out that they are not fixed and defined entities but ones that are constructed, contested and open to negotiation in contexts (see also Wodak et al. 2009; Millar, this volume; Llamas, this volume). In postcolonial Africa in general, and Nigeria in particular, contention exists around notions of 'nation' that are tenuous firstly because they are the result of the arbitrary partitioning of lands and communities in the 1880s, and secondly because they undermine the solidity of pre-existing primary communities. These pre-existing communities, as discussed in earlier sections, generally corresponded closely with linguistic groupings. However, it should be remembered that multilingualism, then as now, was widespread across many ethnic groups.

5. Monolingualism, multilingualism and identity

In the contemporary world monolingualism is increasingly rare. However, it serves the useful purpose of constructing essentialist identities as departure points, a stance Bucholtz (2003) calls 'strategic essentialism'. In Nigeria, multilingualism and multilingual identities are the new reality as the numbers of second and 'foreign' language users of indigenous Nigerian languages increase. However, based on spread alone, two languages – Nigerian English and Nigerian Pidgin English – seem to be most closely associated with national identity in Nigeria, as a result of the emergence of distinct and easily recognisable linguistic features. Among other features, dialect variation in English distinguishes between the major Nigerian ethnic groups. We encounter compounds that are combinations of borrowings from one of Nigeria's constituent ethnocultural worlds and pre-existing English words, such as the phrases 'okada cyclists' (commercial motorcyclists in the public transportation system), 'tokunbo cars' (imported used cars) and 'guber aspirants' (individuals aspiring to the office of governor of a state; see also Jibril 1986, 1991). Other features include the pluralisation of ethnic group names for example, Yorubas, Igbos and so on, as a transferred pattern from nationality labels (like 'Americans', 'Nigerians', 'Germans'), and the use of unique idioms and metaphors such as 'every nook and corner' (for every nook and cranny) and 'baby lawyers' (for legal professionals newly called to the bar).

The pervasiveness of English lexis in Nigerian discourse is of course scarcely surprising, given the language's long-standing and elevated status in Nigeria and other countries of Anglophone Africa. The Nigerian constitution had institutionalised English as the country's sole official language until arrangements were revised in preparation for the inception of the Second Republic in 1979, for which the functional statuses of Hausa, Igbo and Yoruba were raised to broaden their domains of usage to include official contexts. Since then, state radio has broadcast in an additional six languages. In 1998, French was added as a second foreign official language by military decree. Okon (2002) and Omoniyi (2003a) both critique the latter amendment, and make a strong case for enhancing the fortunes of indigenous languages relative to English and French (see also Igboanusi and Pütz 2008).

Another demonstration of Nigeria's linguistic complexity is conveyed by Brann's ethnolinguistic pyramid of Nigeria (Brann 1978: 10, cited in Simire 2003: 233) atop which Arabic sits as a language of religion, followed in descending order by English (official language), Pidgin (contact language), Hausa, Igbo and Yoruba (majority/national languages), Edo, Efik, Fula, Ijo, Kanuri, Nupe, Tiv, and again Hausa, Igbo and Yoruba (inter-regional languages), fifty-one Nigerian languages for administrative educational divisions (over 100,000 speakers each), 100 Nigerian languages with a writing system, and finally at the pyramid's base 400–513 Nigerian languages, not counting dialects. In relation to national identity, however, Brann's pyramid – which includes the greatest fraction of the population in the most multilingual base category – may be interpreted as offering a multilingual national identity as the most tangible option. In other words, no one language or set of powerful languages can in reality convincingly identify Nigeria.

It is evident from Brann's model that linguistic homogeneity is an aberration in contemporary Nigeria, and indeed in many African countries, a reality which necessitates some languages taking on the role of languages of wider communication (Bamgbose

1991) or lingua francas. Banjo (2000: 29) talks of local varieties of English emerging to perform this function among West African elites. Although this class of people runs the administrative machinery of state, there remains a huge rural sector of the economy that is to some extent distant and isolated from an English-dominated mainstream. The latter sector is a source of worry when English is described as a language of national identity or lingua franca. Instantly, two senses of national identity are invoked. The first is the kind of corporate identity that is inscribed on international travel documents (for example, the Nigerian passport), and which led Nigeria to engage with Cameroon in the dispute over the Bakassi Peninsula at the International Court of Justice, The Hague, in 2002 (Omoniyi 2004b). The second is the sense of community defined by shared passions about language, culture, religion, and so on, which binds people together. The indigenous languages potentially feature prominently in the latter form of national identity, fuelling subnational identities such as Ijo, Tiv and Edo, among others.

6. The constitution and national languages

Article 55 of the Constitution of the Federal Republic of Nigeria (1999) stipulates that 'The business of the National Assembly shall be conducted in English, and in Hausa, Ibo and Yoruba when adequate arrangements have been made therefor.' This wording is from the first post-independence constitution of 1960, and it is interesting that, nearly fifty years on, Hausa, Ibo and Yoruba (even though their mention seems tokenistic, considering that over 500 languages are used within the state boundaries) are still not being used in most of the state assemblies, let alone in the National Assembly. The states of Nigeria's south-west geopolitical zone, in which Yoruba is the majority and dominant regional language, have experimented with the use of an indigenous language the most. Lagos State Assembly rejected a Yoruba language bill in 1999 but passed it in 2003, and the Oyo State Assembly introduced Yoruba as a co-official language one day a week (Wednesdays) to coincide with the installation of the Second Republic in 1979. There is no clear rationale for this provision or choice of day of the week, and it therefore may be a merely cosmetic arrangement. The Ogun State Assembly is also a 'bilingual assembly' in the sense that members can address the House in Yoruba as well as in English, but this is again only an occasional occurrence. The state assemblies are bound by the same Constitution as the National Assembly. Thus, the fact that the Ogun State Government has implemented a provision of the national constitution (that Yoruba should be assigned co-official language status alongside English) invests Yoruba with national rather than ethnonational symbolic property identity.

I shall draw this chapter to a close by returning to the epigraph and addressing the questions of whether there is a genuine national identity in Nigeria, and if so, what role language plays in fostering such an identity.

There is certainly a genuine national identity in the context of arbitration in conflicts between nations of the kind we find in Nigeria's dispute with Cameroon over ownership of the Bakassi Peninsula. The identity in question here, though, is a political one, focused on territory rather than people. The extent to which language policy has or has not been an important factor in establishing this identity – or indeed has been an impediment to it – is evident in the criteria upon which judgement was reserved for Cameroon (see further Omoniyi 2004b). In the context of this dispute, it would seem that for the people of Bakassi, whereas national identity is made negotiable in the realm of international politics, their Nigerian identity is weaker than the ethnic identity around which they rally to protest against their inclusion by the International Court of Justice in the Cameroon national community. Here, language choice is a primary symbol of expressing loyalty to an ethnic group/nation.[1]

7. Conclusion

A nation is defined by the aggregate of those who belong to it, even as it defines them. A nation and its people are thus mutually invested. Against this background, Bamgbose's (1991) observation that language policy and ignorance are the principal factors impeding popular participation in the political process would suggest that input into the linguistic construction of national identity will reflect group perceptions of the extent to which policies, including language policy, cater to group needs and desires (see also Omoniyi 2003a, b). Therefore, among groups who perceive their destinies to be inadequately catered for, it is likely that ethnic identity will be a stronger unit of reference than national identity. Depending on the demographic distribution of groups, then, national identity may or may not be superficial. We may discuss this within the frameworks of intra- and inter-national politics. It is within the intra-national political framework that Nigeria's national identity has been described as a mere political expression, as per Obafemi Awolowo's contention in the epigraph at the beginning of this chapter. The upsurge in the activities of ethnic nationalities since the return of democratic governance in 1999 may be considered as validating that claim.

In view of the fact that language policy impacts negatively on the abilities of 'most of the population to participate effectively in the educational, socio-economic and political systems' (Bamgbose 2005), it may be argued that the capacity for emotional investment in the idea of a Nigerian national identity is commensurably limited, especially among uneducated rural people, for whom the indigenous languages meet the bulk of communicative needs as well as frame their ethnocultural worldview. Such people, who ironically constitute the majority of the nation's population, are administratively processed and marked for exclusion through institutional exercises such as electoral register compilation or constitutional debates, the texts of which are written exclusively in English and thereby rendered inaccessible (see Omoniyi 2003c).

From the linguistic point of view, the odds therefore seem stacked against the unification of Nigeria, the most populous and one of the most linguistically diverse countries in Africa, under a single monolithic and collectively agreed definition of nationhood. It remains to be seen whether the future language policies of the Federal Government will address the changing expectations and aspirations of Nigeria's culturally and linguistically heterogeneous population as the twenty-first century unfolds.

Note

1. British Academy Grant No. SG-36820 facilitated the Bakassi study in 2003 and 2004.

22

An Historical National Identity?
The Case of Scots

Robert McColl Millar

1. The nature of the problem: nationalism and language

In *Imagined Communities*, Benedict Anderson (1991) suggested that a shared sense of national identity was a product of a conscious *imagining* by opinion makers in European and American nations in the eighteenth and nineteenth centuries. This imagined community is a particularly powerful construct; so powerful, in fact, that people have been willing to die for it. Central to many imagined communities is the connection of *nation* with *language*, strengthened from the early modern period on through the growth of print capitalism and rammed home by the spread of literacy in the nineteenth century.

This relationship is not always as straightforward as the nationalist project suggests, however. There are many polities which do not have a national language; there may be a number of competing native languages and a language of wider communication left over from a colonial occupation. To analyse this, Fishman (1973) distinguished two forms of national identity: one associated with *nationality*, the other with *nation*. Nationality is defined by adherence to a common ethnic culture, expressed through use of the nationality's language. A nation, conversely, is not an ethnic construct. Citizens may speak different languages and come from different cultural backgrounds; their common, civic bonds will be celebrated, however. While a nationality's language policy will be built upon a single national language, the nation will use a language which is acceptable (or, at least, not unacceptable) to the majority.

This tension between *nationalist* and *nationist* forces can be found in most polities, although it is at its most intense in postcolonial contexts where citizens often share nothing except their former rulers and the rulers' language. In this chapter, however, I will discuss a situation which appears very different from that of, say, Nigeria (see further Omoniyi, this volume): Scotland. A complex relationship between language and (both personal and particularly national) identity exists in the latter country. An old country with a strong sense of a national history, Scotland has only recently gained some degree of autonomy after almost three hundred years of direct rule by a government and parliament dominated by English interests. Without overstressing the point, these changes bear some resemblance to postcolonial developments.

This similarity is particularly pronounced in language use. Unlike many submerged European nations, Scotland does not have one language as potential national symbol; instead, it has two. Moreover, one of these national vernaculars, Scots, is a close relative of the *de facto* official language of the United Kingdom, Standard English, and has been dialectalised into the English system over the last few centuries. This chapter will be primarily concerned with the problematical relationship Scots has with Scottish identity. In order to do this, however, we must first consider the status in the country of the other national language, Gaelic (Gàidhlig), and analyse the effectiveness of some of the non-linguistic symbols of Scottish identity.

2. Gaelic as a national identity symbol

Since the passing of the Gaelic Language Act of 2005, Scotland has been institutionally bilingual. The Scottish Government and Parliament are both officially so, with signage and Hansard (the official parliamentary report) produced both in English and Gaelic. All local councils must have a language plan designed to facilitate the use of services for Gaelic speakers and to raise the profile of that language in their area. One council, that of the Western Isles, has been bilingual since its inception in 1975; in those islands where Gaelic is dominant, Gaelic-only signs are the norm. Gaelic education is encouraged at all levels throughout both the *Gàidhealtachd* (the Gaelic-speaking part of north-western Scotland) and the Lowlands, and Gaelic programming is an integral part of Scottish terrestrial television schedules. Gaelic's importance in Scotland is emphasised by Gaelic-learning programmes such as *Speaking Our Language*, where an explicit connection is made between proficiency in Gaelic and national identity. Yet fewer than 60,000 people spoke Gaelic as a first language in 2001, in a country whose population is over 5 million (MacKinnon 2003).

There is considerable danger that, after centuries of what was, at best, benevolent neglect and was often in fact suppression, the use of Gaelic will become a token gesture, a 'dummy High' variety (Platt 1977) which is brought out to demonstrate national solidarity in a way which excludes a large part of the present Scottish population. Many Scots activists feel aggrieved by the fact that Gaelic appears to be given special treatment – more importantly, funding – when Scots has many more speakers than Gaelic and is spoken in various dialects in all of the counties of Scotland with the exception of the Western Isles. This may be precisely why Gaelic is given support, of course.

3. Non-linguistic expressions of Scottish identity

There are many features of Scottish life which could be analysed as identity symbols. These include institutional differences with England such as Scots Law and the Scottish church, as well as the strong folk song and folk dance traditions found in the country, often associated with festivals largely unknown outside Scotland (or exported by emigrants), such as Hogmanay. Sport also plays a vital role in defining Scottish identity. These can be seen as nationist rather than nationalist, to use Fishman's terms; civic, rather than ethnic, to use Anderson's. Everyone who lives in Scotland can participate, no matter what their ethnic or linguistic origin.

But although these symbols can create a strong sense of identity for Scottish people, they do not possess the force of the ethnic and linguistic nationalisms of Scotland's

Scandinavian neighbours to the north and east. Why is it that Scots, spoken by a large part of the population, cannot be used as such a symbol in as straightforward a way as, say, Swedish? To answer this, the historical development of Scots in Scotland and how the vernacular has been perceived and used in modern times must be analysed.

4. Scots and Scottish identity

4.1 Language status and dialectalisation

The connection between Scots and Scotland has always been fraught. From a linguistic viewpoint, the Germanic dialects of Scotland are sufficiently distinct from Standard English as to be considered part of a separate entity: intelligibility is heavily compromised when denser varieties of Scots are spoken to an English speaker who has had no contact with Scottish varieties. From a sociolinguistic standpoint, however, the relationship between Scots and Standard English is similar to, although subtly different from, that found between the English dialects and the standard. It is this subtle distinction with which the rest of this section will be concerned.

Kloss (1967, 1978; see also Millar 2005) distinguished between two means by which linguistic discreteness can be established: *Abstand* and *Ausbau*. While Abstand is produced through linguistic distinctiveness – the lack of mutual intelligibility – Ausbau is sociolinguistic in origin: a language comes into being through the conscious efforts of its speakers to make it distinct from its relatives. Ausbau is a dynamic process: use of a language variety in a greater number of non-local, scientific or bureaucratic written domains brings it closer to language status. In attempting this, supporters of a language almost inevitably become embroiled in competition, possibly conflict, with the supporters of other language varieties. Most languages have elements of both in their makeup. French is a language because it is sufficiently discrete from its Romance sisters to be perceived as a unit in itself; six hundred years of standardisation and planning have also allowed Parisian French to be employed in contexts closed to other northern Gallo-Romance dialects. For our purposes, however, Kloss's most intriguing contribution to the debate over what constitutes a language was his demonstration (Kloss 1984) that Ausbau status was dynamic. Dialects could become languages, and languages could be *dialectalised*.

Kloss posited a state (*Ausbaudialekt* 'Ausbau dialect' or *kin-tongue*) in between Ausbau language and a 'normal' dialect. Some varieties, which otherwise act as if they are 'normal' dialects of a language (generally the only variety taught as the 'national' one in schools), evince some Ausbau features. They are used in writing beyond humorous prose or verse and may be considered more appropriate than the standard in certain contexts. Practically all of these varieties are close relatives of the national language.

A good example of these processes is Low German (as discussed, for instance, in Francis 2002). The language of the mediaeval Hanseatic League, used around the Baltic and North Seas, it profoundly affected the languages of Scandinavia and influenced both Scots and English varieties. With speakers numbered in the millions, it was also the language of the north European plain from the Netherlands to central Poland. But although a Bible was published in Low German, High German began to encroach on most of its written domains from the Protestant Reformation onward. Low German was gradually dialectalised. The upper and middle classes – particularly in urban areas – switched over to High German. Low German quickly became seen as rural. Urban working-class varieties are generally looked down upon as 'corrupt' by both middle-class and rural speakers. Nevertheless, a considerable literature continues to be written; indeed, Low German has some status in local government in some parts of northern Germany. While being less than a language, it remains much more than a dialect.

4.2 The rise and fall of Scots[1]

Like Gaelic, Scots is not originally native to Scotland. Speakers of Old English first began to infiltrate what is now south-eastern Scotland in the sixth and seventh centuries. By the eighth century most of the lands to the south and east of Linlithgow had been incorporated into Northumbria. The variety of Old English spoken in these provinces was, as both a small amount of contemporary evidence and what we can reconstruct from later dialects demonstrates, already divergent from the West Saxon written variety used in most Old English materials. In the aftermath of the Scandinavian conquest and settlement of the Northumbrian heartland around York, the lands to the north of the Tyne, less affected by the invasions, were left in limbo: provinces without a kingdom.

In the tenth and eleventh centuries, the Gaelic-speaking King of Scots began to extend his power into this vacuum. South-east Scotland was, after all, one of the few parts of the country with long, relatively dry summers, increasing agricultural productivity. There is some evidence that the Anglian landholding class in this area was at least partly Gaelicised in culture and language; this cannot have been true for more lowly residents, given later events. Thus the Anglian dialects of Scotland were not integral to Scotland's original identity.

In the eleventh century Malcolm Canmore sought refuge in England for a considerable period, before seizing the Scottish throne with English support. Malcolm was undoubtedly Anglophile; it would be very surprising if he had not learned English during his exile. These tendencies were encouraged by the arrival in Scotland of the legitimate claimant to the English throne, Edgar Atheling, and his sister Margaret, in exile after the Norman conquest of 1066. Malcolm married Margaret, and their children, a number of whom became king, would all have spoken Gaelic. They would, however, all also have spoken English as – literally – their mother tongue. At the same time, the principal royal seat moved to the south-east. The fact that the people of Edinburgh spoke an Anglian dialect not terribly different from Margaret's Saxon one must have made it attractive.

The Anglian dialects of Lothian were not, therefore, considered markers of Scottish identity, but rather of the connection between England and this part of Scotland, a connection associated with new ideas and structures, foreign to the Scottish status quo.

In early mediaeval Scotland most food was produced at subsistence level; opportunities for trade were highly limited. Money was practically unknown. As the rest of north-west Europe became economically and culturally interconnected, the Kings of Scots became aware that their kingdom would not survive unless it adapted to these new situations. With this in mind, they invited members of the Norman ruling class of England to settle in Scotland, bringing with them followers who had the ability to construct and trade from a fortified marketplace, or *burgh*. The citizens of these burghs were given many inducements to develop trade in their hinterlands. This immigration would not have been possible without the perception of linguistic kinship with England the English-speaking monarchy obviously felt.

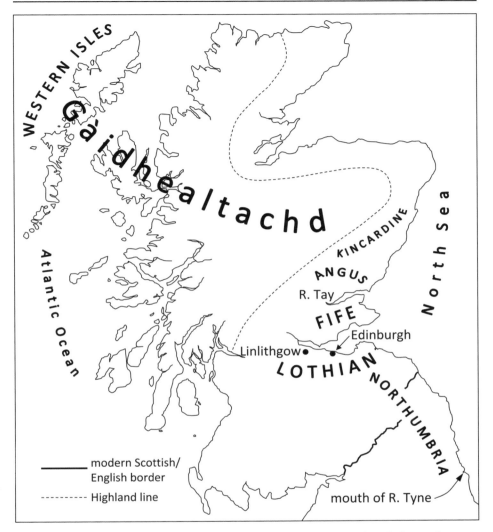

Figure 22.1 Map of Scotland showing places mentioned in the text. Based on Ordnance Survey map data by permission of the Ordnance Survey © Crown copyright 2001.

Most of the new landowners came from the north of England, a smaller number from the Welsh marches. All could develop and defend marginal and contested lands. Their followers would have spoken northern English dialects in the main, dialects affected directly by the Scandinavian settlements, unlike the existing Lothian dialects. Scots is a product of their merger. Again, what would eventually become Scots cannot be analysed as an identity symbol for the Scottish nation. Instead, it was associated with a particular region, particular immigrants and a particular, in many ways Anglophile, party within the ruling class. External, rather than internal, forces changed this.

Without going into needless detail, the good relations Scotland and England enjoyed during this period were destroyed through an attempted English conquest of Scotland in the late thirteenth century. The resistance to this aggression was not focused in the ruling class. Instead, and perhaps for the first time in European history, people's armies were created which mixed Scottish people from many different backgrounds. Modern Scotland was created during this period. The status of Scots shifted as well.

At the time there would still have been Gaelic speakers in the Lowlands, particularly in the hilly territory in Fife and the south-west. The Anglian dialects of the burghs would probably have spread in the more prosperous and fertile areas. There is every chance, nonetheless, that both Gaelic and perhaps still British (Brythonic) speakers were to be found even in the most populous areas. North of the Tay, Gaelic was dominant, but there were Anglian-speaking burghs in Angus and Kincardineshire and, north of the Highland Line, in the north-east. There were also a considerable number of speakers of North Germanic dialects around the periphery of northern Scotland. Many of the aristocracy would have spoken (Norman) French. Speakers of Dutch and Low German would have been regular visitors and might already have begun to settle in the burghs.

In the thirty years of intermittent warfare, people from different parts of Scotland who, we assume, spoke different languages, began to work together in a common cause. Inevitably, casual contacts between people of different cultures and languages became regular, and more intense contacts would have been common. The social chaos created by what was in many ways a civil war would also have encouraged contact. Although it would be difficult to prove, *Inglis*, as the native Germanic dialect was known, must have been employed as the *lingua franca*, acquiring many national trappings. It certainly became the language of most Scots south and east of the Highland line, including the aristocracy.

In the period immediately following independence Scots continued to spread and gain prestige, being used eventually in the *Brus*, an epic life of King Robert I, written by John Barbour (died 1395). What – among other things – Barbour is writing is national history with a propagandistic purpose. The language he uses is part of this nationalising process, although he does not explicitly make the connection between the two. Indeed, no Scottish writer in this period seems to have considered his *Inglis* as absolutely separate from English.

Too much has, perhaps, been made of the influence of Chaucer upon early sixteenth-century Scottish writers such as Dunbar and Henryson. Scottish critics in particular take exception to the phrase 'Scottish Chaucerians', since it implies a slavish imitation of the English writer on the part of *makars* (poets) who should be treated as writers of considerable merit and originality in their own right. Yet influence there certainly was. It is telling that, when higher register styles were employed, forms which represent southern English phonological patterns rather than Scottish ones are regularly found, albeit in an essentially Scottish context. Such style shifts remained common in many writers of the sixteenth century, the high point of autonomous Scots.

With Henryson and Dunbar's somewhat younger contemporary, Gavin Douglas, a different viewpoint appears. In the introduction to his translation of Virgil's *Aeneid* (1513), he explicitly distinguishes his *Scottis* (as he now terms his variety) from *Inglis* or *sudroun* ('southron'). At around the same time, Pedro de Ayala, the Spanish ambassador to Scotland, observed that 'His [King James IV's] own Scottish language is as different from English as Aragonese from Castilian' (Brown [1891] 1978: 39–40). Much has been made of these views; nevertheless, a view which perceived Scots and English as part of the same unit, no matter how loosely defined, was also prevalent, perhaps even dominant.

Thus, even at the height of its autonomy, a consensus on the exact nature of Scots and its relationship to English was never fully achieved. This would have disastrous effects upon the status of the language over the next two hundred years.

From around 1500 onward, Scotland and England became more closely interconnected than had previously been the case – even if the connections were bloody. The defeats at Flodden in 1513 and Solway Moss in 1542 were only the most dramatic of more than half a century's disorder on the marches. Along with the loss of many leading figures, the difficult times, including civil war, caused Scotland's economy to deteriorate. Economic instability meant that fewer printed books were produced in Scotland. It also meant that printers preferred to print works which were attractive to the far more affluent English readership. Inevitably, this encouraged Anglicisation in writing.

Along with many other European countries, Scotland suffered religious turmoil in this period. Scotland's reformation was, unusually, a change led by significant forces within the population rather than the monarchy. Perhaps because of this, there was considerable dissent within the Protestant camp. Religious strife became the norm. There was a linguistic dimension to these changes. In the first place, central to Protestant ideology was the belief that all should have access to the scriptures in their own language. In Scotland, this should have meant the production of a Bible in Scots. Translations were attempted during the Reformation. Eventually, however, the English Geneva Bible was preferred. This was partly expediency: an English translation of some quality was available when the stability necessary to produce Scots translations was absent; but many of the radical ideologues were also unusually Anglophile and Anglophone. The choice of an English Bible had immediate effects on the status of Scots. In a society where the Bible was perceived as the infallible word of God, what language it was written in mattered. Scots inevitably lost authority through not being used in these contexts. Religious radicals were attracted further to using the emerging Standard English in their writings, an encouragement reinforced by the potential market for writings in English in England. From this point, God spoke English in Scotland.

It should be stressed, however, that as far we can tell, all non-Gaelic Scots spoke Scots in the sixteenth century. The Union of the Crowns of Scotland and England in 1603 altered this. In the first place, King James VI (and I of England) moved to London and was followed by many Scottish aristocrats. Although this first generation continued using Scots, the organic link (itself probably compromised or never fully achieved, as we have seen) between Scots and being Scottish was lost. Instead, a (partly) Anglicised elite now ruled a Scots-speaking population. Moreover, the awareness that fortunes could be made in England led to a considerable number of rather less exalted Scots moving south. This shift in the psychological map of Scotland was matched by the awareness that, although Scotland remained in theory an independent country, it had in effect become an English satellite. The ongoing political and religious instability in Scotland did nothing to lessen this effect.

The Anglicisation of written Scots was not an overnight affair. Scots features in orthography, lexis and grammar were gradually replaced by English ones from the mid-sixteenth century on (Meurman-Solin 1993). By about a century later, the process was almost complete: Scots had been dialectalised.

4.3 Scots in the modern age

The result of the 'decline and fall' of Scots as a national language is a complex dialectic between the variety and Scottish national identity. To analyse this relationship, we need to consider both its modern literary use and the activist movement's own construction and relationship to speakers.

4.3.1 Scots Literature and Scottish national identity

I recently gave a conference paper concerning governmental support (or lack thereof) for Scots. At the end of my paper, one delegate said 'So long as there is literature in the language, Scots will survive.' When I demurred, making the Klossian point that the true index of linguistic health was the use of a language in non-literary contexts, he became agitated. I made the point that I was not in any way denigrating Scots literature; I believed literature in Scots was worthwhile in itself, but had little influence on the development or perception of the variety. If anything, the literary canon has been used against many contemporary varieties, their language being compared unfavourably with a 'glorious' literary past. Some lesser-used languages do not have enough literature written in them; with Scots the opposite may be true.

From the revival of writing in Scots in the eighteenth century, a number of use patterns are prevalent (as discussed, for instance, by Corbett 1997). In the first place, most texts entirely in Scots are poetic. When Scots is used in prose fiction, it is generally employed to represent the speech of working-class characters, with the middle and upper classes speaking Standard English (even when the novel is set in a period when most middle-class Scots still spoke Scots). The working-class characters are sympathetic types, demonstrating native simplicity and wit. The exception to this is the association of urban dialects with the dangerous or the sordid. The proverbial goodheartedness of rural dialect speakers is not, of course, a topos confined to Scottish writing. But this concentration on using Scots only for reported speech, as well as encouraging unfortunate social attitudes, inevitably makes the narrative, in Standard English, represent the default voice of authority, a view which was, inevitably, being reinforced through Church, State and the Educational system.

Some scholars would disagree with me. McClure (2000) makes a spirited defence of the view that the 'Scottish Renaissance' of the twentieth century marks the first modern attempt at both corpus and (implicitly) status planning for Scots. But its effect on the populace at large was minimal. For many Scots speakers, Scots as a written medium is associated with the poetry of Robert Burns, with the use of some Scots in popular newspapers and, finally, perhaps, its use in the rather saccharine magazine stories descending from the nineteenth-century 'Kailyard' movement (Nash 2007). I have been to many a Burns Supper, the annual celebration of Scotland's national bard, but never to a dinner in memory of, say, Sydney Goodsir Smith, another poet who wrote chiefly in Scots.

While comparable nations, such as Norway, developed nationalism in the wake of the French Revolution and expressed it through Romantic art works readily accessible to popular taste, Scottish cultural nationalism began in an era of literary experimentation. While that might make many of the writers of the 1920s and 1930s objectively greater artists than those writing a hundred years earlier, it does not make their work any more accessible to the speakers of the language represented. The quality of Scots literature has not been translated into the use of Scots as a national symbol.

4.3.2 Scots language activism

Indeed, this 'literary road' has been particularly damaging to the Scots activist movement. Central institutions, such as the Scots Language Society, were founded as literary societies. Often their influence has not spread beyond these contexts.

The activist movement itself is deeply divided. Of course, this is not unknown in language planning; what is troubling, however, is that controversial issues and decisions can lead to great tension in a relatively small group. Much energy is expended on these quarrels, rather than the language policy and planning supposedly at the movement's heart.

Sometimes these quarrels are caused by regional or age differences, regularly because of differences in temperament and political viewpoint (taken in its broadest sense). The movement is split into two main parties that I have termed (Millar 2005) the *cultural* and the *official*. The cultural party connects status planning for Scots with vernacular culture. Its use in folk song and verse, as well as its omnipresence in many rural areas associated with traditional lifestyles, supports this connection.

There is a problem with the cultural connection, however. Not all Scots speakers participate in Scottish traditional culture. They may even be negatively disposed towards something they consider divorced from their everyday lives. In the town where I live, two music clubs meet weekly: a folk club and a country and western society. Both hold regular 'open mic' nights at which anyone may perform. At the folk club, the members generally speak English but sing in Scots; at the country and western club, conversations in dense Scots are interrupted while participants sing in faux-American accents. Which is more representative of vernacular culture?

Moreover, the industrialisation of Scotland has led to bipolarity in the perception of Scottish culture and language. The majority of Scottish people live in urban environments. People who were nurtured in this environment have typically had little or no unmediated contact with rural traditions. The Scots they speak is also a product of their environment. Although traditional vernacular features survive (Macafee 1994), the influence of colloquial English is considerable. Both traditional speakers and many activists (of any party) are hostile to these urban varieties.

The official party essentially look to the 'capture' for Scots of many of the domains associated with state power: the bureaucracy, the educational system, and so on. The civil service, in particular, would be targeted, with a prescriptive standardised Scots being enforced by their practice. As part of this process, Scots would be promoted through being given 'Part III recognition' under the Council of Europe Charter for Regional or Minority Languages, a status at present only enjoyed by Gaelic. Scots is currently treated as a 'Part II' language (Millar 2006), which affords it a measure of protection, but which is more facilitative than actively promotional. A Scots Language Act to echo the Gaelic Language Act of 2005 would also be passed.

Again, it would be difficult to fault the intention of these policies. There is a glaring flaw in them, however: just because you legislate that something is the case linguistically does not mean that it will actually *be* the case. The case of Irish since 1922 is a good example of this problem. A government-inspired, purist Scots might be offputting to the majority of Scots-speakers, who might not recognise their variety in the new standard. The evidence Hardie (1996) and Fässler (1998) present supports this. There is a good chance that the policies put in place to protect and encourage the language might actually alienate speakers from it.

All of these processes can be analysed as *dislocation* (Millar, forthcoming). The Scottish state is dislocated from Scots speakers; the Scots language movement is dislocated from Scots speakers; Scots speakers may themselves be dislocated from Scots. While this is common to many minority language situations, it is acute for Scots in relation to Scotland. Whether we can still speak of a discrete Scots, and how the national vernacular relates to national identity, is unclear (see further Llamas, this volume).

5. Towards a conclusion

This chapter has attempted an historical, political and cultural survey of the confused relationship between Scots and Scottish identity. Although this confusion can be attributed to a number of causes, it is primarily due to the lack of definition over what the variety is, and what its relationship is to Standard English. Even in its 'glory days', when it was as standardised as any European vernacular, this niggling suspicion about identity and relationship remained. In the period which followed, this uncertainty permitted – perhaps encouraged – the dialectalisation of Scots. The association of its use with purely literary contexts cannot but have encouraged the idea that English was the default in non-literary, everyday domains. The activist movement, with its origins in modernism, contributes to this. Their concerns are rarely those of native speakers. While this is probably true for all language policy and planning initiatives, it is unusual to have such a lack of concordance between the two groups.

Note

1. What follows is generally well-documented – best, perhaps, by Macafee (2002). The interpretation is largely mine, however.

Bibliography

Abercrombie, David (1979), 'The accents of Standard English in Scotland', in Adam J. Aitken and Tom McArthur (eds), *Languages of Scotland*, Edinburgh: Chambers, pp. 65–84.

Abercrombie, Patrick and John Forshaw (1943), *County of London Plan*, London: Macmillan.

Adams, Caroline (1987), *Across Seven Seas and Thirteen Rivers*, London: Tower Hamlets Art Project (THAP) Books.

Afolayan, Adebisi (1976), 'The six-year primary project in Nigeria', in Ayo Bamgbose (ed.), *Mother Tongue Education: The West African Experience*, London: Hodder and Stoughton, pp. 113–34.

Agha, Asif (2003), 'The social life of a cultural value', *Language and Communication*, 23: 231–73.

Agha, Asif (2005), 'Voice, footing, enregisterment', *Journal of Linguistic Anthropology*, 15(1): 38–59.

Agha, Asif (2007), *Language and Social Relations*, New York: Cambridge University Press.

Ahearn, Laura (2001), 'Language and agency', *Annual Review of Anthropology*, 30: 109–37.

Aitken, Adam J. (1979), 'Scottish speech: a historical view with special reference to the Standard English of Scotland', in Adam J. Aitken and Tom McArthur (eds), *Languages of Scotland*, Edinburgh: Chambers, pp. 84–118.

Aitken, Adam J. (1984), 'Scottish accents and dialects', in Peter Trudgill (ed.), *Language in The British Isles*, Cambridge: Cambridge University Press, pp. 94–118.

Aitken, Adam J. (1992), 'Scots', in Tom McArthur (ed.), *The Oxford Companion to the English Language*, Oxford: Oxford University Press, pp. 893–9.

Akindele, Femi and Wale Adegbite (2000), *The Sociology and Politics of English in Nigeria: An Introduction*, Ile-Ife: Obafemi Awolowo University Press.

Alim, H. Sami and John Baugh (2007, eds), *Talkin Black Talk: Language, Education, and Social Change*, New York: Teachers' College Press.

Allard, Emily and Dale Williams (2008), 'Listeners' perceptions of speech and language disorders', *Journal of Communication Disorders*, 41: 108–23.

Allen, John, Doreen Massey and Allan Cochrane (1998), *Rethinking the Region*, London: Routledge.

Altendorf, Ulrike (2003), *Estuary English*, Tübingen: Gunter Narr Verlag.

Alvesson, Mats and Yvonne Billing (1997), *Gender, Work and Organization*, London: Sage.

Al-Wer, Enam (1997), 'Arabic between reality and ideology', *International Journal of Applied Linguistics*, 7: 251–65.

Amadiume, Ifi (1987), *Male Daughters, Female Husbands: Gender and Sex in African Society*, London: Zed Books.

Anderson, Benedict (1991), *Imagined Communities: Reflections on the Origin and Spread of Nationalism*, 2nd edn, London: Verso.

Anderson, Bridget (2002), 'Dialect leveling and /ai/ monophthongization among African American Detroiters', *Journal of Sociolinguistics*, 6: 86–98.

Andres, Claire and Rachel Votta (2007), 'AAE and Anglo vowels in a suburb of Atlanta', paper presented at the Annual Meeting of the Linguistic Society of America, Anaheim, CA, January 2007.

Androutsopoulos, Jannis (2001), 'From the streets to the screen and back again: on the mediated diffusion of ethnolectal patterns in contemporary German', *LAUD Linguistic Agency*, Series A, No. 522, Essen: Universität Essen.

Antaki, Charles and Sue Widdicombe (1998, eds), *Identities in Talk*, London: Sage.

Anwar, Muhammad (1979), *The Myth of Return*, London: Heinemann.

Ash, Sharon and John Myhill (1986), 'Linguistic correlates of inter-ethnic contact', in David Sankoff (ed.), *Diversity and Diachrony (Current Issues in Linguistic Theory 53)*, Amsterdam: John Benjamins, pp. 33–44.

Ashworth, Lauren, Nicholas Miller and Ghada Khattab (2006), 'The perception of foreign accent in low-pass filtered speech', paper presented at the 11th Meeting of the International Clinical Phonetics and Linguistics Association, Dubrovnik, Croatia, June 2006.

Asiwaju, Anthony (1976), *Western Yorubaland under European Rule 1889–1945: A Comparative Analysis of French and British Colonialism*, London: Humanities Press.

Atwood, Elmer (1953), *A Survey of Verb Forms in the Eastern United States*, Ann Arbor: University of Michigan Press.

Auer, Peter (1984), *Bilingual Conversation*, Amsterdam: John Benjamins.

Auer, Peter and Aldo Di Luzio (1992), *The Contextualization of Language*, Philadelphia: John Benjamins.

Austin, John (1962), *How to Do Things with Words*, Cambridge, MA: Harvard University Press.

Awobuluyi, Oladele (1996), 'Language education in Nigeria: theory, policy and practice', *Fafunwa Foundation Internet Journal of Education*, http://awobuluyi.notlong.com (accessed 7 April 2009).

Awolowo, Obafemi (1947), *Path to Nigerian Freedom*, London: Faber and Faber.

Bailey, Guy and Natalie Maynor (1987), 'Decreolization?', *Language in Society*, 16: 449–73.

Bailey, Guy and Jan Tillery (1999), 'The Rutledge Effect: the impact of interviewers on survey results in linguistics', *American Speech*, 74: 389–402.

Bailey, Guy, Tom Wikle, Jan Tillery and Lori Sand (1991), 'The apparent time construct', *Language Variation and Change*, 3: 241–64.

Bakhtin, Mikhail (1981), *The Dialogic Imagination: Four Essays by M.M. Bakhtin*, trans. Caryl Emerson and Michael Holquist, ed. Michael Holquist, Austin, TX: University of Texas Press.

Bakhtin, Mikhail (1984), *Problems of Dostoevsky's Poetics*, ed. Caryl Emerson, Minneapolis, MN: University of Minnesota Press.

Balibar, Etienne and Immanuel Wallerstein (1991), *Race, Nation, Class: Ambiguous Identities*, London: Verso.

Bamgbose, Ayo (1991), *Language and the Nation: The Language Question in Sub-Saharan Africa*, Edinburgh: Edinburgh University Press.

Bamgbose, Ayo (2005), 'Language and good governance', Nigerian Academy of Letters (NAL) convocation lecture, University of Lagos, August 2005.

Bamgbose, Ayo, Ayo Banjo and Andrew Thomas (1995), *New Englishes: A West African Perspective*, Ibadan: Mosuro Publishers.

Bangali, Lamissa (2002), '*We are Tagwa but my Mother is a Smith*': Ethnicity and Identity Transformation among the Sena-Tagwa of Burkina Faso', PhD Thesis: The University of Illinois at Urbana-Champaign.

Banjo, Ayo (2000), 'English in West Africa', *International Journal of the Sociology of Language*, 141: 27–38.

Barrett, Mary and Marilyn Davidson (2006), 'Gender and communication at work: an introduction', in Mary Barrett and Marilyn Davidson (eds), *Gender and Communication at Work*, Aldershot: Ashgate, pp. 1–16.

Barrett, Rusty (1995), 'Supermodels of the world, unite! Political economy and the language of performance among African American drag queens', in William Leap (ed.), *Beyond the Lavender Lexicon: Authenticity, Imagination, and Appropriation in Lesbian and Gay Languages*, Amsterdam: Gordon and Breach, pp. 207–26.

Barrett, Rusty (1999), 'Indexing polyphonous identity in the speech of African American drag queens', in Mary Bucholtz, A.C. Liang and Laurel Sutton (eds), *Reinventing Identities: The Gendered Self in Discourse*, New York: Oxford University Press, pp. 313–31.

Baugh, John (1983), *Black Street Speech: Its History, Structure, and Survival*, Austin, TX: University of Texas Press.

Baum, Shari and Marc Pell (1999), 'The neural bases of prosody: insights from lesion studies and neuroimaging', *Aphasiology*, 13: 581–608.

Bauman, Zygmunt (2000), *Liquid Modernity*, Cambridge: Polity.

Bauman, Zygmunt (2001), *Community: Seeking Safety in an Insecure World*, Cambridge: Polity.

Baxter, Judith (2008), 'Is it all tough at the top? A post-structuralist analysis of the construction of gendered speaker identities of British business leaders within interview narratives', *Gender and Language*, 2(2): 197–222.

Baylor, Carolyn, Kathryn Yorkston and Tanya Eadie (2005), 'The consequences of spasmodic dysphonia on communication-related quality of life: a qualitative study of the insider's experiences', *Journal of Communication Disorders*, 38: 395–419.

Beaken, Michael (1971), *A Study of Phonological Development in a Primary School Population in East London*, PhD thesis, University of London.

Beck, Janet Mackenzie (1999), 'Organic variation of the vocal apparatus', in William Hardcastle and John Laver (eds), *The Handbook of Phonetic Sciences*, Oxford: Blackwell, pp. 256–89.

Beck, Ulrich [1986] (1992), *Risk Society: Towards a New Modernity*, trans. Mark Ritter, London: Sage.

Beck, Ulrich (1999), *World Risk Society*, Cambridge: Polity.

Beck, Ulrich and Elisabeth Beck-Gernsheim (2002), *Individualization: Institutionalized Individualism and its Social and Political Consequences*, London: Sage.

Becker, Alton (1979), 'The figure a sentence makes: an interpretation of a classical Malay sentence', in Talmy Givón (ed.), *Syntax and Semantics, Vol. 12: Discourse and Syntax*, New York: Academic Press, pp. 243–59.

Becker, Kara and Elizabeth Coggshall (2008), 'The vowel phonologies of African American and White New York City residents', paper presented at the Annual Meeting of the Linguistic Society of America, Chicago, January 2008.

Behar, Ruth and Deborah Gordon (1995, eds), *Women Writing Culture*, Berkeley, CA: University of California Press.

Bell, Allan (1984), 'Language style as audience design', *Language in Society*, 13: 145–204.

Bell, Allan (2001), 'Back in style: reworking audience design', in Penelope Eckert and John Rickford (eds), *Style and Sociolinguistic Variation*, Cambridge: Cambridge University Press, pp. 139–69.

Bentahila, Abdelali and Eirlys Davies (2002), 'Language mixing in rai music: localisation or globalisation?' *Language and Communication*, 22(2): 187–207.

Benwell, Bethan and Elizabeth Stokoe (2006), *Discourse and Identity*, Edinburgh: Edinburgh University Press.

Bergvall, Victoria (1999), 'Toward a comprehensive theory of language and gender', *Language in Society*, 28: 273–93.

Bermant, Chaim (1975), *Point of Arrival*, London: Eyre Methuen.

Bernard, John (1969), 'On the uniformity of spoken Australian English', *Orbis*, 18: 63–73.

Bernstein, Basil (1996), 'Sociolinguistics: a personal view', in Basil Bernstein (ed.), *Pedagogy, Symbolic Control and Identity: Theory, Research, Critique*, London: Taylor and Francis, pp. 147–56.

Berthier, Marcelo, Adelaida Ruiz, Maria Massone, Sergio Starkstein and Ramon Leiguarda (1991), 'Foreign Accent Syndrome – behavioral and anatomical findings in recovered and non-recovered patients', *Aphasiology*, 5: 129–47.

Besnier, Niko (2003), 'Crossing genders, mixing languages: the linguistic construction of transgenderism in Tonga', in Janet Holmes and Miriam Meyerhoff (eds), *Handbook of Language and Gender*, Oxford: Blackwell, pp. 279–301.

Besnier, Niko (2004), 'Consumption and cosmopolitanism: practicing modernity at the second-hand marketplace in Nuku'alofa, Tonga', *Anthropological Quarterly*, 77(1): 7–45.

Besnier, Niko (2007), 'Language and gender research at the intersection of the global and the local', *Gender and Language*, 1(1): 67–78.

Bhat, D.N. Shankara (1970), 'Age-grading and sound change', *Word*, 26: 262–70.

Billig, Michael (1995), *Banal Nationalism*, London: Sage.

Bing, Janet and Victoria Bergvall (1996), 'The question of questions: beyond binary thinking', in Victoria Bergvall, Janet Bing and Alice Freed (eds), *Rethinking Language and Gender Research: Theory and Practice*, London: Longman, pp. 1–30.

Bird, Jon (1993), 'Dystopia on the Thames', in Jon Bird, Barry Curtis, Tim Putnam, George Robertson and Lisa Tickner (eds), *Mapping the Futures: Local Cultures, Global Change*, London: Routledge, pp. 120–35.

Bishop, Hywel, Nikolas Coupland and Peter Garrett (2003), '"Blood is thicker than the water that separates us!": dimensions and qualities of Welsh identity in the North American diaspora', *The North American Journal of Welsh Studies*, 3(2): 37–52.

Blatchford, Helen and Paul Foulkes (2006), 'Identification of voices in shouting', *International Journal of Speech, Language and the Law*, 13(2): 241–54.

Block, David (2005), *Multilingual Identities in a Global City: London Stories*, Basingstoke: Palgrave.

Blom, Jan Peter and John Gumperz (1972), 'Social meaning in linguistic structures: code switching in Norway', in John Gumperz and Dell Hymes (eds), *Directions in Sociolinguistics*, New York: Holt, Rinehart and Winston, pp. 407–34.

Blomberg, Mats, Daniel Elenius and Elisabeth Zetterholm (2004), 'Speaker verification scores and acoustic analysis of a professional impersonator', *Proceedings of the 17th Swedish Phonetics Conference (Fonetik 2004)*, University of Stockholm. http:// blombergetal.notlong.com (accessed 7 April 2009).

Blommaert, Jan (1999, ed.), *Language Ideological Debates*, Berlin: Mouton de Gruyter.

Blommaert, Jan (2005), *Discourse: A Critical Introduction*, Cambridge: Cambridge University Press.

Blommaert, Jan (2007), 'Sociolinguistics and discourse analysis: orders of indexicality and polycentricity', *Journal of Multicultural Discourses*, 2: 115–30.

Blondeau, Hélène (2001), 'Real-time changes in the paradigm of personal pronouns in Montreal French', *Journal of Sociolinguistics*, 5: 453–74.

Bloomfield, Leonard (1927), 'Literate and illiterate speech', *American Speech*, 2: 432–39.

Bloomquist, Jennifer (2008), 'African American English in central Pennsylvania's lower Susquehanna Valley: regional phonological accommodation', paper presented at the Annual Meeting of the American Dialect Society, Chicago, January 2008.

Blumstein, Sheila and Kathleen Kurowski (2006), 'The foreign accent syndrome: a perspective', *Journal of Neurolinguistics*, 19: 346–55.

Boberg, Charles (2000), 'Geolinguistic diffusion and the U.S.–Canada border', *Language Variation and Change*, 12: 1–24.

Bockting, Walter (1997), 'Transgender coming out: implications for the clinical management of gender dysphoria', in Bonnie Bullough, Vern Bullough and James Elias (eds), *Gender Blending*, Amherst, NY: Prometheus Books, pp. 48–52.

Boersma, Paul and David Weenink (2009), 'Praat: doing phonetics by computer', (Version 5.1), [Computer program]. http://www.praat.org (accessed 7 April 2009).

Bond, Ross and Michael Rosie (2002), *National Identities in Post-Devolution Scotland*, University of Edinburgh Institute of Governance Online Articles and Papers, http:// bondrosie.notlong.com (accessed 7 April 2009).

Borba, Rodrigo and Ana Cristina Ostermann (2007), 'Do bodies matter? Travestis' embodiment of (trans)gender identity through the manipulation of the Brazilian Portuguese grammatical gender system', *Gender and Language*, 1(1): 131–47.

Bornstein, Kate (1994), *Gender Outlaw: On Men, Women, and the Rest of Us*, New York: Routledge.

Bornstein, Kate [1994] (2006), 'Gender terror, gender rage', in Susan Stryker and

Stephen Whittle (eds), *The Transgender Studies Reader*, New York: Routledge, pp. 236–43.

Bortoni-Ricardo, Stella (1985), *The Urbanization of Rural Dialect Speakers: A Sociolinguistic Study in Brazil*, Cambridge: Cambridge University Press.

Boum, Aomar (2008), 'The political coherence of educational incoherence: the consequences of educational specialization in a southern Moroccan community', *Anthropology and Education Quarterly*, 39(2): 205–23.

Bourdieu, Pierre [1972] (1977), *Outline of a Theory of Practice*, trans. Richard Nice, Cambridge: Cambridge University Press.

Bourdieu, Pierre (1984), *Distinction: A Social Critique of the Judgment of Taste*, trans. Richard Nice, Cambridge, MA: Harvard University Press.

Bourdieu, Pierre (1991), *Language and Symbolic Power: The Economy of Linguistic Exchanges*, trans. Gino Raymond and Matthew Adamson, ed. John B. Thompson, Cambridge: Polity Press.

Bowie, David (2000), *The Effect of Geographic Mobility on the Retention of a Local Dialect*, PhD thesis: University of Pennsylvania.

Bowie, David (2005), 'Language change over the lifespan: a test of the apparent time construct', *University of Pennsylvania Working Papers in Linguistics*, 11(2): 45–58.

Bowie, David (forthcoming), 'Aging and sociolinguistic variation', in Anna Duszak and Urszula Okulska (eds), *Communicating Across Age Groups: Age, Language and Society*, Berlin: Mouton de Gruyter.

Bradley, Harriet (1996), *Fractured Identities: Changing Patterns of Inequality*, Cambridge: Polity.

Brann, Conrad (1978), *Multilinguisme et Éducation au Nigeria*, Quebec: Centre Internationale de Recherche sur le Bilinguisme.

Britain, David (2001), 'Welcome to East Anglia! Two major dialect boundaries in the Fens', in Jacek Fisiak and Peter Trudgill (ed.), *East Anglian English*, Woodbridge: Boydell and Brewer, pp. 217–42.

Britain, David (2005), 'Innovation diffusion, "Estuary English" and local dialect differentiation: the survival of Fenland Englishes', *Linguistics*, 43: 995–1022.

Britain, David (in press a), 'Conceptualisations of geographic space in linguistics', in Alfred Lameli, Roland Kehrein and Stefan Rabanus (eds), *The Handbook of Language Mapping*, Berlin: Mouton de Gruyter.

Britain, David (in press b), 'Contact and dialectology', in Raymond Hickey (ed.), *Handbook of Language Contact*, Oxford: Blackwell.

Britain, David, and Peter Trudgill (1999), 'Migration, new-dialect formation and sociolinguistic refunctionalisation: reallocation as an outcome of dialect contact', *Transactions of the Philological Society*, 97(2): 245–56.

Britain, David and Peter Trudgill (2005), 'New dialect formation and contact-induced reallocation: three case studies from the English Fens', *International Journal of English Studies*, 5(1): 183–208.

Broeders, Ton and Toni Rietveld (1995), 'Speaker identification by earwitnesses', in Angelika Braun and Jens-Peter Köster (eds), *Studies in Forensic Phonetics*, Trier: Wissenschaftlicher Verlag, pp. 24–40.

Brown, Penelope and Stephen Levinson (1987), *Politeness: Some Universals in Language Usage*, Cambridge: Cambridge University Press.

Brown, Peter Hume [1891] (1978), *Early Travellers in Scotland*, Edinburgh: James Thin.

Bucholtz, Mary (1995), 'From mulatta to mestiza: passing and the linguistic reshaping of ethnic identity', in Kira Hall and Mary Bucholtz (eds), *Gender Articulated: Language and the Socially Constructed Self*, New York: Routledge, pp. 351–73.

Bucholtz, Mary (1999a), 'You da man: narrating the racial other in the linguistic production of white masculinity', *Journal of Sociolinguistics*, 3(4): 443–60.

Bucholtz, Mary (1999b), '"Why be normal?": language and identity practices in a community of nerd girls', *Language in Society*, 28: 203–23.

Bucholtz, Mary (2003), 'Sociolinguistic nostalgia and the authentication of identity', *Journal of Sociolinguistics*, 7(3): 398–416.

Bucholtz, Mary and Kira Hall (2004a), 'Language and identity', in Alessandro Duranti (ed.), *A Companion to Linguistic Anthropology*, Oxford: Blackwell, pp. 369–94.

Bucholtz, Mary and Kira Hall (2004b), 'Theorizing identity in language and sexuality research', *Language in Society*, 33(4): 501–47.

Bucholtz, Mary and Kira Hall (2005), 'Identity and interaction: a socio-cultural linguistic approach', *Discourse Studies*, 7(4–5): 585–614.

Buchstaller, Isabelle (2002), 'BE like U.S. English? BE goes U.S. English?', paper presented at New Ways of Analyzing Variation (NWAV) 31, Stanford University.

Buchstaller, Isabelle (2006), 'Diagnostics of age-graded linguistic behaviour: the case of the quotative system', *Journal of Sociolinguistics*, 10: 3–30.

Bull, Ray and Brian Clifford (1984), 'Earwitness voice recognition accuracy', in Gary Wells and Elizabeth Loftus (eds), *Eyewitness Testimony: Psychological Perspectives*, Cambridge: Cambridge University Press, pp. 92–123.

Bull, Ray, Harriet Rathborn and Brian Clifford (1983), 'The voice recognition accuracy of blind listeners', *Perception*, 12: 223–6.

Burda, Angela and Carlin Hageman (2005), 'Perception of accented speech by residents in assisted-living facilities', *Journal of Medical Speech-Language Pathology*, 13: 7–14.

Burgener, Sandy and Barbara Berger (2008), 'Measuring perceived stigma in persons with progressive neurological disease: Alzheimer's dementia and Parkinson's disease', *Dementia*, 7: 31–53.

Burgess, Melinda and George Weaver (2003), 'Interest and attention in facial recognition', *Perceptual and Motor Skills*, 96(2): 467–80.

Butler, Judith (1990), *Gender Trouble: Feminism and the Subversion of Identity*, New York: Routledge.

Butler, Judith (1993), *Bodies That Matter: On the Discursive Limits of 'Sex'*, London: Routledge.

Butler, Judith (1999), *Gender Trouble: Feminism and the Subversion of Identity*, 2nd ed., New York: Routledge.

Butler, Judith (2004), *Undoing Gender*, New York: Routledge.

Butters, Ronald and Ruth Nix (1986), 'The English of Blacks in Wilmington, North Carolina', in Michael Montgomery and Guy Bailey (eds), *Language Variety in the South: Perspectives in Black and White*, Tuscaloosa, AL: University of Alabama Press, pp. 254–63.

Bybee, Joan (2006), 'From usage to grammar: the mind's response to repetition', *Language*, 82: 711–33.

California Style Collective (1993), 'Personal and group style', paper presented at New Ways of Analyzing Variation (NWAV) 22, Ottawa, October 1993.

Calvet, Louis-Jean (1994), *Les Voix de la Ville: Introduction à la Sociolinguistique Urbaine*, Paris: Éditions Payot et Rivales.

Cambier-Langeveld, Tina (2007), 'Current methods in forensic speaker identification: results of a collaborative exercise', *International Journal of Speech, Language and the Law*, 14(2): 223–43.

Cameron, Deborah (2003), 'Gender and language ideologies', in Janet Holmes and Miriam Meyerhoff (eds), *The Handbook of Language and Gender*, Oxford: Blackwell, pp. 447–67.

Cameron, Deborah (2007), 'Unanswered questions and unquestioned assumptions in the study of language and gender: female verbal superiority', *Gender and Language*, 1(1): 15–25.

Cant, Robin (1997), 'Rehabilitation following a stroke: a participant perspective', *Disability and Rehabilitation*, 19: 297–304.

Carbary, T.J., J.P. Patterson and P.J. Snyder (2000), 'Foreign Accent Syndrome following a catastrophic second injury: MRI correlates, linguistic and voice pattern analyses', *Brain and Cognition*, 43: 78–85.

Carlson, Holly and Monica McHenry (2006), 'Effect of accent and dialect on employability', *Journal of Employment Counseling*, 43: 70–83.

Carpenter, Jeannine (2004), *The Lost Community of the Outer Banks: African American Speech on Roanoke Island*, MA dissertation, North Carolina State University.

Chambers, Jack (1992), 'Dialect acquisition', *Language*, 68(4): 673–705.

Chambers, Jack (2000), 'Region and language variation', *English World-Wide*, 21(2): 169–99.

Chambers, Jack (2002), 'Dynamics of dialect convergence', *Journal of Sociolinguistics*, 6(1): 117–30.

Champion, Tony (1998), 'Studying counterurbanisation and the rural population turnaround', in Paul Boyle and Keith Halfacree (eds), *Migration into Rural Areas: Theories and Issues*, Chichester: Wiley and Sons, pp. 21–40.

Champion, Tony (2001), 'Urbanization, suburbanization, counterurbanization and reurbanization', in Ronan Paddison (ed.), *The Handbook of Urban Studies*, London: Sage, pp. 143–61.

Champion, Tony (2005), 'Population movement within the UK', in Roma Chappell (ed.), *Focus on People and Migration*, Basingstoke: Palgrave, pp. 91–114.

Charmaz, Kathy (1995), 'The body, identity, and self: adapting to impairment', *The Sociological Quarterly*, 36: 657–80.

Charmaz, Kathy (2002), 'Stories and silences: disclosures and self in chronic illness', *Qualitative Inquiry*, 8: 302–28.

Chase, Cheryl (1998), 'Hermaphrodites with attitude: mapping the emergence of intersex political activism', *GLQ: A Journal of Lesbian and Gay Studies*, 4(2): 189–211.

Chaski, Carole (2005), 'Who's at the keyboard? Authorship attribution in digital evidence investigations', *International Journal of Digital Evidence*, 4(1): 1–13.

Cheshire, Jenny, Susan Fox and David Britain (2007), *Relatives from the South*, paper presented at the 6th UK Language Variation and Change Conference, Lancaster University, September 2007.

Cheshire, Jenny, Susan Fox, Paul Kerswill and Eivind Torgersen (in press), 'Ethnicity, friendship network, and social practices as the motor of dialect change: linguistic innovation in London', *Sociolinguistica*, 21.

Cheshire, Jenny and Penelope Gardner-Chloros (1998), 'Codeswitching and the sociolinguistic gender pattern', *International Journal of the Sociology of Language* 129: 5–34.

Chetrit, Joseph (1994), 'Structures du mixage linguistique dans les langues secrètes juives du Maroc', in Dominique Caubet and Martine Vanhove (eds), *Actes des Premières Journées Internationales de Dialectologie Arabe de Paris*, Paris: Publications Langues'O, pp. 519–30.

Chetrit, Joseph (2003), 'Configurations morpho-phonétiques dans le parler judéo-arabe de Meknès: prolégomènes à une description du parler', in Jérôme Lentin and Antoine Lonnet (eds), *Mélanges David Cohen: Études sur le langage, les langues, les littératures, offertes par ses élèves, ses collègues, ses amis*, Paris: Maisonneuve et Larose, pp. 159–72.

Childs, Becky, Christine Mallinson, and Jeannine Carpenter (2007), 'Vowel phonology and ethnicity in North Carolina', paper presented at the Annual Meeting of the Linguistic Society of America, Anaheim, CA, January 2007.

Choudhury, Yousuf (1993), *The Roots and Tales of the Bangladeshi Settlers*, Birmingham: Sylheti Social History Group.

Christen, Helen (1997), 'Koiné-Tendenzen im Schweizerdeutschen?', in Gerhard Stickel (ed.), *Varietäten des Deutschen: Regional- und Umgangssprachen*, Berlin: Walter de Gruyter, pp. 346–63.

Christensen, Helen, Ailsa Korten, Anthony Jorm, Scott Henderson, Patricia Jacomb, Bryan Rodgers and Andrew Mackinnon (1999), 'An analysis of diversity in the cognitive performance of elderly community dwellers: individual differences in change scores as a function of age', *Psychology and Aging*, 14: 365–79.

Christoph, D., G. De Freitas, D. Dos Santos, M. Lima, A. Araújo and A. Carota (2004), 'Different perceived foreign accents in one patient after prerolandic hematoma', *European Neurology*, 52: 198–201.

Chun, Elaine (2004), 'Ideologies of legitimate mockery: Margaret Cho's revoicings of mock-Asian', *Pragmatics*, 14: 263–90.

Clark, Herbert (1997), 'Dogmas of understanding', *Discourse Processes*, 25: 567–98.

Clark, J. Alan, P. Dee Boersma and Dawn M. Olmsted (2006), 'Name that tune: call discrimination and individual recognition in Magellanic penguins', *Animal Behavior*, 72(5): 1141–8.

Clark, Jessica and Paul Foulkes (2007), 'Identification of voices in electronically disguised speech', *International Journal of Speech, Language and the Law*, 14(2): 195–221.

Clayton, Tristan (2002), 'Politics and nationalism in Scotland: a Clydeside case study of identity construction', *Political Geography*, 21: 813–43.

Clifford, Brian, Harriet Rathborn and Ray Bull (1981), 'The effects of delay on voice recognition accuracy', *Law and Human Behavior*, 5: 201–8.

Clifford, James and George Marcus (1986, eds), *Writing Culture: The Poetics and Politics of Ethnography*, Berkeley, CA: University of California Press.

Coadou, Marion and Abderrazak Rougab (2007), 'Voice quality and variation in English', *Proceedings of the 16th International Congress of Phonetic Sciences*, Saarbrücken, August 2007, pp. 2077–80.

Coates, Jennifer (1997), 'Competing discourses of femininity', in Helga Kotthoff and

Ruth Wodak (eds), *Communicating Gender in Context*, Amsterdam: John Benjamins, pp. 285–313.

Coe, Neil and Alan Townsend (1998), 'Debunking the myth of localized agglomerations: the development of a regionalized service economy in South-East England', *Transactions of the Institute of British Geographers NS*, 23: 385–404.

Cohen, Anthony (1985), *The Symbolic Construction of Community*, London: Tavistock.

Cohen, Philip (1972), 'Subcultural conflict and working class community', *Working Papers in Cultural Studies 2*, Birmingham: Centre for Contemporary Cultural Studies, pp. 5–53.

Cohen, Philip (1988), 'Perversions of inheritance: studies in the making of multiracist Britain', in Philip Cohen and Harwant Bains (eds), *Multiracist Britain*, Basingstoke: Macmillan, pp. 9–120.

Cook, Susan and John Wilding (2001), 'Earwitness testimony: effects of exposure and attention on the Face Overshadowing Effect', *British Journal of Psychology*, 92: 617–29.

Corbett, John (1997), *Language and Scottish Literature*, Edinburgh: Edinburgh University Press.

Cornelissen, Georg (1999), 'Regiolekte im deutschen Westen', *Niederdeutsches Jahrbuch: Jahrbuch des Vereins für niederdeutsche Sprachforschung*, 122: 91–114.

Coronado Suzán, Gabriela (1999), *Porque Hablar dos Idiomas es Como Saber Más: Sistemas Comunicativos Bilingües Ante el México Plural*, México DF: Conacyt.

Coupland, Nikolas (1980), 'Style-shifting in a Cardiff work-setting', *Language in Society*, 9(1): 1–12.

Coupland, Nikolas (2000), '"Other" representation', in Jef Verschueren, Jan-Ola Östman, Jan Blommaert and Chris Bulcaen (eds), *Handbook of Pragmatics, 1999 Installment*, Amsterdam: John Benjamins, pp. 1–24.

Coupland, Nikolas (2001a), 'Age in social and sociolinguistic theory', in Nikolas Coupland, Srikant Sarangi and Christopher Candlin (eds), *Sociolinguistics and Social Theory*, London: Longman, pp. 185–211.

Coupland, Nikolas (2001b), 'Stylization, authenticity and TV news review', *Discourse Studies*, 3: 413–42.

Coupland, Nikolas (2001c), 'Dialect stylisation in radio talk', *Language in Society*, 30(3): 345–75.

Coupland, Nikolas (2003), 'Sociolinguistic authenticities', *Journal of Sociolinguistics*, 7(3): 417–31.

Coupland, Nikolas (2007), *Style, Variation and Identity*, Cambridge: Cambridge University Press.

Coupland, Nikolas (2008), 'The delicate constitution of identity in face-to-face accommodation: a response to Trudgill', *Language in Society*, 37: 267–70.

Coupland, Nikolas and Adam Jaworski (2009, eds), *The New Sociolinguistics Reader*, Basingstoke: Macmillan.

Coupland, Nikolas and Virpi Ylänne (2006), 'The sociolinguistics of ageing', in Ulrich Ammon, Norbert Dittmar, Klaus Mattheier and Peter Trudgill (eds), *Sociolinguistics: An International Handbook of the Science of Language and Society*, Vol. 3, Berlin: Walter de Gruyter, pp. 2334–40.

Craig, Cairns (1996), *Out of History*, Edinburgh: Polygon.

Craig, Holly and Julie Washington (2006), *Malik Goes to School: Examining the Language Skills of African American Students From Preschool–5th Grade*, Mahwah, NJ: Lawrence Erlbaum Associates.

Critchley, Macdonald (1970), 'Regional "accent", demotic speech and aphasia' (reprinted from *Livre Jubilaire de Ludo van Bogaert* 1962, pp. 182–91, Antwerp), in Macdonald Critchley (ed.), *Aphasiology and Other Aspects of Language*, London: Arnold, pp. 240–7.

Cunningham-Andersson, Una and Olle Engstrand (1989), 'Perceived strength and identity of foreign accent in Swedish', *Phonetica*, 46: 138–54.

Dankovičová, Jana, Jennifer Gurd, John Marshall, Michael MacMahon, Jane Stuart-Smith, John Coleman and A. Slater (2001), 'Aspects of non-native pronunciation in a case of altered accent following stroke (foreign accent syndrome)', *Clinical Linguistics and Phonetics*, 15: 195–218.

da Silva, Emanuel, Mireille McLaughlin and Mary Richards (2007), 'Bilingualism and the globalized new economy: the commodification of language and identity', in Monica Heller (ed.), *Bilingualism: A Social Approach*, New York: Palgrave Macmillan, pp. 183–206.

Davies, Bethan (2005), 'Communities of practice: legitimacy not choice', *Journal of Sociolinguistics*, 9: 557–581.

Davies, Eirlys and Abdelali Bentahila (2008), 'Code switching as a poetic device: examples from rai lyrics', *Language and Communication*, 28(1): 1–20.

de Fina, Anna (forthcoming), 'The negotiation of identities', in Sage Graham and Miriam Locher (eds), *Handbook of Interpersonal Pragmatics*, Berlin: Mouton de Gruyter.

De Mareüil, Philippe Boula and Bianca Vieru-Dimulescu (2006), 'The contribution of prosody to the perception of foreign accent', *Phonetica*, 63: 247–67.

Dessalles, Jean-Louis (2007), *Why We Talk: The Evolutionary Origins of Language*, trans. James Grieve, Oxford: Oxford University Press.

Deser, Toni (1990), *Dialect Transmission and Variation: An Acoustic Analysis of Vowels in Six Urban Detroit Families*, PhD thesis, Boston University.

Diamond, Milton (2003), 'What's in a name? Some terms used in the discussion of sex and gender', *Transgender Tapestry*, 102: 18–21.

Dickson, Sylvia, Rosaline Barbour, Marian Brady, Alexander Clark and Gillian Paton (2008), 'Patients' experiences of disruptions associated with post-stroke dysarthria', *International Journal of Language and Communication Disorders*, 43: 135–53.

Di Dio, Cinzia, Jörg Schulz and Jennifer Gurd (2006), 'Foreign Accent Syndrome: in the ear of the beholder?', *Aphasiology*, 20: 951–62.

Dixon, John, Berenice Mahoney and Roger Cocks (2002), 'Accents of guilt? Effects of regional accent, race, and crime type on attributions of guilt', *Journal of Language and Social Psychology*, 21: 162–8.

Docherty, Gerard, Paul Foulkes, James Milroy, Lesley Milroy and David Walshaw (1997), 'Descriptive adequacy in phonology: a variationist perspective', *Journal of Linguistics*, 33: 275–310.

Domingue, Nicole (1981), 'Internal change in a transplanted language', *Studies in the Linguistic Sciences*, 4: 151–9.

Donnan, Hastings and Thomas Wilson (1999), *Borders: Frontiers of Identity, Nation and State*, Oxford: Berg Publishers.

Doty, Nathan (1998), 'The influence of nationality on the accuracy of face and voice recognition', *American Journal of Psychology*, 111: 191–214.

Du Bois, John (2002), 'Stance and consequence', paper presented at the Annual Meeting of the American Anthropological Association, New Orleans, November 2002.

Du Bois, John (2007), 'The stance triangle', in Robert Englebretson (ed.), *Stancetaking in Discourse: Subjectivity, Evaluation, Interaction*, Amsterdam: John Benjamins, pp. 139–82.

Dudai, Yadin (1997), 'How big is human memory, or on being just useful enough', *Learning and Memory*, 3: 341–65.

Duffy, Joseph (2005), *Motor Speech Disorders*, St Louis, MO: Mosby Press.

Dunbar, Robin (1996), *Grooming, Gossip and the Evolution of Language*, London: Faber and Faber.

Duranti, Alessandro (1997), *Linguistic Anthropology*, Cambridge: Cambridge University Press.

Duranti, Alessandro (2004), 'Agency in language', in Alessandro Duranti (ed.), *A Companion to Linguistic Anthropology*, Malden, MA: Blackwell, pp. 451–73.

Durian, David, Robin Dodsworth, and Jennifer Schumacher (2007), 'Convergence in urban blue collar Columbus AAVE and EAE vowel systems?', paper presented at the Annual Meeting of the Linguistic Society of America, Anaheim, CA, January 2007.

Dyer, Judy (2000), *Language and Identity in a Scottish–English Community: A Phonological and Discoursal Analysis*, PhD thesis, The University of Michigan.

Dyer, Judy (2002), '"We all speak the same round here": dialect levelling in a Scottish-English community', *Journal of Sociolinguistics*, 6(2): 99–116.

Eberhardt, Maeve (2008), 'Still different in the [stɪl] city? African American and White vowel systems in Pittsburgh', paper presented at the Annual Meeting of the Linguistic Society of America, Chicago, January 2008.

Eckert, Penelope (1989), *Jocks and Burnouts: Social Identity in the High School*, New York: Teachers College Press.

Eckert, Penelope (1990), 'The whole woman: sex and gender differences in variation', *Language Variation and Change*, 1: 245–67.

Eckert, Penelope (1997), 'Age as a sociolinguistic variable', in Florian Coulmas (ed.), *The Handbook of Sociolinguistics*, Oxford: Blackwell, pp. 151–67.

Eckert, Penelope (2000), *Linguistic Variation as Social Practice: The Linguistic Construction of Identity at Belten High*, Oxford: Blackwell.

Eckert, Penelope (2003), 'Elephants in the room', *Journal of Sociolinguistics*, 7(3): 392–7.

Eckert, Penelope (2005), 'Variation, convention and social meaning', paper presented at the Annual Meeting of the Linguistic Society of America, Oakland, CA, January 2005.

Eckert, Penelope and Sally McConnell-Ginet (1992), 'Think practically and look locally: language and gender as community-based practice', *Annual Review of Anthropology*, 21: 461–90.

Eckert, Penelope and Sally McConnell-Ginet (2003), *Language and Gender*, Cambridge: Cambridge University Press.

Eckert, Penelope and Sally McConnell-Ginet (2007), 'Putting communities of practice in their place', *Gender and Language*, 1: 27–37.

Eckert, Penelope and John Rickford (2001, eds), *Style and Sociolinguistic Variation*, Cambridge: Cambridge University Press.

Eckert, Penelope and Etienne Wenger (1993), *Seven Principles of Learning*, Palo Alto, CA: Institute for Research on Learning.

Eckert, Penelope and Etienne Wenger (2005), 'What is the role of power in sociolinguistic variation?', *Journal of Sociolinguistics*, 9: 582–9.

Edwards, John (1985), *Language, Society and Identity*, Oxford: Blackwell.

Edwards, Walter (1992), 'Sociolinguistic behavior in a Detroit inner-city black neighborhood', *Language in Society*, 21(1): 93–115.

Edwards, Walter (1997), 'The variable persistence of Southern vernacular sounds in the speech of inner-city Black Detroiters', in Cynthia Bernstein, Thomas Nunnally and Robin Sabino (eds), *Language Variety in the South Revisited*, Tuscaloosa, AL: University of Alabama Press, pp. 76–86.

Egbokhare, Francis (2001), 'The Nigerian linguistic ecology and the changing profiles of Nigerian Pidgin', in Herbert Igboanusi (ed.), *Language Attitudes and Language Conflict in West Africa*, Ibadan: Enicrownfit Publishers, pp. 105–24.

Eira, Christina and Tonya Stebbins (2008), 'Authenticities and lineages: revisiting concepts of continuity and change in language', *International Journal of the Sociology of Language*, 189: 1–30.

Eladd, Eitan, Sima Segev and Yishai Tobin (1998), 'Long-term working memory in voice identification', *Psychology, Crime and Law*, 4(2): 73–88.

Ellis, Alexander (1889), *On Early English Pronunciation (Vol. 5)*, London: Truebner and Co.

Ellis, Stanley (1994), 'The Yorkshire Ripper enquiry: part I', *Forensic Linguistics*, 1(2): 197–206.

Ellis-Hill, Caroline (2000), 'Changes in identity and self-concept: a new theoretical approach to recovery following stroke', *Clinical Rehabilitation*, 14: 279–87.

Endres, W., W. Bambach and G. Flösser (1971), 'Voice spectrograms as a function of age, voice disguise, and voice imitation', *Journal of the Acoustical Society of America*, 49: 1842–8.

Engstrand, Olle, Karen Williams and Francisco Lacerda (2003), 'Does babbling sound native? Listener responses to vocalizations produced by Swedish and American 12- and 18-month-olds', *Phonetica*, 60: 19–46.

Ennaji, Moha (2005), *Multilingualism, Cultural Identity, and Education in Morocco*, New York: Springer.

Equality and Human Rights Commission (2008), *Sex and Power 2008*, London: Equality and Human Rights Commission.

Eriksson, Anders and Pär Wretling (1997), 'How flexible is the human voice? A case study of mimicry', *Proceedings of the 5th European Conference on Speech Communication and Technology (Eurospeech '97)*, Rhodes, Greece, September 1997, pp. 1043–6.

Fasold, Ralph (1972), *Tense Marking in Black English: A Linguistic and Social Analysis*, Washington, DC: Center for Applied Linguistics.

Fasold, Ralph and Walt Wolfram (1970), 'Some linguistic features of Negro dialect, in Ralph Fasold and Roger Shuy (eds), *Teaching English in the Inner City*, Washington, DC: Center for Applied Linguistics, pp. 41–86.

Fässler, Isabel (1998), *The Evolution of Written Scots and the Perception of Spelling Standardisation in the North-East of Scotland*, MA dissertation, University of Lausanne.

Feagin, Crawford (2002), 'Entering the community: fieldwork', in Jack Chambers, Peter Trudgill and Natalie Schilling-Estes (eds) *The Handbook of Language Variation and Change*, Oxford: Blackwell, pp. 20–39.

Feinberg, Leslie [1992] (2006), 'Transgender liberation: a movement whose time has come', in Susan Stryker and Stephen Whittle (eds), *The Transgender Studies Reader*, New York: Routledge, pp. 205–20.

Fenstermaker, Sarah and Candace West (2002, eds), *Doing Gender, Doing Difference: Social Inequality, Power, and Resistance*, New York: Routledge.

Ferguson, Charles (1991), 'Epilogue: diglossia revisited', *Southwest Journal of Linguistics*, 10(1): 214–34.

Fichte, Johann [1808] (1968), *Addresses to the German Nation*, trans. R.F. Jones and G.H. Turnbull, ed. George Kelly, New York: Harper Torch Books.

Figueiredo, Ricardo Molina de and Helena de Souza Britto (1996), 'A report on the acoustic effects of one type of disguise', *Forensic Linguistics*, 3: 168–75.

Figueroa, Esther (1994), *Sociolinguistic Metatheory*, Oxford: Pergamon Press.

Findlay, Allan, Aileen Stockdale, Anne Findlay and David Short (2001), 'Mobility as a driver of change in rural Britain: an analysis of the links between migration, commuting and travel to shop patterns', *International Journal of Population Geography*, 7: 1–15.

Finnegan, Katie (forthcoming), *Dialect Levelling in Sheffield English*, PhD thesis, University of Sheffield.

Fish, Stanley (1980), *Is There a Text in this Class?*, Cambridge, MA: Harvard University Press.

Fishman, Joshua (1965), 'Who speaks what language to whom and when?' *La Linguistique*, 1(2): 67–88 (reprinted in Li Wei [ed.], *The Bilingualism Reader*, London: Routledge, 2000, pp. 89–106).

Fishman, Joshua (1971, ed.), *Advances in the Sociology of Language*, The Hague: Mouton.

Fishman, Joshua (1973), *Language and Nationalism*, Rowley: Newbury House.

Fishman, Joshua [1989] (1997), *Language and Ethnicity in Minority Sociolinguistic Perspective*, Clevedon: Multilingual Matters. (Extracted as 'Language ethnicity and racism', in Nikolas Coupland and Adam Jaworski [eds], *Sociolinguistics: A Reader and Coursebook*, Basingstoke: Macmillan, 1997, pp. 329–40).

Fishman, Joshua (1991), *Reversing Language Shift: Theory and Practice of Assistance to Threatened Languages*, Clevedon: Multilingual Matters.

Fishman, Joshua (1999, ed.), *Handbook of Language and Ethnic Identity*, Oxford: Oxford University Press.

Fitzsimons, Annette (2002), *Gender as a Verb: Gender Segregation at Work*, Aldershot: Ashgate.

Fong, Terry, Marcia Finlayson and Nadine Peacock (2006), 'The social experience of aging with a chronic illness: perspectives of older adults with multiple sclerosis', *Disability and Rehabilitation*, 28: 695–705.

Fordham, Signithia and John Ogbu (1986), '"Black students" school success: coping with the burden of "acting white"', *Urban Review*, 18: 176–206.

Forman, Charlie (1989), *Spitalfields: A Battle for Land*, London: Hilary Shipman.

Foucault, Michel (1972), *The Archaeology of Knowledge*, London: Routledge.

Foulkes, Paul and Anthony Barron (2000), 'Telephone speaker recognition amongst members of close social network', *Forensic Linguistics*, 7: 180–98.

Foulkes, Paul and Gerard Docherty (1999a, eds), *Urban Voices: Accent Studies in the British Isles*, London: Arnold.

Foulkes, Paul and Gerard Docherty (1999b), 'Urban voices – overview', in Paul Foulkes and Gerard Docherty (eds), *Urban Voices: Accent Studies in the British Isles*, London: Arnold, pp. 1–24.

Fox, Barbara (1999), 'Directions in research: language and the body', *Research on Language and Social Interaction*, 32(1/2): 51–9.

Fox, Susan (2007), *The Demise of Cockneys? Language Change in London's East End*, PhD thesis, University of Essex.

Francis, Timothy (2002), '"Vnse Sassische sprake": evidence for the status and use of Low German in the period of decline, 1500–1650', PhD thesis, University of London.

Francom, Claudia (2009), *Elección de Lengua en Encuentros de Servicio en una Comunidad Bilingüe*, MS, University of Arizona.

Frankenberg, Ruth and Lata Mani (1996), 'Crosscurrents, crosstalk: race, "postcoloniality", and the politics of location', in Smadar Lavie and Ted Swedenburg (eds), *Displacement, Diaspora, and Geographies of Identity*, Durham, NC: Duke University Press, pp. 273–93.

French, Peter, Philip Harrison and Jack Windsor-Lewis (2007), 'R -v- John Samuel Humble: the Yorkshire Ripper Hoaxer trial', *International Journal of Speech, Language and the Law*, 13(2): 255–73.

Fridland, Valerie (2003), 'Network strength and the realization of the Southern Shift among African-Americans in Memphis, Tennessee', *American Speech*, 78: 3–30.

Fridland, Valerie and Kathy Bartlett (2006), 'The social and linguistic conditioning of back vowel fronting across ethnic groups in Memphis, Tennessee', *English Language and Linguistics*, 10: 1–22.

Frumkin, Lara (2007), 'Influences of accent and ethnic background on perceptions of eyewitness testimony', *Psychology, Crime and Law*, 13: 317–31.

Gafaranga, Joseph (2007), *Talk in Two Languages*, New York: Palgrave Macmillan.

Gal, Susan (1978), 'Variation and change in patterns of speaking: language shift in Austria', in David Sankoff (ed.), *Linguistic Variation: Models and Methods*, New York: Academic Press, pp. 227–38.

Gal, Susan (1979), *Language Shift: Social Determinants of Linguistic Change in Bilingual Austria*, New York: Academic Press.

Gal, Susan and Judith Irvine (1995), 'The boundaries of languages and disciplines: how ideologies construct difference', *Social Research*, 62: 967–1001.

Galtung, Johan (1971), 'A structural theory of imperialism', *Journal of Peace Research*, 8(2): 81–117.

Gardner-Chloros, Penelope (1991), *Language Selection and Switching in Strasbourg*, Oxford: Oxford University Press.

Garrett, Peter, Nikolas Coupland and Angie Williams (2003), *Investigating Language Attitudes: Social Meanings of Dialect, Ethnicity and Performance*, Cardiff: University of Wales Press.

Garrido, Lúcia, Frank Eisner, Carolyn McGettigan, Lauren Stewart, Disa Sauter, J. Richard Hanley, Stefan Schweinberger, Jason Warren and Brad Duchaine (2009),

'Developmental phonagnosia: a selective deficit to vocal identity recognition', *Neuropsychologia*, 47(1): 123–31.

Gaudio, Rudolf (1997), 'Not talking straight in Hausa', in Anna Livia and Kira Hall (eds), *Queerly Phrased: Language, Gender, and Sexuality*, New York: Oxford University Press, pp. 416–29.

Gaudio, Rudolf (2005), 'Male lesbians and other queer notions in Hausa', in Andrea Cornwall (ed.), *Readings in Gender in Africa*, Bloomington, IN: Indiana University Press, pp. 47–52.

Gaudio, Rudolf (2007), 'Out on video: gender, language and new public spheres in Islamic Northern Nigeria', in Bonnie McElhinny (ed.), *Words, Worlds, and Material Girls: Language, Gender, Globalization*, Berlin: Mouton de Gruyter, pp. 237–77.

Gee, James (2005), 'Meaning making, communities of practice and analytical toolkits', *Journal of Sociolinguistics*, 9: 590–4.

Gerstorf, Denis, Nilam Ram, Christina Röcke, Ulman Lindenberger and Jacqui Smith (2008), 'Decline in life satisfaction in old age: longitudinal evidence for links to distance-to-death', *Psychology and Aging*, 23: 154–68.

Gfroerer, Stefan (1994), 'Häufigkeit und Art forensischer Stimmverstellungen' [Frequency and type of forensic voice disguises], MS, Bundeskriminalamt Wiesbaden, Germany.

Giegerich, Heinz (1992), *English Phonology*, Cambridge: Cambridge University Press.

Gilroy, Paul (1987), *There Ain't No Black in the Union Jack*, London: Hutchinson.

Gilroy, Paul and Errol Lawrence (1988), 'Two-tone Britain: white and black youth and the politics of anti-racism', in Philip Cohen and Harwant Bains (eds), *Multiracist Britain*, Basingstoke: Macmillan, pp. 121–55.

Glauser, Beat (1974), *The Scottish–English Linguistic Border: Lexical Aspects*, Basel: Francke Verlag Bern.

Glisky, Elizabeth, Lee Ryan, Sheryl Reminger, Oliver Hardt, Scott Hayes and Almut Hupbach (2004), 'A case of psychogenic fugue: I understand, aber ich verstehe nichts', *Neuropsychologia*, 42: 1132–47.

Glynn, Sarah (2002), 'Bengali Muslims: the new East End radicals?', *Ethnic and Racial Studies*, 25(6): 969–88.

Gobl, Christer and Ailbhe Ní Chasaide (1992), 'Acoustic characteristics of voice quality', *Speech Communication*, 11: 481–90.

Goffman, Erving [1974] (1986), *Frame Analysis: An Essay on the Organization of Experience*, Boston: Northwestern University Press.

Goggin, J.P., C.P. Thompson, G. Strube and L.R. Simental (1991), 'The role of language familiarity in voice identification', *Memory and Cognition*, 19: 448–58.

Goldstein, Alvin, Paul Knight, Karen Bailis and Jerry Conover (1981), 'Recognition memory for accented and unaccented voices', *Bulletin of the Psychonomic Society*, 17(5): 217–20.

Goodwin, Charles (1986), 'Gesture as a resource for the organization of mutual orientation', *Semiotica*, 62(1/2): 29–49.

Goodwin, Charles (2003), 'Pointing as situated practice', in Sotaro Kita (ed.), *Pointing: Where Language, Culture and Cognition Meet*, Mahwah, NJ: Lawrence Erlbaum Associates, pp. 217–41.

Goodwin, Marjorie Harness (2006), *The Hidden Life of Girls: Games of Stance, Status, and Exclusion*, Malden, MA: Blackwell.

Gordon, Elizabeth (1983), 'New Zealand English pronunciation: an investigation into some early written records', *Te Reo: Journal of the Linguistic Society of New Zealand*, 26: 29–42.

Gordon, Matthew J. (2000), 'Phonological correlates of ethnic identity: evidence of divergence?', *American Speech*, 75: 115–36.

Gordon, Matthew J. (2004), 'Investigating chain shifts and mergers', in Jack Chambers, Peter Trudgill and Natalie Schilling-Estes (eds), *The Handbook of Language Variation and Change*, Oxford: Blackwell, pp. 244–66.

Grant, Tim (2008), 'Approaching questions in forensic authorship analysis', in John Gibbons and Maria Teresa Turell (eds), *Dimensions of Forensic Linguistics*, Amsterdam: Benjamins, pp. 215–31.

Green, Anne, Terence Hogarth and Ruth Shackleton (1999), 'Longer distance commuting as a substitute for migration in Britain: a review of trends, issues and implications', *International Journal of Population Geography*, 5: 49–67.

Green, Lisa (2002), *African American English: A Linguistic Introduction*, Cambridge: Cambridge University Press.

Gumperz, John (1982), *Discourse Strategies*, Cambridge: Cambridge University Press.

Gumperz, John (1996), 'The linguistic and cultural relativity of conversational inference', in John Gumperz and Stephen Levinson (eds), *Rethinking Linguistic Relativity*, Cambridge: Cambridge University Press, pp. 374–406.

Gurd, Jennifer, Nicola Bessell, R.A.W. Bladon and J.M. Bamford (1988), 'A case of Foreign Accent Syndrome, with follow-up clinical, neuropsychological and phonetic descriptions', *Neuropsychologia*, 26: 237–51.

Gurd, Jennifer, John Coleman, Angela Costello and John Marshall (2001), 'Organic or functional? A new case of foreign accent syndrome', *Cortex*, 37: 715–18.

Guy, Gregory (1980), 'Variation in the group and the individual: the case of final stop deletion', in William Labov (ed.), *Locating Language in Time and Space*, New York: Academic Press, pp. 1–36.

Haeri, Niloofar (1991), *Sociolinguistic Variation in Cairene Arabic: Palatalization and the 'Qaf' in the Speech of Men and Women*, PhD thesis, University of Pennsylvania.

Haeri, Niloofar (2003), *Sacred Language, Ordinary People: Dilemmas of Culture and Politics in Egypt*, New York: Palgrave.

Hall, Kira (1995), *Hijra/Hijrin: Language and Gender Identity*, PhD thesis, University of California at Berkeley.

Hall, Kira (1997), '"Go suck your husband's sugarcane!": hijras and the use of sexual insult', in Anna Livia and Kira Hall (eds), *Queerly Phrased: Language, Gender, and Sexuality*, New York: Oxford University Press, pp. 430–60.

Hall, Kira (2003a), 'English, sexuality, and modernity in Hindi-speaking India', paper presented at Words, Worlds, and Material Girls: A Workshop on Language, Gender, and Political Economy, University of Toronto, October 2003.

Hall, Kira (2003b), 'Exceptional speakers: contested and problematized gender identities', in Miriam Meyerhoff and Janet Holmes (eds), *The Handbook of Language and Gender*, Oxford: Blackwell, pp. 352–80.

Hall, Kira (2005), 'Intertextual sexuality: parodies of class, identity, and desire in liminal Delhi', *Journal of Linguistic Anthropology*, 15(1): 125–44.

Hall, Kira and Veronica O'Donovan (1996), 'Shifting gender positions among Hindi-speaking hijras', in Victoria Bergvall, Janet Bing and Alice Freed (eds), *Rethinking Language and Gender Research: Theory and Practice*, London: Longman, pp. 228–66.

Hammersley, Richard and J. Don Read (1985), 'The effect of participation in a conversation on recognition and identification of the speakers' voices,' *Law and Human Behavior*, 9(1): 71–81.

Hardie, Kim (1996), 'Lowland Scots: issues in nationalism and identity', in Charlotte Hoffman (ed.), *Language, Culture and Communication in Contemporary Europe*, Clevedon: Multilingual Matters, pp. 61–74.

Harris, Roxy (2006), *New Ethnicities and Language Use*, Basingstoke: Palgrave.

Hastings, Adi and Paul Manning (2004), 'Introduction: acts of alterity', *Language and Communication*, 24: 291–311.

Hastings, Adrian (1997), *The Construction of Nationhood: Ethnicity, Religion and Nationalism*, Cambridge: Cambridge University Press.

Haviland, John (2004), 'Gesture', in Alessandro Duranti (ed.), *A Companion to Linguistic Anthropology*, Malden, MA: Blackwell, pp. 197–221.

Hayashi, Makoto (2003), 'Language and the body as resources for collaborative action: a study of word searches in Japanese conversation', *Research on Language and Social Interaction*, 36(2): 109–41.

Hazen, Kirk (2000), *Identity and Ethnicity in the Rural South: A Sociolinguistic View Through Past and Present Be*, Durham, NC: Duke University Press.

Hebdige, Dick (1987), *Cut 'n' Mix: Culture, Identity and Caribbean Music*, London: Comedia.

Heeringa, W., J. Nerbonne, H. Niebaum, R. Nieuweboer and P. Kleiweg (2000), 'Dutch–German contact in and around Bentheim', in D.G. Gilbers, J. Nerbonne and J. Scheeken (eds), *Languages in Contact*, Amsterdam: Rodopi, pp. 145–56.

Heller, Monica (2001), 'Critique and sociolinguistic analysis of discourse', *Critique of Anthropology*, 21(2): 117–41.

Heller, Monica (2005), 'Language skill and authenticity in the globalized new economy', *Noves SL: Revista de Sociolingüística*, Winter 2005, http://heller2005.notlong.com (accessed 8 April 2009).

Heller, Monica (2007), 'Bilingualism as ideology and practice', in Monica Heller (ed.), *Bilingualism: A Social Approach*, New York: Palgrave Macmillan, pp. 1–22.

Heller, Monica (2010), 'Language as resource in the globalised new economy', in Nikolas Coupland (ed.), *The Handbook of Language and Globalisation*, Malden, MA: Blackwell.

Herbst, Jeffrey (2000), *States and Power in Africa: Comparative Lessons in Authority and Control*, Princeton, NJ: Princeton University Press.

Herdt, Gilbert (1993a, ed.), *Third Sex, Third Gender: Beyond Sexual Dimorphism in Culture and History*, New York: Zone Books.

Herdt, Gilbert (1993b), 'Introduction: third sexes and third genders', in Gilbert Herdt (ed.), *Third Sex, Third Gender: Beyond Sexual Dimorphism in Culture and History*, New York: Zone Books, pp. 21–82.

Hernández-Campoy, Juan Manuel and Juan Andrés Villena-Ponsoda (2009), 'Standardness and non-standardness in Spain: dialect attrition and revitalisation of regional dialects of Spanish', *International Journal of the Sociology of Language*, 196/197: 181–214.

Heslop, R. Oliver (1892), *Northumberland Words. A Glossary of Words Used in the County of Northumberland and on the Tyneside*, London: English Dialect Society/Kegan Paul, Trench, Trübner and Co.

Hewitt, Roger (1986), *White Talk Black Talk*, Cambridge: Cambridge University Press.

Hill, Jane (1995), 'The voices of Don Gabriel: responsibility and self in a modern Mexicano narrative', in Bruce Mannheim and Dennis Tedlock (eds), *The Dialogic Emergence of Culture*, Urbana, IL: University of Illinois Press, pp. 97–147.

Hill, Jane (2005), 'Intertextuality as source and evidence for indirect indexical meanings', *Journal of Linguistic Anthropology* 15(1): 113–24.

Hill, Russell and Robin Dunbar (2003), 'Social network size in humans', *Human Nature* 14(1): 53–72.

Hinton, Linette and Karen Pollock (2000), 'Regional variations in the phonological characteristics of African American Vernacular English', *World Englishes*, 19: 59–71.

Hirson, Allen and Martin Duckworth (1995), 'Forensic implications of vocal creak as voice disguise', in Angelika Braun and Jens-Peter Köster (eds), *Studies in Forensic Phonetics*, Trier: Wissenschaftlicher Verlag Trier, pp. 67–76.

Hirson, Allen, Peter French and David Howard (1995), 'Speech fundamental frequency over the telephone and face-to-face: some implications for forensic phonetics', in Jack Windsor-Lewis (ed.), *Studies in General and English Phonetics: Essays in Honour of Professor J.D. O'Connor*, London: Routledge, pp. 230–40.

Hobsbawm, Eric (1990), *Nations and Nationalism since 1780: Programmes, Myth, Reality*, Cambridge: Cambridge University Press.

Hoffman, Katherine (2008), *We Share Walls: Language, Land and Gender in Berber Morocco*, Malden, MA: Blackwell.

Holland, Robert (1886), *A Glossary of Words Used in the County of Chester*, London: English Dialect Society/Trübner and Co.

Hollien, Harry (2002), *Forensic Voice Identification*, San Diego, CA: Academic Press.

Hollien, Harry, Wojciech Majewski and E. Thomas Doherty (1982), 'Perceptual identification of voices under normal, stress, and disguised speaking conditions', *Journal of Phonetics*, 10: 139–48.

Hollien, Harry and Reva Schwartz (2001), 'Speaker identification utilizing noncontemporary speech', *Journal of Forensic Science*, 46(1): 63–7.

Holly, Werner, Ulrich Püschel and Jörg Bergmann (2001, eds), *Die sprechende Zuschauer*, Wiesbaden: WV.

Holmes, Janet (1995), *Women, Men and Politeness*, London: Longman.

Holmes, Janet (1997), 'Women, language and identity', *Journal of Sociolinguistics*, 1: 195–224.

Holmes, Janet (2005), 'Power and discourse at work: is gender relevant?', in Michelle Lazar (ed.), *Feminist Critical Discourse Analysis*, Basingstoke: Palgrave Macmillan, pp. 31–60.

Holmes, Janet (2006), *Gendered Talk at Work*, Oxford: Blackwell.

Holmes, Janet and Paul Kerswill (2008), 'Contact is not enough: a response to Trudgill', *Language in Society*, 37(2): 273–7.

Holmes, Janet and Meredith Marra (2005), 'Narrative and the construction of professional identity in the workplace', in Joanna Thornborrow and Jennifer Coates (eds), *The Sociolinguistics of Narrative*, Amsterdam: Benjamins, pp. 193–213.

Holmes, Janet and Maria Stubbe (2003), *Power and Politeness in the Workplace: A Sociolinguistic Analysis of Talk at Work*, Harlow: Pearson.

Hopper, Paul (1988), 'Emergent grammar and the a priori grammar postulate', in Deborah Tannen (ed.), *Linguistics in Context: Connecting Observation and Understanding*, Norwood, NJ: Ablex, pp. 117–34.

Hornsby, David (2009), 'Dedialectalization in France: convergence and divergence', *International Journal of the Sociology of Language*, 196/197: 157–80.

Horvath, Barbara and Ronald Horvath (2001), 'A geolinguistics of short A in Australian English', in David Blair and Peter Collins (eds), *English in Australia*, Amsterdam: John Benjamins, pp. 341–55.

Hosoda, Megumi, Eugene Stone-Romero and Jennifer Walter (2007), 'Listeners' cognitive and affective reactions to English speakers with standard American English and Asian accents', *Perceptual and Motor Skills*, 104: 307–26.

House of Lords Select Committee on the Constitution (2009), *Surveillance: Citizens and the State, Vol. I: Report*, London: The Stationery Office, http://surveillance.notlong. com (accessed 8 April 2009).

Hudson, Amelia and Anthony Holbrook (1981), 'A study of the reading fundamental vocal frequency of young black adults', *Journal of Speech and Hearing Research*, 24: 197–200.

Hudson, Richard (1975), 'The meaning of questions', *Language*, 51(1): 1–31.

Hudson, Richard (1996), *Sociolinguistics*, 2nd edn, Cambridge: Cambridge University Press.

Hudson, Richard and Anne Holloway (1977), *Variation in London English: Final Report to the Social Sciences Research Council*, London: Department of Phonetics and Linguistics, University College London.

Hultgren, Anna Kristina (2008), 'Reconstructing the sex dichotomy in language and gender research: call centre workers and "women's language"', in Kate Harrington, Lia Litosseliti, Helen Sauntson and Jane Sunderland (eds), *Gender and Language: Research Methodologies*, Basingstoke: Palgrave, pp. 29–42.

Hutcheon, Linda (1995), 'Colonialism and the postcolonial condition: complexities abounding', *Proceedings of the Modern Language Association*, 110(1): 7–16.

Hutchins, Edwin (1995), *Cognition in the Wild*, Cambridge, MA: MIT Press.

Hymes, Dell (1975), 'Breakthrough into performance', in Dan Ben-Amos and Kenneth Goldstein (eds), *Folklore: Performance and Communication*, The Hague: Mouton, pp. 11–74.

Igboanusi, Herbert and Martin Pütz (2008), 'The future of French in Nigeria's language policies', *Journal of Multilingual and Multicultural Development*, 29(3): 235–59.

Inoue, Miyako (2004), 'What does language remember? Indexical inversion and the naturalized history of Japanese women', *Journal of Linguistic Anthropology*, 14(1): 39–56.

Irvine, Judith (2001), '"Style" as distinctiveness: the culture and ideology of linguistic differentiation', in Penelope Eckert and John Rickford (eds), *Style and Sociolinguistic Variation*, Cambridge: Cambridge University Press, pp. 21–43.

Jakobson, Roman (1960), 'Concluding statement: linguistics and poetics', in Thomas Sebeok (ed.), *Style in Language*, Cambridge, MA: MIT Press, pp. 350–77.

Jenkins, Richard (1997), *Rethinking Ethnicity: Arguments and Explorations*, London: Sage.

Jessen, Michael (2007), 'Forensic reference data on articulation rate in German', *Science and Justice*, 47: 50–67.

Jibril, Munzali (1986), 'Sociolinguistic variation in Nigerian English', *English World-Wide* 7: 47–75.

Jibril, Munzali (1991), 'The sociolinguistics of prepositional usage in Nigerian English', in Jenny Cheshire (ed.), *English Around the World: Sociolinguistic Perspectives*, Cambridge: Cambridge University Press, pp. 519–44.

Johnson, Keith and Misty Azara (2000), *The Perception of Personal Identity in Speech: Evidence from the Perception of Twins' Speech*, http://johnsonazara.notlong.com (accessed 8 April 2009).

Johnson, Nadine (2006), *An Examination of the Concrete Ceiling: Perspectives of Ten African American Women Managers and Leaders*, Boca Raton, FL: Dissertation.Com.

Johnston, Paul (1997), 'Regional variation', in Charles Jones (ed.), *The Edinburgh History of the Scots Language*, Edinburgh: Edinburgh University Press, pp. 433–513.

Johnston, Ron (1991), *A Question of Place: Exploring the Practice of Human Geography*, Oxford: Blackwell.

Johnstone, Barbara (1994), *Repetition in Discourse: Interdisciplinary Perspectives*, Norwood, NJ: Ablex.

Johnstone, Barbara (1996), *The Linguistic Individual: Self-Expression in Language and Linguistics*, New York: Oxford University Press.

Johnstone, Barbara (forthcoming), 'Stance, style, and the linguistic individual', in Alexandra Jaffe (ed.), *Sociolinguistic Perspectives on Stance*, Oxford: Oxford University Press.

Johnstone, Barbara, Jennifer Andrus and Andrew Danielson (2006), 'Mobility, indexicality, and the enregisterment of "Pittsburghese"', *Journal of English Linguistics*, 34(2): 77–104.

Johnstone, Barbara, Neeta Bhasin and Denise Wittkofski (2002), '"Dahntahn Pittsburgh": monophthongal /aw/ and representations of localness in southwestern Pennsylvania', *American Speech*, 77: 148–66.

Johnstone, Barbara and Scott Kiesling (2008), 'Indexicality and experience: exploring the meanings of /aw/-monophthongization in Pittsburgh', *Journal of Sociolinguistics*, 12(1): 5–33.

Jones, Jamila and Dennis Preston (forthcoming), 'AAE and identity: constructing and deploying linguistic resources', to appear in *Journal of African Language Learning and Teaching*, http://jonespreston.notlong.com (accessed 8 April 2009).

Jones, Simon (1988), *Black Culture White Youth*, Basingstoke: Macmillan.

Joseph, John (2004), *Language and Identity: National, Ethnic, Religious*, Basingstoke: Palgrave Macmillan.

Joseph, John and Talbot Taylor (1990, eds), *Ideologies of Language*, London: Routledge.

Kanter, Rosabeth (1977), *Women and Men of the Corporation*, New York: Basic Books.

Kaplan, Robert and Richard Baldauf (1997), *Language Planning: From Theory to Practice*, Clevedon: Multilingual Matters.

Kay, Billy (1986), *Scots: The Mither Tongue*, Edinburgh: Mainstream Publishing.

Kempler, Daniel and Diana Van Lancker (2002), 'Effect of speech task on intelligibility in dysarthria: a case study of Parkinson's disease', *Brain and Language*, 80: 449–64.

Kendall, Shari (2004), 'Framing authority: gender, face and mitigation at a radio network', *Discourse and Society*, 15(1): 55–79.

Kendon, Adam (1997), 'Gesture', *Annual Review of Anthropology*, 26: 109–28.

Kendon, Adam (2000), 'Language and gesture: unity or duality?', in David McNeill (ed.), *Language and Gesture*, Cambridge: Cambridge University Press, pp. 162–85.

Kendon, Adam (2004), 'Some contrasts in gesticulation in Neapolitan speakers and speakers in Northamptonshire', in Roland Posner and Cornelia Mueller (eds), *The Semantics and Pragmatics of Everyday Gesture*, Berlin: Weidler Buchverlag, pp. 173–93.

Kerstholt, José, Noortje Jansen, Adri Van Amelsvoort and Ton Broeders (2004), 'Earwitnesses: effects of accent, retention and telephone', *Applied Cognitive Psychology*, 20(2): 187–97.

Kerswill, Paul (1994), *Dialects Converging: Rural Speech in Urban Norway*, Oxford: Clarendon Press.

Kerswill, Paul (1996), 'Children, adolescents, and language change', *Language Variation and Change*, 8(2): 177–202.

Kerswill, Paul (2002), 'Models of linguistic change and diffusion: new evidence from dialect levelling in British English', *Reading Working Papers in Linguistics*, 6: 187–216.

Kerswill, Paul (2003), 'Dialect levelling and geographical diffusion in British English', in David Britain and Jenny Cheshire (eds), *Social Dialectology: In Honour of Peter Trudgill*, Amsterdam: Benjamins, pp. 223–43.

Kerswill, Paul and Ann Williams (2000), 'Creating a new town koine: children and language change in Milton Keynes', *Language in Society*, 29: 65–115.

Kerswill, Paul and Ann Williams (2002), '"Salience" as an explanatory factor in language change: evidence from dialect levelling in urban England', in Mari Jones and Edith Esch (eds), *Language Change: The Interplay of Internal, External and Extra-linguistic Factors*, Berlin: Mouton de Gruyter, pp. 81–110.

Kerswill, Paul, Eivind Torgersen and Susan Fox (2008), 'Reversing "drift": innovation and diffusion in the London diphthong system', *Language Variation and Change*, 20: 451–91.

Kessler, Suzanne (1990), 'The medical construction of gender: case management of inter-sexed infants', *Signs: Journal of Women in Culture and Society*, 16(1): 3–26.

Kiely, Richard, David McCrone, Frank Bechhofer and Robert Stewart (2000), 'Debatable land: national and local identity in a border town', *Sociological Research Online* 5(2), http://www.socresonline.org.uk/5/2/kiely.html (accessed 8 April 2009).

Kiesling, Scott (1998), 'Men's identities and sociolinguistic variation: the case of fraternity men', *Journal of Sociolinguistics*, 2: 69–99.

Kiesling, Scott (2005), 'Variation, stance, and style: word-final -er, high rising tone, and ethnicity in Australian English', *English World-Wide*, 26: 1–44.

Kiesling, Scott and Marc Wisnosky (2003), 'Competing norms, heritage prestige, and /aw/-monophthongization in Pittsburgh', poster presented at New Ways of Analyzing Variation (NWAV) 32, Philadelphia, October 2003.

Kinzler, Katherine, Emmanuel Dupoux and Elizabeth Spelke (2007), 'The native language of social cognition', *Proceedings of the National Academy of Sciences of the United States of America*, 104: 12577–80.

Klompas, Michelle and Eleanor Ross (2004), 'Life experiences of people who stutter, and the perceived impact of stuttering on quality of life: personal accounts of South African individuals', *Journal of Fluency Disorders*, 29: 275–305.

Kloss, Heinz (1967), '"Abstand Languages" and "Ausbau Languages"', *Anthropological Linguistics*, 9: 29–41.

Kloss, Heinz (1968), 'Notes concerning a language/nation typology', in Joshua Fishman, Charles Ferguson and Jyotirindra Das Gupta (eds), *Language Problems of Developing Nations*, New York: Wiley, pp. 69–85.

Kloss, Heinz (1978), *Die Entwicklung neuer germanischer Kultursprachen seit 1800*, 2nd edn, Düsseldorf: Schwann.

Kloss, Heinz (1984), 'Interlingual communication: danger and chance for the smaller tongues', *Scottish Studies*, 4: 73–77.

Koch, Barbara Johnstone (1984), 'Repeating yourself: discourse paraphrase and the generation of language', in *Proceedings of the First Eastern States Conference on Linguistics*, Columbus, OH: The Ohio State University, pp. 250–9.

Kontra, Miklós (2003), 'Changing mental maps and morphology', in David Britain and Jenny Cheshire (eds), *Social Dialectology: In Honour of Peter Trudgill*, Amsterdam: Benjamins, pp. 173–90.

Köster, Olaf and Niels Schiller (1997), 'Different influences of the native language of a listener on speaker recognition', *Forensic Linguistics*, 4: 18–28.

Kreiman, Jody and Bruce Gerratt (2000), 'Sources of listener disagreement in voice quality assessment', *Journal of the Acoustical Society of America*, 108: 1867–76.

Krikorian, Mark (2002), 'Alingual education: young victims of mass immigration', *National Review*, June 13th 2002, http://krikorian.notlong.com (accessed 8 April 2009).

Kroll, Judith and Annette De Groot (2005), *Handbook of Bilingualism: Psycholinguistic Approaches*, Oxford: Oxford University Press.

Kroskrity, Paul (2000, ed.), *Regimes of Language: Ideologies, Polities, and Identities*, Santa Fe, NM: School of American Research Press.

Kulick, Don (1997), 'The gender of Brazilian transgendered prostitutes', *American Anthropologist*, 99(3): 574–85.

Künzel, Hermann (1989), 'How well does average fundamental frequency correlate with speaker height and weight?', *Phonetica*, 46: 117–25.

Künzel, Hermann (2000), 'Effects of voice disguise on speaking fundamental frequency', *International Journal of Speech, Language and the Law*, 7(2): 149–79.

Kurowski, Kathleen, Sheila Blumstein and Michael Alexander (1996), 'The foreign accent syndrome: a reconsideration', *Brain and Language*, 54: 1–25.

Kwon, Miseon and Jong Kim (2006), 'Change of dialect after stroke: a variant of foreign accent syndrome', *European Neurology*, 56: 249–52.

Labov, William (1963), 'The social motivation of a sound change', *Word*, 19: 273–309.

Labov, William (1966), *The Social Stratification of English in New York City*, Washington, DC: Center for Applied Linguistics.

Labov, William (1972a), 'The isolation of contextual styles', in William Labov (ed.), *Sociolinguistic Patterns*, Philadelphia: University of Pennsylvania Press, pp. 70–109.

Labov, William (1972b), *Sociolinguistic Patterns*, Philadelphia: University of Pennsylvania Press.

Labov, William (1972c), *Language in the Inner City: Studies in the Black English Vernacular*, Philadelphia: University of Pennsylvania Press.

Labov, William (1982), 'Objectivity and commitment in linguistic science: the case of the Black English trial in Ann Arbor', *Language in Society*, 11: 165–201.

Labov, William (1991), 'The intersection of sex and social class in the course of linguistic change', *Language Variation and Change*, 2: 205–51.

Labov, William (1994), *Principles of Linguistic Change, Volume 1: Internal Factors*, Oxford: Blackwell.

Labov, William (2001), *Principles of Linguistic Change, Volume 2: Social Factors*, Oxford: Blackwell.

Labov, William, Paul Cohen, Clarence Robins and John Lewis (1968), *A Study of the Non-Standard English of Negro and Puerto Rican Speakers in New York City*, New York: Columbia University Press.

Labov, William, Sharon Ash and Charles Boberg (2006), *Atlas of North American English*, New York: Mouton de Gruyter.

Ladefoged, Peter and Jenny Ladefoged (1980), 'The ability of listeners to identify voices', *UCLA Working Papers in Phonetics*, 49: 43–51.

Lakoff, Robin (1973), 'Language and woman's place', *Language in Society*, 2: 45–80.

Lakoff, Robin (1975), *Language and Woman's Place*, New York: Harper and Row.

Lakoff, Robin (2003), 'Language, gender and politics: putting "women" and "power" in the same sentence', in Janet Holmes and Miriam Meyerhoff (eds), *The Handbook of Language and Gender*, Oxford: Blackwell, pp. 161–78.

Lakoff, George and Mark Johnson (1980), *Metaphors We Live By*, Chicago: University of Chicago Press.

Lang, Sabine (1998), *Men as Women, Women as Men: Changing Gender in Native American Cultures*, trans. John Valentine, Austin, TX: University of Texas Press.

Laqueur, Thomas (1990), *Making Sex: Body and Gender from the Greeks to Freud*, Cambridge, MA: Harvard University Press.

Laver, John (1980), *The Phonetic Description of Voice Quality*, Cambridge: Cambridge University Press.

LeMaster, Barbara (2006), 'Language contraction, revitalization and Irish women', *Journal of Linguistic Anthropology*, 16(2): 211–28.

Lenneberg, Eric (1967), *Biological Foundations of Language*, New York: Wiley.

Le Page, Robert and Andrée Tabouret-Keller (1985), *Acts of Identity: Creole-Based Approaches to Language and Ethnicity*, Cambridge: Cambridge University Press.

Lerner, Gene (2003), 'Selecting next speaker: the context-sensitive operation of a context-free organization', *Language in Society*, 32(2): 177–201.

Levinson, Steven (1983), *Pragmatics*, Cambridge: Cambridge University Press.

Levy, Robert (1973), *Tahitian: Mind and Experience in the Society Islands*, Chicago: University of Chicago Press.

Lillie, Diane (1998), *The Utah Dialect Survey*, MA dissertation, Brigham Young University.

Lindemann, Stephanie (2003), 'Koreans, Chinese or Indians? Attitudes and ideologies about non-native English speakers in the United States', *Journal of Sociolinguistics*, 7: 348–64.

Livia, Anna and Kira Hall (1997), '"It's a girl!": bringing performativity back to linguistics', in Anna Livia and Kira Hall (eds), *Queerly Phrased: Language, Gender, and Sexuality*, New York: Oxford University Press, pp. 3–18.

Li Wei (1998), 'The "why" and "how" questions in the analysis of conversational code-switching,' in Peter Auer (ed.), *Code Switching in Conversation: Language, Interaction and Identity*, Routledge: London, pp. 156–79.

Li Wei (2007, ed.), *The Bilingualism Reader*, 2nd edn, New York: Routledge.

Llamas, Carmen (1999), 'A new methodology: data elicitation for social and regional language variation studies', *Leeds Working Papers in Linguistics and Phonetics*, 7: 95–118.

Llamas, Carmen (2001), *Language Variation and Innovation in Teesside English*, PhD thesis, University of Leeds.

Llamas, Carmen (2006), 'Shifting identities and orientations in a border town', in Tope Omoniyi and Goodith White (eds), *The Sociolinguistics of Identity*, London: Continuum, pp. 92–112.

Llamas, Carmen (2007a), 'Age', in Carmen Llamas, Louise Mullany and Peter Stockwell (eds), *The Routledge Companion to Sociolinguistics*, London: Routledge, pp. 69–76.

Llamas, Carmen (2007b), '"A place between places": language and identities in a border town', *Language in Society*, 36(4): 579–604.

Llamas, Carmen, Daniel Johnson and Dominic Watt (2008), 'Rhoticity in four Scottish/English border localities', paper presented at Sociolinguistics Symposium 17, Amsterdam, April 2008, http://llamasetal2008.notlong.com (accessed 8 April 2009).

Llamas, Carmen, Dominic Watt and Daniel Johnson (forthcoming), 'Linguistic accommodation and the salience of national identity markers in a border town', to appear in *Journal of Language and Social Psychology*.

Low, Ee-Ling, Esther Grabe and Francis Nolan (2001), 'Quantitative characterisations of speech rhythm: syllable-timing in Singapore English', *Language and Speech*, 43(4): 377–401.

Lum, Carmel and Andrew Ellis (1999), 'Why do some aphasics show an advantage on some tests of nonpropositional (automatic) speech?', *Brain and Language*, 70: 95–118.

Macafee, Caroline (1983), *Varieties of English Around the World: Glasgow*, Amsterdam: Benjamins.

Macafee, Caroline (1994), *Traditional Dialect in the Modern World: A Glasgow Case Study*, Frankfurt: Peter Lang.

Macafee, Caroline (2002), 'A history of Scots to 1700', in *A Dictionary of the Older Scottish Tongue, Vol. 12*, Oxford: Oxford University Press, pp. xxi–clvi.

Macaskill, Mark (2008), 'Blind taught to "see" like a bat', *The Sunday Times*, 10th February 2008, http://macaskill.notlong.com (accessed 8 April 2009).

Macaulay, Ronald (2001), '"You're like 'why not?'" The quotative expressions of Glasgow adolescents', *Journal of Sociolinguistics*, 5(3): 3–21.

MacKinnon, Kenneth (2003), *Census 2001 Scotland: Gaelic Language – First Results, Bòrd Gàidhlig na h-Alba: New Thinking for a Fresh Start?*, http://newthinking.notlong.com (accessed 10 April 2009).

Magen, Harriet (1998), 'The perception of foreign-accented speech', *Journal of Phonetics*, 26: 381–400.

Maguire, Warren (2005), 'The "NURSE-NORTH merger" in Tyneside English: origin, status and "reversal"', paper presented for University of Aberdeen Centre for Linguistic Research seminar series, April 2005, http://maguire.notlong.com (accessed 8 April 2009).

Maguire, Warren, April McMahon and Paul Heggarty (2008), 'Integrating social and geographical variation by phonetic comparison and network analysis', poster presented at the 13th International Conference on Methods in Dialectology, University of Leeds, August 2008.

Makoni, Sinfree and Alastair Pennycook (2005), 'Disinventing and reconstituting languages', *Critical Inquiry in Language Studies*, 2(3): 137–56.

Mann, Thomas (1903), *Tonio Kröger*, Berlin: S. Fischer.

Mann, Virginia, Rhea Diamond and Susan Carey (1979), 'Development of voice recognition: parallels with face recognition', *Journal of Experimental Child Psychology*, 27: 153–65.

Mäntylä, Timo (1997), 'Recollections of faces: remembering differences and knowing similarities', *Journal of Experimental Psychology: Learning, Memory and Cognition*, 23: 1203–16.

Markham, Duncan (1999), 'Listeners and disguised voices: the imitation and perception of dialectal accent', *Forensic Linguistics*, 6(2): 289–99.

Marra, Meredith, Stephanie Schnurr and Janet Holmes (2006), 'Effective leadership in New Zealand workplaces', in Judith Baxter (ed.), *Speaking Out: The Female Voice in Public Contexts*, Basingstoke: Palgrave, pp. 240–60.

Martín Rojo, Luisa and Concepción Gómez Esteban (2005), 'The gender of power: the female style in labour organizations', in Michelle Lazar (ed.), *Feminist Critical Discourse Analysis*, Basingstoke: Palgrave, pp. 66–89.

Martínez, Glenn (2003), 'Perceptions of dialect in a changing society: folk linguistics along the Texas–Mexico border', *Journal of Sociolinguistics*, 7(1): 38–49.

Martínez, Oscar (1994), *Border People*, Tucson, AZ: University of Arizona Press.

Massey, Doreen (1985), 'New directions in space', in Derek Gregory and John Urry (eds), *Social Relations and Spatial Structures*, London: Macmillan, pp. 9–19.

Masthoff, Herbert (1996), 'A report on a voice disguise experiment', *Forensic Linguistics*, 3: 160–7.

Mæhlum, Brit (1996), 'Semi-migration in the Arctic – a theoretical perspective on the dialect strategies of children on Spitsbergen', in Per Sture Ureland and Iain Clarkson (eds), *Language Contact Across the North Atlantic*, Tübingen: Max Niemeyer Verlag, pp. 313–31.

McCarty, Christopher, Peter Killworth, H. Russell Bernard and Eugene Johnsen (2001), 'Comparing two methods for estimating network size', *Human Organization*, 60(1): 28–39.

McClelland, Elizabeth (2008), 'Voice recognition within a closed set of family members', paper presented at the International Association for Forensic Phonetics and Acoustics 2008 Conference, Lausanne, July 2008.

McClure, J. Derrick (2000), *Language, Poetry and Nationhood*, East Linton: Tuckwell Press.

McConnell-Ginet, Sally (2000), 'Breaking through the glass ceiling: can linguistic awareness help?', in Janet Holmes (ed.), *Gendered Speech in Social Context: Perspectives from Gown to Town*, Wellington: Victoria University Press, pp. 259–82.

McDougall, Kirsty and Francis Nolan (2007), 'Discrimination of speakers using the formant dynamics of /uː/ in British English', *Proceedings of the 16th International Congress of Phonetic Sciences*, Saarbrücken, pp. 1825–8.

McElhinny, Bonnie (2002), *Policing Gender: Linguistic Strategies in Language and Gender*, London: Longman.

McElhinny, Bonnie (2003), 'Theorizing gender in sociolinguistics and linguistic anthropology', in Janet Holmes and Miriam Meyerhoff (eds), *The Handbook of Language and Gender*, Oxford: Blackwell, pp. 21–42.

McGehee, Frances (1937), 'The reliability of the identification of the human voice', *Journal of General Psychology*, 17: 249–71.

McIntosh, Janet (2002), *The Edge of Islam: Religion, Language, and Essentialism on the Kenya Coast*, PhD thesis, University of Michigan.

McNeil, Malcolm, Patrick Doyle and Julie Wambaugh (2000), 'Apraxia of speech: a treatable disorder of motor planning and programming', in Stephen Nadeau, Leslie Gonzalez Rothi and Bruce Crosson (eds), *Aphasia and Language: Theory to Practice*, New York: Guilford Press, pp. 221–66.

McNeill, David (1997), 'Growth points cross-linguistically', in Jan Nuyts and Eric Pederson (eds), *Language and Conceptualization, Vol. 1: Language, Culture and Cognition*, New York: Cambridge University Press, pp. 190–212.

Mees, Inger (1987), 'Glottal stop as a prestigious feature in Cardiff English', *English World-Wide*, 8: 25–39.

Mendoza-Denton, Norma (1997), *Chicana/Mexicana Identity and Linguistic Variation: An Ethnographic and Sociolinguistic Study of Gang Affiliation in an Urban High School*, PhD thesis, Stanford University.

Mendoza-Denton, Norma (1999), 'Sociolinguistic and linguistic anthropological studies of US Latinos,' *Annual Review of Anthropology*, 28: 375–95.

Mendoza-Denton, Norma (2002), 'Language and identity', in Jack Chambers, Peter Trudgill and Natalie Schilling-Estes (eds), *The Handbook of Language Variation and Change*, Oxford: Blackwell, pp. 475–99.

Mendoza-Denton, Norma (2004), 'The anguish of normative gender', in Mary Bucholtz (ed.), *Language and Woman's Place II: Text and Commentaries*, 2nd edn, Oxford: Oxford University Press, pp. 343–55.

Mendoza-Denton, Norma (2008), *Homegirls: Language and Cultural Practice Among Latina Youth Gangs*, London: Wiley-Blackwell.

Meudell, Peter, Bernice Northen, Julie Snowden and David Neary (1980), 'Long term memory for famous voices in amnesic and normal subjects', *Neuropsychologia*, 18(2): 133–39.

Meurman-Solin, Anneli (1993), *Variation and Change in Early Scottish Prose*, Helsinki: Suomalainen Tiedeakatemia.

Meyerhoff, Miriam (2002), 'Communities of practice', in Jack Chambers, Peter Trudgill and Natalie Schilling-Estes (eds), *The Handbook of Language Variation and Change*, Malden, MA: Blackwell Publishing, pp. 526–48.

Meyerhoff, Miriam (2005), 'Biographies, agency and power', *Journal of Sociolinguistics*, 9: 595–601.

Meyerhoff, Miriam and Nancy Niedzielski (2003), 'The globalization of vernacular variation', *Journal of Sociolinguistics*, 7(1): 534–55.

Michele de Oliveira, Sandi (2002), 'Discourses of identity at the Spanish/Portuguese border: self-identification strategies of centre and periphery', *National Identities*, 4(3): 245–56.

Millar, Robert McColl (2005), *Language, Nation and Power*, Basingstoke: Palgrave Macmillan.

Millar, Robert McColl (2006), '"Burying alive": unfocused governmental language policy and Scots', *Language Policy*, 5: 63–86.

Millar, Robert McColl (forthcoming), '*Dislocation*: is it presently possible to envisage an economically based language policy for Scots in Scotland?', in John Kirk and Dónall Ó Baóill (eds), *Language and Economic Development: Northern Ireland, the Republic of Ireland, and Scotland*, Belfast: Cló Ollscoil na Banríona.

Miller, Nicholas (2000), 'Changing ideas in apraxia of speech', in Ilias Papathanasiou (ed.), *Acquired Neurogenic Communication Disorders*, London: Whurr, pp. 173–202.

Miller, Nicholas, Anja Lowit and Helen O'Sullivan (2006a), 'What makes acquired foreign accent syndrome foreign?', *Journal of Neurolinguistics*, 19: 385–409.

Miller, Nicholas, Emma Noble, Diana Jones and David Burn (2006b), 'Life with communication changes in Parkinson's disease', *Age and Ageing*, 35: 235–9.

Miller, Nicholas, Emma Noble, Diana Jones, Liesl Allcock and David Burn (2008), 'How do I sound to me? Perceived changes in communication in Parkinson's disease', *Clinical Rehabilitation*, 22: 14–22.

Mills, Sara (1997), *Discourse*, London: Routledge.

Milroy, James (1992), *Linguistic Variation and Change*, Oxford: Blackwell.

Milroy, James and Lesley Milroy (1985a), 'Linguistic change, social network and speaker innovation', *Journal of Linguistics*, 21: 339–84.

Milroy, James and Lesley Milroy (1985b) *Authority in Language: Investigating Language Prescription and Standardisation*, London: Routledge.

Milroy, James and Lesley Milroy (1998), 'Mechanisms of change in urban dialects: the role of class, social network and gender', in Peter Trudgill and Jenny Cheshire (eds), *The Sociolinguistics Reader, Vol. 1: Multilingualism and Variation*, London: Arnold, pp. 179–95.

Milroy, James, Lesley Milroy, Sue Hartley and David Walshaw (1994a), 'Glottal stops and Tyneside glottalisation: competing patterns of variation and change in British English', *Language Variation and Change*, 6: 327–58.

Milroy, James, Lesley Milroy and Sue Hartley (1994b), 'Local and supra-local change in British English: the case of glottalisation', *English World-Wide*, 15: 1–33.

Milroy, Lesley (1980), *Language and Social Networks*, Oxford: Blackwell.

Milroy, Lesley (1987), *Language and Social Networks*, 2nd edn, Oxford: Blackwell.

Milroy, Lesley (1999), 'Women as innovators and norm-creators: the sociolinguistics of dialect levelling in a northern English city', in Suzanne Wertheim, Ashlee Bailey and Monica Corston-Oliver (eds), *Engendering Communication: Proceedings of the 5th Berkeley Women and Language Conference*, Berkeley, CA: BWLG Publications, pp. 361–76.

Milroy, Lesley (2000), 'Two nations divided by the same language and different language ideologies,' *Journal of Linguistic Anthropology*, 9(1): 1–34.

Milroy, Lesley (2002), 'Social networks', in Jack Chambers, Peter Trudgill and Natalie Schilling-Estes (eds), *The Handbook of Language Variation and Change*, Malden, MA: Blackwell, pp. 549–72.

Milroy, Lesley (2004), 'Language ideologies and linguistic change', in Carmen Fought (ed.), *Sociolinguistic Variation: Critical Reflections*, Oxford: Oxford University Press, 161–77.

Milroy, Lesley (2008), 'Off the shelf or under the counter? On the social dynamics of sound changes', in Christopher Cain and Geoffrey Russom (eds), *Studies in English Historical Linguistics III – Managing Chaos: Strategies for Identifying Change in English*, Berlin: Mouton de Gruyter, pp. 149–72.

Modood, Tariq (1999), 'New forms of Britishness: post-immigration ethnicity and hybridity in Britain', in Rosemarie Sackmann, Bernhard Peters and Thomas Faist (eds), *Identity and Integration: Migrants in Western Europe*, Farnham: Ashgate Press, pp. 77–90.

Monrad-Krohn, Georg (1947), 'Dysprosody or altered melody of language', *Brain*, 70: 405–15.

Montgomery, Chris (2006), *Northern English Dialects: A Perceptual Approach*, PhD thesis, University of Sheffield.

Montgomery, Chris (forthcoming), 'Mapping language perceptions', in Alfred Lameli, Roland Kehrein and Stefan Rabanus (eds), *Handbook of Language Mapping*, Berlin: Mouton de Gruyter.

Moonis, M., J.M. Swearer, S.E. Blumstein, K. Kurowski, R. Licho, P. Kramer, A. Mitchell, D.L. Osgood and D.A. Drachman (1996), 'Foreign accent syndrome following a closed head injury: perfusion on single photon emission tomography with normal magnetic resonance imaging', *Neuropsychiatry, Neuropsychology and Behavioral Neurology*, 9: 272–9.

Moore, Emma (2003), *Learning Style and Identity: A Sociolinguistic Analysis of a Bolton High School*, PhD thesis, University of Manchester.

Moore, Emma (2004), 'Sociolinguistic style: a multidimensional resource for shared identity creation', *Canadian Journal of Linguistics*, 49: 375–96.

Moore, Emma (2006), '"You tell all the stories": using narrative to explore hierarchy within a community of practice', *Journal of Sociolinguistics*, 10: 611–40.

Moore, Emma and Robert Podesva (in preparation), '"We do say *in' he?*, don't we?": using tag questions to explore social meaning and style'.

Moosmüller, Sylvia (1997), 'Phonological variation in speaker identification', *Forensic Linguistics*, 4: 29–47.

Morrison, Ann, Randall White and Ellen van Velsor (1987), *Breaking the Glass Ceiling: Can Women Reach the Top of America's Largest Corporations?* Reading, MA: Addison-Wesley.

Morrison, Geoffrey (2008), 'Forensic voice comparison using likelihood ratios based on polynomial curves fitted to the formant trajectories of Australian English /aɪ/', *International Journal of Speech, Language and the Law*, 15(2): 247–64.

Moyer, Melissa and Luisa Martín Rojo (2007), 'Language migration and citizenship: new challenges in the regulation of bilingualism', in Monica Heller (ed.), *Bilingualism: A Social Approach*, New York: Palgrave Macmillan, pp. 137–60.

Mühlhäusler, Peter (1980), 'Structural expansion and the process of creolization', in Albert Valdman and Arnold Highfield (eds), *Theoretical Orientations in Creole Studies*, London: Academic Press, pp. 19–55.

Mullany, Louise (2006), 'Narrative constructions of gendered and professional identities', in Goodith White and Tope Omoniyi (eds), *The Sociolinguistics of Identity*, London: Continuum, pp. 157–72.

Mullany, Louise (2007), *Gendered Discourse in the Professional Workplace*, Basingstoke: Macmillan.

Mullany, Louise (2008), '"The wee girl in the office": direct indexing of gender in the Cambridge and Nottingham Business English Corpus', paper presented at International Gender and Language Association Conference 5, Victoria University, Wellington, New Zealand, July 2008.

Murray, Craig and B. Harrison (2004), 'The meaning and experience of being a stroke survivor: an interpretative phenomenological analysis', *Disability and Rehabilitation*, 26: 808–16.

Muysken, Pieter (2000), *Bilingual Speech*, Cambridge: Cambridge University Press.

Myers-Scotton, Carol (1983), 'The negotiation of identities in conversation: a theory of markedness and code-choice', *International Journal of the Sociology of Language*, 44: 432–43.

Myers-Scotton, Carol (1988), 'Code-switching as indexical of social negotiation', in Monica Heller (ed.), *Code-Switching: Anthropological and Sociolinguistic Perspectives*, Berlin: Mouton de Gruyter, pp. 151–86.

Myers-Scotton, Carol (1993a), *Social Motivations for Codeswitching: Evidence From Africa*, Oxford: Clarendon.

Myers-Scotton, Carol (1993b), *Duelling Languages: Grammatical Structure in Codeswitching*, Oxford: Clarendon.

Nahkola, Kari and Marja Saanilahti (2004), 'Mapping language changes in real time: a panel study on Finnish', *Language Variation and Change*, 16: 75–92.

Namaste, Ki (1996), '"Tragic misreadings": queer theory's erasure of transgender subjectivity', in Brett Beemyn and Mickey Eliason (eds), *Queer Studies: A Lesbian, Gay, Bisexual, and Transgender Anthology*, New York: New York University Press, pp. 183–203.

Nanda, Serena (1985), 'The hijras of India: cultural and individual dimensions of an institutionalized third gender role', *Journal of Homosexuality*, 11(34): 35–54.

Nanda, Serena (1990), *Neither Man nor Woman: The Hijras of India*, Belmont, CA: Wadsworth Publishing.

Nash, Andrew (2007), *Kailyard and Scottish Literature*, Amsterdam: Rodopi.

National Audit Office (2008), *Widening Participation in Higher Education*, London: National Audit Office.

Needs, Chris (2001), *Like It Is: My Autobiography*, Talybont: Y Lolfa.

Neuhauser, Sara and Adrian Simpson (2007), 'Imitated or authentic? Listeners' judgments of foreign accents', *Proceedings of the 16th International Congress of Phonetic Sciences*, Saarbrücken, August 2007, pp. 1805–8.

Newbrook, Mark (1986), *Sociolinguistic Reflexes of Dialect Interference in West Wirral*, Frankfurt: Peter Lang.

Nichols, Patricia (1986), 'Prepositions in Black and White English of coastal South Carolina', in Michael Montgomery and Guy Bailey (eds), *Language Variety in the South: Perspectives in Black and White*, Tuscaloosa, AL: University of Alabama Press, pp. 73–84.

Nicholson, Linda (1994), 'Interpreting gender', *Signs: Journal of Women in Culture and Society*, 20: 79–105.

Nnoli, Okwudiba (1978), *Ethnic Politics in Nigeria*, Enugu: Fourth Dimension Publishers.

Nolan, Francis (1983), *The Phonetic Bases of Speaker Recognition*, Cambridge: Cambridge University Press.

Nolan, Francis (1993), 'Auditory and acoustic analysis in speaker recognition', in John Gibbons (ed.), *Language and the Law*, London: Longman, pp. 326–45.

Nolan, Francis (2005), 'Forensic speaker identification and the phonetic description of voice quality', in William Hardcastle and Janet Mackenzie Beck (eds), *A Figure of Speech: A Festschrift for John Laver*, Mahwah, NJ: Lawrence Erlbaum Associates, pp. 385–411.

Nolan, Francis and Catalin Grigoras (2005), 'A case for formant analysis in forensic speaker identification', *International Journal of Speech, Language and the Law*, 12(2): 143–73.

Nolan, Francis and Tomasina Oh (1996), 'Identical twins, different voices', *Forensic Linguistics*, 3: 39–49.

Novak, Deanna and Mara Mather (2007), 'Aging and variety seeking', *Psychology and Aging*, 22: 728–37.

Ochs, Elinor (1992), 'Indexing gender', in Alessandro Duranti and Charles Goodwin (eds), *Rethinking Context: Language as an Interactive Phenomenon*, New York: Cambridge University Press, pp. 335–58.

Ochs, Elinor (1993), 'Indexing gender', in Barbara Miller (ed.), *Sex and Gender Hierarchies*, Cambridge: Cambridge University Press, pp. 146–69. (Reprint of 'Indexing gender' in Alessandro Duranti and Charles Goodwin [eds], *Rethinking Context: Language as an Interactive Phenomenon*, New York: Cambridge University Press, 1992, pp. 335–58).

Ochs, Elinor, Emanuel Schegloff and Sandra Thompson (1996, eds), *Interaction and Grammar*, Cambridge: Cambridge University Press.

Ocumpaugh, Jaclyn (2001), *The Variable Chapter in the Story of R: An Acoustic Analysis of a Shift in Final and Pre-Consonantal Instances of American /r/ Production in Louisburg, North Carolina*, MA dissertation, North Carolina State University.

Okon, M. (2002), 'French: Nigeria's second official language?', *Calabar Journal of Liberal Studies*, 5(11): 59–71.

Omoniyi, Tope (2003a), 'Language ideology and politics: a critical appraisal of French as a second official language in Nigeria', in Sinfree Makoni and Ulrike Meinhof (eds), *Africa and Applied Linguistics: AILA Review* 16, pp. 13–25.

Omoniyi, Tope (2003b), 'Local policies, global forces: multiliteracy and Africa's indigenous languages', *Language Policy*, 2: 133–52.

Omoniyi, Tope (2003c), 'Biliteracy for democracy: Nigeria's identity card scheme', paper presented at the 4th International Symposium on Bilingualism, Arizona State University, Tempe, AZ, April 2003.

Omoniyi, Tope (2004a), *The Sociolinguistics of Borderlands: Two Nations, One Community*, Trenton, NJ: Africa World Press.

Omoniyi, Tope (2004b), 'Identity constructs in a contested borderland: the Bakassi Peninsula', in Duro Oni, Suman Gupta, Tope Omoniyi, Efurosibina Adegbija and Segun Awonusi (eds), *Nigeria in the Age of Globalization: Contemporary Discourses and Texts*, Lagos: CBAAC, pp. 171–93.

Omoniyi, Tope (2006), 'Societal multilingualism and multifaithism: a sociology of language and religion perspective', in Tope Omoniyi and Joshua Fishman (eds), *Explorations in the Sociology of Language and Religion*, Amsterdam: Benjamins, pp. 121–40.

Orchard, Tara and A. Daniel Yarmey (1995), 'The effects of whispers, voice-sample duration, and voice distinctiveness on criminal speaker identification', *Applied Cognitive Psychology*, 9(3): 249–60.

Orcutt-Gachiri, Heidi (2008), 'Shrubbing and the evaluation of expertise in Kenyan

English and Kiswahili: placing Kenyan indigenous languages at risk', paper presented at the Annual Meeting of the American Anthropological Association, San Francisco, November 2008.

Orton, Harold (1962), *Survey of English Dialects: An Introduction*, Leeds: E.J. Arnold.

Ortan, Harold and Eugen Dieth (1962–71, eds), *Survey of English Dialects: Introduction and 4 Volumes in 3 Parts*, Leeds: E.J. Arnold.

Orton, Harold and Philip Tilling (1969–71, eds), *The Survey of English Dialects: The Basic Material, Vol. 3.1 – East Midland Counties and East Anglia*, Leeds: E.J. Arnold.

Orton, Harold and Wilfred Halliday (1962), *Survey of English Dialects (B): the Basic Material. The Six Northern Counties and the Isle of Man. Vol. 1*, London: E.J. Arnold.

Osborne, Dana (2008), *Identifying the Pitch and Duration Ranges for Enregistered Utterances: Mexicano and White Voice*, MS, University of Arizona.

Osmond, John and Jessica Mugaseth (2004), 'Community approaches to poverty in Wales', in *Overcoming Disadvantage: An Agenda for the Next 20 Years*, York: Joseph Rowntree Foundation.

Ostermann, Ana Cristina (2003), 'Communities of practice at work: gender, facework and the power of *habitus* at an all-female police station and a feminist crisis intervention center in Brazil', *Discourse and Society*, 14(4): 473–505.

Oswalt, Philipp and Tim Rieniets (2006), 'Introduction/Einführung', in Philipp Oswalt and Tim Rieniets (eds), *Atlas of Shrinking Cities/Atlas der Schrumpfenden Städte*, Berlin: Kulturstiftung des Bundes, pp. 6–7.

Påhlsson, Christer (1972), *The Northumbrian Burr: a Sociolinguistic Study*, Lund: Gleerup.

Parish, William (1875), *A Dictionary of the Sussex Dialect and Collection of Provincialisms in Use in the County of Sussex*, Lewes: Farncombe and Co.

Parker, Janat, Elizabeth Haverfield and Stephanie Baker-Thomas (2006), 'Eyewitness testimony of children', *Journal of Applied Social Psychology*, 16(4): 287–302.

Parr, Susie (2001), 'Psychosocial aspects of aphasia: whose perspectives?', *Folia Phoniatrica et Logopaedica*, 53: 266–88.

Patrick, Peter (2002), 'The speech community', in Jack Chambers, Peter Trudgill and Natalie Schilling-Estes (eds), *The Handbook of Language Variation and Change*, Malden, MA: Blackwell, pp. 573–97.

Pederson, Lee, Susan Leas McDaniel, Guy Bailey, Marvin Basset, Carol Adams, Caisheng Liao and Michael Montgomery (1986–1992, eds), *The Linguistic Atlas of the Gulf States* (7 vols.), Athens, GA: University of Georgia Press.

Pell, Marc (2006), 'Cerebral mechanisms for understanding emotional prosody in speech', *Brain and Language*, 96: 221–34.

Perfect, Timothy, Laura Hunt and Christopher Harris (2002), 'Verbal overshadowing in voice recognition', *Applied Cognitive Psychology*, 16(8): 973–80.

Perry, Theresa and Lisa Delpit (1997, eds), *The Real Ebonics Debate: Power, Language, and the Education of African American Children*, Boston: Beacon Press.

Peys, Stéphanie (2001), *In Pursuit of Cockney Speak*, MA dissertation, Université de Pau et des Pays de L'Adour.

Philippon, Axelle, Julie Cherryman, Ray Bull and Aldert Vrij (2007), 'Lay people's and police officers' attitudes towards the usefulness of perpetrator voice identification', *Applied Cognitive Psychology*, 21(1): 103–15.

Pinto, José Antonio, Renato José Corso, Ana Guilherme, Sílvia Pinho, and Monica de Oliveira Nóbrega (2004), 'Dysprosody nonassociated with neurological diseases – a case report', *Journal of Voice*, 18: 90–6.

Platt, John (1977), 'A model for polyglossia and multilingualism (with special reference to Singapore and Malaysia)', *Language in Society*, 6: 361–78.

Pollack, I., J.M. Pickett and W.H. Sumby (1954), 'On the identification of speakers by voice', *Journal of the Acoustical Society of America*, 26(3): 403–6.

Poplack, Shana and Sali Tagliamonte (2001), *African-American English in the Diaspora*, Oxford: Blackwell.

Pratt, Mary Louise (1987), 'Linguistic utopias', in Nigel Fabb, Derek Attridge, Alan Durant and Colin MacCabe (eds), *The Linguistics of Writing*, Manchester: Manchester University Press, pp. 48–66.

Pred, Allan (1985), 'The social becomes the spatial, the spatial becomes the social: enclosures, social change and the becoming of places in the Swedish province of Skåne', in Derek Gregory and John Urry (eds), *Social Relations and Spatial Structures*, London: Macmillan, pp. 337–65.

Prompapakorn, Praparat (2005), *Dialect Contact and New Dialect Formation in a Thai New Town*, PhD thesis, University of Essex.

Przedlacka, Joanna (2002), *Estuary English? A Sociophonetic Study of Teenage Speech in the Home Counties*, Frankfurt: Peter Lang.

Purnell, Thomas (2008), 'AAE in Milwaukee: contact at a vowel shift frontier', paper presented at the Annual Meeting of the Linguistic Society of America, Chicago, January 2008.

Putnam, Robert (2000), *Bowling Alone: The Collapse and Revival of American Community*, New York: Simon and Schuster.

Queen, Robin (2004), '"I am woman, hear me roar": the importance of linguistic stereotype for lesbian linguistic identity performances', in Mary Bucholtz (ed.), *Language and Women's Place: Text and Commentaries*, Oxford: Oxford University Press, pp. 289–95.

Quintos-Pozos, David (2006), *Contact between Mexican Sign Language and American Sign Language in Two Texas Border Areas*, PhD thesis, University of Texas at Austin.

Quiroga, Rodrigo, L. Reddy, Gabriel Kreiman, Christof Koch and Itzhak Fried (2005), 'Invariant visual representation by single neurons in the human brain', *Nature*, 435: 1102–07.

Raheja, Gloria and Ann Gold (1994), *Listen to the Heron's Words: Reimagining Gender and Kinship in North India*, Berkeley, CA: University of California Press.

Rampton, Ben (1983), 'Some flaws in educational discussion in the English of Asian schoolchildren in Britain', *Journal of Multilingual and Multicultural Development*, 4(1): 15–28.

Rampton, Ben (1995), *Crossing: Language and Ethnicity Among Adolescents*, London: Longman.

Rampton, Ben (1998), 'Speech community', in Jef Verschueren, Jan-Ola Östman, Jan Blommaert and Chris Bulcaen (eds), *Handbook of Pragmatics*, Amsterdam: John Benjamins, pp. 1–34.

Rampton, Ben (1999), 'Crossing', *Journal of Linguistic Anthropology*, 9(1–2): 54–6.

Rampton, Ben (2005), *Crossing: Language and Ethnicity Among Adolescents*, 2nd edn, Manchester: St. Jerome Press.

Rampton, Ben (2006), *Language in Late-Modernity: Interaction in an Urban School*, Cambridge: Cambridge University Press.

Rampton, Ben (2009), 'Speech community and beyond', in Nikolas Coupland and Adam Jaworski (eds), *The New Sociolinguistics Reader*, London: Palgrave Macmillan, pp. 694–713.

Rauniomaa, Mirka (2003), 'Stance accretion', paper presented at the Language, Interaction, and Social Organization Research Focus Group, University of California, Santa Barbara, February 2003.

Raymond, Janice (1979), *The Transsexual Empire: The Making of the She-Male*, Boston: Beacon Press.

Reay, Diane (1998), 'Rethinking social class: qualitative perspectives on class and gender', *Sociology*, 32(2): 259–75.

Reich, Alan (1981), 'Detecting the presence of vocal disguise in the male voice', *Journal of the Acoustical Society of America*, 69(5): 1458–61.

Reich, Alan and James Duke (1979), 'Effects of selected vocal disguises upon speaker identification by listening', *Journal of the Acoustical Society of America*, 66: 1023–28.

Remez, Robert (forthcoming), 'Spoken expression of individual identity and the listener', in Ezequiel Morsella (ed.), *Expressing Oneself/Expressing One's Self: A Festschrift in Honor of Robert M. Krauss*, London: Taylor and Francis.

Rhodes, Penny, Neil Small, Hanif Ismail and John Wright (2008), '"What really annoys me is people take it like it's a disability": epilepsy, disability and identity among people of Pakistani origin living in the UK', *Ethnicity and Health*, 13: 1–21.

Richardson, Elaine (2003), *African-American Literacies*, New York: Routledge.

Richardson, Elaine (2006), *Hip-Hop Literacies*, New York: Routledge.

Rickford, John (1986), 'The need for new approaches to social class analysis in sociolinguistics', *Journal of Communication*, 6: 215–21.

Rickford, John (1999), *African American Vernacular English: Features, Evolution, Educational Implications*, Oxford: Blackwell.

Rickford, John, Arnetha Ball, Raina Jackson Blake and Naomi Martin (1991), 'Rappin on the copula coffin: theoretical and methodological issues in the analysis of copula variation in African American Vernacular English', *Language Variation and Change*, 3: 103–32.

Rickford, John and Elizabeth Traugott (1985), 'Symbol of powerlessness and degeneracy, or symbol of solidarity and truth? Paradoxical attitudes toward pidgins and creoles', in Sidney Greenbaum (ed.), *The English Language Today*, Oxford: Pergamon, pp. 252–61.

Rickford, John, Julie Sweetland and Angela Rickford (2004), 'African American English and other vernaculars in education: a topic-coded bibliography', *Journal of English Linguistics*, 32(3): 230–320.

Rickford, John and Russell Rickford (2000), *Spoken Soul*, New York: Wiley.

Riggins, Stephen (1997, ed.), *The Language and Politics of Exclusion: Others in Discourse*, Thousand Oaks, CA: Sage.

Rivera-Gaxiola, Maritza, Lindsay Klarman, Adrian Garcia-Sierra and Patricia Kuhl (2005), 'Neural patterns to speech and vocabulary growth in American infants', *Neuroreport*, 16: 495–8.

Rodman, Robert and Michael Powell (2000), 'Computer recognition of speakers who disguise their voice', *Proceedings of the International Conference on Signal Processing*

Applications and Technology 2000 (ICSPAT 2000), Dallas, TX, October 2000, http://rodmanpowell.notlong.com (accessed 8 April 2009).

Rogers, Everett (2003), *Diffusion of Innovations*, 5th edn, New York: Free Press.

Rogers, Everett and F. Floyd Shoemaker (1971), *Communication of Innovations: A Cross-Cultural Approach*, New York: Free Press.

Rogers, Henry (1998), 'Foreign accent in voice discrimination: a case study', *Forensic Linguistics*, 5: 203–8.

Romaine, Suzanne (1978), 'Postvocalic /r/ in Scottish English: sound change in progress?', in Peter Trudgill (ed.), *Sociolinguistic Patterns in British English*, London: Arnold, pp. 144–57.

Romaine, Suzanne (1995), *Bilingualism*, 2nd edn, Oxford: Blackwell.

Romaine, Suzanne and Euan Reid (1983), 'Glottal sloppiness? A sociolinguistic view of urban speech in Scotland', in Michael Stubbs and Hilary Hillier (eds), *Readings on Language, Schools and Classrooms: Contemporary Sociology of the School*, London: Taylor and Francis, pp. 70–81.

Roscoe, Will (1991), *The Zuni Man-Woman*, Albuquerque, NM: University of New Mexico Press.

Roscoe, Will (1998), *Changing Ones: Third and Fourth Genders in Native North America*, New York: St. Martin's Press.

Rose, Mary (2006), *Language, Place, and Identity in Later Life*, PhD thesis, Stanford University.

Rose, Mary and Devyani Sharma (2002), 'Introduction: ideology and identity in practice', in Sarah Benor, Mary Rose, Devyani Sharma, Julie Sweetland and Qing Zhang (eds), *Gendered Practices in Language*, Stanford, CA: CSLI Publications, pp. 1–20.

Rose, Philip (2006), 'Technical forensic speaker recognition: evaluation, types and testing of evidence', *Computer Speech and Language*, 20: 159–91.

Ross, Elliott and Marilee Monnot (2008), 'Neurology of affective prosody and its functional-anatomic organization in right hemisphere', *Brain and Language*, 104: 51–74.

Rossini, Nicla (2004), 'Sociolinguistics in gesture: how about the *mano a borsa?*', *International Communication Studies*, 13(3): 144–54.

Roth, Elliot, Kathleen Fink, Leora Cherney and Kelly Hall (1997), 'Reversion to a previously learned foreign accent after stroke', *Archives of Physical Medicine and Rehabilitation*, 78: 550–2.

Rousseau, Pascale and David Sankoff (1978), 'Advances in variable rule methodology', in David Sankoff (ed.), *Linguistic Variation: Models and Methods*, New York: Academic Press, pp. 57–69.

Røyneland, Unn (2009), 'Dialects in Norway – catching up with the rest of Europe?', *International Journal of the Sociology of Language*, 196/197: 7–30.

Rubin, Gayle (1975), 'The traffic in women: notes on the political economy of sex', in Rayna Reiter (ed.), *Toward an Anthology of Women*, New York: Monthly Review Press, pp. 157–210.

Ryan, Ellen Bouchard (1979), 'Why do low-prestige language varieties persist?', in Howard Giles and Robert St. Clair (eds), *Language and Social Psychology*, Oxford: Blackwell, pp. 145–57.

Sadiqi, Fatima (2003), *Women, Gender and Language in Morocco*, Leiden: Brill Academic Press.

Sagay, Itse (no date), 'Nigeria: federalism, the constitution and resource control', paper presented at the 4th Sensitisation Programme organised by the Ibori Vanguard, Lagos, http://sagay.notlong.com (accessed 6 April 2009).

Said, Edward (1978), *Orientalism*, London: Routledge and Kegan Paul.

Sancier, Michele and Carol Fowler (1997), 'Gestural drift in a bilingual speaker of Brazilian Portuguese and English', *Journal of Phonetics*, 25: 421–36.

Sankoff, David (1988), 'Variable rules', in Ulrich Ammon, Norbert Dittmar, and Klaus Mattheier (eds), *Soziolinguistik: Ein internationalisches Handbuch zur Wissenschaft von Sprache und Gesellschaft*, Berlin: Walter de Gruyter, pp. 984–97.

Sankoff, Gillian and Hélène Blondeau (2007), 'Language change across the lifespan: /r/ in Montreal French', *Language*, 83: 560–88.

Sankoff, Gillian, Hélène Blondeau and Anne Charity (2001), 'Individual roles in a real-time change: Montreal (r → R) 1947–1995', *Etudes et Travaux*, 4: 141–57.

Sauntson, Helen (2008), 'The contribution of queer theory to gender and language research', in Kate Harrington, Lia Litosseliti, Helen Sauntson and Jane Sunderland (eds), *Gender and Language Research Methodologies*, Basingstoke: Palgrave, pp. 271–82.

Savage, Mike (2007), 'An alternative history of class identities in post-war Britain', paper presented at ESRC Identities and Social Action Programme, London Metropolitan University, March 2007.

Sayers, Dave (2009), *Reversing Babel: Declining Linguistic Diversity and the Flawed Attempts to Protect It*, PhD thesis, University of Essex.

Schegloff, Emanuel (1998), 'Body torque', *Social Research*, 65(3): 535–95.

Schieffelin, Bambi and Rachelle Charlier Doucet (1998), 'The 'real' Haitian Creole: ideology, metalinguistics, and orthographic choice,' in Bambi Schieffelin, Kathryn Woolard and Paul Kroskrity (eds), *Language Ideologies: Theory and Practice*, Oxford: Oxford University Press, pp. 285–316.

Schieffelin, Bambi, Kathryn Woolard and Paul Kroskrity (1998, eds), *Language Ideologies: Practice and Theory*, Oxford: Oxford University Press.

Schiller, Niels and Olaf Köster (1996), 'Evaluation of a foreign language speaker in forensic phonetics: a report', *Forensic Linguistics*, 3: 176–85.

Schilling-Estes, Natalie (2004), 'Constructing ethnicity in interaction', *Journal of Sociolinguistics*, 8(2): 163–95.

Schilling-Estes, Natalie and Walt Wolfram (1994), 'Convergent explanation and alternative regularization patterns: *were/weren't* leveling in a vernacular English variety', *Language Variation and Change*, 6: 273–302.

Schlichter, Hélène (1996), 'Comparaison prosodique et acoustique de trois imitations vocales', *Travaux de l'Institut de Phonétique de Strasbourg*, 26: 115–44.

Schlichting, Frank and Kirk Sullivan (1997), 'The imitated voice – a problem for voice line-ups?', *Forensic Linguistics*, 4: 148–65.

Schnurr, Stephanie (forthcoming), '"Decision made, let's move on!": negotiating gender and professional identity in Hong Kong workplaces', in Markus Bieswanger, Heiko Motschenbacher and Susanne Mühleisen (eds), *Language in its Socio-Cultural Context: New Explorations in Global, Medial and Gendered Uses*, Berlin: Peter Lang.

Schulte, Brigid (2002), 'Trapped between two languages – poor and isolated, many immigrants' children lack English', *Washington Post*, http://earthops.org/immigration/alingual1.html (accessed 8 April 2009).

Schweitzer, Nicholas and Michael Saks (2007), 'The CSI Effect: popular fiction about forensic science affects public expectations about real forensic science', *Jurimetrics*, 47: 357–64.

Searle, John (1969), *Speech Acts: An Essay in the Philosophy of Language*, Cambridge: Cambridge University Press.

Sebba, Mark (2007), 'Identity and language construction in an online community: the case of "Ali G"', in Peter Auer (ed.), *Style and Social Identities: Alternative Approaches to Linguistic Heterogeneity*, Berlin: Mouton de Gruyter, pp. 361–92.

Self, Abigail (2008, ed.), *Social Trends 2008*, London: Office for National Statistics.

Serano, Julia (2007), *Whipping Girl: A Transsexual Woman on Sexism and the Scaping of Femininity*, Emeryville, CA: Seal Press.

Shadden, Barbara (2005), 'Aphasia as identity theft: theory and practice', *Aphasiology*, 19: 211–23.

Shaffer, L.H. (1978), 'Timing in the motor programming of typing', *Quarterly Journal of Experimental Psychology*, 30: 333–45.

Shenk, Petra Scott (2007), '"I'm Mexican remember?": constructing ethnic identities via authenticating discourse, *Journal of Sociolinguistics*, 11: 194–220.

Shipton, Martin (2008), 'Storm over attack on Welsh medium schools', *Wales Online* 29th December 2008, http://welshmedium.notlong.com (accessed 6 April 2009).

Shirt, Marion (1984), 'An auditory speaker-recognition experiment', *Proceedings of the Institute of Acoustics*, 6(1): 101–4.

Shuy, Roger (1990), 'Dialect as evidence in law cases', *Journal of English Linguistics*, 23(1/2): 195–208.

Sidnell, Jack (2006), 'Coordinating gesture, talk, and gaze in reenactments', *Research on Language and Social Interaction*, 39(4): 377–409.

Silverstein, Michael (1976), 'Shifters, linguistic categories, and cultural description', in Keith Basso and Henry Selby (eds), *Meaning in Anthropology*, Albuquerque, NM: University of New Mexico Press, pp. 11–55.

Silverstein, Michael (1979), 'Language structure and linguistic ideology', in Paul Clyne, William Hanks and Carol Hofbauer (eds), *The Elements: A Parasession on Linguistic Units and Levels*, Chicago: Chicago Linguistic Society, pp. 193–247.

Silverstein, Michael (1985), 'Language and the culture of gender: at the intersection of structure, usage, and ideology', in Elizabeth Mertz and Richard Parmentier (eds), *Semiotic Mediation: Socio-cultural and Psychological Perspectives*, Orlando, FL: Academic Press, pp. 219–59.

Silverstein, Michael (1993), 'Metapragmatic discourse and metapragmatic function', in John Lucy (ed.), *Reflexive Language*, Cambridge: Cambridge University Press, pp. 33–58.

Silverstein, Michael (1995), 'Indexical order and the dialectics of sociolinguistic life', paper presented at SALSA III: the 3rd Symposium About Language and Society, Austin, TX, April 1995.

Silverstein, Michael (2003), 'Indexical order and the dialectics of sociolinguistic life', *Language and Communication*, 23: 193–229.

Simire, G.O. (2003), 'Developing and promoting multilingualism in public life and society in Nigeria', *Language, Culture and Curriculum*, 16(2): 231–43.

Simo Bobda, Augustin, Hans-Georg Wolf and Peter Lothar (1999), 'Identifying regional and national origin of English-speaking Africans seeking asylum in Germany', *Forensic Linguistics*, 6(2): 300–19.

Sivertsen, Eva (1960), *Cockney Phonology*, Oslo: Oslo University Press.

Sjöström, Maria, Erik Eriksson, Elisabeth Zetterholm and Kirk Sullivan (2006), 'A switch of dialect as disguise', *Proceedings of the 19th Swedish Phonetics Conference (Fonetik 2006)*, University of Stockholm, pp. 113–16.

Skeggs, Beverley (1997), *Formations of Class and Gender*, London: Sage.

Skeggs, Beverley (2004), *Class, Self, Culture*, London: Routledge.

Smith, Anthony (1998), *Nationalism and Modernism: A Critical Survey of Recent Theories of Nations and Nationalism*, London: Routledge.

Smith, Dai (1999), *Wales: A Question for History*, Bridgend: Seren.

Smitherman, Geneva and John Baugh (2002), 'The shot heard from Ann Arbor: language and public policy in African America', *Howard Journal of Communications*, 13(1): 5–24.

Sommer, Doris (2004), *Bilingual Aesthetics: A New Sentimental Education*, Durham, NC: Duke University Press.

Sommer, Elisabeth (1986), 'Variation in Southern urban English', in Michael Montgomery and Guy Bailey (eds), *Language Variety in the South: Perspectives in Black and White*, Tuscaloosa, AL: University of Alabama Press, pp. 180–201.

Southwood, M. Helen and James Flege (1999), 'Scaling foreign accent: direct magnitude estimation versus interval scaling', *Clinical Linguistics and Phonetics*, 13: 335–49.

Spolsky, Bernard (2004), *Language Policy*, Cambridge: Cambridge University Press.

Stokoe, Elizabeth (2008), 'Categories, actions and sequences', in Kate Harrington, Lia Litosseliti, Helen Sauntson and Jane Sunderland (eds), *Gender and Language Research Methodologies*, London: Palgrave Macmillan, pp. 139–57.

Stokoe, Elizabeth and Janet Smithson (2001), 'Making gender relevant: conversation analysis and gender categories in interaction', *Discourse and Society*, 12(2): 217–44.

Streeck, Jürgen (1993), 'Gesture as communication I: its coordination with gaze and speech', *Communication Monographs*, 60: 275–99.

Stryker, Susan (1994), 'My words to Victor Frankenstein above the village of Chamounix: performing transgender rage', *GLQ: A Journal of Lesbian and Gay Studies*, 1: 237–54.

Stryker, Susan (2004), 'Transgender studies: queer theory's evil twin', *GLQ: A Journal of Lesbian and Gay Studies*, 10(2): 212–15.

Stryker, Susan (2006), '(De)subjugated knowledges: an introduction to transgender studies', in Susan Stryker and Stephen Whittle (eds), *The Transgender Studies Reader*, New York: Routledge, pp. 1–17.

Stryker, Susan (2008), 'Transgender history, homonormativity, and disciplinarity', *Radical History Review*, 100: 144–57.

Stuart-Smith, Jane (1999), 'Glasgow: accent and voice quality', in Paul Foulkes and Gerry Docherty (eds), *Urban Voices: Accent Studies in the British Isles*, London: Arnold, pp. 201–20.

Stuart-Smith, Jane (2003), 'The phonology of modern urban Scots', in John Corbett, J. Derrick McClure and Jane Stuart-Smith (eds), *The Edinburgh Companion to Scots*, Edinburgh: Edinburgh University Press, pp. 110–37.

Stuart-Smith, Jane (2005), 'Is TV a contributory factor in accent change in adolescents?', final report on UK Economic and Social Research Council grant no. R000239757, http://stuart-smith.notlong.com (accessed 7 April 2009).

Stuart-Smith, Jane (2006), 'The influence of media on language', in Carmen Llamas, Louise Mullany and Peter Stockwell (eds), *The Routledge Companion to Sociolinguistics*, London: Routledge, pp. 140–8.

Stuart-Smith, Jane (2008), 'Scottish English: phonology', in Bernd Kortmann and Clive Upton (eds), *Varieties of English: The British Isles*, Berlin: Mouton de Gruyter, pp. 48–70.

Stuart-Smith, Jane and Claire Timmins (2006), '"Tell her to shut her moof": the role of the lexicon in TH-fronting in Glaswegian adolescents', in Graham Caie, Carole Hough and Irené Wotherspoon (eds), *The Power of Words: Essays in Lexicography and Lexicology in Honour of Christian Kay*, Amsterdam: Rodopi, pp. 171–83.

Stuart-Smith, Jane, Claire Timmins, Gwylim Pryce and Barrie Gunter (in progress, a), *Television is a Factor in Language Change: Evidence from Glasgow*.

Stuart-Smith, Jane, Claire Timmins, Gwylim Pryce and Barrie Gunter (in progress, b), *Mediating the Local: Language Change and the Media*.

Stuart-Smith, Jane, Claire Timmins and Fiona Tweedie (2007), '"Talkin' Jockney?": accent change in Glaswegian', *Journal of Sociolinguistics*, 11: 221–61.

Sullivan, Nikki (2006), 'Transmogrification: (un)becoming other(s)', in Susan Stryker and Stephen Whittle (eds), *The Transgender Studies Reader*, New York: Routledge, pp. 552–64.

Sunderland, Jane (2004), *Gendered Discourses*, Basingstoke: Palgrave.

Surridge, Paula (2007), 'Class belonging: a quantitative exploration of identity and consciousness', *British Journal of Sociology*, 58(2): 207–26.

Sweetland, Julie (2002), 'Unexpected but authentic use of an ethnically-marked dialect', *Journal of Sociolinguistics*, 6(4): 514–36.

Tajfel, Henri (1978), 'Social categorization, social identity and social comparison', in Henri Tajfel (ed.), *Differentiation Between Social Groups: Studies in the Social Psychology of Intergroup Relations*, London: Academic Press, pp. 61–76.

Tajfel, Henri and John Turner (1979), 'An integrative theory of inter-group conflict', In William Austin and Stephen Worchel (eds), *The Social Psychology of Intergroup Relations*, Monterey, CA: Brookes/Cole, pp. 33–47.

Tannen, Deborah (1987), 'Repetition in conversation: toward a poetics of talk', *Language*, 63: 574–605.

Tannen, Deborah (1993, ed.), *Framing in Discourse*, Oxford: Oxford University Press.

Tanner, Dennis and Dean Gerstenberger (1988), 'The grief response in neuropathologies of speech and language', *Aphasiology*, 2: 79–84.

Tate, Donna (1979), 'Preliminary data on dialect in speech disguise', in Harry Hollien and Patricia Hollien (eds), *Current Issues in the Phonetic Sciences*, Amsterdam: Benjamins, pp. 846–50.

Taylor, Talbot (1997), *Theorizing Language: Analysis, Normativity, Rhetoric, History*, New York: Pergamon.

Terzulo, C.A. and P. Viviani (1980), 'Determinants and characteristics of motor patterns used for typing', *Neuroscience*, 5: 1085–1103.

Thomas, Erik (1989/1993), 'Vowel changes in Columbus, Ohio', *Journal of English Linguistics*, 22: 205–15.

Thomas, Erik (2001), *An Acoustic Analysis of Vowel Variation in New World English*, Durham, NC: Duke University Press.

Thomas, Erik (2007), 'Phonological and phonetic characteristics of African American Vernacular English', *Language and Linguistics Compass*, 1: 450–75.

Thomas, Erik and Guy Bailey (1998), 'Parallels between vowel subsystems of African American Vernacular English and Caribbean creoles', *Journal of Pidgin and Creole Languages*, 13: 267–96.

Thomason, Sarah and Terrence Kaufman (1988), *Language Contact, Creolization, and Genetic Linguistics*, Berkeley, CA: University of California Press.

Thompson, Charles (1987), 'A language effect in voice identification', *Applied Cognitive Psychology*, 1: 121–31.

Thompson, Edward (1978), *The Poverty of Theory and Other Essays*, London: Merlin Press.

Thornborrow, Joanna and Jennifer Coates (2005), *The Sociolinguistics of Narrative*, Amsterdam: Benjamins.

Tillery, Jan and Guy Bailey (2003), 'Approaches to real time in dialectology and sociolinguistics', *World Englishes*, 22: 351–65.

Tolfree, Thomas (2004), *Identifying the Local Housing Markets of South East England, Part C: Analysis and Initial Hypothesis*, Reading: DTZ Pieda Consulting.

Tollfree, Laura (1999), 'South East London English: discrete versus continuous modelling of consonantal reduction', in Paul Foulkes and Gerard Docherty (eds), *Urban Voices: Accent Studies in the British Isles*, London: Arnold, pp. 163–84.

Tomaney, John (1998), 'New Labour and the English question', *University of Sheffield Political Economy Research Centre Occasional and Working Papers*, Policy Paper 13.

Tomaney, John and Neil Ward (2001), 'Locating the region: an introduction', in John Tomaney and Neil Ward (eds), *A Region in Transition: North East England at the Millennium*, Aldershot: Ashgate, pp. 1–23.

Torgersen, Eivind and Paul Kerswill (2004), 'Internal and external motivation in phonetic change: dialect levelling outcomes for an English vowel shift', *Journal of Sociolinguistics*, 8: 24–53.

Torstensson, Niklas, Erik Eriksson and Kirk Sullivan (2004), 'Mimicked accents – do speakers have similar cognitive prototypes?', *Proceedings of the 10th Australian International Conference on Speech Science and Technology*, Sydney, December 2004, pp. 271–6.

Towle, Evan and Lynn Morgan (2002), 'Romancing the transgender native: rethinking the use of the "third gender" concept', *GLQ: A Journal of Lesbian and Gay Studies*, 8(4): 469–97.

Traunmüller, Hartmut (1990), 'Analytical expressions for the tonotopic sensory scale', *Journal of the Acoustical Society of America*, 88: 97–100.

Trudgill, Peter (1974), *The Social Differentiation of English in Norwich*, Cambridge: Cambridge University Press.

Trudgill, Peter (1978), 'Introduction: sociolinguistics and sociolinguistics', in Peter Trudgill (ed.), *Sociolinguistic Patterns in British English*, London: Edward Arnold, pp. 1–18.

Trudgill, Peter (1986), *Dialects in Contact*, Oxford: Blackwell.

Trudgill, Peter (1988), 'Norwich revisited: recent linguistic changes in an English urban dialect', *English World-Wide*, 9: 33–49.

Trudgill, Peter (1992), 'Dialect typology and social structure', in Ernst Håkon Jahr (ed.),

Language Contact: Theoretical and Empirical Studies, Berlin: Mouton de Gruyter, pp. 195–212.

Trudgill, Peter (2002), *Sociolinguistic Variation and Change*, Edinburgh: Edinburgh University Press.

Trudgill, Peter (2004), *New Dialect Formation: The Inevitability of Colonial Englishes*, Edinburgh: Edinburgh University Press.

Trudgill, Peter (2008), 'Colonial dialect contact in the history of European languages: on the irrelevance of identity to new-dialect formation, *Language in Society*, 37(2): 241–54.

Turner, John (1991), *Social Influences*, Buckingham: Open University Press.

Turner, John, Michael Hogg, Penelope Oakes, Stephen Reicher and Margaret Wetherell (1987, eds), *Rediscovering the Social Group: A Self-Categorization Theory*, Oxford: Blackwell.

Vadnais, Janelle Chaundre (2006), *A Cross-Regional Study of Locative* to *in North Carolina*, MA dissertation, North Carolina State University.

Valdes, Guadalupe (1981), 'Code-switching as a deliberate verbal strategy: a microanalysis of direct and indirect request among Chicano bilingual speakers', in Richard Duran (ed.), *Latino Language and Communication Behavior*, Norwood, NJ: Ablex Press, pp. 95–108.

Vanags, Thea, Marie Carroll and Timothy Perfect (2005), 'Verbal overshadowing: a sound theory in voice recognition?', *Applied Cognitive Psychology*, 19: 1127–44.

Vandekerckhove, Reinhild (2005), 'Interdialectal convergence between West-Flemish urban dialects', in Nicole Delbecque, Johan van der Auwera, Dirk Geeraerts (eds), *Perspectives on Variation: Sociolinguistic, Historical, Comparative*, Berlin: Mouton de Gruyter, pp. 111–27.

Van Lancker, Diana, Jeffrey Cummings, Jody Kreiman and Bruce Dobkin (1988), 'Phonagnosia: a dissociation between familiar and unfamiliar voices', *Cortex*, 24(2): 195–209.

Van Putten, Steffany and Judy Walker (2003), 'Production of emotional prosody in varying degrees of severity of apraxia of speech', *Journal of Communication Disorders*, 36: 77–95.

Verschueren, Jef (1999, ed.), *Language and Ideology: Selected Papers from the 6th International Pragmatics Conference*, Antwerp: International Pragmatics Association.

Vickery, Chad, Arash Sepehri and Clea Evans (2008), 'Self-esteem in an acute stroke rehabilitation sample: a control group comparison', *Clinical Rehabilitation*, 22: 179–87.

Visweswaran, Kamala (1994), *Fictions of Feminist Ethnography*, Minneapolis, MN: University of Minnesota Press.

Wagner, Isolde and Olaf Köster (1999), 'Perceptual recognition of familiar voices using falsetto as a type of disguise', *Proceedings of the 14th International Congress of Phonetic Sciences*, San Francisco, August 1999, pp. 1381–4.

Wahlin, Willhelmina (2007), 'Women in the workplace', *J@pan.Inc*, 73, http://wahlin.notlong.com (accessed 7 April 2009).

Wales, Katie (2006), *Northern English: A Social and Cultural History*, Cambridge: Cambridge University Press.

Wales, Katie (2008), 'Regional variation in English in the new millennium: looking to the future', in Miriam Locher and Jürg Strässler (eds), *Standards and Norms in the English Language*, Berlin: Mouton de Gruyter, pp. 47–67.

Walker, Janine, Henry Jackson and Geoffrey Littlejohn (2004), 'Models of adjustment to chronic illness: using the example of rheumatoid arthritis', *Clinical Psychology Review*, 24: 461–88.

Wallerstein, Immanuel (1991), 'The construction of peoplehood: racism, nationalism, ethnicity', in Etienne Balibar and Immanuel Wallerstein (eds), *Race, Nation, Class: Ambiguous Identities*, London: Verso, pp. 71–85.

Walton, Julie and Robert Orlikoff (1994), 'Speaker race identification from acoustic cues in the vocal signal', *Journal of Speech and Hearing Research*, 37: 738–45.

Wassink, Alicia Beckford (1999), 'Historic low prestige and seeds of change: language attitudes toward Jamaican Creole', *Language in Society*, 28(1): 57–92.

Wassink, Alicia Beckford and Anne Curzan (2004), 'Addressing ideologies around African American English', *Journal of English Linguistics*, 32(3): 171–85.

Wassink, Alicia Beckford and Judy Dyer (2004), 'Language ideology and the transmission of phonological change: changing indexicality in two situations of language contact', *Journal of English Linguistics*, 32(1): 3–30.

Watson, Kevin (2007), 'Liverpool English', *Journal of the International Phonetic Association*, 37: 351–60.

Watt, Dominic (1998), *Variation and Change in the Vowel System of Tyneside English*, PhD thesis, Newcastle University.

Watt, Dominic (2002), '"I don't speak with a Geordie accent, I speak, like, the Northern accent": contact-induced levelling in the Tyneside vowel system', *Journal of Sociolinguistics*, 6(1): 44–63.

Watt, Dominic and Lesley Milroy (1999), 'Patterns of variation and change in three Tyneside vowels: is this dialect levelling?', in Paul Foulkes and Gerard Docherty (eds), *Urban Voices: Accent Studies in the British Isles*, London: Arnold, pp. 25–46.

Webb, Victor and Kembo-Sure (2000), 'The languages of Africa', in Victor Webb and Kembo-Sure (eds), *African Voices: An Introduction to the Languages and Linguistics of Africa*, Oxford: Oxford University Press, pp. 26–54.

Wells, John (1982), *Accents of English* (3 vols.), Cambridge: Cambridge University Press.

Wendt, Beate, Ines Bose, Michael Sailer, Henning Scheich and Hermann Ackermann (2007), 'Speech rhythm of a woman with foreign accent syndrome (FAS)', *Proceedings of the 16th International Congress of Phonetic Sciences*, Saarbrücken, Germany, August 2007, pp. 2009–12.

Wenger, Etienne (1998), *Communities of Practice: Learning, Meaning and Identity*, Cambridge: Cambridge University Press.

Werbner, Richard (1996), 'Introduction: multiple identities, plural arenas', in Richard Werbner and Terence Ranger (eds), *Postcolonial Identities in Africa*, London: Zed Books, pp. 1–25.

Werbner, Richard and Terence Ranger (1996, eds), *Postcolonial Identities in Africa*, London: Zed Books.

West, Candace and Don Zimmerman (1991), 'Doing gender', in Judith Lorber and Susan Farrell (eds), *The Social Construction of Gender*, Newbury Park, CA: Sage, pp. 13–37.

Whitehead, Harriet (1981), 'The bow and the burden-strap: a new look at institutionalized homosexuality in Native America', in Sherry Ortner and Harriet Whitehead (eds), *Sexual Meanings: The Cultural Construction of Gender and Sexuality*, New York: Cambridge University Press, pp. 80–115.

Wikan, Unni (1982), *Behind the Veil in Arabia: Women in Oman*, Baltimore, MD: Johns Hopkins University Press.

Wilchins, Riki Anne (1997), *Read My Lips: Sexual Subversion and the End of Gender*, Ithaca, NY: Firebrand Books.

Williams, Ann and Paul Kerswill (1999), 'Dialect levelling: change and continuity in Milton Keynes, Reading and Hull', in Paul Foulkes and Gerard Docherty (eds), *Urban Voices: Accent Studies in the British Isles*, London: Arnold, pp. 141–62.

Williams, Gwyn (1985), *When was Wales?*, London: Black Raven Books.

Williams, Raymond (1977), *Marxism and Literature*, Oxford: Oxford University Press.

Williams, Raymond (2003), *Who Speaks for Wales? Nation, Culture, Identity*, Cardiff: University of Wales Press.

Williams, Walter (1986), *The Spirit and the Flesh: Sexual Diversity in American Indian Culture*, Boston: Beacon Press.

Williamson, Juanita (1968), *A Phonological and Morphological Study of the Speech of the Negro in Memphis, Tennessee*, Tuscaloosa, AL: University of Alabama Press.

Willis, Paul (1977), *Learning to Labour: How Working Class Kids Get Working Class Jobs*, Hampshire: Gower.

Windsor-Lewis, Jack (1994), 'The Yorkshire Ripper Enquiry: part II', *Forensic Linguistics*, 1: 207–16.

Winford, Donald (2003), *An Introduction to Contact Linguistics*, Oxford: Blackwell.

Wodak, Ruth (1989, ed.), *Language, Power and Ideology*, Amsterdam: John Benjamins.

Wodak, Ruth, Rudolf de Cillia, Martin Reisigl and Karin Liebhart (1999), *The Discursive Construction of National Identity*, trans. Angelika Hirsch and Richard Mitten, Edinburgh: Edinburgh University Press.

Wodak, Ruth, Rudolf de Cillia, Martin Reisigl and Karin Liebhart (2009), *The Discursive Construction of National Identity*, 2nd edn, Edinburgh: Edinburgh University Press.

Wolfram, Walt (1969), *A Sociolinguistic Description of Detroit Negro Speech*, Washington, DC: Center for Applied Linguistics.

Wolfram, Walt (1998), 'Language ideology and dialect: understanding the Ebonics controversy', *Journal of English Linguistics*, 26(2): 97–107.

Wolfram, Walt (2007), 'Sociolinguistic folklore in the study of African American English', *Language and Linguistics Compass*, 1(4): 292–313.

Wolfram, Walt and Erik Thomas (2002), *The Development of African American English*, Oxford: Blackwell.

Wolfram, Walt and Natalie Schilling-Estes (1998), *American English: Dialects and Variation*, Malden, MA: Blackwell.

Woodward, John, Nicholas Orlans and Peter Higgins (2003), *Biometrics: Identity Assurance in the Information Age*, Berkeley, CA: McGraw Hill Osborne Media.

Woolard, Kathryn (1999), 'Simultaneity and bivalency as strategies in bilingualism', *Journal of Linguistic Anthropology*, 8(1): 3–29.

Woolhiser, Curt (2005), 'Political borders and dialect divergence/convergence in Europe', in Peter Auer, Frans Hinskens and Paul Kerswill (eds), *Dialect Change: Convergence and Divergence in European Languages*, Cambridge: Cambridge University Press, pp. 236–62.

Wright, Joseph (1896–1905), *The English Dialect Dictionary*, 6 vols., Oxford: Clarendon.

Wroblewski, Michael, Thea Strand and Sylvie Dubois (2007), 'African American and non-African American vowels in Cajun country', paper presented at the Annual Meeting of the Linguistic Society of America, Anaheim, CA, January 2007.

Yarmey, A. Daniel (2004), 'Eyewitness recall and photo identification: a field experiment', *Psychology, Crime and Law*, 10: 53–68.

Yarmey, A. Daniel, Meagan Yarmey and Leah Todd (2008), 'Frances McGehee (1912–2004): the first earwitness researcher', *Perceptual and Motor Skills*, 106(2): 387–94.

Yieke, Felicia (2005), 'Gender and discourse: topic organisation on workplace management committee meetings in Kenya', paper presented at Theoretical and Methodological Approaches to Gender BAAL/CUP Seminar, University of Birmingham, November 2005.

Yule, Henry and Arthur Coke Burnell (1886), *Hobson-Jobson: A Glossary of Colloquial Anglo-Indian Words and Phrases, and of Kindred Terms, Etymological, Historical, Geographical and Discursive*, London: Murray (reprinted as Henry Yule, Arthur Coke Burnell and William Crooke [1985], *Hobson-Jobson: The Anglo-Indian Dictionary*, London: Routledge and Kegan Paul).

Zentella, Ana Celia (1997), *Growing Up Bilingual: Puerto Rican Children in New York*, Oxford: Blackwell.

Zetterholm, Elisabeth (2003), *Voice Imitation: A Phonetic Study of Perceptual Illusions and Acoustic Success*, PhD thesis, Lund University.

Zetterholm, Elisabeth, Mats Blomberg and Daniel Elenius (2004), 'A comparison between human perception and a speaker verification system score of a voice imitation', *Proceedings of the 10th Australian International Conference on Speech Science and Technology*, Sydney, December 2004, pp. 393–7.

Zimman, Lal (2008), 'Contesting gender, (re)constructing sex: semantic variation in transgender communities', paper presented at 15th Annual Lavender Languages and Linguistics Conference, Washington DC, February 2008.

Zimman, Lal (in preparation), 'Gender on the body, sex in the mind: ideology and practice in talk about transgender embodiment', to appear in Lal Zimman, Joshua Raclaw and Jenny Davis (eds), *Queer Excursions: New Directions in Language, Gender, and Sexuality Research*.

Index